CLINICAL IMPLICATIONS
OF ATTACHMENT

CHILD PSYCHOLOGY

A series of books edited by **David S. Palermo**

CLINICAL IMPLICATIONS
OF ATTACHMENT

Editors

Jay Belsky
The Pennsylvania State University

Teresa Nezworski
University of California, Santa Barbara

LEA LAWRENCE ERLBAUM ASSOCIATES, PUBLISHERS
1988   Hillsdale, New Jersey   Hove and London

Lawrence Erlbaum Associates, Inc., Publishers
365 Broadway
Hillsdale, New Jersey 07642

Library of Congress Cataloging-in-Publication Data
Clinical implications of attachment.

  (Child psychology)
  Includes indexes.
  1. Attachment behavior in children. 2. Security
(Psychology) in children. 3. Mother and child. 4. Mental
illness—Forecasting. I. Belsky, Jay, 1952-
II. Nezworski, Teresa M. III. Series. [DNLM: 1. Mother-
Child Relations. 2. Object Attachment. WS 105.5.F2C641]
RJ507.A77C57   1988   155.4′18   86-29312
ISBN 0-89859-778-1

Printed in the United States of America
10   9   8   7   6   5   4   3

CONTENTS

PART IV: CLINICAL IMPLICATIONS

CONTRIBUTORS

JOHN E. BATES • Department of Psychology, University of Indiana, Bloomington, IN 47405

KATHRYN BAYLES • Department of Psychology, University of Indiana, Bloomington, IN 47405

JAY BELSKY • Department of Individual and Family Studies, College of Health and Human Development, The Pennsylvania University, University Park, PA 16802

CATHRYN L. BOOTH • Child Development and Mental Retardation Training Center, University of Washington, Seattle, WA 98195

JUDE CASSIDY • Department of Psychology, University of Illinois at Urbana-Champaign, 603 E. Daniel St., Champaign, IL 61820

PATRICIA M. CRITTENDEN • Mailman Center for Child Development, University of Miami Medical School, Miami, FL 33101

MARK T. GREENBERG • Department of Psychology, NI-25, University of Washington, Seattle, WA 98117

STANLEY I. GREENSPAN • Department of Psychiatry and Behavioral Sciences, George Washington University Medical Center, Washington, DC 20037

RUSSELL ISABELLA • Department of Family and Human Development, Utah State University, Logan, UT 84322

R. ROGERS KOBAK • Department of Psychology, University of Denver, Denver, CO 80208

ALICIA F. LIEBERMAN • Department of Psychiatry, Infant–Parent Program, San Francisco General Hospital, 1001 Potrero Ave., Ward 95, San Francisco, CA 94110

SUSAN P. LOLLIS • Department of Psychology, University of Waterloo, Waterloo, Ontario N1H 1T2 Canada

TERESA NEZWORSKI • Counseling Psychology Clinic, 1113 Phelps Hall, University of California, Santa Barbara, Santa Barbara, CA 93106

JEREE H. PAWL • Department of Psychiatry, Infant–Parent Program, San Francisco General Hospital, 1001 Potrero Ave., Ward 95, San Francisco, CA 94110

KENNETH H. RUBIN • Department of Psychology, University of Waterloo, Waterloo, Ontario N2L 3G1 Canada

MATTHEW L. SPELTZ • Department of Psychology, NI-25, University of Washington, Seattle, WA 98117

SUSAN J. SPIEKER • Child Development and Mental Retardation Training Center, University of Washington, Seattle, WA 98117

L. ALAN SROUFE • Institute of Child Development, University of Minnesota, Minneapolis, MN 55455

WILLIAM J. TOLAN • Meadows Psychiatric Center, RD #1, Centre Hall, PA 16828

PREFACE

In the summer of 1983, while Jay Belsky was directing a research program focused on families rearing firstborn infants, two research reports indicating a possible link between insecure attachment and the subsequent development of child behavior problems (Erickson, Egeland, & Sroufe, 1985;[1] Lewis, Feiring, McGuffog, & Jaskir, 1984[2]) came to our attention. Neither of the studies described in these reports demonstrated that insecurity caused subsequent behavior problems in preschool and early school-age children. However, each indicated that under certain conditions, 12- to 18-month-old children who were evaluated as insecurely attached to their mothers in the Strange Situation were at heightened risk for displaying internalizing and/or externalizing behavior problems as older children.

At the time that these investigations came to our attention, we were in the midst of completing attachment assessments on the infants whose families were enrolled in our second longitudinal study and were about to initiate assessments of a third sample. Upon enrolling families in all of our investigations, we promised parents that we would share with them any concerns about their child's development that might surface in the course of our research. Not only did we see such an offer as an inducement to parents to become involved, but in virtually every case this was a motivating factor for them. Even before we informed parents of our policy that the information we obtained on their children belonged to them and was not something that we would keep for ourselves, many queried us about the feedback we would give them concerning our findings.

Having established this implicit social contract to share information, we

---

[1]Erickson, M., Egeland, B., & Sroufe, L. A. (1985). The relationship between quality of attachment and behavior problems in preschool in high risk sample. In I. Bretherton & E. Waters (Eds.), Growing points in attachment theory and research (pp. 147-186). *Monographs of the Society for Research in Child Development, 50* (1-2, Serial No. 209).

[2]Lewis, M., Feiring, C., McGuffog, C., & Jaskir, J. (1984). Predicting psychopathology in six-year-olds from early social relations. *Child Development, 55,* 123-137.

felt obligated, as a result of the Lewis et al. (1984) and Erickson et al. (1985) studies, to share with parents some of what was being discovered about the developmental correlates of insecure attachment. What we remained uncertain about was exactly what we should tell them and how we should share with them our developing concerns about the implications of early insecurity as assessed in the Strange Situation. In the course of our deliberations as a research team, which by this time included Teresa Nezworski, a child clinician who had recently come to Penn State, we came to realize that the clinical implications of attachment had not been explored very much in the developmental literature and so, did not provide the guidance we felt we needed. As we moved to develop a clinical intervention for families participating in our third longitudinal study (described in chapter 11), we desperately sought consultation from other experts in the field regarding what the implications of the research evidence was on infant–mother attachment.

At about this same time, the annual announcement of the Study Group Program from the Society for Research in Child Development appeared. This led one of our students, Russell Isabella, to suggest that we seek funds to organize a study group to consider the clinical implications of attachment. And so, this volume emerged. We sought to invite to our study group developmental psychologists and child psychiatrists and clinicians who not only were knowledgeable about attachment theory and research but who also had experience treating young children and their families. Our goal for the study group was to explore a variety of issues related to attachment, including the predictive utility of Strange Situation assessments, the conditions under which insecurity is related to subsequent difficulties, the origins of individual differences in attachment security, and intervention strategies that might prove useful in ameliorating the developmental risks that appeared to be associated with insecure attachment relationships. Perhaps wisely, perhaps unwisely, we specifically requested that participants refrain from writing formal papers in advance of the study group in hopes that this would permit more open and informal discussion.

Whatever the consequences of this strategy for the study group process itself, it proved problematical when it came to putting together a volume to address the issues considered in the group. Some participants, as we should have expected, never wrote a paper and others were very late in completing theirs. It is for this reason that it has taken far longer than we desired to have this volume appear in print. To be honest, there were times when it was uncertain whether the volume would materialize. Fortunately, we were able to attract contributions from individuals who were not included in the study group but who felt they had something to say on the topic at hand. In considering the contributions of these persons, it is clear to us that they not only have greatly improved the volume, but also would have made valuable contributions to our study group deliberations.

Beyond the debt we owe to the contributors of this book, we need to extend our thanks to the Society for Research in Child Development, which manages the Study Group Program, and to the Foundation for Child Development, which has generously supported this program. Intellectual gratitude should also be extended to John Bowlby, Mary Ainsworth, and L. Alan Sroufe whose seminal theoretical and empirical work has been largely, if not entirely, responsible for current interest in attachment.

Jay Belsky
Teresa Nezworski

GENERAL ISSUES

1
Clinical Implications
of Attachment

Jay Belsky
The Pennsylvania State University

Teresa Nezworski
University of California, Santa Barbara

Only a decade ago, students of human development were routinely taught that individual differences in infant functioning in the first year of life were not predictive of later development. Despite this, many continued to pursue the question of the origins of individual differences that emerge after the period of infancy and that are so evident in human functioning across the lifespan. In fact, even in the face of all too consistent evidence indicating that individual differences were not stable from infancy to the childhood years, either in domains of intelligence or social and affective functioning, the collection of data that could radically alter this state of knowledge continued unabated.

In the absence of much evidence that individual differences were stable, clearly articulated positions emerged as to why such continuity should not be expected and could not be found. One point of view with respect to cognitive development was that the transition from sensorimotor intelligence, characteristic of the infant years, to symbolic intelligence, characteristic of the child, adolescent, and adulthood years, was qualitative in nature and, therefore, relatively impervious to stable individual differences (McCall, 1979). Additional theoretical support for this conclusion came from evolutionary arguments that asserted that development in the opening year or two of life was highly canalized and that unless the individual encountered gross deprivation in his/her rearing environment, normative variation in sensorimotor intelligence would not be predictive of variation in later intelligence (Scarr-Salapatek, 1976).

In the realm of social and affective development, stable individual differences were also strikingly difficult to document from infancy through preschool years. This led some to argue that the period of infancy was one of getting started and that it made little sense from an evolutionary perspective for variation beyond the range of the most serious dysfunction to have important implications for future development. In further developing this line of reasoning, Kagan (Kagan, Kearsley, & Zelazo, 1978) went so far as to argue, in his most eloquent and compelling manner, that the very notion of connectivity from early to later development was a figment of Western imagination grounded more in our cultural heritage and collective belief system than in the empirical world.

In view of this history, it seems reasonable to argue that over the past decade a virtual revolution has taken place in our understanding of early human development. This is because in both the cognitive and socioemotional realms of development there now exist sizeable bodies of evidence demonstrating that individual differences measured within the first year of life are, in fact, predictive of later development. With respect to cognitive development, a number of studies conducted in a variety of laboratories across the country have revealed that individual differences in information processing capabilities in the third through sixth months of life (and possibly earlier) are predictive—to a surprisingly large degree—of variation in psychometric intelligence (i.e., IQ) measured as late as the eighth year of life. Thus, infants who more quickly discriminate between novel and familiar stimuli, as has been revealed by a number of attention-habituation paradigms, score more highly on tests of intelligence as they grow older (see Bornstein & Sigman, 1986, for a review of the relevant research). In fact, these associations between early information processing and later intelligence are so robust and have been replicated so often that efforts are underway to develop and deploy screening tests to identify infants who might be at risk for later cognitive deficits that currently go unnoticed (Fagan, 1984).

In the realm of socioemotional development, it is the measurement of security of infant–mother attachment that has proved equally successful in documenting systematic associations between development at the end of the first year of life and subsequent functioning as late as the early school-age years. Studies carried out by Sroufe and his colleagues at the University of Minnesota (building upon the seminal work of Mary Ainsworth and the theorizing of John Bowlby), as well as investigations carried out in a number of laboratories around the county, clearly have demonstrated that infants whose relationships with their mothers can be characterized as secure as opposed to insecure using the Strange Situation paradigm generally look more competent as toddlers, preschoolers, and even as children beginning public school (see Bretherton, 1985 and Lamb, Thompson, Gardner, Charnov, & Estes, 1984, for reviews of the relevant data). All this is not to imply that individual differences in the security of attachment are deterministic of later development, but rather that theoretically meaningful associations between development in infancy and later functioning have been repeatedly established in studies focusing upon socio-affective functioning.

In recent years, the meaning of these associations has been the subject of great debate. Although they were anticipated on the basis of attachment theory, which stipulated that feelings of security and control growing out of the infant–mother relationship would contribute to the regulation of affect, the establishment of other social relationships, and the child's negotiation of subsequent developmental tasks, it was never assumed that the child would be impervious to subsequent experience or that early attachment security would determine—in any unmediated fashion—the course of later development. Nevertheless, this is exactly what some critics of the theory and the research tradition it generated so often imply (Lamb et al., 1984), if not state directly (Skolnick, 1986). But as Sroufe makes eminently clear in his contribution to this volume, in which he clarifies many misconceptions that have been attributed to attachment theory, the basic assumption guiding attachment research is not that the relationship between mother and infant inevitably affects later development, but rather that the child's initial relationship experience with mother probabilistically predicts later social development because it affects his/her expectations about others and relationships, feelings about self, and social skills used in other social contexts.

In reading contemporary criticism of attachment theory, one gets the sense not only that simplistic notions of development are being attributed to students of attachment, but also that there is little appreciation for the empirical contributions that this tradition has generated. The very fact that there is today a need to consider and debate why it is that early relationships predict subsequent functioning is in large measure a direct consequence of the success of the attachment paradigm in demonstrating that lawful relations do exist between security of infant–mother attachment and development in the toddler, preschool, and school-age years. That is, only because it has been demonstrated that there is continuity in socioemotional development has attention shifted to the conditions of such continuity. In our minds, the work of Erickson, Sroufe, and Egeland, (1985) is most instructive in this regard not only because it demonstrates an appreciation among students of attachment theory for these conditions of continuity, but because it indicates that the predictive power of assessments of attachment security, in large measure, depend on experiences that ensue in the post-infancy years. In showing that the association between insecurity and subsequent social difficulties is mitigated when mothers become more available and supportive of their offspring and that the association between security and subsequent competence is attenuated when the quality of maternal care deteriorates during the toddler and early preschool years, the work by the Minnesota group goes a long way toward modeling basic principles of attachment theory as well as of the developmental process more generally. More specifically, it underscores the fact that there is continuity in development when future experiences maintain developmental trajectories that have been established and that discontinuity characterizes the developmental process when experiences inconsistent with these trajectories are encountered.

This interpretation of the Erickson et al. research and this analysis of what is meant by the phrase "conditions of continuity" should not be read to imply that earlier experiences are insignificant and that only concurrent experiences are developmentally influential. The reason for this, clarified by the attachment theory, is that the child is by no means a passive recipient of experience (see Sroufe, this volume). Rather, the child is an active constructor of reality who both creates experiences and differentially attends to diverse information in his/her social world. After all, it was Bowlby's contention in articulating the concept of "internal working models" that experience in the attachment relationship generates expectations of self and of others and that these are used to guide behavior and interpret experience. Evidence that this process is indeed at work in social development is suggested quite strongly by Dodge's (Dodge & Richard, 1985) recent research on aggressive children. In demonstrating that such school-age boys are biased in their interpretations of the behavior of agemates by perceiving malicious intent and hostility when no such motives are present, it becomes clear that attributional processes not unlike those subsumed by the term *internal working model* do affect social functioning in important ways. Moreover, the fact that aggressive children are known to come from homes in which discipline is harsh and punitive (Parke & Slaby, 1983) is quite consistent with the notion that these models that guide behavior may well derive from earlier experiences in the parent–child relationship.

The possibility that there is a relationship between the processes that Dodge is studying and those that have traditionally been the focus of attachment researchers is suggested by the very research that stimulated the convening of a study group sponsored by the Society for Research on Child Development concerning Clinical Implications of Attachment, which resulted in the current volume. As a result of two separate investigations documenting a link between early insecurity and subsequent behavioral problems (Erickson et al., 1985; Lewis, Feiring, McGuffog, & Jaskir, 1984), it became clear that the concept of attachment, which had proven so useful to developmental psychologists studying normal developmental processes, might well have some clinical implications. That this might indeed be the case was certainly evident in Bowlby's early writings, but it took the research of Erickson et al. and Lewis et al. to convincingly demonstrate a linkage between early insecurity, as measured in the Strange Situation, and subsequent behavioral problems. In neither of these studies, it is important to note, was it the case that insecurity inevitably led to externalizing or internalizing behavioral problems; the seminal contribution of this work, however, was the empirical demonstration that childhood problems long thought to have their roots in difficulties in the early infant–mother relationship were indeed related to insecurity of attachment.

Actually, when one carefully examines earlier research on the developmental correlates of attachment security, it becomes apparent that the associations documented by Erickson et al. and Lewis et al. were very much foreshadowed by earlier findings in the literature, though never cast in terms of behavioral problems per se. Consider, in this regard, the fact that Matas, Arend, and Sroufe (1978) found, in studying toddlers' behaviors during a problem-solving task, that those with histories of anxious-resistant attachment were whiney, negativistic, and easily frustrated, and that those with anxious-avoidant histories were neither compliant nor cooperative. Similarly, Maslin and Bates (1982) observed that 2-year-old who had been classified as insecurely attached to their mothers at 13 months of age engaged in more conflict with their mothers than infants evaluated as securely attached.

When one considers these findings linking early insecurity with behavioral functioning that is often associated with referrals to child guidance clinics, and then reflects upon the recent emergence of interest in developmental psychopathology, it is not difficult to realize why we believe that one of the major contributions of research and theory on attachment has been the drawing together of students of normal and abnormal development. In fact, we wonder whether the resurgence of interest in developmental psychopathology that we have witnessed in the past few years (Cicchetti, 1984; Sroufe & Rutter, 1984) would have taken place without the seminal contribution of attachment research. This is not to say that the basic concepts underlying the notion of developmental psychopathology have not been around for some time, but only that it took evidence documenting associations between normal and abnormal processes, which attachment research did much to provide, for the interrelation of the normal and dysfunctional and the developmental roots of psychopathology to capture once again the attention of mainstream developmental psychology.

In the chapters contributed to this volume, clinical implications of attachment theory are examined. In overviewing some of the primary contributions of these chapters we find it useful to think in terms of characteristics, consequences, and determinants of attachment security, as well as to consider the direct clinical applications of concepts derived from attachment theory in the provision of services to children and families. In the remainder of this chapter we outline what we view as some of the most important issues addressed in these chapters.

CHARACTERIZING VARIATION IN ATTACHMENT SECURITY

For many years now it has been traditional to employ the standard Strange Situation laboratory procedure when infants are 12 to 18 months of age in order to assess the security of the infant–parent attachment relationship. In distinguishing secure and insecure relationships, there has been some confusion about the interpretation of maladaptation applied to insecure attachments. As Sroufe, Crittenden, Lieberman and Greenspan, and Bates and Bayles all make clear in their chapters, the term *maladaptation* is employed within the attachment framework in terms of the child's future development. All of these authors recognize the fact that insecurely attached infants have established relationships that must be considered adapted to the circumstances of their rearing, even if they prove to be problematical as they move into the world beyond the family. Thus, insecure relationships are considered to be functional in that they serve to protect the child against anxiety, which arises in the face of a caregiver who may be less than optimally available. When seen in this light, avoidance, for example, serves as a strategy for avoiding anger that may evoke negative responses from the caregiver (see Cassidy & Kobak, this volume).

Until recently, behavior observed in the Strange Situation was used to characterize the infant–mother relationship in terms of one of three kinds of attachments: secure, anxious-avoidant, and anxious-resistant. In recent years, investigators working in a number of labs have identified subgroups of infants that fall outside of these traditional groupings. One particular subgroup that has attracted a great deal of attention is comprised of infants displaying both heightened avoidance of the mother when reunited with her following a brief separation as well as heightened resistance. As Crittenden demonstrates in her chapter, unless an A/C coding category is employed to capture such relationships, these children can be classified erroneously as secure. Particularly noteworthy in this regard is Crittenden's findings that such infants are disproportionately likely to have been abused and/or neglected. Such findings merit special attention from the standpoint of clinical concerns particularly when it is noted that children of depressed mothers also are disproportionately likely to be classified into this category when it is available for consideration (Radke-Yarrow, Cummings, Kucynski, & Chapman, 1985). The possibility that this classification is especially likely to be associated with disturbances on the part of the mother is strongly suggested by Speiker and Booth in their chapter, which devotes exclusive attention to the caregivers of infants with A/C classifications (see the following).

ORIGINS OF ATTACHMENT SECURITY

This discussion of the maternal correlates of attachment relationships that are classified A/C draws attention to one of the major debates that has always surrounded consideration of individual differences in infant–mother attachment security; namely, what are the determinants of variation in the quality of these relationships. By tradition, this issue has been cast in terms of characteristics of the infant versus the nature of the care provided by mother. Proponents of either point of view clearly recognize, however, that these viewpoints are not mutually exclusive, but do reflect differential emphases placed upon the role of the mother and of the infant in determining the course of the relationship that develops between them. Several contributors to this volume address this issue of the origins of individual differences in attachment security.

The role of temperament is empirically considered in the Belsky and Isabella chapter, which indicates that various indices of temperament do not directly distinguish secure from insecure relationships. More in-depth analyses of the attachment relationship, which are the focus of their chapter in this volume, as well as of another sample do reveal, however, that temperament does play a most apparent role in the behavior displayed by the infant in the Strange Situation, even if it does not determine attachment security per se (i.e., the organization of attachment behavior). Indeed, findings reported by Belsky and Rovine (1987) clearly show that infant temperament does not so much determine whether or not a relationship is secure or insecure, but rather influences the way in which security and insecurity may be expressed.

Such findings are consistent with points of view articulated by Sroufe and by Rubin and Lollis in their respective chapters contributed to this volume. Rubin and Lollis, in particular, draw attention to the role that infant inhibition may play in contributing to the development of anxious-resistant attachment when a caregiver proves insensitive to this temperamental attribute of the child. It is strongly argued in both this chapter and in that by Sroufe, however, that insecurity does not derive directly from the behavioral inclinations of the baby, as virtually any infant is considered to be capable of developing a secure relationship with its principle caregiver as long as a sensitive regimen of care is provided. Rather, it is principally when the temperamental dispositions of the infant are insensitively responded to that insecurity is likely to emerge as a central characteristic of the infant–mother relationship.

One important implication of these ideas is that it may be necessary, in pursuing the actual interactional antecedents of variation in attachment security, to distinguish between infants of varying temperaments. This is because it may well be that what it takes to establish a secure relationship and, thereby, generate a sense of felt security in one infant who, for example, might be very susceptible to distress, may well be quite different from what is required in the case of another baby whose temperamental qualities make him/her far less vulnerable to distress. The failure of research in the past to make distinctions such as these may be one important reason why, as Belsky and Isabella note in their chapter, that even though ratings of maternal sensitivity have consistently been found to discriminate attachment groups, the results from more detailed codings of maternal behavior have proven far less consistent.

In considering the determinants of attachment security, several contributions to this volume underscore the need to attend to factors and processes not subsumed by infant temperament or maternal behavior. In several chapters, special attention is drawn to characteristics of the mother as a person outside the mother–infant relationship and to sources of stress in the family that may undermine mother's ability to be emotionally available to her infant. Speiker and Booth, in reviewing data bearing on the incidence of insecure attachments across samples, note, for example, that although economic stress (as indicated by socioeconomic status) does not appear to be a major determinant of attachment security, psychological characteristics of the mother do seem to play a role in the etiology of the A/C attachment pattern. Of particular importance is their observation that mothers of these infants may be disposed to focusing upon stress and other negative aspects of their lives, a finding consistent with evidence reported by Isabella and Belsky (1985) in a follow-up analysis of data first examined as part of their contributions to this volume.

In observing that changes in marital quality across the transition to parenthood distinguished secure and insecure attachment groups, with mothers of the latter experiencing a more precipitous decline than mothers of the former, Isabella and Belsky (1985) wondered whether the marital relationships of women who went on to rear securely and insecurely attached infants differed prior to the infant's birth in ways that were not evident in a simple analysis of mean differences. As it turned out, they did, with mothers of secure infants seeming to rely more upon what was going well in their marriages when it came to appraising their overall satisfaction with their spousal relationships before their infants were born and mothers of insecure infants relying more upon feelings of ambivalence and experiences of conflict in making their prenatal appraisals of marital satisfaction. As Speiker and Booth point out in their chapter in this volume, these results, like their own, suggest that some women whose babies establish insecure relationships with them may be more disposed to focus upon negative events, feelings, and circumstances rather than more positive ones. In view of the fact that there is much in the behavior of the young infant that is negative and much in the transition to parenthood that is stressful, it is not difficult to imagine how a woman prone to focus upon the negative would not only foster a more pronounced decline in marital quality, but also be insensitive to her infant.

To the extent that dispositional characteristics of the mother do contribute to the likelihood that her infant will establish a secure or insecure relationship with her, probably as a result of the quality of care she provides—as the chapters by Belsky and Isabella, Speiker and Booth, and Cassidy and Kobak suggest—there is a need to consider the very origins of these dispositions. Several contributors to the present volume draw attention to the quality of care that the mother herself received while growing up and thus her expectations about relationships and her inclination to interpret the behavior of others, be it the infant or a service provider, in particular ways (see chapters by Sroufe; Nezworski, Tolan, & Belsky; Lieberman & Greenspan). In the only empirical analysis of this issue appearing in this volume, however, Belsky and Isabella were unable to distinguish attachment groups using retrospective reports of child-rearing history. In view of the success that others have achieved in this area (see reviews of prior work in chapters just cited) and the limits that Belsky and Isabella acknowledge regarding their methodology, it would seem inappropriate to disregard entirely a basic premise of the construct of internal working models in attachment theory; namely, that past relationship experiences affect the way in which individuals process interpersonal information and thereby influence the nature of relationships established beyond the family of origin and across the lifespan.

CONSEQUENCES OF ATTACHMENT SECURITY

As noted at the outset of this introductory chapter, the success that has been achieved in predicting individual differences in development during the toddler, preschool, and school-age years using Strange Situation assessments of attachment security has constituted, at least in our opinion, an unrecognized revolution in the study of early human development. We suspect that one major reason for the success of the attachment paradigm, beyond its theoretical power and appeal, has been the fact that distinctions between relationships during infancy have been kept to a minimum. For the most part, predictive validity studies have distinguished simply between secure and insecure relationships, usually disregarding the nature of the difference between anxious-avoidant and anxious-resistant attachments, and virtually always disregarding the subgroups within each of the three major attachment classifications. Although some might regard this approach as too global, we are of the opinion that all too often "hairs are split" when distinctions are not fully understood. There seems to be good sense, then, in not turning up the power of the microscope to 5,000 power until what can be observed at 500 power is sufficiently appreciated. If one was a biologist first peering into the cell and found oneself focused upon the inside of the cell nucleus, much of the potential knowledge so obvious to us now would likely be unrecognized. Without having first examined the cell at a lower power and observed the outer wall of the cell and the structure inside that would eventually be labeled the nucleus, there would be little way of knowing what one was looking at when peering inside of the nucleus.

Although some might be distressed by an analogy such as this that suggests our knowledge of infant development is, in some respects at least, not much advanced over that of the early biologists just discovering the basic structures of cells, we find this situation much less disconcerting. Not only is it a far cry from the not too distant past when we assumed that individual differences were not stable from infancy onward (i.e., didn't know that cells had a nucleus), but given the progress in biology that followed the discovery of basic cell structures, we are buoyed by the prospects of a developmental science now capable of characterizing individual differences in relationship experience that prove even modestly predictive of later development. All this, of course, leads us to be both humble and proud of the progress that has been made in a relatively short period of time in studying individual differences in attachment and their developmental consequences. It seems to us that some critics have been all too unappreciative of the very real achievements that have been made and all too willing to focus on the limits of our field's accomplishments (Lamb et al., 1984). Balance thus seems to be called for, not only among critics of attachment research and theory, but advocates as well.

We noted at the outset of this chapter that this volume and the study group from which it derived were stimulated by the empirical discovery that behavioral problems in early childhood could be predicted by assessments of attachment security in infancy. The inconsistency that is evident in the two reports that document this association and the failure to replicate this finding even at a general level in a third study (Bates, Maslin, & Frankel, 1985) clearly indicates, then, that there are very real limits to the robustness of the relation between early insecurity and subsequent behavioral problems. Besides differences between samples and across methods, there are a number of reasons why this inconsistency exists across researches. A number of these are discussed by Bates and Bayles, Greenberg and Spitz, and Rubin and Lollis in their chapters dealing with the developmental consequences of attachment security.

All of these authors underscore the most important point made earlier, namely, that an association between insecurity and behavioral problems is not inevitable, but only probabilistic. And the reason for this, they all stress, is that contextual systems must sustain earlier effects for them to be maintained. When quality of care changes in a manner that is inconsistent with developmental trajectories, some degree of change in developmental functioning should be expected. This point is central to Greenberg and Spitz' analysis of models of continuity in their chapter, one that endeavors to recast behavioral approaches to externalizing problems in terms of attachment theory, with particular emphasis on working models and the acting-out-child's lack of control in his/her relationships. This issue of the conditions of continuity is also central to Rubin and Lollis' analysis of the potential linkage between temperamental inhibition, anxious-resistant attachment, and social withdrawal in 4, 5, and 6-year olds. In developing a model that characterizes the conditions under which these separate entities are tied together over time, these authors continually point to conditions that will increase or decrease the likelihood that these phenomenon will be associated with one another.

Whereas the chapters by Greenberg and Spitz and by Rubin and Lollis represent theoretical attempts to account for why and when a relation between insecurity and behavioral problems develops, those by Bates and Bayles and by Cassidy and Kobak in the section of the book on consequences of attachment have somewhat different foci. The former report 5 and 6-year follow-up data linking maternal assessments of temperament and behavioral problems from an ongoing longitudinal study that failed to document an association between insecurity and behavioral problems (Bates et al., 1985). Cassidy and Kobak, in contrast, address neither a particular form of behavioral problems such as externalizing or internalizing disorders (as Greenberg and Spitz and Rubin and Lollis do, respectively), nor the conditions of continuity, but rather focus upon the meaning, origins, and consequences of a particular form in which insecurity is expressed, namely anxious-avoidance. In arguing that avoidance serves as a mechanism of defense, these authors strongly assert that researchers and clinicians studying the consequences of attachment relationships need to pay particular attention to inconsistencies in the performance of older children and adults. In highlighting the performance inconsistency often evident in individuals displaying avoidant interpersonal styles, Cassidy and Kobak once again underscore the need to examine the organization of behavior, not just the frequency of its occurrence—a point Waters (1978) made long ago as the key to recognizing developmentally significant differences in attachment behavior.

CLINICAL APPLICATIONS

Appreciation of the fact that continuity in socio-affective functioning from infancy to the childhood years is dependent on the context of development should make us aware that, even if some developmental trajectories pose risks to the developing child, these risks can be reduced. If the nature and quality of care provided to the child is changed and/or the child's or adult's working model of self and of relationships is modified, then, according to attachment theory, we should expect that developmental outcomes anticipated on the basis of early assessments of attachment security should not necessarily emerge. Although such contextual and/or personal changes may be difficult to evoke, they are presumed not only to be possible but also to have expectable outcomes. Indeed, under the right conditions, one might anticipate change in developmental trajectories and thus appropriately speak of "lawful discontinuity."

It is the assumption that lawful discontinuity is possible that provides clinical meaning to much attachment theory and research. If developmental trajectories can be redirected, and if this, in theory at least, can be done by affecting the child's caregiving environment and working model, then the goals of intervention become rather evident. It is one thing to be clear about goals, however, and quite another to be clear about means. In two chapters appearing in the final section of this volume, Lieberman and Pawl and Nezworski and her colleagues describe two distinct but not unrelated approaches to providing services to families whose infants are considered to be at risk on the basis of their attachment relationships. Although there are other factors in the family systems that provide the rationale for intervention in addition to the quality of the attachment bond, the services provided in both cases are based upon assumptions derived from attachment theory; namely, that the mother's way of relating to her infant is based, in part, upon her own working model of relationships forged in her own relationship history. In addition, the two intervention efforts described recognize the role of contemporary stressors, both within the family and beyond, which affect the caregiver's perception of her child and thus her pattern of mothering. Although neither report provides evidence that a particular intervention strategy is effective in ameliorating all difficulties encountered by parents and their infants, each highlights the way in which concepts derived from attachment theory and research inform clinical practice.

A major issue raised in the third chapter appearing in the section of the book dealing with clinical applications of attachment theory has to do with the clinical and diagnostic utility of the Strange Situation paradigm. Put rather simply, if attachment classifications are, to a degree, predictive of later behavioral problems, can they be used to diagnose infants at-risk and initiate services for them and their families? Greenspan and Lieberman, in the course of outlining their own approach to developmental assessment, strongly articulate a position that we ourselves subscribe to; namely, that this research procedure is neither sufficiently powerful, accurate, nor comprehensive to be employed as a diagnostic clinical tool. This is not to say, however, that it cannot prove informative; as the chapter by Nezworski and her colleagues points out, not only did collateral research information reveal families of insecure infants to be under particular stress, but so too did the actual therapeutic sessions provided to mothers of insecure infants. If assessments of attachment security are to be used in making clinical diagnoses, they should not be used in isolation. To be noted, also, is the fact that the Strange Situation is by no means necessarily the best, and certainly not the only, way to evaluate the attachment relationship.

CONCLUSIONS

The discovery that individual differences in the security of infant–mother attachment possess some power in predicting later developmental difficulties serves to underscore the fact that attachment theory and research are of clinical significance. In this chapter we have sought to highlight what some of these central implications are and particularly those that are addressed in the chapters of this volume. As we have seen, they pertain to the characterization of variation in attachment relationships, the origins of such variation, the developmental consequences of attachment and, finally, explicit applications of the attachment framework to diagnosis and service delivery.

REFERENCES

Bates, J., Maslin, C., & Frankel, K. (1985). Attachment security, mother–child interaction, and temperament as predictors of behavior problem ratings at age three years. In I. Bretherton & E. Waters (Eds.), *Growing points in attachment theory and research. Monographs of the Society for Research in Child Development* (pp. 167–193), Vol. 50, Nos. 1–2.

Belsky, J., & Rovine, M. (1987). Temperament and attachment security in the Strange Situation: An empirical rapproachement. *Child Development, 58.*

Bornstein, M., & Sigman, M. (1986). Continuity in mental development from infancy. *Child Development, 57,* 251–1274.

Bretherton, I. (1985). Attachment theory: Retrospect and prospect. In I. Bretherton & E. Waters (Eds.), *Growing points in attachment theory and research. Monographs of the Society for Research in Child Development* (pp. 3–36), Vol. 50, Nos. 209.

Cicchetti, D. (1984). The emergence of developmental psychopathology. *Child Development, 55* 1–7.

Dodge, K., & Richard, B. (1985). Peer perceptions, aggression, and the development of peer relations. In J. Pryor & J. Day (Eds.), *The development of social cognition.* New York: Springer-Verlag.

Erickson, M., Sroufe, A., & Egeland, B. (1985). The relationship between quality of attachment and behavior problems in preschool in a high-risk sample. In I. Bretherton & E. Waters (Eds.), *Growing points in attachment theory and research. Monographs for the Society for Research in Child Development* (pp. 147–166), Vol. 50, Nos. 1–2.

Fagan, J. (1984). *Infants' attention to visual novelty and the prediction of later intellectual deficit.* Paper presented at the International Conference on Infant Studies, New York.

Isabella, R., & Belsky, J. (1985). Marital change across the transition to parenthood and security of infant–parent attachment. *Journal of Family Issues, 6,* 505–522.

Kagan, J., Kearsley, R., & Zelazo, P. (1978). *Infancy: Its place in human development.* Cambridge, MA: Harvard University Press.

Lamb, M. E., Thompson, R. A., Gardner, W., Charnov, E. L., & Estes, D. (1984). Security of infantile attachment as assessed in the "Strange Situation": Its study and biological interpretation. *Behavioral and Brain Sciences, 7,* 127–147.

Lewis, M., Feiring, C., McGuffog, C., & Jaskir, J. (1984). Predicting psychopathology in six-year-olds from early social relations. *Child Development, 55,* 123–136.

Maslin, L., & Bates, J. (1982). *Anxious attachment as a predictor of disharmony in the mother–toddler relationship.* Paper presented at the International Conference on Infant Studies, Austin, TX.

Matas, L., Arend, R., & Sroufe, L. (1978). Continuity in adaptation in the second year: The relationship between quality of attachment and later competence. *Child Development, 49,* 547–556.

McCall, R. (1979). The development of intellectual functioning in infancy and the prediction of later IQ. In J. Osofsky (Ed.), *Handbook of infant development* (pp. 707–741). New York: Wiley.

Parke, R., & Slaby, R. (1983). The development of aggression. In M. E. Hetherington (Ed.), *Handbook of child psychology: Socialization, personality, and social development* (Vol. 4). New York: Wiley.

Radke-Yarrow, M., Cummings, E. M., Kucynski, L., & Chapman, M. (1985). Patterns of attachment in two- and three-year-olds in normal families and families with parental depression. *Child Development, 56,* 884–893.

Scarr-Salapatek, S. (1976). An evolutionary perspective on infant intelligence: Species patterns and individual variations. In M. Lewis (Ed.), *Origins of intelligence* (pp. 165–197). New York: Plenum.

Skolnick, A. (1986). Early attachment and personal relationships. In P. Baltes, D. Featherman, & R. Lerner (Eds.), *Life-span development and behavior* (Vol. 7, pp. 173–206). Hillsdale, NJ: Lawrence Erlbaum Associates.

Sroufe, L. A., & Rutter, M. (1984). The domain of developmental psychopathology. *Child Development, 55,* 17–29.

Waters, E. (1978). The reliability and stability of individual differences in infant–mother attachment. *Child Development, 49,* 483–494.

2

The Role of Infant–Caregiver Attachment in Development

L. Alan Sroufe
Institute of Child Development University of Minnesota

> *At all developmental levels maturationally guided processes are turned into developmental processes as a result of the adaptations enforced by exchanges with the surround and the organism's response to them . . . Maturation is a useful concept, but in reality there is only development.*

—Spitz, Emde, & Metcalf (1970)

In Bowlby's theory it was proposed that all human infants, however treated, become attached to persons who care for them (Bowlby, 1969/ 1982). The quality of such attachment relationships varies, however, depending on the quality of care the infant has experienced. Further, the quality of this early experience, and the relationship to which it leads, exercises an important influence on later development. Theoretically, this is because in the context of this developing relationship the infant forms initial expectations concerning self and other, or what bowlby (1973, 1980) called *inner working models.* Such models concerning the availability of others and, in turn, the self as worthy or unworthy of care, provide a basic context for subsequent transactions with the environment, most particularly social relationships.

Bowlby's ideas concerning working models recently have received increased attention, primarily due to the efforts of Main and Bretherton (Bretherton, 1985; Main, Kaplan, & Cassidy, 1985). Our own theoretical perspective (Sroufe, 1979; Sroufe & Fleeson, 1986) is closely related to, and draws heavily from Bowlby's theory. Differences are primarily a matter of emphasis. For example, we have emphasized how *relationships* are internalized, in addition to generalized expectations concerning self and others. Nonetheless, Bowlby's ideas that such experiences are

18

abstracted and represented (that such representations are active constructions) and that as working models they influence later experience and are subject to change, have strongly influenced my own research on attachment.

AN OVERVIEW OF SOME RECENT
ATTACHMENT RESEARCH

From the beginning, attachment research has been guided by the notion that Ainsworth attachment assessments (Ainsworth, Blehar, Waters, & Wall, 1978) capture not only aspects of infant behavior, but the relationship between infant and caregiver, and therefore provide entrée to the infant's inner working models of self, others, and relationships. In an early study my colleagues and I showed that quality of attachment in infancy predicted both the quality of maternal support as well as enthusiasm, persistence, compliance, and other aspects of toddler behavior (Matas, Arend, & Sroufe, 1978). A dissertation followed in which it was demonstrated that mothers' reported histories of nurturance in their own childhoods, could predict the quality of their infants' attachments (Morris, 1980, 1983). Thus, from infant behavior in the Strange Situation one can predict infant behavior. Other investigators also have obtained such results (Cox, Owen, Lewis, Riedel, Scalf-McIver, & Suster, in press; Main & Goldwyn, 1984; Ricks, 1985), and Main has beautifully articulated the process by which such relationship patterns are represented and carried forward.

The bulk of my work since these early studies has been addressed to later development outside of the home of children with known attachment histories. Still, these studies have been specifically guided by Bowlby's theoretical concepts. The most detailed work occurred in the context of the Minnesota preschool project. Forty children were brought together to look at their inner sense of confidence and their relationships with peers and teachers. It is in these domains that attachment theory makes its strongest claims.

The child's inner world was assessed in three basic ways. First, based on the composited Q-sorts of three teachers who were blind to attachment history, self-esteem scores were derived by comparing actual Q-sort descriptions to a self-esteem ideal Q-sort developed by Everett Waters. Dramatic differences were found between those preschoolers assessed in infancy as securely attached and those who had been anxiously attached— especially those with histories of avoidant attachment, where there was almost no overlap between groups (Sroufe, 1983). Even individual

Q-sort items, such as "appears to feel unworthy" were significantly discriminating.

A second aspect of the data on the child's inner world concerned the child's fantasy play. Two coders, blind to attachment history or any other data on the children, coded qualitative aspects and content of the children's fantasy play. Not only were there significant differences in the elaborateness, flexibility and overall quality of the fantasy play, but there were important content differences as well (Rosenberg, 1984). Most striking, for children having a history of avoidant attachment there was an almost total absence of fantasy themes concerning people, which was in sharp contrast to the play of securely attached children. Also, the play of secure children had fewer conflict themes, and, more importantly, when problems or conflicts were introduced into the play, they far more frequently were brought to satisfactory resolution than was the case for children with histories of anxious attachment. For example, a child with a secure history might have a theme of injury to a child—"Oh, no! He broke his leg"; but this would be followed by reparation—"Here comes the ambilens. They take him to the hospital. Zoom . . . they fixed it!".

Finally, we examined teacher, observer, and clinician's judgments of depression in these children, with coders again being blind and independent. There was substantial agreement among these independent sources (Garber, Cohen, Bacon, Egeland, & Sroufe, 1985), and the results with regard to attachment history were clear; depressive symptoms were associated with anxious attachment and avoidant attachment in particular.

In the preschool project, the child's expectations or models concerning self with others were explored by examining relationships with peers and with teachers. It was reported earlier that those with secure attachment histories are viewed by observers and teachers as being more competent with peers, more positive, more empathic, and more likely to develop friendships (Sroufe, 1983). They also rank higher on peer sociometrics. Beyond this it was found that their relationships with peers are deeper and less likely to be tinged with hostility (Pancake, 1985). Recently, Troy and Sroufe (in press) examined in detail an exploitative aspect of some relationships that we call victimization. The data clearly showed that children with histories of secure attachment neither victimized nor were they victimized by assigned play partners. In sharp contrast, children with avoidant histories were quite likely to victimize, and children with either anxious/avoidant or anxious/resistant histories were targeted for victimization. In fact, in each of 5 play pairs observed where the avoidant pattern was combined with either a second child with an avoidant history or a child with a resistant history, victimization occurred, and it occurred in none of the other 14 play pairs. Again, coders in all these studies were blind and contributed no other data to the study.

The power of inner models is perhaps even better illustrated by our recent analysis of preschool child–teacher relationships. We reasoned that if children bring forward models of self and relationships, these should be reflected in differential reactions of teachers. Although there would be interaction between teacher relationship history and child relationship history, there is a certain sense in which our preschool teachers, having relationships with all 40 children, were constants. Previously, we demonstrated that those with histories of anxious attachment were more emotionally dependent on preschool teachers (Sroufe, Fox, & Pancake, 1983). A new set of coders examined the involvement, affection, nurturance, anger, expectations for compliance, and tolerance for immature or inappropriate behavior of each of two teachers with each child. A clear picture emerged (Motti, 1986). The teachers treated those with secure histories in a matter-of-fact, yet warm way. They exercised little control over these children, yet clearly expected compliance with their directives and held high maturity standards for them (cf. Baumrind's, 1967, "authoritative" parenting). Children with anxious histories received much more control, and the teachers showed little expectation that they would comply. Whereas with the secure group, teachers turned and went about their business after giving a directive (being confident the child will comply), directives to those with anxious histories often were repeated and intensified even before the child had time to comply. Some interesting distinctions also are emerging between the avoidant and resistant groups. Teacher anger, although rare, was directed almost exclusively toward those with avoidant histories. In contrast, ratings of nurturance were quite high for the resistant group, as was tolerance for the child's immature behavior. The teachers seemed to see them as needy and not yet able to fully comply with classroom demands; therefore, they made allowances for them. Apparently, teachers, too, form expectations or models of particular children, and these models relate in complex ways to the children's attachment histories.

One final piece of research concerns a follow-up of 28 children in third grade. This study represents the most long-range prediction we have reported and, like the previous studies, it illustrates how Bowlby's model and a relationship perspective guide this research. The study involved Q-sort descriptions based on 3 days of school observation. Observers had never seen the children before and knew nothing about them. Deliberately, the focus was on two variables: anxiety/security and peer competence. Relevant items were composited for each variable (cf. Block & Block, 1979), and in both cases significant differences were obtained between those with secure and those with anxious histories (Bergmann, Egeland, & Sroufe, submitted). For the combined index, attachment history accounted for 20% of the variance. Given the developmental span covered and the challenges of demonstrating continuity with a poverty sample, we find these results impressive. There is, of course, also substantial change. This issue is dealt with in the following section.

IMPLICATIONS OF ATTACHMENT THEORY AND RESEARCH FOR UNDERSTANDING DEVELOPMENT

The complexity of the development viewpoint underlying attachment theory at times has not been sufficiently appreciated. When Bowlby's concept of inner working model is embraced, a new perspective on the issue of continuity and change emerges, an alternative to two extreme perspectives. One of these suggests that quality of adaptation is primarily a product of current circumstances; early experience especially is unlikely to exert much lasting influence because it effect will be washed out by later experience. Little continuity from the early years to later childhood is expected (Kagan, 1982). Any apparent continuity is illusory and occurs merely because the environment was unchanged (Lamb, 1984). The other equally extreme viewpoint would be a rigid critical-period hypothesis. According to this view, one's attachment and basic pattern of adaptation are fixed early in life and determine, in a linear way, later behavior. Although it is difficult to find anyone who holds this position, it has sometimes been attributed wrongly to attachment researchers, including myself (Lamb, 1984), despite clear statements to the contrary in all my published papers (see Appendix). Perhaps this misconception derives from the belief that infinite elasticity and complete fixity are the only options. But Bowlby's view and my own view are in sharp contrast to either of these positions.

   The idea of *working* models means both that such models are active constructions forged over time and they are subject to change. The inner aspect is meant to imply that the model is not simply formed and reshaped from the outside; rather, new experiences are engaged from within the framework of models already constructed, and change is an active rather than a passive process. Bowlby's is a sophisticated sensitive period hypothesis. One's models of self, others, and relationships begin to emerge in the first year and have some firmness even before leaving infancy. They become increasingly firm as their structuring is broadened and elaborated and as they are supported by more experience. By adolescence they have become quite firm, although new models of thinking here may also provide new opportunities for change (Main et al., 1985). The increasing firmness of models derives from the fact that with development the child becomes more of a force in creating his own environment (by choosing which relationships are sought out, which activities are engaged in, etc.)

and because an increasing range of experiences may be interpreted within (assimilated to) preexisting models.

Later experiences, of course, influence these inner models, but later experiences do not occur in a vacuum. As Bowlby (1973) has suggested, at each point development is a product of current circumstances and preceding development. Moreover, later experiences are not independent of preexisting models. The child seeks, creates, shapes, and interprets experience. What is rejection to one child is benign to another. What is warmth to a second child is confusing or ambiguous to another. For example, a child approaches another and asks to play. Turned down, the child goes off and sulks in a corner. A second child receiving the same negative reaction skips on to another partner and successfully engages him in play. Their experiences of rejection are vastly different. Each receives confirmation of quite different inner working models.

It is, of course, the case that change can and does take place, despite these forces toward continuity, and this point has been made repeatedly in our published papers (see Appendix). Moreover, we have several times provided clear data on changing adaptation and the role of relationships in such change (Egeland, Jacobvitz, & Sroufe, in press; Erickson, Egeland, & Sroufe, 1985; Vaughn, Egeland, Waters, & Sroufe, 1979). In particular, when our poverty mothers form stable relationships with a partner, child adaptation improves. Certainly in the early years, when family relationships undergo major change, so does child behavior and, presumably, so do the child's inner working models. Changing adaptation is fully consistent with, and poses no problem to, Bowlby's theory.

Even with respect to change, however, Bowlby's view is distinct from complete elasticity theories. First, once inner working models emerge, the child becomes a dramatically more active force in the parent–child relationship itself. Should an inconsistent parent become consistent in a later period, certainly the child would respond positively to this change. However, when the child holds models of the parent as unpredictable, and self as lacking in efficacy, difficult behavior results, calling for an unusual degree of consistency in the parent, which makes such change more difficult. Second, even should both relationship situation and child change, prior models are viewed as transformed but not erased. One of the most pressing research questions of our time concerns the differential stress resistance of groups of equally well-functioning children who differ in terms of their history of support. A related question concerns the nature of special issues retained by individuals even when quality of adaptation changes; for example, issues concerning abandonment, loss, and the expression of angry feelings.

It is sometimes useful for understanding the implications of the inner working model concept to make an analogy to a scientific theory, as

Epstein (1973) has proposed with regard to the self. In the early stages of theory construction, one may dramatically alter or abandon the theory in the face of some piece of new evidence. As the theory becomes more refined and as it is borne out repeatedly by wide-ranging evidence, one becomes more committed to it and more skeptical of disconfirming data. If one then has experience with such apparent disconfirmations evaporating, in time one's conviction deepens further. Ultimately, rather massive disconfirmation is required to abandon a robust and widely substantiated theory. Change remains possible but it becomes less likely; moreover, aspects of the theory may be carried forward to the new formulation.

To summarize here, attachment theory is *not* a critical period theory. Inner working models are constructed over time and are continually elaborated and, at times, fundamentally changed. At the same time, inner working models become somewhat firm even in early childhood, and such beginning models influence both the child's experiences and how these experiences are processed. Thus, there is a great deal of force on the side of basic continuity—that is, continuity in terms of the core features of one's representations of self, others, and relationships. Moreover, even when fundamental change occurs, it is presumed that early experience retains influence. This may take the form of a tendency to resume the previous pattern in the face of loss or other serious stress, or it may take the form of issues which remain salient or challenging for the individual.

MISCONCEPTIONS AND CLARIFICATIONS

We have discussed a major misconception appearing in the literature— that a critical-period hypothesis is embodied in Bowlby's attachment theory. A corollary to this is the idea that Ainsworth's A, B, and C categories are viewed as fixed patterns, that security in infancy guarantees healthy development and that patterns of anxious attachment scar one for life. I know of no one who believes in such fixity or simple-minded determinism, and it certainly does not characterize my own position (see Appendix). As is discussed in the psychopathology section, most anxiously attached infants would not be expected to be psychiatrically disturbed, and some children who were securely attached will show serious malfunctioning and notable pathology. Secure attachment is only a start toward healthy development, though it may indeed be a good start. What the probabilities for pathology for various attachment groups actually are remains to be fully tested.

There also has been confusion concerning A and C patterns as adaptations to the environment. As I (Sroufe, 1983) have written previously,

"Each child is making a particular and unique adaptation to his or her world" (p. 76). A and C patterns, of course, represent children's efforts to fit into the environments they have encountered. Main (1977) has argued that the avoidant pattern may even represent a required strategy for not alienating and for keeping an unresponsive or rejecting caregiver minimally accessible and thus maintaining, to some extent, the protective function of the attachment relationship. Certainly, A and C patterns are *adaptations,* and we presume them to be the best adaptations possible under the circumstances that prevail. Still, it is proposed that in an important sense they are *mal*adaptations. It is argued that these patterns compromise the capacity for dealing with subsequent developmental issues, especially those surrounding intimate social relationships and parenting, though not generally to the extent of influencing reproductive success. The test of this has been and remains the developmental consequences of these patterns (Waters & Sroufe, 1983). What may serve infants in some ways may not serve the same children well later, especially in other contexts. As Sroufe and Rutter (1984) have put it:

> thus, a given pattern of early adaptation could lead a child to isolate himself from peers or to alienate them, to avoid emotionally complex and stimulating social commerce, or to respond to such complexity in an impulsive or inflexible manner. Even such patterns may not be viewed a pathological (in the clinical sense) and certainly may be viewed as "adapted," in the sense that the child continues to strive toward a "fit" with the environment. (p. 23)

Another misconception regarding attachment research concerns whether factors other than primary attachments influence development. First, clearly there are aspects of parenting that influence child behavior and development beyond the provision of an available, emotionally responsive presence that leads to secure attachment. One important example concerns the socialization of impulse control. Parents differ enormously both in terms of their goals and their styles of limit setting, discipline, and control, and such differences are to some extent orthogonal to attachment pattern. I view basic responsiveness and warmth (and consequent secure attachment) as representing a core substrate, from which develops the child's inner sense of confidence, efficacy, and empathic regard for others. But on top of this substrate, layered around it as it were, are parental control and support for autonomy. The two are not totally unrelated, because children with histories of secure attachment are more likely to respond to parental directives and comply with parental boundaries (Londerville & Main, 1981; Matas et al., 1978; Stayton, Hogan, & Ainsworth, 1971). Nonetheless, the particular styles by which parents deal with issues of impulse expression and control will interact with attachment security in the personality formation process.

Second, it clearly is not the case that primary attachment relationships are all-important, with other relationships being irrelevant. We all agree that development is profoundly influenced by the network of family relationships and, beyond these, by relationships with peers, teachers, and others. Not only are children strongly influenced by their relationships with secondary caregivers, siblings, and so forth, but they also are impacted by the relationships among these other persons. In fact, I have been struck by the observation that in our poverty sample, which has a large proportion of single parents, the most healthy and the most extremely disturbed children often are from intact families. A relationship system may be far more powerful than a single relationship in shaping development toward health *or* pathology. There is nothing in attachment theory that says that only attachment status or only the caregiver's behavior influences development. To the contrary, I think one reason attachment assessments have proven to be such powerful predictors is precisely because they tap into a broader network of influence—relationship stability, available social support, life stress, and so forth.

In a similar vein, there is no implication of blaming mothers within this research. Yes, mothers commonly are primary caregivers. Yes, the quality of their care influences the quality of the attachment relationship and this, in turn, predicts subsequent adaptation, for reasons clarified earlier. Yet the quality of care provided depends on a host of factors including social support, preparation for parenthood and the caregiver's own developmental history and the consequent models of relationships that have been forged. To blame a mother is to blame her own mother and so on in infinite regress. Blaming the mother would be as inappropriate as blaming the child. At the same time, a strong case can be made that anxious attachment is not the responsibility of the infant. It is our societal obligation to insure that caregivers have the resources required for adequate parenting.

BOUNDARIES ON ATTACHMENT THEORY

There is also a need to clarify the predictive claims of attachment theory and to resist the tendency to seek any and all relationships between attachment security and other variables. Otherwise there is the risk of discrediting the theory through inappropriate overextension.

As previously stated, the specific claims of attachment theory concern the child's developing sense of inner confidence, efficacy and self-worth, and aspects of intimate personal relationship (the capacity to be emotionally close, to seek and receive care, and to give care to others). There are a range of corollaries to be sure. Thus, children with secure histories have been predicted (and found) to be more self-reliant, more empathic and less hostile with peers, and more cooperative with adults and so forth. but this range of corollaries is not without limit. Anxious attachment predicts retention in kindergarten, and I expect it to predict a number of aspects of school adjustment difficulties, but I do not expect that it will ultimately predict school grades. Ultimately, I expect no correlation with IQ, and to the extent that modest relationships are found with cognitive tests in the early years this may be because of different degrees of comfort with the examiner. Thus, in a sense, such relationships are indirect or even spurious. For the most part I would expect the unfolding of cognitive *competence* (in contrast to performance) to be robust with respect to attachment security.

Consider the example of language acquisition and language expression. Language acquisition seems to be influence heavily by the presence of language in the environment. If people talk to children they acquire language. One could imagine that some chronically depressed, uninvolved caregivers might fail to provide an adequate language environment. Such a pattern of caregiving might also lead to avoidant attachment. In general, one could therefore obtain a modest relationship between secure attachment and language acquisition. But predicting mean length of utterances or other aspects of language acquisition really isn't central in testing attachment theory, and the failure to find such relationships would not call Bowlby's theory into question. Far more relevant is the quality of the child's relationship with others, which can, of course, be expressed in part through language.

As another example, consider the confusion at present concerning the relationship between age of emergence of self-recognition and security of attachment. Lewis, Brooks-Gunn, and Jaskir (1985) report that anxiously attached children show self-recognition earlier; Cicchetti (1986) reports that it is earlier for those who are securely attached. In our own sample of 190 infants we found no relationship. Is this inconsistency problematic for attachment theory? Not at all. Emergence of self-recognition is probably tied to general cognitive/developmental processes (Mans, Cicchetti, & Sroufe, 1978), and it is not clear what claim concerning it would be derived from attachment theory. Self-awareness arises in every child and every child has a sense of self. it is not whether or when these appear, but their quality that is within the domain of attachment theory. Attachment theory strongly predicts that feelings of efficacy and inner worth should be related to secure attachment. I know of no claims concerning the age of emergence of self-concept.

In general, we need to be constrained in the predictions that we make from attachment theory. There are those who will some day count the number of "hits" and "misses," disregarding the precision of theoretical derivation. If we want to adequately test the theory and contribute to its evolution, our empirical efforts need to be thoughtfully guided. This may be especially true as we now begin to examine the links between quality of attachment in infancy and later psychopathology.

ATTACHMENT AND PSYCHOPATHOLOGY

Anxious attachment classifications are not equivalent to psychiatric diagnoses of infants. A and C patterns should not be viewed as forms of psychopathology; moreover, it remains likely that only a minority of such cases will ever develop psychiatric diagnoses. Even if such patterns are viewed as pathogenic, it remains the case, as discussed earlier, that they are subject to change. Moreover, multiple factors beyond primary attachment influence development, most notably other relationships, and many serious adult disorders (schizophrenia, depression) are thought to involve biological as well as experiential factors. Anxious attachment is not equivalent to psychopathology nor is it properly viewed as causing psychopathology in a linear way.

Yet, attachment theory and attachment research are vitally important to the discipline of developmental psychopathology (Cicchetti, 1984; Sroufe, 1986; Sroufe & Rutter, 1984). According to Sroufe (1986), developmental psychopathology is an integrative discipline, traversing the normal and abnormal and focusing on the process and source of individual patterns of adaptation:

> The focus of developmental psychopathology is not just childhood disorders but the course of individual differences in adaptation, normal and pathological. Developmental psychopathologists seek to understand the developmental roots of adult disorder, experiences that leave individuals vulnerable or buffered with respect to stressful life circumstances, and the capacity of individuals to draw strength from available social support. Bowlby's work, emphasizing vital human relationships, the quality of early adaptation, attachment, separation and loss, and the connectivity in experience, is central to this enterprise. It provides a framework for looking at psychopathology in a truly developmental manner. (p. 843)

From the point of view of developmental psychopathology there are several ways in which to view the relation between attachment and psychopathology:

1. Anxious attachment may be conceived as a marker variable or risk factor, suggesting that development is proceeding along a pathway that

may be probabilistically related to later problems. Analogous to inadequate peer relations in middle childhood, which has been identified as a "sturdy" predictor of adult maladjustment (Kohlberg, LaCrosse, & Ricks, 1972; Robins, 1978; Roff, Sells, & Golden, 1972), anxious attachment is of importance if it increments outcome predictions. The recent demonstration of a correlation between anxious attachment in infancy and peer competence in third grade takes on added significance from this perspective. Anxious attachment does not cause later pathology, for many anxious infants are not clinically disturbed as children, but it may place individuals at greater risk for pathology. Those few children in our longitudinal study who have shown clear psychiatric disturbance were indeed anxiously attached.

Lewis (1986) has reported recently that anxious attachment alone did not predict behavioral problems in school-age children. However, anxious attachment, combined with high stress, did predict behavioral problems. This is consistent with the view of anxious attachment history as a risk factor.

2. The other side of the risk equation concerns protective factors. Individuals differ in terms of their capacity to establish bases of social support, to seek support when required, and to draw strength from it. It would be hypothesized that secure attachment history, and consequent models of self as worthy of and effective in obtaining care, and others as available, would be an important factor in buffering individuals with respect to stress and their ability to cope with stress when it did occur.

3. Related to the aforementioned, individuals with a basic sense of inner security and confidence may more readily recover from debilitating stress and continue to "expect well" even in malevalent circumstances. One of the strongest associations ever uncovered in my research is between secure attachment and "ego-resiliency" (Sroufe, 1983), which is the capacity to flexiby engage the environment, to maintain organized behavior in the face of high arousal, and to recoup following stress.

4. Finally, a fruitful area for future research concerns the nature or quality of symptoms when individuals do become disordered. Even were it the case that attachment history did not predict strongly the presence or absence of disorder, it may still be related to the *type* of symptoms occurring in those individuals who do show disorder. Demonstrations of associations between avoidant attachment and depressive symptoms and conduct disorders in young children were not based on shots in the dark; such relationships make sense based on presumed inner-working models of children who have experienced chronic emotional unavailability or rejection. Such behaviors and even severe antisocial symptoms would be predicted for adolescents who become disordered and have avoidant histories. Conversely, from Bowlby's theory, sociopathic behavior in

individuals with histories of secure attachment would seem highly unlikely, regardless of degree of psychopathology. The first critical prospective studies through the adolescent period will be completed in the next decade.

CONCLUSION

Bowlby's claims concerning the central role of primary attachment relationships for certain core aspects of development have received strong support. In particular, the literature is congruent with Bowlby's idea that from primary relationships the child forges working models of self and other and that these models, although subject to change, exert an active influence on the child's ongoing transactions with the environment. Later experience does not wash over the child, but rather occurs in the context of preceding development.

It is on this basis that it is reasonable to expect some degree of continuity from the early years to middle childhood, adolescence, and even adulthood. Relationships will be complex and at times subtle; they will exist more notably at the level of the inner structuring of the self than in terms of manifest behavior, and they will be mediated by other factors such as encountered life stress. Relations between attachment and later behavior, normal and pathological, are not best viewed in linear, causal terms. Anxious attachment does not cause later peer incompetence, anxiety, antisocial behavior, or depression, but it may likely represent a developmental context that makes the emergence of such problems more likely.

ACKNOWLEDGMENT

Preparation of the chapter was supported in part by a grant from the National Institute of Mental Health (1 R01 MN/HD40864–01).

APPENDIX: ATTACHMENT, PATTERNS OF ADAPTATION, CONTINUITY AND CHANGE

The following are a series of quotations, beginning with the 1977 paper and continuing through papers published in 1986.

A. DOES ATTACHMENT PATTERN CAUSE LATER BEHAVIORS OR DOES CONTINUITY BETWEEN ATTACHMENT PATTERN AND

LATER BEHAVIOR REQUIRE ONGOING ENVIRONMENTAL SUPPORT? (IS QUALITY OF ADAPTATION CHANGEABLE?)

Behavior is dependent on environmental support. . . . (p. 1187).

> Sroufe, L. A., & Waters, E. (1977). Attachment as an organizational construct. *Child Development, 48,* 1184–1199.

Within our model of continuity, however, the issue is not stability but the coherence of individual development. We would not expect a child to be permanently scarred by early experience or permanently protected from environmental assaults. Early experience cannot be more important than later experience, and life in a changing environment should alter the quality of a child's adaptation (p. 56).

> Sroufe, L. A. (1978). Attachment and the roots of competence. *Human Nature, 1*(10), 50–57.

The issue of continuity of maternal variables is at least as important as continuity of infant variables.

Thus, it was expected that mothers of securely attached infants would be more sensitive when the infant was 2. . . .

During this time the continued emotional availability of the caregiver is essential if the child's autonomous ego is to attain optimal functional capacity, while his reliance on magic omnipotence recedes (p. 555).

> Matas, L., Arend, R. A., & Sroufe, L. A. (1978). Continuity of adaptation in the second year: The relationship between quality of attachment and later competence. *Child Development, 49,* 547–556.

Thus, continuity in quality of adaptation is seen as resulting from the child's functioning with respect to developmentally salient issues and its subsequent effects on later adaptation in conjunction with environmental support (p. 957).

> Arend, R., Gove, F. L., & Sroufe, L. A. (1979). Continuity of individual adaptation from infancy to kindergarten: A predictive study of ego resiliency and curiosity in preschoolers. *Child Development, 50,* 950–959.

Demonstrating coherence in individual development does not rest on continuity alone. Change may be comprehended as well. . . .

In contrast with our middle-class samples, these children experience noticeably fluctuating environmental circumstances. . . .

These fluctuating circumstances appear linked to the child's quality of adaptation (p. 840).

Sroufe, L. A. (1979). The coherence of individual development: Early care, attachment, and subsequent developmental issues. *American Psychologist, 34*(10), 834–841

Changes in circumstances can lead to changes in interaction and therefore to changes in relationships (p. 974).

Vaughn, B., Waters, E., Egeland, B., & Sroufe, L. A. (1979). Individual differences in infant–mother attachment at twelve and eighteen months: Stability and change in families under stress. *Child Development, 50,* 971–974.

Without doubt, experiences within the 3 years between infancy and preschool have a powerful influence on development.

In addition, the quality of a child's adaptation in the preschool likely is influenced by the ways parents managed the child's impulses and feelings during the transition from infancy to childhood.

There is no doubt that such styles of dealing with the toddler's impulses and feelings will impact upon the quality of adaptation in complex ways.

I believe there are three reasons for the demonstrated coherence. First, fortunately and unfortunately, there is often continuity in the quality of care. Parents who are inconsistent in responding to the infant's signals commonly are inconsistent and unclear in setting and maintaining limits for their toddler, and so forth.

It is sometimes concluded that the strong evidence in our research for continuity of individual adaptation (or even a downward spiral of maladaptation; Egeland & Sroufe, 1981b) suggests a pessimism concerning intervention. This is certainly not the case.

I have no doubt that in the preschool years the vast majority of these troubled children could be helped in a fundamental way toward healthier development (pp. 72–77).

Sroufe, L. A. (1983). Infant caregiver attachment and patterns of adaptation in preschool: The roots of maladaptation and competence. In M. Perlmutter (Ed.), *The Minnesota Symposia on Child Psychology* (Vol. 16, pp. 41–83). Hillsdale, NJ: Lawrence Erlbaum Associates.

It is, of course, not being argued that anxious attachment *causes* later overdependency; that is, were the caregiving environment substantially changed we would expect greatly reduced continuity in adaptation (cf. Vaughn et al., 1979). It is likely that caregivers that promoted formation of secure attachment continue to support the child in the preschool (Sroufe, 1979). Quality of attachment in infancy does, however, *predict* later dependency behavior (as nothing else has yet been shown to do), and it seems reasonable to assume that behavioral organization builds upon earlier foundations in a coherent manner (p. 1625).

Sroufe, L. A., Fox, N., & Pancake, V. (1984). Attachment and dependency in developmental perspective. *Child Development, 54,* 1615–1627

In modern terms personality is not a collection of static traits or even behavioral dispositions. It is not a thing or even a collection of things that person "have" in certain degrees (p. 51).

Sroufe, L. A., & Fleeson, J. (1986). Attachment and the construction of relationships. In W. Hartup & Z. Rubin (Eds.), *Relationships and development* (pp. 51–71) Hillsdale, NJ: Lawrence Erlbaum Associates.

B. ANXIOUS PATTERNS OF ATTACHMENT AS ADAPTATIONS

Each child is making a particular and unique adaptation to his or her world. Even children with very disturbed behavior became understandable. Even the most disturbed children must be viewed in terms of their particular patterns of adaptation (p. 76).

Sroufe, L. A. (1983). Patterns of individual adaptation from infancy to preschool: The roots of maladaptation and competence. In M. Perlmutter (Ed.), *Minnesota Symposia on Child Psychology* (Vol. 16, pp. 41–83). Hillsdale, NJ: Lawrence Erlbaum Associates.

For each child these adaptations (the accomplished "fit" between child and this aspect of environment) are unique.

Thus a given pattern of early adaptation could lead a child to isolate himself from peers or to alienate them, to avoid emotionally complex and stimulating social commerce, or to respond to such complexity in an impulsive or inflexible manner. Even such patterns may not be viewed as pathological (in the clinical sense) and certainly may be viewed as "adapted," in the sense that the child continues to strive toward a "fit" with the environment (p. 23).

Sroufe, L. A., & Rutter, M. (1984). The domain of developmental psychopathology. *Child Development, 55,* 17–29.

C. HOW IS EARLY EXPERIENCE OF SPECIAL IMPORTANCE?

Still, early experience may be of special importance in two ways. First, the child is engaged in active transactions with the environment. The child not only interprets experience, the child creates experience. As Alfred Adler has suggested, the child is both the artist and the painting. If because of early experience the preschooler isolates himself from the peer group, he removes himself further from positive social experiences. Second, if self-esteem and trust are established early, children may be more resilient in the face of environmental stress. They may show poor adaptation during an overwhelming crisis, but when the crisis has passed and the environment is again positive, they may respond more quickly. Even when floundering, some children may not lose their sense that they can affect the environment and that, ultimately, they will be all right (p. 45).

Sroufe, L. A. (1978). Attachment and the roots of competence. *Human Nature, 1*(10), 50–57.

Second, since children interact with the environment in terms of their previous adaptation, a self-perpetuating cycle is maintained. The C baby, for example commonly is a difficult toddler who taxes the patience of the parent, and later is a highly dependent or impulsive preschooler who alienates others. The A baby learns not to seek the emotional support it needs and later keeps others at a distance through emotional isolation or hostility.

Finally, development is hierarchical; it is not a blackboard to be erased and written upon again. Even when children change rather markedly, the shadows of the earlier adaptation remain and, in times of stress, the prototype itself may be clear (pp. 73–74).

Sroufe, L. A.(1983). Patterns of individual adaptation from infancy to preschool: The roots of maladaptation and competence. In M. Perlmutter (Ed.), *Minnesota Symposia on Child Psychology* (Vol. 16, pp. 41–83). Hillsdale, NJ: Lawrence Erlbaum Associates.

But if the adaptation compromises the normal developmental process whereby children are increasingly able to draw emotional support from agemates (as well as give it), and to stay engaged in social commerce despite the frequent emotional challenge of doing so, the individual may be sacrificing an important buffer against stress and, ultimately, psychopathology (p. 23).

Sroufe, L. A., & Rutter, M. (1984). The domain of developmental psychopathology. *Child Development, 55,* 17–29.

REFERENCES

Ainsworth, M. D. S., Blehar, M., Waters, E., & Wall, S. (1978). *Patterns of attachment.* Hillsdale, NJ: Lawrence Erlbaum Associates.

Arend, R., Gove, F., & Sroufe, L. A. (1979). Continuity of individual adaptation from infancy to kindergarten: A predictive study of ego-resiliency and curiosity in preschoolers. *Child Development, 50,* 905–959.

Baumrind, D. (1967). Child care practices anteceding three patterns of preschool behavior. *Genetic Psychology Monographs, 75,* 43–88.

Bergmann, S., Egeland, B., & Sroufe, L. A. (1986). *Peer competence and anxiety in middle childhood: Prediction from infant–caregiver attachment.* Unpublished manuscript.

Block, J. H., & Block, J. (1979). The role of ego-control and ego-resiliency in the organization of behavior. In W. A. Collins (Ed.), *Minnesota Symposia on Child Psychology* (Vol. 13, pp. 39–101). Hillsdale, NJ: Lawrence Erlbaum Associates.

Bowlby, J. (1982). *Attachment and loss,* Vol. 1: *Attachment* (2nd ed.). New York: Basic Books. (Originally published 1969)

Bowlby, J. (1973). *Attachment and loss,* Vol. 2: *Separation.* New York: Basic Books.

Bowlby, J. (1980). *Attachment and loss,* Vol. 3: *Loss, sadness and depression.* New York: Basic Books.

Bretherton, I. (1985). Attachment theory: Retrospect and prospect. In I. Bretherton & E. Waters (Eds.), *Growing points in attachment theory and research. Monographs of the Society for Research in Child Development, 50,* (Serial No. 209).

Cicchetti, D. (1984). The emergence of developmental psychopathology. *Child Development, 55,* 1–5.

Cicchetti, D. (1986, April). *Organization of the self system in atypical populations.* Paper presented at the Biennial Meeting of the International Conference on Infant Studies, Los Angeles.

Cox, M., Owen, M., Lewis, J., Riedel, C., Scalf-McIver, L., & Suster, A. (in press). Intergenerational influences on the parent–infant relationship in the transition to parenthood. *Journal of Family Issues.*

Egeland, B., Jacobvitz, D., & Sroufe, L. A. (in press). Breaking the cycle of abuse. *Child Development.*

Epstein, S. (1973). The self-concept revisited, or a theory of a theory. *American Psychologist, 28,* 404–416.

Erickson, M., Egeland, B., Sroufe, L. A. (1985). The relationship between quality of attachment and behavior problems in preschool in a high risk sample. In I. Bretherton & E. Waters (Eds.), *Growing points in attachment theory and research. Monographs of the Society for Research in Child Development, 50,* (Serial No. 209), 147–186.

Garber, J., Cohen, E., Bacon, P., Egeland, B., & Sroufe, L. A. (1985). *Depression in preschoolers: Reliability and validity of a behavioral observation measure.* Paper presented at the Society for Research in Child Development, Toronto.

Kagan, J. (1982). *Psychological research on the human infant: An evaluative summary.* New York: W. T. Grant Foundation.

Kohlberg, L., LaCrosse, J., & Ricks, D. (1972). The predictability of adult mental health from childhood behavior. In B. Wolman (Ed.), *Manual of child psychopathology* (pp. 1217–1284). New York: McGraw-Hill.

Lamb, M. (1984). Fathers, mothers, and childcare in the 1980s: Family influences on child development. In K. Borman, D. Quarm, & S. Gideonese (Eds.), *Women in the workplace: Effects on families* (pp. 61–88). Norwood, NJ: Ablex.

Lewis, M., Brooks-Gunn, J., & Jaskir, J. (1985). Individual differences in visual self-recognition as a function of mother–infant attachment relationship. *Developmental Psychology, 21,* 1181–1183.

Londerville, S., & Main, M. (1981). Security of attachment, compliance, and maternal training methods in the second year of life. *Developmental Psychology, 17,* 289–299.

Main, M. (1977). Analysis of a peculiar form of reunion behavior seen in some daycare children: Its history and sequaelae in children who are home reared. In R. Webb (Ed.), *Social development in daycare* (pp. 33–78). Baltimore: Johns Hopkins University Press.

Main, M., & Goldwyn, R. (1984). Predicting rejection of her infant from mother's representation of her own experience: Implications for the abused-abusing intergenerational cycle. *Child Abuse and Neglect, 8,* 203–217.

Main, M., Kaplan, N., & Cassidy, J. (1985). Security in infancy, childhood and adulthood: A move to the level of representation. In I. Bretherton & E. Waters (Eds.) *Growing points in attachment theory and research. Monographs of the Society for Research in Child Development, 50* (Serial No. 209), 66–104.

Mans, L., Cicchetti, D., & Sroufe, L. A. (1978). Mirror reactions of Down's syndrome infants and toddlers. Cognitive underpinnings of self-recognition. *Child Development, 49,* 1247–1250.

Matas, L. Arend, R., & Sroufe, L. A. (1978). Continuity of adaptation in the second year: The relationship between quality of attachment and later competent functioning. *Child Development, 49,* 547–556.

Morris, D. (1980). *Infant attachment and problem solving in the toddler: Relations to mothers' family history.* Unpublished doctoral dissertation, University of Minnesota.

Morris, D. (1983). Attachment and intimacy. In G. Stricker & M. Fisher (Eds.), *Intimacy* (pp. 305–323). New York: Plenum.

Motti, F. (1986). *Relationships of preschool teachers with children of varying developmental histories.* Unpublished doctoral dissertation, University of Minnesota.

Pancake, V. R. (1985, April). *Continuity between mother–infant attachment and ongoing dyadic peer relationships in preschool.* Paper presented at the Biennial meeting of the Society for Research in Child Development, Toronto.

Ricks, M. (1985). The social transmission of parental behavior. Attachment across generations. In I. Bretherton & E. Waters (Eds.), *Growing points in attachment theory and research. Monographs of the Society for Research in Child Development, 50,* (Serial No. 209), 211–227.

Robins, L. (1978). Sturdy childhood predictors of adult antisocial behavior: Replications from longitudinal studies. *Psychological Medicine, 8,* 611–622.

Roff, M., Sells, S., & Golden, M. (1972). *Social adjustment and personality development in children.* Minneapolis: University of Minnesota Press.

Rosenberg, D. (1984). *The quality and content of preschool fantasy play: correlates in concurrent social-personality function and early mother–child attachment relationships.* Unpublished doctoral dissertation, University of Minnesota.

Spitz, R., Emde, R., & Metcalf, D. (1970). Further prototypes of ego formation. *Psychoanalytic Study of the Child, 25,* 417–444.

Sroufe, L. A. (1979). The coherence of individual development. *American Psychologist, 34,* 834–841.

Sroufe, L. A. (1983). Infant–caregiver attachment and patterns of adaptation in the preschool: The roots of competence and maladaptation. In M. Perlmutter (Ed.), *Minnesota Symposia in Child Psychology* (Vol. 16, pp. 41–83). Hillsdale, NJ: Lawrence Erlbaum Associates.

Sroufe, L. A. (1986). Bowlby's contribution to psychoanalytic theory and developmental psychopathology. *Journal of Child Psychology and Psychiatry, 27,* 841–849.

Sroufe, L. A., & Fleeson, J. (1986). Attachment and the construction of relationships. In W. Hartup & Z. Rubin (Eds.), *Relationships and development* (pp. 51–71). Hillsdale, NJ: Lawrence Erlbaum Associates.

Sroufe, L. A., Fox, N., & Pancake, V. (1983). Attachment and dependency in developmental perspective. *Child Development, 54,* 1615–1627.

Sroufe, L. A., & Rutter, M. (1984). The domain of developmental psychopathology. *Child Development, 55,* 17–29.

Stayton, D., Hogan, R., & Ainsworth, M. (1971). Infant obedience and maternal behavior: The origins of socialization reconsidered. *Child Development, 42,* 1057–1069.

Troy, M., & Sroufe, L. A. (in press). Victimization among preschoolers: The role of attachment relationship history. *Journal of the American Academy of Child Psychiatry.*

Waters, E., & Sroufe, L. A. (1983). A developmental perspective on competence. *Developmental Review, 3,* 79–97.

Vaughn, B., Egeland, B., Waters, E., Sroufe, L. A. (1979). Individual differences in infant–mother attachment at 12 and 18 months: Stability and change in families under stress. *Child Development, 50,* 971–975.

II

DETERMINANTS OF ATTACHMENT SECURITY AND INSECURITY

3

Maternal, Infant, and Social-Contextual Determinants of Attachment Security

Jay Belsky
The Pennsylvania State University

Russell Isabella
Utah State University

As noted in the introductory chapter to this volume, it was only a decade or so ago that students of infancy and early childhood were taught that individual differences in child development could not be predicted on the basis of information obtained during the first year of life. Yet today, on the basis of just 10 years' worth of theoretically informed empirical inquiry into the developmental "consequences" of attachment security (and insecurity), such a conclusion is regarded by most as patently false. In point of fact, critics as well as proponents of the Strange Situation procedure (used for measuring security of infant–parent attachment) acknowledge the predictive power of 12 to 18 month attachment classifications (Bretherton, in press; Lamb, Thompson, Gardner, Charnov, & Estes, 1984), even if they are in disagreement as to why such prediction from infancy to early childhood is successful.

Although inquiry into the consequences of individual differences in attachment security has captured the interest of a great many clinicians and researchers, and has spawned new approaches to thinking about and studying continuity and discontinuity in early development (see Chapter 1), it has not been the only attachment-related issue that has generated a great deal of theoretically informed research. The second major issue that has long occupied theoretician and researcher alike, and that serves as the focus of this chapter, involves the developmental antecedents responsible for the individual differences in security of attachment that are so readily observed in the Strange Situation at 1 year.[1] The prevailing notion holds

---

[1]The Strange Situation procedure was developed for use with infants ranging in age from

41

that it is mothers' sensitivity to their children that leads to the development of secure attachment relationships. That is, mothers who perceive, accurately interpret, and respond in a prompt and appropriate manner to their infants' communications cultivate secure attachment relationships by providing an environment for the infant that is predictable and controllable, and which thereby promotes his/her regulation of arousal and sense of efficacy (cf. Ainsworth, Bell, & Stayton, 1974; Sroufe, 1979a, 1979b). It is further assumed within this framework that the infant contributes to the development of the attachment relationship to the extent that his/her endogenously based behavioral dispositions (globally referred to as infant temperament) influence mother's care by making it more or less difficult for mother to meet the infant's idiosyncratic needs. It is presumed by theoreticians such as Ainsworth and Sroufe, as well as by ourselves and many others, however, that mother holds the balance of influential power in the relationship; that is, mother ultimately determines when and how interactions will transpire, at least until the infant has developed the capacity for mobility (Ainsworth, 1972). Thus, the infant's temperament is acknowledged as playing a role in the development of the attachment relationship, but primarily in terms of the extent to which it influences the probability that mother will provide sensitive, security-promoting care (Sroufe, 1985).

Although the theory regarding the role of maternal sensitivity in the development of infant–mother attachment is quite clear if not compelling, the data available to substantiate it are neither as strong nor as consistent as those concerning the consequences of individual differences in attachment (Lamb et al., 1984). Nor are they as clear and compelling as some proponents of the role of maternal sensitivity contend (e.g., Ainsworth et al., 1974; Sroufe, 1985). This is not to say, however, that there is justification in concluding, as some have, that little if any empirical evidence exists for the theory outlined (Lamb et al., 1984). Rather, it must be stated that although the general notion of maternal sensitivity and its significance in the development of secure attachment relationships has been demonstrated (cf. Sroufe, 1985), operationalization of the sensitivity construct has not been uniformly successful in documenting specific behavioral antecedents of 12-month infant–mother attachment. That is, although data are available that highlight the theoretically expected linkages

---

12 to 18 months (Ainsworth, Blehar, Waters, & Well, 1978). In the course of our chapter, general discussion of attachment quality as assessed in the Strange Situation, in those cases where reference to either or both ages would be appropriate, refer to 12 months only. It must be understood, therefore, that discussions regarding 12-month attachment classifications are expected to hold true for assessments occurring between 12 and 18 months as well. In the case of reported research findings, reference to age at attachment quality assessments are specific.

between sensitive mothering and secure attachment, not all data that address this topic provide such support.

As Sroufe (1985) noted recently in a critical review of theories that posit temperament as the sole determinant of individual differences in attachment, four distinct studies have replicated Ainsworth's seminal findings (summarized in Ainsworth et al., 1978) in showing that *highly detailed* clinical ratings of maternal sensitivity taken during the infant's first year distinguish secure and insecure attachment groups at 12 months (Bates, Maslin, & Frankel, 1985; Egeland & Farber, 1984; Grossman, Grossman, Gottfried, Spangler, Suess, & Unzer, 1985). It is important to recognize that these studies have been carried out by different groups of researchers, in different countries (including Germany; Grossman et al., in press), and all have reported, as predicted, that mothers whose infants have developed secure attachments by 12 months are *rated* as significantly more sensitive in interactions with their infants during all or part of their first year of life than mothers whose infants become insecurely attached (see also Barglow & Hoffman, 1985, for a fifth replication using 9-month ratings during a feeding interaction).

Having presented support for the clinically measured (i.e., evaluative ratings) construct of maternal sensitivity as a significant predictor of 12-month infant–mother attachment security, it must be pointed out, as previously stated, that efforts to examine maternal sensitivity with more specific, behaviorally detailed data collection procedures have not provided uniform and unambiguous results. Although some studies that rely on behavioral codes rather than clinical ratings provide support for the mother-as-influential-agent thesis, others do not. A brief summary of some of the significant findings is needed, given the tendency of opponents as well as proponents of this thesis to selectively consider the evidence in efforts to show that sensitive mothering is or is not influential.

Ainsworth's seminal work resulted in the presentation of evidence indicating that mothers of securely attached 1-year-olds were more affectionate, tender, careful, and less inept while in close bodily contact with their infants during the first and fourth quarters of the first year, and were more likely to contingently pace their behaviors during face-to-face interactions and feedings within the infant's first 3 months of life than mothers of insecure 1-year-olds (Ainsworth, Blehar, Waters, & Wall, 1978). In addition to this early work, Maslin and Bates (1983), Crockenberg (1981), Miyake, Chen, and Campos (in press), and Belsky, Rovine, and Taylor (1984), to name but a few, have subsequently reported theoretically meaningful covariation between maternal behavior during the first year and infant behavior observed in the Strange Situation at 12 months. Crockenberg's 3-hour, in-home observations of mothers and their 3-month-olds revealed, for example, that mothers who responded most promptly to their infants' distress signals had 1-year-olds who exhibited significantly more proximity-seeking and significantly less resistance to mother in the Strange Situation than those infants whose distress signals were not promptly responded to at 3 months. These findings are consistent with those of Belsky et al., which indicated that infants who at 1 year were classified as securely attached had mothers who were more responsive to their cries and vocalizations at 3 and 9 months than mothers of insecure 1-year-olds. Looking at mother–infant interaction at 6 months, Bates and his colleagues reported that securely attached 13-month-olds experienced significantly higher levels of affectionate contact from their mothers than did their insecurely attached agemates (Maslin & Bates, 1983) and were involved in more mutually positive face-to-face interaction (Kiser, Bates, Maslin, & Bayles, 1986). In addition, mothers of securely attached infants were quicker to respond to their infants' cries and social elicitations than were mothers of insecurely attached infants (Bates, Maslin, & Frankel, 1985). As a final example of supportive evidence for the thesis proposed, Miyake et al. (1985) found that during a 7-month laboratory situation, those Japanese infants who would develop secure attachments had mothers who were significantly less intrusive, i.e., less likely to interrupt their baby's ongoing behavior, and who held their infants longer than those mothers whose infants developed insecure-resistant attachment relationships.[2]

It should be noted, however, that in contrast to what we and others would have predicted, Miyake et al. (1985) found no differences between mothers of secure and insecure infants with respect to their responsiveness to infant behaviors and effectiveness of infant stimulation. Similarly, Maslin and Bates (1983) failed to discern differences between attachment groups as a function of mothers' type and degree of stimulation of their infants, as well as their amount of nonaffectionate communication with their infants. As a final example of nonsupportive findings, Egeland and Farber (1984) could not distinguish mothers of secure and insecure 1-year-olds in terms of their quality of physical contact, facility in caretaking, or positive regard for the infant during 3 and 6-month feeding observations,

---

[2]It should be noted that serious concerns have been raised about the administration of the Strange Situation to the Japanese infants Miyake et al. studied. Not only was it the case that these infants had virtually no experience with separation given cultural child-rearing practices, but probably as a consequence, their reactions to separation were extreme. As Sroufe (personal communication, 1985) notes, having observed the videotapes, "these babies were blown out by the procedure and therefore determining, A, B, and C (attachment classifications) was impossible." Indeed, he goes on to point out the original scorer of the videotapes in Japan, Keuko Takahashi, felt the same way.

nor as a function of their patience or amount of reciprocal play with infant during a 6-month standardized play observation.

In summary, although there is an abundance of antecedent data that are consistent with the mother-as-influential-agent thesis, evidence that fails to support this contention is also available—often in the very same studies that show differences in behaviors of mothers of secure and insecure infants. Our inclination is to consider the trends in the data, particularly in view of the diverse samples and methods that have been employed to address the issue or origins of individual differences in attachment and the inherent difficulty encountered in attempting to operationalize a construct as subtle as maternal sensitivity. To our reading the trends are clear, even if not compelling to the skeptic: Mother's behavior during the first year does consistently (but not universally) covary with security of attachment as assessed at 1-year in the Strange Situation, suggesting that mothers of secure infants are more accepting of, responsive to, positively affectionate toward, and thereby more sensitive to their infants. In sum, we think there is enough consistency, even in the absence of uniformity, to treat the sensitivity-security linkage as, at the very least, a viable working hypothesis.

BEYOND MOTHER–INFANT INTERACTION

To the extent that maternal behavior and sensitivity play a major role in the development of secure infant–parent attachment, it stands to reason that factors beyond the specific interactions that transpire between mother and infant also serve to influence the development of attachment security, if only because they are likely to affect the very behavioral exchanges that take place between mother and infant that are considered to be the medium through which the relationship develops. That this is indeed the case is most apparent in data indicating that the proportion of secure attachments is considerably smaller in impoverished samples living under chronic stress than in middle-class samples. Whereas the rate of secure attachments tends to fall between 65% and 75% in most middle-class samples studied (e.g., Ainsworth et al., 1978; Belsky, Rovine, & Taylor, 1984; Maslin & Bates, 1983; Weber, Levitt, & Clark, in press), investigations such as that of Egeland and Farber (1984) report considerably lower rates (i.e., 55%) for lower class, high-risk samples (see also Lyons-Ruth, Connell, Grunebaum, Botein, & Zoll, 1984; Spieker & Booth, 1985). Such data suggest to us that forces beyond the immediate interactions between mother and infant influence the development of the infant–mother attachment relationship, probably by affecting the extent and nature of mother's physical and psychological availability to her baby.

Interesting to note is the fact that, to our knowledge, no studies have linked such distal influences (e.g., socioeconomic status, SES) to proximal processes (e.g., mother–infant interaction) and, thereby, to individual differences in security of attachment as would be required to test this thesis. Although the ultimate goal of our own research program is to pursue such linkages from distal forces (e.g., social network, maternal personality, marital relationship) to proximal forces (i.e., actual mother–infant interaction), to security of attachment, in this chapter we merely initiate the pursuit of this goal. That is, we attempt to link distal influences directly to attachment while we explore elsewhere the relation between these distal forces and observed mother–infant interaction (Belsky, Hertzog, & Rovine, 1986) and between observed interaction and attachment (Belsky, 1984).

Although the social class comparisons cited earlier draw attention to the role that such distal factors may play in the development of security, it happens to be the case that much less empirical, if not theoretical, attention has been paid to these factors, especially in comparison to studies of maternal behavior as antecedents of attachment or studies of the predictive power of attachment for later child development. Unfortunately, when potential contextual influences have been studied, they have been examined in isolation, i.e., one at a time (e.g., Durrett, Otaki, & Richards, 1984), or attempts to relate multiple potential influences to attachment have been empirically and theoretically problematic (e.g., Maslin & Bates, 1983). Most important in this regard is the fact that investigators have failed to distinguish sufficiently between different sources of influence. Rather than examining the distinct association between attachment security and maternal personality, social network support, or stressful life events, for example, multiple measures of these and many other constructs are virtually "thrown at" attachment security using multivariate data analytic techniques in order to see which individual variables, in which combinations, discriminate groups. The utilization of analytic strategies that fail to maintain conceptually important distinctions, besides looking (and functioning) like empirical fishing expeditions, leaves one with the sense that the very thoughtfulness that seems to have guided initial study design and instrument selection is all but forgotten when the critical time comes to analyze the very data that were so wisely and arduously gathered. It is as if the high-speed computer, which is so seductive in its capacity to "handle" greater quantities of information, deludes the investigator into believing that statistics can replace theory.

We believe that this potential pitfall can be avoided—and consciously so—by articulating a conceptual framework to guide empirical inquiry and using such a framework to form data analysis and interpretation; this is exactly our strategy for the present chapter, which deals with factors beyond mother–infant interactions. The framework we draw upon is based on a process model of the determinants of parenting (Belsky, 1984) that is depicted in Fig. 3.1. The model presumes that the parent–child relationship is directly influenced by forces emanating from within the individual parent (child-rearing history and personality), within the individual child (child characteristics of individuality), and from the broader social context in which the parent–child relationship is embedded, specifically, marital relations, social networks, and occupational experiences of parents. Further, the model assumes that parents' developmental histories, marital relations, social networks, and jobs influence their individual personalities and general psychological well-being and, thereby, what transpires between them and their children. Basic to this guiding framework is the notion that individual differences in the quality of parent–child relations are multiply determined. We proceed now, therefore, to consider available evidence indicating that characteristics of the mother, her infant, and the broader social context in which the mother–infant relationship is embedded are systematically related to individual differences in attachment security. Upon completion of this review, we examine the relationship between these potential determinants of attachment security and actual attachment security using data from a longitudinal study designed to address this very issue.

Characteristics of the Mother

Belsky's (1984) model of the determinants of parenting depicted in Fig. 3.1 draws attention to two distinct aspects of mothers as individuals that may be related to the quality of the relationships they establish with their infants; these are their own experiences during childhood, most especially the way they were reared in their families of origin (i.e., developmental history), and their personal psychological resources (i.e., personality). To

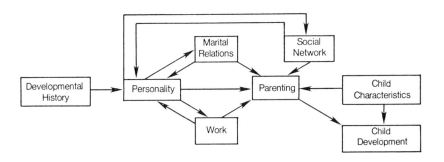

FIG. 3.1.   Process model of the determinants of parenting (from Belsky, 1984).

date, only a handful of studies have included measures sufficient to permit examination of the influence of these maternal characteristics as they relate to infant–mother attachment security. In fact, to our knowledge, only four investigations address the issue of mothers' experiences in their own childhoods. Each is limited by the fact that information on developmental history was gather retrospectively, long after the mother had moved away from her parents' home. Because the validity of such reports is unknown, the results of these investigations can only be considered suggestive with respect to the influence of mothers' childhood experiences in their families of origin on subsequent mother–infant relationship development. In view of the absence of prospective data, however, these studies merit careful consideration.

In the very first investigation examining the developmental history of mothers of securely and insecurely attached infants, Morris (1980, 1981) gathered family history data by means of a 160-item family-of-origin interview designed by a family therapist. An objective scoring of this clinical interview (Morris, 1981) revealed that "mothers of anxiously attached children came from families where there was an emotionally intense father–daughter relationship with her or a sister, and a 'role reversal' between daughter and mother" (p. 316). In contrast, "mothers of securely attached children were likely to be positively identified with their mothers and to perceive them as strong, nurturant, and emotionally available. The generational boundaries were more clearly drawn and children's emotional needs were more likely to be met without jeopardizing parental self-esteem" (p. 316).

Consistent with these findings are those emanating from a study of some 28 mothers' recollections of their own parents' acceptance of them during childhood. Ricks (1985b) found that mothers of securely attached 1-year-olds recalled significantly more acceptance and less rejection from each of their parents than did mothers of insecurely attached 1-year-olds. In another investigation, however, this one of low income families, reports of parental warmth (in family of origin) failed to distinguish mothers of secure and insecure-avoidant infants (Lyons-Ruth et al., 1984); in fact, a discriminant function analysis actually revealed that mothers of secure infants reported more family conflict than those of insecure-avoidant infants. In the fourth study to examine the relationship between recollected child-rearing history and attachment security, Main and Goldwyn (1984) reported results consistent with those of Ricks in an investigation in which developmental history data were gathered during in-depth clinical interviews carried out 4 years *after* the actual assessment of infant–mother attachment. Infants who displayed heightened avoidance in the Strange Situation at 1 year had mothers who had trouble recalling their childhoods or, when they did recall them, tended to idealize their mothers (i.e., denying negative attributes), to be disorganized in their presentation of the kinds of people their mothers were, or to report that their mothers were less attentive toward them during their childhoods.

Although all the data under consideration emanate from correlational and retrospective investigations and are not completely consistent, the Morris, Ricks, and Main findings do provide support for the conclusion that experiences during childhood are associated with, and may even causally influence the quality of the relationship a mother and infant establish. This is not to say, however, that stressful child-rearing experiences inevitably put the mother at risk in terms of the relationship she establishes with her own infant. Indeed, Main and Goldwyn discovered that those mothers whose childhood experiences were problematic did not have insecure infants if the women could express anger toward their own mothers during the clinical interviews. It seems, the, that the mothers who had psychologically worked through their earlier experiences had reduced the potential of these histories for exerting a detrimental effect on their own maternal role performance. This line of reasoning suggests, like the model depicted in Fig. 3.1, that the influence of childhood experience on infant–mother attachment is likely to result from the effect of childhood experiences on personality development and, thereby, patterns of mother–infant interaction.

In view of this analysis, it is especially unfortunate that the relationship between maternal personality and attachment security has not been extensively researched. Nonetheless, four of six investigations that do address this issue to some degree provide some support for the contention that women who are psychologically healthier are more likely to raise infants who establish secure attachment relationships with them. In the previously mentioned Ricks (1985b) study, it was found that mothers of secure infants displayed significantly higher levels of general self-esteem on a standard personality inventory than did mothers of insecure 1-year-olds; and in the previously cited Lyons-Ruth study, discriminant function analysis revealed that mothers of insecure-avoidant infants experienced more depression than those of secure infants (Lyons-Ruth et al., 1984). More recently, Benn (1985) reported that working mothers of securely attached 18-month-olds were rated higher than working mothers of insecurely attached toddlers on a scale of emotional integration (based on a clinical interview) that assessed general level of competence, emotional responsivity, warmth, and acceptance of motherhood. In Maslin and Bates' (1983) longitudinal study of some 160 mother–infant pairs, mothers who appeared, on a series of personality tests, more nurturant, more understanding, more autonomous, less aggressive, more dependent, and who seemed to be more inquisitive, to enjoy physical sensation, and to be responsive to stimuli, also had infants more likely to be classified as securely attached to them. This was also true of mothers who displayed little tendency to dominate others or to be self-centered (as revealed by dominance-exhibitionism scores).

Two final studies of which we are aware failed to provide strong evidence of a relationship between maternal personality and attachment security. Levitt, Weber, and Clark (in press) reported that several indices of maternal well-being, including life satisfaction, affect balance, positive affect, and negative affect, did not covary with 13-month quality of attachment assessments. These authors did point out, however, that despite nonsignificant univariate results, a contrast between mothers of secure and anxious-resistant infants showed that the latter group of mothers reported significantly higher levels of negative affect. In addition, in a related report on this same sample, which examined the relative predictive power of maternal and infant temperament, it was observed that only indices of mothers' temperament significantly covaried with attachment classifications and attachment behaviors directed toward mother in the Strange Situation at 13 months. More specifically, mothers who evaluated themselves as temperamentally more reactive to stimulation had infants who were more likely to be classified as insecure-avoidant. Additionally, mothers who evaluated themselves as less adaptable to new situations had infants who cried more and were more likely to involve themselves in proximal interactions than were infants of more adaptable mothers.

Egeland and Farber (1984) found that personality measures of maternal aggression, suspiciousness, impulsiveness succor, and social desirability did not differentiate attachment groups. It did turn out to be the case, however, that when the stability/instability of attachment classifications at 12 and 18 months was examined, those babies who changed from secure to insecure, in contrast to those who remained secure over time, had mothers who scored higher prenatally and/or at 3-months postpartum on personality measure of aggression and suspicion; this was true whether the child changed from secure to insecure-avoidant or from secure to insecure-resistant. Why maternal personality differences should emerge with respect to changes in attachment over time, but not to 12-month attachment, is by no means clear. Nevertheless, it should be noted that neither in this study, nor any other, do data emerge that suggest that mothers of insecure infants look psychologically healthier or more mature than those of secure infants.

The fact that mothers of secure infants appear more psychologically healthy than those of insecure infants (when group differences are found) is consistent with the general tenet of attachment theory that underscores the preeminent role of maternal sensitivity in promoting attachment security. After all, being sensitive involves being empathic, appropriately responsive and psychologically available; if a mother is to provide care of this kind she must be able to decenter from self, appraise the needs of another, and meet those needs in a nonnarcissistic manner. In many respects, being psychologically mature means being able to do just such things. Empirical evidence in support of this contention can be found in Benn's (1985) recent study. Not only did the measure of psychological integration predict maternal sensitivity, but when this maternal personality measure was statistically controlled, the relationship between sensitivity and attachment security was strongly reduced, whereas the same degree of attenuation was not discerned when sensitivity variance was partialled from the personality-attachment relationship. Thus, it would seem to be the case, as the aforementioned logic would dictate, that maternal personality (i.e., integration) influences mothering (i.e., sensitivity), which in turn influences the security of the attachment relationship.

Characteristics of the Infant

The study of infant temperament and particularly its influence on infant development continues to be a source of heated debate among developmentalists (Chess & Thomas, 1982; Sroufe, 1985). With regard to the question of temperament-attachment associations, there are two general schools of thought concerning the role that temperament plays in the development and assessment of individual differences in infant–mother attachment relationships. Some, as noted earlier, contend that temperament does not directly influence the quality of attachment that develops between infant and mother, because even a difficult infant, given the "right" care, can become secure—there are multiple pathways to security. It is recognized, nevertheless, that some infants are more difficult than others to care for in a sensitive, security-promoting manner, and that even infants with "easy" temperaments, if provided insensitive care, can develop insecure relationships. This line of argument suggests, of course, that temperament does not exert a "main" effect in determining attachment quality. In support of this notion, Crockenberg (1981) reported that the effect of infant temperament on the developing attachment relationship was dependent on the extent to which mothers received social support from their environments. More specifically, highly irritable infants were more likely to develop insecure attachment relationships only when their mothers experience low levels of social support.

   The possibility does exist, even within this line of theorizing, that although temperament does not determine whether an infant will be securely or insecurely attached, the "kind" of secure or insecure attachment that develops may be a function of temperament. One reasonable hypothesis, for example, is that temperamentally less irritable babies, if cared for in a sensitive manner, will display B_1 or B_2 type secure attachments, whereas if cared for in an insensitive manner will develop insecure-avoidant attachments. Common to each of these relationship types is a lower susceptibility to distress upon separation. In contrast, babies characterized by high levels of irritability would be expected to display B_3 or B_4 type secure attachments when cared for in a sensitive manner, and to develop insecure-resistant attachments when they receive insensitive care. Common to each of these relationship types is a greater susceptibility to distress upon separation. Recent work by Belsky and Rovine (in press) provide some support for this line of argument.

The second school of thought regarding the temperament-attachment association, articulated most clearly by Kagan (1982) and Chess and Thomas (1982), reflects the belief not only that an infant's temperament directly affects the development of the attachment relationship via the impact it exerts on mother–infant interactions, but also that the very behaviors that define temperament (e.g., susceptibility to distress) determine attachment classifications in the Strange Situation such that security of attachment, as assessed in this laboratory context, is principally determined by temperament. This argument is often advanced with the claim that infants classified as securely attached are less disturbed by separation in the Strange Situation whereas those infants classified as insecurely attached are more distressed—despite the fact that both secure *and* insecure infants display the same kinds of discrete behaviors in the Strange Situation assessment (i.e., crying). To support the position that attachment assessments and classifications are seriously confounded with temperament, Kagan cites Miyake et al.'s (1986) findings, which indicate that Japanese infants are more likely to be classified as anxious-resistant than secure or anxious-avoidant. Since anxious-resistant infants cry more than *some* secure infants and virtually all anxious-avoidant infants, Kagan concludes that the Strange Situation is picking up constitutionally based racial differences in temperament rather than relationship differences resulting from early experiences within and beyond the family. What Kagan has not acknowledged, although making this inference that *sounds* sensible, is that research on constitutional differences between Japanese-Oriental and North American-Caucasian infants would lead to the prediction that Japanese infants should be least resistant, not more resistant, if, indeed, attachment classification is principally a function of temperament. This is because the available data clearly indicated that Japanese newborns are actually *less* subject to distress than North American-Caucasian infants (Callagahn, 1981; Caudill & Weinstein, 1969; Freedman, 1974; Kuchner, 1980). In other words, quite a complex theory of development is called for if we are to assume that the heightened resistance of Japanese infants is a product of constitutionally based temperament because somehow we have to explain how a reduced propensity to become distressed as a neonate turns into an increased propensity as a 1-year-old, at least in the Strange Situation.

In point of fact, the data on infant temperament and its association with infant attachment are mixed. If one looks to maternal reports of infant temperament, most studies discern little, if any, covariation (Bates, in press). Using the Dimensions of Temperament Survey (DOTS; Lerner, Palermo, Spiro, & Nesselroade, 1982), Belsky, Rovine, and Taylor (1984) found no relationship between infant activity, attention span, vigor, or adaptability at 3, 9, and 12-month attachment. Similar null findings have been reported by Weber et al. (in press) using the DOTS at 12 months; Egeland and Farber (1984) using the Carey (1970) Infant Temperament Questionnaire at 6 months (which measures activity level, rhythmicity, approach, adaptability, threshold of responsiveness, intensity of reaction, quality of mood, distractibility, attention span, and persistence); and Bates, Maslin, and Frankel (1985) using the Infant Characteristics Questionnaire (which assesses fussiness/difficult temperaments, unpredictability, unadaptability, and dullness). In only one study has a reliable association between mothers' reports of infant temperament and infant–mother attachment been reported. Frodi (1983) found that infants classified as anxious-resistant at 12 months were reported by their mothers as being more difficult (using Infant Temperament Questionnaire) than secure and anxious-avoidant infants. It must be noted that both the attachment relationship and infant temperament were assessed at 12 months. Thus, maternal reports of infant temperament cannot be considered antecedents of the attachment relationship, and may indeed reflect more of the relationship than temperament per se.

In considering the general absence of association between reports of infant temperament and attachment, two points must be stressed. First, similar failures to reject the null hypothesis may exist, yet remain unpublished because such data are difficult to have published in archival journals, which set a premium on the discovery of associations rather than on their absence. In addition, there is some debate regarding exactly what many maternal questionnaire assessments of infant temperament are actually measuring—the baby's individuality (Chess & Thomas, 1982), the mother's personality (Vaughn, 1983), or the interaction of the two as revealed in mother's perceptions of her baby (Bates, 1980; Bates & Bayles, 1984).

Investigators who have relied on actual behavioral assessments of newborns and infants have proven somewhat more successful in linking "temperament" and attachment, though by no means are the data entirely consistent. In one of the earliest studies to address this issue, Waters, Vaughn, and Egeland (1980) found, during newborn behavioral assessments using the Brazelton (1973) scale on the seventh day of life, that infants who would develop insecure-resistant attachments with their mothers were less capable of orienting and regulating their state, and were more motoricallly immature than babies who would develop secure attachment relationships. Difficult to understand in view of these associations is why they very same neonatal behavioral assessment carried out 3 days later failed to distinguish attachment groups. Consistent with the 7-day findings of Waters et al., though, are those emanating from a more recent study of Japanese infants whose reactions to the interruption of sucking at days 2 and 5 were evaluated. Miyake et al. (1985) reported that newborns, who 1 year later were classified as anxious-resistant in their attachments, reacted with greater distress to this disturbing procedure; that is, although they took longer to cry initially, infants who would develop insure attachment relationships cried for longer periods once they became distressed (see footnote 2). Also consistent with some of the findings of Waters et al. are those from another cross-cultural study, this one carried out in Germany (Grossman et al., 1985). Newborns who were later classified as securely attached displayed higher levels of orientation during the Brazelton assessment on days 5 and 8 than those infants who eventually developed anxious-avoidant relationships. It should be noted, however, that in the Grossman et al. study, no relationship between neonatal irritability and attachment classifications was discerned. This is contrary to a report by Holmes, Roble, Kowalski, and Lavesen (1984), which indicated that insecure infants cried more during their first 48 hours following hospital discharge than during their opening days of life. In a final relevant study, Egeland and Farber (1984) relied on ratings made by nurses who worked in the newborn nursery and found that newborns who would develop insecure attachment relationships were regarded as significantly more difficult to care for than those newborns who later developed secure attachments.

In considering these data, one is left to conclude, at least at the most general level, that although *reports* of temperament routinely fail to distinguish attachment groups, *behavioral evaluations* of newborns sometimes do distinguish these groups. Indeed, the evidence tends to suggest that newborns destined to become secure are generally more alert and responsive, whereas those destined to become insecure *and* to express their insecurity in a *resistant* manner are generally more irritable. At this point, two qualifications must be considered. First, even in those studies in which early temperamental differences have been discerned between groups, only one or, at most, two among many variables emerge to account for these distinctions. The fact, however, that these few discriminating variables *are* conceptually meaningful should not be discounted, as differences in alertness and susceptibility to distress are far more interpretable than differences involving habituation or reflex strength. Crockenberg's study (1981) strongly suggests, though, that the contribution of temperament showing up in these studies may actually be most influential in interaction with other contextual factors likely to determine the extent to which mothers will be sensitively responsive to the initial differences that characterize their infants at birth. Indeed, an intriguing finding by Levitt, Weber, and Clark (1986) provides additional support for this contention. In exploring the interaction effects between infant temperament and maternal support on 13-month infant behavior in the Strange Situation, these authors reported that temperamentally difficult infants whose mothers reported less satisfactory relationships with their own mothers were significantly more likely to avoid mothers at reunion. It must be noted, however, that, as the authors themselves pointed out, this result was the only significant correlation of several, and thus might be a result of chance.

In the face of the Levitt et al. data, along with those of Crockenberg, we are forced to wonder about the extent to which the apparent main effects chronicled by Miyake et al., Grossman et al., and others would themselves be qualified by interactions between infant characteristics and characteristics of the mother or the social context in which she and her infant were embedded. That is, to what extent was newborn irritability not related to later resistance, for example, when mothers were psychologically mature and involved in harmonious marriages and supportive social networks and, thus, highly likely to provide sensitive, security-promoting care? Analogously, to what extent was neonatal alertness not related to later security when mothers were psychologically immature and involved in unsupportive adult relationships?

Characteristics of the Social Context

As our analysis through this point makes clear, most debate regarding the origins of individual differences in attachment has focused attention on mother's and child's contributions. Crockenberg's (1981) much cited investigations, the questions just raised, and a general contextual orientation to development (Bronfenbrenner, 1979) compels us to look beyond proximal determinants of attachment and consider the social milieu in which mothers and babies find themselves. Most important in this regard may be the support that mothers have available to them, which, in theory at least, ought to influence their availability and responsiveness to their infants. Particularly significant are likely to be mothers' relationships with their husbands (Belsky, 1981) and their relationships with significant others (Cochran & Brassard, 1979). Although the mother's marital relationship and her social network have not received the attention they merit from investigators interested in the origins of attachment, the evidence that is available clearly suggests that these aspects of the mother's social context may play a significant role in the establishment of a secure infant–mother attachment relationship.

Marriage. Four investigations have examined the association between attachment and some aspect of the marital relationship; three of four provide some evidence of linkage between these two family relationships. In one cross-sectional study of 75 families with 20-month-old toddlers, Goldberg and Easterbrooks (1984) observed that secure attachments (to mother as well as to father) were more likely when marital adjustment was high, whereas insecure attachments were more frequent than would be expected by chance when marital adjustment was low. In another cross-sectional study, this one carried out in Japan, Durret et al. (1984) found that mothers of insecure-avoidant 1-year-olds reported receiving the least support from their husbands; of special interest was the unexpected finding that mothers of both secure *and* anxious-resistant infants experienced significantly greater, but not different, levels of spousal support than did those of anxious-avoidant infants. In the third investigation, Egeland and Farber (1984) found no direct relationship between the presence of a husband/boyfriend during the infants' first year and 12-month infant–mother attachment classification. What they did discover, however, using this admittedly rough index of the marital relationship (i.e., presence or absence of a husband/boyfriend), was that infants whose attachment classifications changed from secure to insecure between 12 and 18 months were more likely to have mothers who were not living with their husbands/boyfriends than were those infants who maintained secure attachment relationships across this 6-month period. The fourth and final study to be considered did not provide evidence in support of the association between the attachment and marital relationships. Levitt, Weber, and Clark (1986) measured maternal support from husband—both emotional and caretaking—along with quality of infant–mother attachment at 13 months. None of the various support measures were related to attachment quality. It is of interest to mention, however, that consistent with the framework presented earlier (Belsky, 1984), maternal support from husband was related to maternal well-being, as was evidenced by significant correlations between husband support measures and maternal satisfaction in the marital relationship and the amount of assistance received. Additionally, regression equations indicated that husband support accounted for a significant 21% of the variance in a measure of mother's affect balance, along with 28% of the variance in a measure of mother's life satisfaction.

Consideration of these findings clearly suggests that some association between marriage and attachment probably exists and that measures assessing the quality of the marital relationship, rather than mere presence of a partner, are reliable correlates of attachment security. Such a conclusion is consistent with thinking that links these two family relationships because it is presumed to be the emotional support and instrumental assistance that the husband provides the mother, rather than his presence or mere existence, that influences the quality of care mother provides the child and, thereby, the security of the relationship that develops between infant and mother (Belsky, 1981). What these investigations do not and cannot tell us, however, because they are all cross-sectional in design, is whether the marriage differences precede the emergence of secure and insecure attachment relationships. Because the research we report in this chapter involved the assessment of marriage prior to and following the baby's birth, this is an issue we are in an ideal position to address.

Social Network.   It is not only support from a spouse or boyfriend that seems important to the development of the mother–infant relationship, but that which is provided by other significant individuals in a mother's life, as well. Evidence to this effect has already been presented in the several discussions of Crockenberg's (1981) work discussed earlier. We are aware of no other study, however, that attempts to link this aspect of the social context with the security of the infant–mother attachment relationship. Nevertheless, there exist sufficient data linking social network support and positive patterns of mother–child interactions (for review, see Belsky & Vondra, in press), and there are additional grounds for expecting a reliable association to exist.

Consideration of this more general association between social network support and parenting, as well as between marriage and parenting (which we have documented elsewhere: Belsky, 1984; Belsky & Vondra, in press), rather than the specific association between these aspects of the social context and attachment security per se, raises the possibility that these latter associations may be a function of processes other than the hypothesized influence of emotional support and instrumental assistance on parenting. Indeed, the possibility must be entertained that it is some "third variable," possibly the mother's ability to establish and maintain harmonious social relationships in general, that is responsible for the associations discerned between marriage or social network and attachment security. Quite conceivably, women who are skilled in providing sensitive care to their babies may simply be deploying a more general social skill that derives from their awareness of the needs of others, and their abilities to meet those needs—be they needs of a husband, a friend, or an infant. Such a interpretation is certainly consistent with the model of the determinants of parenting outlined earlier and, indeed, leads to the prediction, advanced elsewhere (Belsky, 1984), that when it comes to considering the relative influence of characteristics of the mother, the infant, and the social context, all determinants of attachment security are not "created equal."

Because the general relationship skills mentioned previously are presumed to reside in the individual, to be deployed where required, and to stem from the mother's own relationship history in her family of origin, we would expect to find that characteristics of the mother are the most influential determinants of attachment security. Because these are presumed to directly influence the marital and social network relationships she establishes, we would further expect that the characteristics of the social context would be next in importance. Finally, it is our expectation, given the greater behavioral maturity and thus absolute "power" of the mother, that characteristics of the infant would be, relatively speaking, least significant in their influence of the three general sources of influence we have considered. In the research to be reported in the remainder of this chapter, we not only endeavor to examine the extent to which the sources of influence we have considered individually distinguish attachment groups, but also to test this set of hypotheses in an effort to model a process whereby multiple sources of influence determine whether the infant–mother attachment relationship will be secure, as revealed by the Strange Situation.

THE PENNSYLVANIA INFANT AND FAMILY DEVELOPMENT PROJECT

The research presented in this chapter is drawn from a three-cohort longitudinal investigation of infant and family development. Beginning in the last trimester of pregnancy, we have followed more than 200 families as they bear and rear their first child through his/her first year of life. In this chapter we report results of families from the second of our three cohorts, 51 of which we have data sufficient to address the contextual issues raised in the introduction—namely, the role that characteristics of the mother, the infant, and the broader social context play in influencing (or at least predicting) security of infant–mother attachment.

The subject pool for this study consisted of 64 Caucasian families participating in the second cohort of The Pennsylvania Infant and Family Development Project (Belsky, 1985; Belsky, Lang, & Rovine, 1985). All couples were expecting their first child at the time of enrollment; all marriages were intact. The largest obstetrical practice in the community provided us with names and telephone numbers of their patients, and provided patients with introductory letters outlining our project. All families were telephoned, and those displaying an interest in learning more about our project were sent a detailed follow-up letter. Within a week of mailing these letters, parents were telephones and a 1½-hour prenatal enrollment visit was scheduled for those expressing interest in participating. Forty percent of those eligible for participation agreed to enroll in the project.

Enrollment visits occurred during the third trimester of pregnancy and consisted of a detailed explanation of the study along with a couple interview. Upon completion of the interview, each parent was given a set of questionnaires to complete and return by mail to our project office. Couple interviews and individual parental questionnaires were administered again at 3- and 9-months postpartum. Additionally, at 1-, 3-, and 9-months postpartum, two separate in-home, naturalistic observations were carried out: one when mother was alone with the infant and another when both parents were present. At 12-months postpartum, each mother–infant dyad was seen in the Ainsworth and Wittig (1969) Strange Situation.

The Strange Situation is a standardized procedure that exposes infants to increasing degrees of stress as a means of examining the extent to which they effectively rely on their mothers to provide comfort, and thus a secure base from which they may explore (Ainsworth et al., 1978). This 21-minute procedure consists of seven, 3-minute episodes in which: (a) mother and infant are alone in a room in which mother sits in a chair and infant plays with toys; (b) an unfamiliar, female adult enters the room and sits across from mother; (c) mother leaves room, thus leaving infant with stranger; (d) mother returns and stranger leaves; (e) mother leaves, thus leaving infant alone; (f) stranger returns; and (g) mother returns. On the basis of infants' exploratory behavior in this situation, their orientation toward the stranger, and especially their way of reacting to reunion with mother following separation, infant–parent relationships are classified into one of three types of attachments. Babies who positively greet the mother following reunion and/or move toward her and who are comforted by her contact if distressed are classified as securely attached. Infants who move away from the mother or avoid interaction with her (e.g., avert gaze) are classified as having insecure-avoidant attachments. And, finally, infants who have difficulty being comforted by mother upon reunion and who both seek and resist contact with mother are classified as having insecure-resistant attachments.

All Strange Situations were videotaped, and each videotape was coded following the procedures described in Ainsworth et al.'s (1978) *Patterns of*

Attachment volume (1978). The primary coder was trained directly by Alan Sroufe and was unaware of the information provided by parents in their individual questionnaires. Inter-judge reliability was assessed by comparing the primary coder's scores with those of Brian Vaughn on 23 of 99 randomly selected tapes. Across the avoidant (A), secure (B), and resistant (C) major group typology, a 91% rate of agreement was achieved; all disagreements were resolved by conference.

It is important to note that at 12 months, attachment ratings were available on a total of 55 mother–infant dyads. Overall, 60% of the attachment classifications were rated as secure and 40% were rated as insecure (18% avoidant, 22% resistant), showing a distribution very similar to those reported by others studying predominantly middle-class samples. The distribution was virtually the same for the 51 dyads whose data are reported, with 59% secure and 41% insecure (18% avoidant, 23% resistant) attachment relationships.

In order to obtain information on mothers, infants, and their social contexts, multiple methods of data collection were employed. In the following pages, we describe each of the three broad domains of interest, along with the specific constructs within each, that were assessed.

Characteristics of Mother

As delineated in the introduction, the conceptual framework that guided our research highlights two distinct aspects of mothers as individuals that may serve to influence the development of the infant–mother relationship. These are developmental history, which consists of mothers' experiences during childhood in the context of their families of origin, and personality, which may be conceptualized as the nature and extent of mothers' personal psychological resources.

Child-Rearing History. As part of the prenatal data collection, parents completed a 60-item, self-report questionnaire *retrospectively* assessing the child-rearing they themselves experienced while growing up. This measure, the Parental Acceptance-Rejection Questionnaire, was developed and validated by Rohner (1980); it yields four theoretically significant subscales: (1) warmth/affection (20 items); (2) hostility/ aggression (15 items); (3) indifference/neglect (15 items); and (4) undifferentiated rejection (10 items). These four subscales, which in the current sample had high internal consistency (range: .82 to .94) were positively and significantly intercorrelated (after reverse scoring the warmth scale) (range: .77 to .89). A high score on all four variables would indicate that the mother had experiences care that she recalled as being cold, rejecting, hostile, and indifferent.

In responding to this questionnaire, mothers were required to evaluate the degree to which each of 60 statements characterized the rearing they experienced between 7 and 12 years of age. Responses were coded along a 4-point scale: "almost always true of my parents," "sometimes true of my parents," "rarely true of my parents," and "almost never true of my parents." Questionnaire items included statements such as "my parents nagged and scolded me when I was bad," "ridiculed and made fun of me," "praised me to others," "talked to me in a warm affectionate way," "forgot important events that I thought they should remember," "respected my point of view and encouraged me to express it," "let me know they loved me," and "paid a lot of attention to me."

As should be evident from such statements, the questionnaire assessed both global characterizations of recollections of one's own child rearing (e.g., "treated me harshly") and more specific actions and behavior (e.g., "were unsympathetic to me when I was having trouble," "yelled at me when they were angry"). It is important to emphasize, however, that the current study design did not allow for a determination of the extent to which these reports are valid with respect to the childrearing these parents actually experienced while growing up. In this regard it might be useful to think of these assessments as measures of parents' *perceptions* of the rearing they experienced. Having said this, however, it is also worth noting that from a functional standpoint, the absolute accuracy of these retrospective reports may be less important than their perceived accuracy because a mother's sense of how she was treated while growing up may be developmentally more influential than how she actually was reared by her parents.

Personality.   Four scales, selected from three personality inventories, were included in the prenatal questionnaire battery; selection of these scales was based upon each scale's theoretical relevance to the nature of maternal care and the extensive research base documenting its reliability and validity. The first personality scale consisted of 16 items taken from Cattell's 16 Personality Factor Questionnaire (16PF; Cattell, Eber, & Tatsuoka, 1970) that assess *ego strength.* Mothers responded to statements about themselves and their feelings toward themselves (e.g., "People treat me less reasonably than my good intentions deserve"; "In my personal life I reach the goals I set almost all the time"; "Some people seem to ignore or avoid me, although I don't know why"). A low score on this personality scale is indicative of high ego strength, which Cattell characterizes in terms of emotional stability and maturity. The person with a high level of ego strength is one who does not allow emotional needs to obscure the realities of a situation. A high score on this scale (i.e., low level of ego strength) is indicative of a person who is emotionally labile, easily upset, tends to become emotional when upset, and who tends to "give up" as a means of evading responsibilities.

The remaining three personality scales employed in this study came from two inventories developed by Jackson (Jackson, 1976, 1980), both of which were designed to provide a set of scores for an individual's personality traits that are relevant to functioning in a wide variety of situations. All of these scales are primarily focused upon areas of normal functioning (rather than pathological functioning). The *nurturance* scale was taken from the Personality Research Form (Jackson, 1980) and assesses the extent to which a person cares for and is concerned about making a contribution to the lives of others. This scale consists of 16 true–false items (e.g., "I have never done volunteer work for charity"; "People like to tell me their troubles because they know I will help them"; "Seeing an old or helpless person makes me feel that I would like to take care of him"); a low score indicated high levels of nurturance. The *interpersonal affect* and *self-esteem* scales were taken from the Jackson Personality Inventory (Jackson, 1976); both consist of 20 true–false items. The interpersonal affect scale assesses the nature and extent of an individual's feelings toward others, using items such as : "I am so sensitive to the moods of my friends that I can almost feel what they are feeling"; and "I don't waste my sympathy on people who have caused their own problems." A low score on this scale indicates high levels of interpersonal affect.

The final personality scale—self-esteem—assesses the way in which a person feels about him/herself in relation to others. A low score on this scale indicates that a person has high self-esteem and thus perceives self as socially adequate and worthy of the interest and care of others. For the current sample, the internal consistencies of the three Jackson scales were .70, .78, and .73 for nurturance, interpersonal affect, and self-esteem, respectively.

Characteristics of the Infant

In an attempt to examine the extent to which infant characteristics influence the relationship that develops between infant and mother during the first year, our investigation assessed infant temperament, both behaviorally (neonatal period, 1, 3, and 9 month) and via maternal reports (3 and 9 months).

Neonatal Behavior. The Neonatal Behavioral Assessment Scale (NBAS) (Brazelton, 1973) was administered by a trained examiner to each infant, in the hospital, between 1 and 3 days postpartum. Based on the virtual convergence of factor analytic findings from several studies (Kaye, 1978; Lester, Als, & Brazelton, 1982; Sameroff, Krafchuk, & Bakow, 1978), the NBAS items were grouped into six clusters, five of which were selected for subsequent analyses:[3] *orientation* (items 5–10); *range of state* (items 17–19, 24); *regulation of state* (items 14, 16, 25, 26); *autonomic stability* (items 21–23); and *motor tonus* (items 11, 12, 13, 15, 20). (See Lester et al., 1982, for specific scoring criteria.)

Reported Infant Temperament.   At 3 and 9 months, each mother completed the Infant Characteristics Questionnaire (ICQ; Bates, Freeland, & Lounsbury, 1979). The ICQ is a 24-item questionnaire designed to assess infant characteristics, particularly with regard to how difficult the infant is. The instrument yields four subscales—*fussy-difficult, unadaptable, dull,* and *unpredictable* (Bates et al., 1979)—with internal consistencies ranging from .30 to .80, with an $\overline{X}$ of .61 across the two times of measurement with this sample.

Infant Behaviors.   Infant behaviors were observed during the course of two in-house, naturalistic observations carried out when infants were 1, 3, and 9-months of age. At each age of measurement, one 45-minute observation was conducted when the child was home alone with mother and a second, 60-minute observation was conducted when both mother and father were home with the infant. (For more details on observation systems, see Belsky, Gilstrap, & Rovine, 1984; Belsky, Taylor, & Rovine, 1984.)

Five of the individual behavioral categories recorded during the mother–infant observations, and coded using a continuous 15-second time-sampling system, are the focus of this report: infant vocalization, infant looking at mother, infant fuss/cry, infant explore (i.e., looking at or manipulating an object), and infant response/explore (i.e., looking at or manipulating an object as a direct result of mother's directing infant's attention to that object). For the mother–father–infant observations there are four individual behavior categories of importance to this study, each coded using a 15-second observe/5-second record, time-sampling system: infant vocalization, infant fuss/cry, infant explore (i.e., looking at or manipulating an object), and infant smile/excite (i.e., smile, laugh, or exhibit excited body movements such as flailing of the arms).

In order to reduce the subject-variable ratio, observational measures of infant behavior were summarized to create indices of two infant

---

[3]Habituation was left out of all analyses due to the fact that many infants were awake during administration of the NBAS. This being the case, our *n* for Habituation items was too small to allow for meaningful, generalizable analyses.

individuality dimensions. *Fussiness* was created by summing the frequency (i.e., number of 15-second time sampling intervals) with which the infant fussed or cried during the dyadic and triadic observation at each age of measurement. To develop a composite index of *alertness/social responsiveness,* behaviors that were positively intercorrelated and presumed to be indicative of such an orientation (cf. Sameroff, Seifer, & Elias, 1982; Sostek & Anders, 1977) were summed across observation situations at each time of measurement. These included, from the dyadic observation, measures of infant vocalization, explore, and response/explore; and from the triadic observation, measures of infant vocalization, explore, and smile/excite. Aggregation of these many behaviors, all thought to reflect infant alertness and responsiveness to the environment, was employed in order to create a composite variable that would be a more representative and reliable index of individual differences than any single measure (Epstein, 1980; Rushton, Brainerd, & Pressley, 1983).

The Social Context

Information on mothers' perceptions of their marriages and social networks was collected repeatedly over the course of the study. Because one of the major goals of the Infant and Family Development Project was to gain insight into how marriages changed across the transition to parenthood, much more data were gathered on the marital relationship than on mothers' relationships with friends, relatives, and neighbors.

Marital Relations.   Three instruments specifically selected to assess marital activity and sentiment were included in a battery of questionnaires individually administered to spouses during the last trimester of pregnancy and again at 3 and 9-months postpartum. One 14-item scale developed by Huston (1983; Huston, McHale, & Crouter, 1986) assessed satisfaction/dissatisfaction with marital interactions and produced two scales measuring satisfaction with the extent to which *negative* and *positive* interpersonal events/activities occurred in the marital relationship (e.g., partner expressing approval, partner acting bored while the other talks). This instrument required respondents to use a 7-point scale in assessing the extent to which they would like specific relationship events to occur more or less often than they typically do. The scale responses ranged from "a great deal more than it does now" to "a great deal less than it does now," with the midpoint defined by "about the same as it does now." A low score on these indices indicated that the respondent would like his/her partner to engage in more positive and fewer negative activities than he/she currently did. Thus, the higher the score on each scale, the "better" the marriage. Internal consistency for these scales ranged from .53 to .83, with a mean of .73 across the three times of measurement.

Spouses completed Braiker and Kelley's (1979) 4-factor scale of intimate relations as a means of assessing two additional marital activities—*Maintenance* and *conflict,*—as well as two marital sentiments—*love* and *ambivalence.* This 25-question instrument tapped the interpersonal character of the relationship with specific regard to the extent to which spouses actively attempt to enrich, improve, and thereby maintain the relationship and the extent to which couples engage in marital disputes. In addition, feelings of love and ambivalence toward the spouse and the relationship were assessed. On this scale, questions such as "to what extent do you have a sense of 'belonging' with your partner" (love), "how often do you and your partner argue" (conflict), and "how much do you tell your partner what you want or need from the relationship" (maintenance) were answered using a 9-point scale ranging from "very little or not at all" to "very much or extremely." The internal consistency of these four subscales, across the three measurement periods, ranged from .61 to .90, with a mean of .76.

The third instrument, also developed by Huston (1983), assessed a final sentiment, *marital satisfaction.* This single-score measure employed a series of 11 bipolar items (e.g., boring–interesting, miserable–enjoyable, hopeful–discouraging) to assess individual spouse's subjective response to the marital relationship in away that was free of assumptions about the specific behavioral patterns underlying the evaluation (Huston & Robins, 1982). The internal consistency of this scale ranged from .86 to .94 across the three times of measurement, with a mean of .91.

In order to reduce the subject-variable ratio while at the same time creating more reliable indices of marriage (Rushton et al., 1983), all seven marital measures were subjected to exploratory factor analyses at each measurement occasion using promax rotation to yield an oblique solution. At the prenatal, 3-month and 9-month times of measurement, one of the two factors to emerge had salient loadings on love (.69/.74/.72), maintenance (.66/.69/.66), and positive events (.64/.52/.64); these individual variables were summed in order to create a composite index of *Positive Activities and Sentiments.* The second factor that emerged had salient loadings, at each time of measurement, on conflict (.70/.73/.71), ambivalence (.50/.59/.61), negative events (−.38/−.67/−.60) and satisfaction (−.59/−.58/−.64). A summary variable labeled *Negative Activities and Sentiments* was created by subtracting scores of the last two variables from the sum of scores from the first two. This resulted in a distribution of negative scores (due to scaling differences across measures) in which lower, that is, more negative values, were indicative of "better" marriages. It should be noted that the inclusion of the satisfaction variable on the second factor is consistent with much of the literature on the behavioral determinants of overall marital satisfaction, which indicates that negative aspects of the marriage are, in general, more important determinants of marital satisfaction than are positive aspects of the marriage (e.g., Gottman, 1979).

Social Network Support. In addition to the three marital assessment instruments included in the prenatal, 3, and 9-month maternal questionnaires, a fourth instrument assessing social network support was specifically developed for this project and included in the questionnaire. This 4-item scale assessed the degree to which mothers spoke with persons other than husband about parenting and nonparenting concerns, and the extent to which mothers felt that such discussions were of assistance to them. Two of the four items on the prenatal scale were: "Do you talk to someone other than your partner (such as a friend or relative) about pregnancy, child-rearing, and your feelings about becoming a parent?"; and "Do you find that talking to this person (or these people) helps you during pregnancy or in your feelings about becoming a parent?" Mothers responded to each question on a 5-point scale that ranged from "very often" or "yes, a great deal" to "never" or "no, not at all" for the two sample questions, respectively. Internal consistencies for this scale ranged from .80 to. 87 across the three times of measurement.

Social Milieu. A final measure of the social context in which mother and infant were embedded was based upon parents' responses, during the prenatal couple interview, to seven questions regarding their perceptions of their neighbors. Mothers and fathers jointly responded to each question (e.g., "Some of the neighbors are friendly"; "some of the neighbors are helpful"; "Some of the neighbors are unfriendly or mean") on a 5-point scale ranging from "very false" to "very true," with "somewhat false, somewhat true" defined as the middle point. A high score on this scale indicated that husband and wife perceived their neighbors as being both friendly and helpful, and thus suggested a perception of a positive social milieu. The internal consistency was .77 for the current sample.

RESULTS AND DISCUSSION

In order to examine the maternal, infant, and social-contextual antecedents of individual differences in infant–mother attachment, three sets of analyses were carried out. In the first set of analyses, we endeavored to determine the extent to which variables from each domain under study (i.e., maternal characteristics, infant characteristics, social context) individually and collectively distinguished the three attachment groups. The second set of analyses built upon the first and was designed to test the hypothesis that characteristics of the mother would be more powerful in distinguishing secure and insecure relationships that would characteristics of the social context, which were expected to be more powerful in distinguishing groups than characteristics of the infant. In the third and final set of analyses, we extended the prior data analyses by testing a path analytic model of the determinants of attachment in hopes of illuminating the dynamic process by which maternal characteristics, infant characteristics, and social context influence the security of the infant–mother attachment relationship. It should be noted that prior to conducting these analyses, a comparison of attachment groups was made on family demographic measures in order to determine whether any differences distinguished the groups at the outset of the study. No such initial differences were discerned on a host of demographic indicators (e.g., mother's age, age at marriage, years of education, years married, planned pregnancy).

Analysis of Distinct Domains of Determination

As part of the first set of analyses, each domain of variables was subjected to a multivariate analysis of variance (MANOVA) in order to determine whether the three attachment groups differed and whether the secure versus insecure comparison was significant. Each MANOVA typically involved a one-time-of-measurement model comparing the three attachment groups on a particular set of variables. In the case of construct measured on more than one occasion (e.g., marriage, temperament), however, the model was amended to a 3 (Time) × 3 (Attachment) repeated measures MANOVA, with time of measurement serving as the single repeated measure factor in the statistical model. Finally, in addition to examining mean differences between attachment groups, multiple regression analyses were also carried out on each set of variables in order to determine the extent to which variables in a set collectively predicted attachment security; for these analyses, a linear variable of attachment security was created by assigning a score of 1 for insecurity and 2 for security.

Characteristics of Mother

Two sets of variables that characterized the mother were subjected to MANOVA and multiple regression analyses: developmental history and personality. The results of these analyses are displayed in Table 3.1. Inspection of the top half of the table reveals that neither individually nor collectively did the developmental history variables distinguish the

TABLE 3.1
Variation in Attachment as a Function of Characteristics of Mother

| | Attachment Group | | | F Ratios | | |
	A	B	C	ABC	SEC/INS	r^a
1. Developmental History	(n=9)	(n=30)	(n=12)	(df=2,48)	(df=1,49)	
Warmth	31.33	29.10	30.73	0.17	0.32	−.08
Aggression	51.83	50.45	52.46	0.16	0.33	−.08
Negative	53.83	52.83	53.36	0.38	0.45	−.08
Rejection	33.83	33.79	34.82	0.11	0.07	−.04
Multivariate				0.62^b	0.88^c	R=.27
2. Personality^d						
Nurturance	20.89	20.97	21.67	0.24	0.17	−.06
Affection	28.67	25.60	28.50	4.73**	9.64**	−.41**
Ego Strength	27.56	24.87	24.92	3.85*	2.30	−.21
Self-Esteem	30.22	29.27	27.42	0.97	0.22	−.07
Multivariate				3.05**	4.46**	R=.53**

*$p < .05$
**$p < .01$
^{a}To calculate the correlation coefficient, insecurity was coded 1 and security was coded 2.
^{b}Multivariate analyses of A, B, C group differences, for both developmental history and personality measures, have $df = 8,88$.
^{c}Multivariate analyses of secure/insecure group differences, for both developmental history and personality measures, have $df = 4,46$.
^{d}Low scores on these scales reflect more optimal functioning.

secure/insecure attachment groups; that is, we found no evidence that mothers of infants who developed secure attachment relationship recollected more positive child-rearing experiences in their own families of origin than mothers of infants who developed insecure attachment relationships.

Although retrospective reports of child-rearing experience did not distinguish attachment groups, personality assessments of the mothers before their babies were born clearly did. As the data displayed in the bottom half of Table 3.1 indicate, mothers of secure infants scored better (lower) on interpersonal affection than mothers of insecure infants ($F 1,49 = 9.64$, $p < .01$). In addition, mothers of avoidant infants displayed significantly poorer (higher) levels of ego strength than mothers of either secure of resistant infants ($F 2,48 = 3.85$, $p < .05$). Additionally, although neither nurturance nor self-esteem were found to differentiate the attachment groups when considered individually, the four personality scores collectively accounted for 28% of the variance in attachment security as revealed by a multiple $R = .52$ ($p < .01$).

In summary, the data on mothers obtained prenatally provide evidence that characteristics of the mother distinguish the infant–mother relationships that eventually develop; these associations seem to be a function of maternal personality rather than developmental history, at least as assessed in the current investigation. The fact that recollected child-rearing histories were unrelated to attachment classification may well be a function of the measurement system employed in this investigation, particularly in view of the findings of Main and Goldwyn (1984). It should be recalled that these investigators, relying upon in-depth clinical interviews, found not only that mothers of insecure infants recalled more rejection, but also that they had more trouble recollecting their childhood experiences, were more incoherent in their presentation of the childrearing they themselves had experienced, and tended to idealize their own mothers by denying their negative attributes. All this suggests to us that a procedure such as that employed in the current study, in which some 60 statements were answered using a questionnaire format, may simply not be sensitive to the kinds of recall difficulties that some mothers of insecure infants seem to display (at least under certain conditions). Quite conceivably, the incoherence of recollections and the denial of negative attributes that Main and Goldwyn observed may generate a great deal of error in a questionnaire such as the one we employed.

Another finding of Main and Goldwyn (1984) also leads us to be cautious in interpreting the absence of group differences on the developmental history measures used in this study. They found that when mothers who experienced rejection as children displayed understanding of their own parents' harsh rearing of them and had "worked through" their feelings with respect to the care they received, they were less at risk for raising insecurely attached infants than were similarly reared parents who had not come to terms with the unsupportive care they had experienced during their own childhoods. On the basis of these findings, the absence of a simple relationship between the kind of rearing experienced and security of attachment becomes more understandable. Had our questionnaire assessed not only past rearing experiences, but current feelings about them, it is quite conceivable that the mothers of securely and insecurely attached infants could have been distinguished.

Although child-rearing history failed to distinguish attachment groups—and for good reason—this was not the case with respect to personality. Indeed, our findings concerning maternal personality make good sense. In view of the role that maternal sensitivity is presumed to play in the development of attachment security, it stands to reason that mothers who are more empathic and concerned with others should be more likely to rear securely attached infants; it is just such personal attributes that the interpersonal affection scale measured. The same line of reasoning leads us to regard the lower ego strength of mothers of avoidant infants as logical. Women who are less emotionally stable and less psychologically mature should, in our view, have greater difficulty establishing a harmonious, synchronous, and thereby security-promoting relationship with their infants. Why it should be, however, that low ego strength characterizes only mothers of insecure-avoidant infants rather than mothers of insecure infants more generally is at this time unclear. Perhaps future studies that reveal additional personality differences of mothers of avoidant and resistant infants will enhance our understanding of the current findings.

Characteristics of Infant

Both the research reviewed in the introduction and the distinct theoretical opinions reflected there suggest that the security of the infant—mother attachment relationship is not solely a function of who mother is as a person before the child is born. Rather, it seems likely, at least theoretically, that the child plays a role in the development of his/her attachment relationship with mother. To address this issue, three sets of data were available for examination. The first of these involved newborn behavior as assessed by the Brazelton Neonatal Behavioral Assessment Scale (NBAS; Brazelton, 1973). Recall that this scale measures infants' orientation, motor tonus, range of state, regulation of state, and autonomic stability. In the current sample, our analyses revealed no evidence of early newborn differences; that is none of the individual NBAS a priori cluster scores differentiated attachment groups, nor did they collectively predict attachment security, as revealed by a multiple $R = .14$ ($p < .10$). (See Table 3.2 for mean values by attachment group along with univariate analyses of variance results.)[4] These findings are, of course, inconsistent with other investigations that have suggested that, as newborns, anxious-resistant infants are more susceptible to distress, whereas secure infants are more alert and responsive (Grossman et al., 1985; Miyake et al., 1985; Waters et al., 1980).

Also available to us (beyond the neonatal period) were data based on infants' behaviors observed ruing two home visits carried out at each of three ages: 1, 3, and 9 months. Data on the frequency of observed infant

---

[4]Since this chapter was written, reanalyses of Brazelton data using a different scoring system have revealed some differences between attachment groups in terms of their newborn behavior. Most noteworthy is the fact that these analyses reveal that newborn behavior predicts the way in which security and insecurity will be expressed rather than whether infants establish secure of insecure attachments to their mothers (see Belsky & Rovine, in press).

fussiness and alertness (both in the mother–infant and mother–father–infant setting) were subjected to a repeated measures MANOVA. Examination of Table 3.2 reveals that, as was the case for neonatal behavior, neither fussiness nor alertness discriminated the A, B., and C attachment classification groups or the secure/insecure groups. Additionally, there were no significant Time $\times$ Attachment interaction effects observed for either fussiness or alertness ($F\,2,41 = 1.48, p > .05; F\,2,41 = 2.56, p > .05$, respectively), in other words, none of the *behavioral* data we collected that can be considered to reflect infant temperament (broadly conceived) during the first year were predictive of attachment classifications.

The final set of data available regarding infant characteristics derive from maternal *reports* of infant temperament provided at 3 and 9-months

TABLE 3.2
Variation in Attachment as a Function of Characteristics of Infant:
Neonatal Behavior

	Attachment Group			*F Ratios*	
	A	*B*	*C*	*ABC*	*SEC/INS*
Neonatal Behaviors	(*n*=9)	(*n*=30)	(*n*=12)	(*df*=2,48)	(*df*=1,49)
Orientation	4.81	4.42	4.79	0.29	0.58
Motor Tonus	4.68	5.11	5.35	2.92	0.07
Range of State	3.84	3.75	3.70	0.11	0.00
Regulation of State	5.02	4.86	4.61	0.32	0.05
Automatic Stability	5.25	5.82	5.91	1.08	0.36

TABLE 3.3
Variation in Attachment as a Function of Characteristics of Infant:
Infant Behavior*

		Attachment Group		
		A	*B*	*C*
Infant Behaviors		(*n*=9)	(*n*=30)	(*n*=12)
Fussiness:	1 month	42.87	41.20	40.55
	3 months	26.00	40.88	34.36
	9 months	16.87	18.08	23.91
Alertness:	1 month	147.7	103.8	119.1
	3 months	284.9	216.6	232.9
	9 months	353.1	357.3	308.7

*See text for results of repeated measures MANOVA.

postpartum. Of the four temperament subscales subjected to repeated measures analysis, none resulted in significant main effects for attachment group (A vs. B vs. C; B vs. A and C). Such results are consistent with the evidence reviewed earlier, which indicate that maternal reports are unrelated to attachment classification. If should be noted, however, that in the case of two temperament subscales significant Time $\times$ Attachment (secure/insecure) interactions emerged: unpredictable (F 2,48 = 11.16; $p < .01$) and unadaptable (F 2,48 = 4.23, $p < .05$). The nature of these interactions is depicted graphically in Fig. 3.2 and 3.3, which reveal that mothers' appraisals of their infants changed as a function of whether infants developed secure or insecure attachments to them. Although infants "destined" to become secure were regarded as *less* adaptable (more unadaptable) when they were 3 months of age than those destined to be insecure (F 1,49 = 3.92, $p < .05$—follow-up test), 6 months later the two groups of infants were indistinguishable on this temperament dimension. Thus, over time, mothers whose infants developed secure attachments to them came to regard their babies as less of a challenge to care for (in terms of unadaptability), whereas those mothers whose infants developed insecure attachments experienced their infants as becoming more of a challenge.

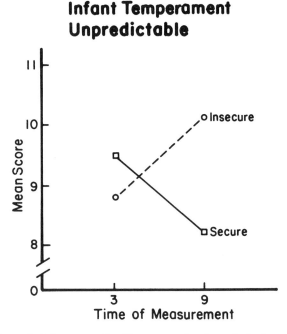

FIG. 3.2.   Change in infant unpredictableness as a function of attachment security.

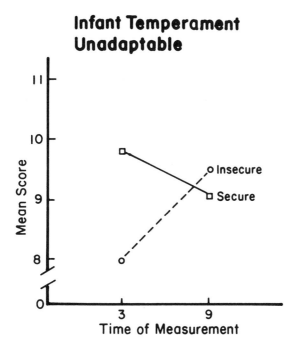

FIG. 3.3.   Change in infant unadaptableness as a function of attachment security.

A similar developmental process is evident in the case of the temperament dimension unpredictability. This time, however, no differences were discerned between groups at 3 months, but by 9 months, postpartum mothers of infants who were developing insecure attachments viewed their children as more unpredictable (F 1,49 = 6.86, $p <$ .01—follow-up test). Thus, we find no evidence, at least in terms of maternal reports, that infants who develop insecure attachments have more attractive temperaments to begin with; if anything, just the opposite is discerned (in the case of adaptability). Yet we do find that by the end of the third quarter of the first year, those infants who will behave in an avoidant or resistant manner in the Strange Situation three months later are regarded by their mothers as more of a challenge to care for.[5] These

---

[5]It is not just the measure of unpredictableness that reveals this pattern of increasing difficultness over time for the insecure group. Although neither the main effect of attachment group nor the Time × Attachment interaction in the repeated measures ANOVA is significant in the case of the fussy/difficult temperament subscale, the babies who behaved insecurely at 12 months were rated significantly more fussy by their mothers at 9 months (19.6 vs. 16.9) as indicated by a single time of measurement analysis of the 9-month data (F 1,49 = 5.91, $p <$ .05); the same was not observed when the 3-month fussy/difficult scores

findings are somewhat consistent with Frodi's (1983) 12-month findings in showing that, in the last quarter of the first year, at least some mothers involved in insecure relationships see their infants as being more difficult.

In considering the data at hand regarding the characteristics of the infant and individual differences in attachment classification, two things are eminently clear. First, there are no differences in objectively observed neonatal, 1, 3, and 9-month behavioral functioning of infants who at 1 year of age differ in their security of attachment—at least as measured in this study. Thus, no support whatsoever is provided for those theorists who contend that security/insecurity is a function of organismic differences in fussiness or other behavioral manifestations of temperament. Indeed, contrary to the expectations of what temperament theorists predict, it was infants destined to become secure who were regarded by their mothers as having less attractive temperaments (i.e., unadaptable, unpredictable) early in life, rather than those who would later develop insecure attachment relationships (see Fig. 3.2 and 3.3). The second point worth noting is that although objective behavioral assessments of infant functioning during the first year (as made in this study) did not distinguish attachment groups, mothers did differentially perceive those infants who became secure and insecure. Particularly striking is the consistent tendency for mothers with babies who could be evaluated as securely attached in the Strange Situation to experience their infants as *becoming more adaptable and predictable* over time, whereas those mothers with infants who could later be judged to be insecurely attached experienced their babies as *becoming less adaptable and predictable* over time.

Such findings clearly raise the possibility that by 9 months of age, distinct relationship patterns have developed that will be evident to researchers in a standard separation-reunion situation 3 months later. Indeed, it is quite possible that our behavioral observation did not pick up these emerging differences due to limitations of our methodology, especially relative to the wealth of information and experience available to mothers. Of particular importance is the fact that although maternal reports of infant temperament may have as much to do with mothers' relationships with their children as with children's actual behavior, our objective measures, which did not distinguish between attachment groups, had only to do with children's behavior. Because the Strange

were analyzed separately. Although it is problematic to extract data from repeated occasions for separate (i.e., one-time-of-measurement) analysis (as just reported), these results are worthy of consideration because they and the data on predictability are perfectly consistent with the results emanating from our first longitudinal study in which we observed that insecurely attached infants did not begin life crying more than securely attached infants, but by 9 months were crying more (Belsky, Rovine, & Taylor, 1984).

Situation assesses the security of the infant–parent attachment *relationship*, it is not unreasonable that data bearing on the relationship (i.e., mothers' perceptions of the child's temperament) should be associated with Strange Situation classifications more strongly and systematically than data obtained from an observational methodology that focuses solely upon discrete behavior. Although this has not been observed in other work (see Chapter 1), it is also true that other investigators have not carried out longitudinal analyses of maternal perceptions of infant temperament vis-á-vis attachment security.

In reflecting upon our absence of temperamental differences between attachment groups, it occurred to us that significant behavioral differences might have merged, especially by 9 months of age, had we coded infant behavior in a more contextually sensitive manner. Conceivably, if fussiness resulting from physical pain (e.g., a bumped head) had been distinguished from that which was more psychologically determined, like being put down too soon following being picked up, or not being picked up at all, then attachment-group differences might have emerged. Under such circumstances, however, we would have a difficult time labeling such differences *temperamental* in origin.

It is also conceivable that temperament effects do exist, but simply did not emerge in our analyses of the Brazelton and home observation data because our analyses tested for "main effects" only. As we argued at the outset of this chapter, the infant's constitutional characteristics of individuality probably function in interaction with other sources of influence on relationship development if they do play a role in the development of secure and insecure attachments. We are currently pursuing just this possibility in order to determine whether less behaviorally attractive infants are more at risk for insecurity under certain contextual conditions (e.g., low maternal ego strength, poor marriage, lack of social support), as well as whether more behaviorally attractive infants are more likely to end up secure under certain contextual conditions (e.g., healthy maternal personality, harmonious marriage). Unfortunately, space limitations preclude consideration of this most important issue in any more detail in this chapter.

An alternative way of looking at the discerned associations between maternal temperament reports and attachment classification draws attention to the possibility that changing appraisals made by mothers of their infants' temperaments may be more a function of their own personalities than they are actual reflections of how their babies behave. In this regard it must be reemphasized that mothers' *perceptions* and *evaluations* of the babies' behaviors are being measured rather than their babies' behaviors per se. This is not to say, however, that the temperament questionnaires are unrelated to observed behavior (see Bates & Bayles,

1984), but only to underscore the fact that maternal reports are likely to be influenced by subjective factors (such as personality) as well as by the child's actual behavior (see Bates, 1980; Bates & Bayles, 1984; Vaughn, 1983).

Although data from the current sample, such as those reported by Vaughn (1983), reveal little association between reports of infant temperament and observed infant behavior (Isabella, Ward, & Belsky, 1985), it happens to be the case, unlike Vaughn (1983), that we discerned no association between mother's personality and her temperament reports. It may well be that the personality scales employed in this study simply do not tap the psychological processes that influence mothers' temperament appraisals. Alternatively, it may be the case that the changing appraisals of temperament capture true behavioral differences in infants to which our observational system was not sensitive. In either event, we find no evidence to suggest that insecure babies begin life with more difficult temperaments, whereas secure babies begin life with more easy temperaments.

Social Context

As articulated in the introduction, a contextual view of parent–child relationships and child development underscores the need to look beyond characteristics of the parent and infant in order to understand what transpires between them. Thus, the question we now address is whether attachment groups can be distinguished in terms of mothers' marital relationships, relationships with others, and general social milieu.

Marriage. Our first step in addressing this issue was to subject the prenatal, 3, and 9-month positive and negative marital activities and sentiment composite scores to multivariate analyses of variance. In the case of both measures, the Time × Attachment Group interaction proved significant ($F_{2,48} = 6.99, p < .01; F_{2,48} = 3.54, p < .05$; for positive and negative composites, respectively), revealing the fact that mothers of insecure infants experienced more pronounced decline in positive activities and sentiments and a greater increase in negative activities and sentiments than mothers of secure infants (see Fig. 3.4 and 3.5). This interpretation was confirmed by a follow-up test indicating that the combined A and C slopes were not parallel to the B slope ($t_{49} = 2.53, p < .05; t_{49} = 2.63, p < .05$; for positive and negative composites, respectively).

Consideration of these findings indicates that insecure infant–mother relationships are most likely to develop in families in which mothers display the greatest decline in the quality of their marital relationships, as

FACTOR 1: POSITIVE MARITAL ACTIVITIES AND SENTIMENTS

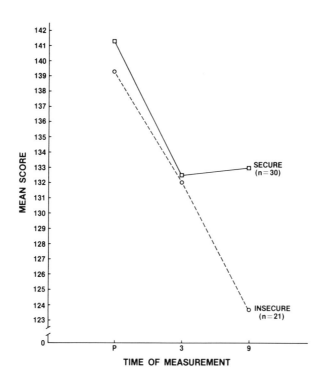

FIG. 3.4. Change in positive marital activities and sentiments as a function of attachment security.

reflected both in positive and negative aspects of their marriages. Careful examination of Fig. 3.4 and 3.5 reveals, however, that mothers of infants who develop secure and insecure attachments apparently do not differ in their marital evaluations prior to the baby's birth, and essentially follow the same course of modest decline in initial response to the transition (e.g., first 3 months). These findings thus clarify issues raised in the three previously cited studies linking marital quality with attachment security at 12 and 20 months. Our data indicate that marital differences do not precede the baby's birth or even accompany the opening months of his/her life. Rather, these differences emerge sometime after the third month, but well prior to the 12 and 20-month dates identified in the prior studies (Durett et al., 1984; Goldberg & Easterbrooks, 1984; Soloman, 1983). More specifically, the quality of the marriage begins to change differentially sometime during the second and third quarters of the first year, a period during which the baby becomes increasingly social and generally positive in affect (Emde, Gaensbauer, & Harmon, 1976).

Thus, although all three groups under study evidenced some decline in overall marital quality during the first half of the 1-year transition period, it was mothers who seemed to terminate this normative "descent" who were fostering the development of secure attachments. It therefore appears that although the birth of a child generally exerts a stress on the marital relationship, some time during the second and third quarters of

FACTOR 2:   NEGATIVE MARITAL ACTIVITIES AND SENTIMENTS

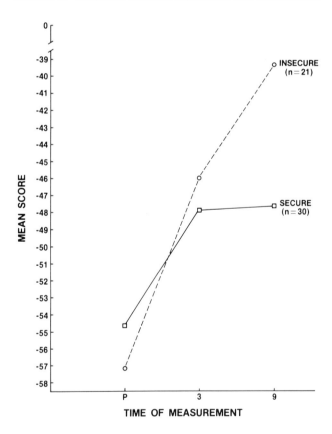

FIG. 3.5.   Change in negative marital activities and sentiments as a function of attachment security. (Note: The more negative the score, the "better" the marriage.)

the first year of the infant's life most mothers manage to pool the resources necessary to maintain a degree of love for their spouses and satisfaction with their marriages that are conducive to the development of secure infant–mother attachment relationships. As predicted by Belsky's (1981, 1984) models of the family system and of the multiple determinants of parenting, and as suggested by the other marriage-attachment work, perhaps husbands' love for and support of their wives provides a significant portion of the resources these mothers possess, and explains the apparent halt to the decline initially observed in feelings regarding husband and the marital relationship.

The fact that marital change was more negative in the case of insecure attachment groups is particularly intriguing in view of the repeatedly discerned association in the clinical literature between marital discord and child behavior problems during preschool and elementary school years (see Emery, 1982, for review). Because, as is noted repeatedly in this volume, there is some degree of association between insecurity in infancy and later behavior problems (Erickson, Sroufe, & Egeland, 1986; Lewis, Feiring, McGuffog, & Jaskir, 1984), and because we discerned a relationship between negative change in marriage and attachment insecurity, it seems quite possible, at least in terms of logical inference, that we may be picking up in the first year of life what is later destined to become the marital-discord/child-behavior-problem relationship so frequently observed by clinical investigators.

Social Network. Having discerned an association between marriage and attachment, a related question concerns the association between attachment and mother's relationships with other members of her social network and her extra-familial social context more generally. With respect to social networks, reports of mothers' prenatal, 3-, and 9-month frequency of supportive contact with others were also compared as a function of 12-month attachment classification. No evidence emerged from these analyses that the social worlds of mothers of secure and insecure infants differed from one another at any of the three times of measurement, nor were differential patterns of change discerned over time.

Our failure to discern differences in the social networks of mothers of secure and insecure infants must be considered in terms of the limits of our measurement system, as it is certainly conceivable that differences could have emerged had other dimensions of the social network been studied, either singularly or in combination. Indeed, if we had it to do again, we would inquire not simply about frequency of contact with and support provided by friends, relatives, and neighbors, but also about difficulties, stresses, and strains generated by these relationships. Clinical experience with the families participating in our third cohort reveals the debilitating effects that such presumably unsupportive relations often engender (see Nezworski, Vondra, & Tolan, this volume).

Social Milieu. The final social context dimension we examined as it related to attachment security was social milieu. Recall that social milieu was assessed prenatally by asking families about their perceptions of their neighbors as friendly and/or helpful. Analyses revealed that secure and insecure groups differed on this measure ($F\,1,49 = 4.45, p < .05$) such that families whose infants established secure attachment relationships scored significantly higher than families whose infants developed insecure attachments ($\overline{X} = 29.0$ and 26.4 respectively). These data indicate that parents of secure infants perceive their social milieu as being more supportive (before their infants are born) than do parents of insecure infants.

Prenatal differences between secure and insecure infants' families on the social milieu measure certainly suggest that it is not just what goes on in the family beyond the mother–infant dyad, i.e., the marriage, that may contribute to the development of secure and insecure attachment relationships. We should not, however, on the basis of these social milieu data, conceive of some neighborhoods as inherently more promoting of optimal family relationships and infant development. Although this is likely to be true in certain cases (crime-ridden, inner-city ghettos vs. suburban neighborhoods), it must be recognized that the items comprising the social milieu measure assessed the extent to which each family *felt* that their neighbors were friendly and helpful. In many cases, the perception of such support—which we have seen distinguishes secure and insecure attachment groups—is a function of the family itself. It is likely, for example, that the quality of social interaction contributed by a husband and wife within their neighborhood strongly influences the quality of neighbors' reciprocal interactions. In addition, the social milieu measure was a subjective one, which leads to the further suggestion that parents' perceptions of their neighbors may indeed be a function of their own social actions. Neighborhood support may therefore be a phenomenon of the family's own making rather than something that is passively experienced and not subject to self-control.

A CONFIGURATIONAL APPROACH TO THE DETERMINANTS OF ATTACHMENT

Through this point in our presentation, the conceptually informed analysis of distinct domains of influence on attachment security has revealed several individual measures that discriminated attachment groups. Having identified these distinguishing variables, our second data analytic procedure involved the examination of a set of theoretical propositions previously advanced by us regarding the probability of parents and children functioning well in various situations (Belsky, 1984; Belsky, Robins, & Gamble, 1984). In this earlier theoretical work, we drew attention to three general sources of influence on parent–child relationships (parent characteristics, child characteristics, social context) and argued that parent–child relationships would function more optimally the more these subsystems worked to promote rather than undermine parental competence. Further, we theorized that characteristics of the mother would be more influential in determining the quality of parent–child relations than characteristics of the social context, which themselves were expected to be more influential than characteristics of the child.

In an effort to test these hypotheses, our second set of analyses involved the creation of three composite variables, each comprised of the individual variables that distinguished attachment groups in our prior set of analyses: one represented maternal personality (interpersonal affection plus ego strength); a second represented the social context of marriage (sum of changes, from pregnancy through 9 months, in positive and negative marital activities and sentiments); and a third represented infant temperament (actually, change in temperament: sum of changes in predictability and unadaptability). Each composite was split at the median, with scores above the median for personality, change in marriage, and change in temperament indicative of "poor" functioning in which the individual looked relatively "unhealthy," marital quality "deteriorated" greatly over time, and infants became especially "difficult" over time; the reverse was true of scores below the median. These three dimensions and six scoring categories enabled us to create eight configurational patterns depending on whether each dimension reflected good (+) or poor (−) functioning. In one subgroup of families, then, scores on all three composite variables reflected positive functioning (Personality +, Marriage +, Temperament +); in three subgroups of families, scores on two of three composite variables reflected positive functioning (P+, M+, T−; P+, M−, T+; P−, M+, T+); in three additional subgroups, scores on only one of three composite variables reflected positive functioning (P+, M−, T−; P−, M+, T−; P−, M−, T+); and finally, in one last subgroup scores on all three composite variables reflected poor functioning (P−, M−, T−).

Using these family types, we examined the eight subgroups in terms of the degree to which they "produced" secure and insecure infant–mother attachments. The results of our configurational analysis are displayed in Table 3.4. Inspection of this table reveals, most obviously and importantly, that, as predicted, the more these three subsystems of influence (parent characteristics, child characteristics, social context) functioned in a supportive mode (+), the more likely it was for the attachment relationship to be secure. Indeed, chi-square analysis comparing the groups with 0, 1, 2, or 3 composite scores in the supportive mode indicated that these groups significantly differed from one another (X^2 (3) = 16.45, $p < .001$: 17% vs. 38% vs. 83% vs. 92% secure, respectively). Beyond this most general observation, several features of Table 3.4 merit particular attention. First, when all three subsystems functioned in a supportive mode only a single instance of insecurity was discerned (11 of 12 secure), and when all subsystems functioned in a stressful mode, all but one relationship was insecure (5 of 6 insecure).

Also worth noting is the fact that the differences between rate of security are much more pronounced between groups that have 1 versus 2 sources of stress (38% vs. 83%) than between groups that have 0 versus 1 source of stress (0 vs. 38%) or those that have 2 versus 3 sources of stress (83% vs. 92%). This nonlinear relationship between sources of stress and rates of insecurity is quite consistent with the theoretical notions guiding this inquiry (Belsky, 1984). More specifically, it appears that sources of sup-

TABLE 3.4
Configurational Analysis of Sources of Stress and Support in Relation to Attachment Security*

| Subgroup | Characteristics of: | | | Frequency: Attachment Security | | | % Secure |
| | Mother | Social Context | Infant | | | | |
	Personality[a]	Marriage[b]	Temperament[c]	A	B	C	
1	+	+	+	0	11	1	92
2	+	+	−	1	3	1	60
3	+	−	+	0	5	0	100
4	−	+	+	0	2	0	100
5	+	−	−	1	4	3	50
6	−	+	−	2	2	2	33
7	−	−	+	2	2	3	29
8	−	−	−	3	1	2	17

*A plus sign (+) indicates that the score on a particular variable was reflective of positive functioning, whereas a minus sign (−) indicates that the score was reflective of negative functioning.

[a]Personality = The sum of interpersonal affection and ego strength.

[b]Marriage = The sum of changes in positive marital activities and sentiments and negative marital activities and sentiments.

[c]Temperament = The sum of changes on the unadaptable and unpredictable subscales of the temperament questionnaire.

port can quite effectively buffer the mother–infant relationship from sources of stress, provided that multiple sources of stress are not in evidence. When, however, sources of stress multiply, so too does the risk of insecurity of attachment in a pattern quite like a classic interaction effect in an analysis of variance model.

A final point to be made with respect to the data depicted in Table 3.4 is that no specific configurational pattern seemed to be related to a particular form of insecurity. Nor was it the case, contrary to our theorizing (Belsky, 1984) that characteristics of the parent (i.e., personality) were more powerful in distinguishing secure and insecure attachments than those of the social context (i.e., marriage), and those of the child (i.e., temperament). For our expectations to have been confirmed, we would have had to observe, for example, decreasing rates of security in groups 2, 3, and 4, as well as in groups 5, 6, and 7. Although the rates of security are in accordance with our predictions in the case of groups 5, 6, and 7, this was not true with regard to groups 2, 3, and 4. In the absence of complete confirmation of our anticipated ranking of groups, it is worth recalling comments made earlier regarding what our temperament variables may actually be measuring; that is, the change in temperament scores utilized in the described analysis may be more a reflection of the mothers' perceptions of the child and, thus, of her relationship with him/her, than of the child's temperament per se. To the extent that this is the case, and we suspect it is, the index of temperament used in this configurational analysis would not be expected to emerge as the weakest predictor.

A DYNAMIC PROCESS MODEL

On the basis of the conceptual framework that guided this inquiry from the outset and that underscored the need to consider characteristics of the mother, the child, and the social context as determinants of infant–mother attachment, we were led to implement one final analysis that built upon and extended the preceding analyses. More specifically, we tested a process model using path analytic techniques which we believed depicted influences on attachment in a more dynamic manner than that offered by the conceptually informed, yet static configuration analysis reported previously. Thus, using path analytic techniques, we sought to model a process whereby the influence of maternal personality on attachment is both direct and mediated by changes in marriage and temperament reports. We based this model on our assumption that the mothers' personalities before their babies are born influence how they experience the transition to parenthood (marital change) and how they experience their

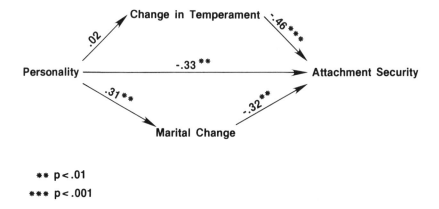

FIG. 3.6.   Path analysis of the determinants of parenting. (Note: The higher the personality score the less "healthy" the individual; the higher the change-in-temperament score, the more "difficult" the infant became over time; the higher the marital change score, the more marital quality "deteriorated" over time; insecure attachment is coded with a value of 1 and secure attachment is coded with a value of 2.)

children (change in temperament), and thus both directly and indirectly affect the nature of the relationships they establish with their children, i.e., security of attachment.

The results of the path analysis are depicted in Fig. 3.6. The numbers on the diagram represent standardized regression coefficients; the model depicted accounts for a total of 48% of the variance in attachment security. Maternal personality is treated as an exogenous variable that is not explained by any other factor in the model. The change in marriage and change in temperament measures represent mediating variables linking prenatal personality and attachment security. Thus, this model addresses two basic questions: Do mothers' changing appraisals of their babies and their marriages mediate the influence of personality on attachment? Does personality exert a direct effect on attachment security, apart from its influence on changing marriage and temperament appraisals?

The network of path coefficients indicates that mothers' prenatal personality exerted both a reliable direct and indirect influence on attachment security; the indirect influence was mediated solely by changes in marital activity and sentiment because prenatal maternal affection was not related to changes in temperament, even though changes in temperament were related to attachment security. From a more substantive standpoint, the path analysis reveals that mothers who scored poorly (received high scores) on ego strength and interpersonal affection prenatally were likely to experience the most negative change in their marriages and that such personality characteristics and marital experience contributed to the development of an insecure infant–mother relationship. Although the effect of marital change on attachment security seemed to derive at least in part from the influence of personality on marital change, this was not the case with respect to changes in temperamental evaluations. Although the absence of a relationship between personality and temperament reports does not support the contention that changes in the latter may be influenced by the psychological characteristics of the person doing the reporting, it would be inappropriate to accept the null hypothesis and conclude that mother's personality has no influence on her changing appraisals of her baby. As noted earlier, it is possible, had other personality indices been available, that associations between personality and temperament reports would have been discerned; in future work we hope to address this issue.

CONCLUSION

In this chapter we have examined the association between security of infant–mother attachment and several sources of influence likely to shape the development of the mother–infant relationship. It should be noted that the strategy adopted to pursue this issue in the current investigation differed in several important respects from most other efforts to illuminate empirically the origins of individual differences in attachment. Most obvious in this regard is the fact that, rather than examining the actual interactional determinants of attachment security, we focused in this chapter on maternal, infant, and contextual sources of stress and support presumed to influence the day-to-day experiences that mother and baby have with each other and, thereby, the security of the attachment relationship. As noted in the introduction to this chapter, one goal of our research program is to link the sources of stress and support we have now found to covary with attachment security directly to observed interaction between mother and infant and, thereby, to individual differences in attachment. Although a great deal of work still needs to be done in order to realize this goal, the findings to emerge from this phase of our inquiry clearly suggests where our next efforts should be directed. Having discovered, for example, that marital change, change in temperamental appraisal, and maternal personality discriminate between attachment groups, we need to understand how these sources of influence relate to observed patterns of mother–infant interaction during the infant's first year of life. Once such linkages are established, we can then proceed to examine associations between observed interaction and attachment security. Such progressive inquiry should enable us to develop a process model linking distal sources of influence (e.g., maternal personality, marital change) to proximal sources of influence (i.e., observed interaction between mother and infant) and thereby to individual differences in infant–mother attachment.

Most prior work that has attempted to link maternal personality, marital quality, or infant temperament to attachment security has focused upon single sources of influence to the exclusion of others or has pursued multiple determinants of attachment security in a relatively atheoretical manner, relying upon sophisticated data analytic techniques such as discriminant function analyses to identify variables that most powerfully distinguish attachment groups. The research reported in this chapter differs from this past work not simply as a result of its focus upon multiple sources of stress and support, but also because it was guided by a conceptual framework that specified, a priori, which sources of influence merited special attention as potential determinants of attachment security. Indeed, the determinants of parenting model proposed by Belsky (1984) not only drew attention to characteristics of the mother, the infant, and the social context (most notably the marriage and the social network), but also suggested specific ways in which these sources of stress and support should be empirically examined. Recall that after assessing the ability of each variable *within* a set to discriminate attachment groups on an *individual basis,* the *collective* influence of the discriminating variables was then examined. In fact, once a configurational analysis revealed the risk of insecurity increased as sources of stress in the family increased, a path analysis was implemented in order to model the dynamic processes through which maternal personality, marital change, and change in temperament influenced the developing mother–infant relationship (as indexed by security of attachment).

The results of the path analysis, which underscored the direct and indirect influence of maternal personality on attachment security, begin to illuminate the dynamic nature of the family and the complex processes through which the mother–infant relationship develops. Recall that the results of this final set of analyses indicated that mothers who were more interpersonally sensitive and emotionally stable prior to their infants birth were more likely to rear infants who developed secure relationships with them, in part because these mothers experienced less marital stress as a result of the transition to parenthood. Certain women, it would appear, are predisposed to navigate the transition successfully and maintain relatively positive relationships with both their husbands and their infants across the child's first year of life. This observation underscores one of the major conclusions to emerge from this inquiry: Not only do developmentalists need to consider the patterns of interaction that characterize and influence parent–infant relationships, but they also need to recognize that parenting is but one activity mothers engage in; how mothers treat their babies, and the manner in which the mother–infant relationship develops is likely to be, in large measure, a function of who the mother is as a psychological agent before the baby is born and of the nature of her relationship with her spouse. It would seem, then, that the mother–infant relationship has a developmental history, if not a developmental trajectory, even before the child encounters the mother for the first time.

It would be a mistake to overinterpret the results of the path analysis and presume that pathways of influence in the parent–child relationship and family system are unidirectional. Although the analysis suggests that material personality, marital change, and change in temperament each directly influence the parent–child relationship, it must be understood that we are dealing with a dynamic system characterized by patterns of reciprocal feedback. The complexity of the actual system is, therefore, likely to far exceed that suggested by any of our data analytic methods. Mother–infant relationships that are experiencing difficulty are likely to create stress for the marriage, which, when experienced by individuals whose interpersonal sensitivity and emotional stability is less than would be ideal, is likely to feedback to further undermine the child-rearing relationship. Unfortunately, our ability to think in terms of such complex systems far exceeds our current ability to model them empirically, even when the available longitudinal data are at hand. Thus, the results of the study reported in this chapter should be considered to illuminate aspects of the dynamic individual and family systems that contribute to the development of secure and insecure infant–mother attachment relationships rather than depict them in their entirety.

Now that we have discovered that maternal personality characteristics measured even before the baby is born, mother's changing perceptions of the infant's temperament, marital change across the transition to parenthood, as well as characteristics of the neighborhood, all relate to attachment-security in a theoretically meaningful manner, we need to consider the implications of these findings. The most obvious implication is that the determinants of attachment-security are many. This means, as our configurational analysis revealed, not only that sources of stress can be buffered by sources of support, that risk is greatest when multiple sources of stress exist, but also that a multiplicity of avenues are available as targets of interventions. Although some might interpret our findings concerning maternal personality as evidence that in-depth psychotherapy is called for in the case of parent–child relationships at risk, we would not draw this conclusion ourselves. Indeed, our reading of the data leads us to emphasize the need to target a variety of contributing processes—and this is exactly what we have been engaged in as part of an experimental intervention effort that is described in Chapter 9, by Nezworski and colleagues (this volume). Basic to this effort is the notion, articulated earlier, that the parent–infant relationship is embedded in a family system comprised of individuals and the marital relationship. This conceptualization, when coupled with the findings emerging from the analyses reported herein, lead us to focus upon the mother's own psychological needs, the interpretations she makes of her infant's behavior, and the nature of her relationship with her spouse and her friends and relatives. The task as we see it is to recognize the mother as a psychological agent in her own right—apart from her role as mother or wife—and then deal with her family and extrafamilial relationships in the context of such understanding.

ACKNOWLEDGMENTS

Work on this chapter and the research reported herein were supported by grants from the National Science Foundation (No. SES-8108886), the National Institute of Mental Health (No. R01MH39740-01), the March of Dimes Birth Defects Foundation (Social and Behavior Science Branch, No. 12–64), and by an NIMH Research Scientist Development Award (K02-MH00486) to the first author. The authors would like to thank Alan Sroufe, Jack Bates, and Jerome Kagan for their thoughtful comments on earlier drafts of this chapter.

REFERENCES

Ainsworth, M. D. S. (1972). Attachment and dependency: A comparison. In J. L. Gewirtz (Ed.), *Attachment and dependency.* Washington, DC: V. H. Winson & Sons.

Ainsworth, M. D. S., Bell, S. M., & Stayton, D. J. (1974). Infant–mother attachment and social development: "Socialization" as a product of reciprocal responsiveness to signals. In M. P. M. Richards (Ed.), *The integration of a child into a social world.* Cambridge, MA: Cambridge University Press.

Ainsworth, M. D. S., Blehar, M. C., Waters, E., & Wall, S. (1978). *Patterns of attachment.* Hillsdale, NJ: Lawrence Erlbaum Associates.

Ainsworth, M. D. S., & Wittig, B. (1969). Attachment and exploratory behavior of one-year-olds in a strange situation. In B. M. Foss (Ed.), *Determinants of infant behavior* (Vol. 4). London: Methuen.

Barglow, P., & Hoffman, M. (1985, May). *Mother's effect upon oral phase ego development and attachment.* Paper presented at the meeting of the American Psychoanalytic Society, Denver.

Bates, J. E. (1980). The concept of difficult temperament. *Merrill-Palmer Quarterly, 26,* 299–319.

Bates, J. E. (in press). Temperament in infancy. In J. Osofsky (Ed.), *Handbook of infant development* (2nd ed.). New York: Wiley.

Bates, J. E., & Bayles, K. (1984). Objective and subjective components in mothers' perceptions of their children from age 6 months to 3 years. *Merrill-Palmer Quarterly, 30,* 111–130.

Bates, J. E., Freeland, C. A. B., & Lounsbury, M. L. (1979). Measurement of infant difficultness. *Child Development, 50,* 794–803.

Bates, J. E., Maslin, C., & Frankel, K. (1985). Attachment security, mother-child interaction, and temperament as predictors of behavior problem ratings at age three years. In I. Bretherton & E. Waters (Eds), *Growing points in attachment theory and research. Monographs for the Society for Research in Child Development, 50* (Serial No. 209, pp. 167–193).

Belsky, J. (1981). Early human experience: A family perspective. *Developmental Psychology, 17,* 3–23.

Belsky, J. (1984). The determinants of parenting: A process model. *Child Development, 55,* 83–96.

Belsky, J. (1985). Experimenting with the family in the newborn period. *Child Development, 56,* 407–401.

Belsky, J., Gilstrap, B., & Rovine, M. (1984). The Pennsylvania Infant and Family Development Project I: Stability and change in mother–infant and father–infant interaction in a family setting at 1-to-3-to-9 months. *Child Development, 55,* 692–704.

Belsky, J., Hertzog, C., & Rovine, M. (1986). The multiple determinants of parenting: Empirical and methodological advances. In M. Lamb, A. Brown, & B. Rogoff (Eds.), *Advances in developmental psychology* (Vol. IV, pp. 153–202). Hillsdale, NJ: Lawrence Erlbaum Associates.

Belsky, J., Lang, M., & Rovine, M. (1985). Stability and change in marriage: A second study. *Journal of Marriage and the Family, 47,* 855–866.

Belsky, J., Robins, E., & Gamble, W. (1984). The determinants of parenting: Toward a contextual theory. In M. Lewis & L. Rosenblum (Eds.), *Beyond the dyad: Social connections* (pp. 251–280). New York: Plenum.

Belsky, J., & Rovine, M. (in press). Temperament and attachment security in the Strange Situation: An empirical rapprochement. *Child Development.*

Belsky, J., Rovine, M., & Taylor, D. (1984). The Pennsylvania Infant and Family Development Project II: Origins of individual differences in infant–mother attachment: Maternal and infant contributions. *Child Development, 55,* 706–717.

Belsky, J., Taylor, M., & Rovine, M. (1984). The Pennsylvania Infant and Family Development Project II: Development of reciprocal interaction in the mother–infant dyad. *Child Development, 55,* 718–772.

Belsky, J., & Vondra, J. (in press). Lessons from child abuse: The determinants of parenting. In C. Cichetti & V. Carlson (Eds.), *Handbook of child maltreatment: Theory and research.* Boston, MA: Cambridge University Press.

Benn, R. K. (1985, April). *Factors associated with security of attachment in dual career families.* Paper presented at the biennial meeting for the Society for Research in Child Development, Toronto.

Braiker, H., & Kelley, H. (1979). Conflict in the development of close relationships. In R. Burgess & T. Huston (Eds.), *Social exchange and developing relationships.* New York: Academic Press.

Brazelton, R. B. (1973). *Neonatal behavioral assessment scale.* London: Heineman.

Bretherton, I. (in press). Attachment theory: Retrospect and prospect. In I. Bretherton & E. Waters (Eds.), *Growing points in attachment theory and research. Monographs of the Society for Research in Child Development,* 50 (Serial No. 209, pp. 3–38).

Bronfenbrenner, U. (1979). *The ecology of human development.* Cambridge, MA: Harvard University Press.

Callaghan, J. W. (1981). A comparison of Anglo, Hopi, and Navajo mothers and infants. In T. M. Field, A. M. Sostek, P. Vietze, & P. H. Leiderman (Eds.), *Culture and early interactions.* Hillsdale, NJ: Lawrence Erlbaum Associates.

Carey, W. B. (1970). A simplified model of measuring infant temperament. *The Journal of Pediatrics, 77,* 188–194.

Cattell, R. B., Eber, H. W., & Tatsuoka, M. M. (1970). *Handbook for the Sixteen Personality Factor Questionnaire (16PF).* Champaign, IL: Institute for Personality and Ability Testing.

Caudill, W., & Weinstein, H. (1969). Maternal care and infant behavior in Japan and America. *Psychiatry, 32,* 12–43.

Chess, S., & Thomas, A. (1982). Infant bonding: Mystique and reality. *American Journal of Orthopsychiatry, 52,* 213–222.

Cochran, M., & Brassard, J. (1979). Child development and personal social networks. *Child Development, 50,* 601–616.

Crockenberg, S. (1981). Infant irritability, mother responsiveness, and social support influences on the security of infant–mother attachment. *Child Development, 52,* 857–869.

Durrett, M. E., Otaki, M., & Richards, P. (1984). Attachment and the mother's perception of support from the father. *International Journal of Behavioral Development, 7,* 169–176.

Egeland, B., & Farber, E. A. (1984). Infant–mother attachment: Factors related to its development and changes over time. *Child Development, 55*(3), 753–771.

Egeland, B., & Sroufe, L. (1981). Attachment and early maltreatment. *Child Development, 52,* 44–52.

Emde, R., Gaensbauer, T., & Harmon, R. (1976). Emotional expression in infancy: A biobehavioral study. *Psychological Issues, 10* (1, Monograph 37).

Emery, R. E. (1982). Marital turmoil: Interparental conflict and the children of discord and divorce. *Psychological Bulletin, 92,* 310–330.

Epstein, S. (1980). The self-concept: A review and the proposal of an integrated theory of personality. In E. Staub (Ed.), *Personality: Basic aspects and current research.* Englewood Cliffs, NJ: Prentice-Hall.

Erikson, M., Sroufe, A., & Egeland, B. (1986). The relationship between quality of attachment and behavior problems in preschool in a high risk sample. In I. Bretherton & E. Waters (Eds.), *Growing points in attachment theory and research. Monographs for the Society for Research in Child Development,* 50 (Serial No. 209, pp. 147–166).

Freedman, D. G. (1974). *Human infancy: An evolutionary perspective.* New York: Wiley.

Frodi, A. (1983). Attachment behavior and sociability with strangers in premature and full-term infants. *Infant Mental Health Journal, 4,* 13–22.

Goldberg, W. A., & Easterbrooks, M. A. (1984). The role of marital quality in toddler development. *Developmental Psychology, 20,* 504–514.

Gottman, J. (1979). *Marital interaction: Experimental investigations.* New York: Academic Press.

Grossmann, K., Grossmann, K. E., Spangler, G., Suess, G., & Unzer, J. (in press). Maternal sensitivity and newborns' orientation responses as related to quality of attachment in northern Germany. In I. Bretherton & E. Waters (Eds.), *Growing points in attachment theory and research. Monographs for the Society for Research in Child Development,* 50, (Serial No. 209, pp. 233–256).

Holmes, D., Ruble, N., Kowalski, J., & Lavesen, B. (1984, April). *Predicting quality of attachment at one year form neonatal characteristics.* Paper presented at the International Conference of Infant Studies, New York.

Huston, T. (1983, July 19). *The topography of marriage: A longitudinal study of change in husband-wife relationships over the first year.* Plenary address to the International Conference on Personal Relationships, Madison, WI.

Huston, T., McHale, S., & Crouter, A. (1986). When the honeymoon's over: Changes in the marriage relationship over the first year. In R.

Gilmour & S. Duck (Eds.), *The emerging fields of personal relationships* (pp. 109–144). Hillsdale, NJ: Lawrence Erlbaum Associates.

Huston, T., & Robins, E. (1982). Conceptual and methodological issues in studying close relationships. *Journal of Marriage and the Family, 44,* 901–925.

Isabella, R. A., Ward, M. J., & Belsky, J. (1985). An examination of the convergence between multiple sources of information on infant individuality: Neonatal behavior, infant behavior, and temperament reports. *Infant Behavior and Development, 8,* 283–291.

Jackson, D. (1976). *Jackson personality inventory.* Gaslen, NY: Research Psychologists Press.

Jackson, D. (1980). *Personality research form.* Port Huron, MI: Research Psychologists Press.

Kagan, J. (1982). *Psychological research on the human infant: An evaluative summary.* New York: W. T. Grant Foundation.

Kagan, J., Kearsley, R., & Zelazo, P. (1978). *Infancy: Its place in human development.* Cambridge: Harvard University Press.

Kaye, K. (1978). Discriminating among normal infants by multivariate analysis of Brazelton scores: Lumping and smoothing. In A. J. Sameroff (Ed.), *Organization and stability of newborn behavior: A commentary on the Brazelton Neonatal Behavior Assessment Scale. Monographs of the Society for Research in Child Development, 43* (5–6, Serial No. 177).

Kiser, L., Bates, J., Maslin, C., & Bayles, K. (1986). Mother–infant play at six months as a predictor of attachment security at thirteen months. *Journal of the American Academy of Child Psychiatry.*

Kuchner, J. F. R. (1980). *Chinese-American and European-American: A cross-cultural study of infant and mothers.* Unpublished doctoral dissertation, University of Chicago.

Lamb, M. E., Thompson, R. A., Gardner, W., Charnov, E. L., & Estes, D. (1984). Security of infantile attachment as assessed in the "Strange Situation": Its study and biological interpretation. *Behavioral and Brain Sciences, 7,* 127–147.

Lerner, R., Palermo, M., Spiro, A., & Nesselroade, J. (1982). The dimensions of temperament survey: A life-span instrument. *Child Development, 53, 149–159.*

Lester, B. M., Als, H., & Brazelton, T. B. (1982). Regional obstetric anesthesia and newborn behavior: A reanalysis toward synergistic effects. *Child Development, 53,* 687–692.

Levitt, M. J., Weber, R. A., & Clark, M. C. (1986). Social network relationships as sources of maternal support and well-being. *Developmental Psychology, 22,* 310–316.

Lewis, M., Feiring, C., McGuffog, C., & Jaskir, J. (1984). Predicting psychopathology in six-year-olds from early social relations. *Child Development, 55,* 123–136.

Lyons-Ruth, K., Connell, D., Grunebaum, H., Botein, S., & Zoll, D. (1984). Maternal family history, maternal caretaking, and infant attachment in multiproblem families. *Journal of Preventive Psychiatry, 2*(3 & 4), 403–425.

Main, M., & Goldwyn, R. (1984). Predicting rejection of her infant from mother's representation of her own experience: Implications for the abused-abusing intergenerational cycle. *Child Abuse and Neglect, 8,* 203–217.

Maslin, C. A., & Bates, J. E. (1983), April). *Precursors of anxious and secure attachments: A multivariate model at age 6 months.* Paper presented at the biennial meeting of the Society for Research in Child Development, Detroit.

Miyake, K., Chen, S., & Campos, J. J. (1985). Infant temperament, mother's mode of interaction, and attachment in Japan: An interim report. In I. Bretherton & E. Waters (Eds.), *Growing points in attachment theory and research. Monographs for the Society for Research in Child Development,* 50 (Serial No. 209, pp. 276–297).

Morris, D. (1980). *Infant attachment and problem solving in the toddler: Relations to mother's family history.* Unpublished doctoral dissertation, University of Minnesota.

Morris, D. (1981). Attachment and intimacy. In G. Stricker (Ed.), *Intimacy* (pp. 305–323). New York: Plenum.

Ricks, M. (1985). The social transmission of parental behavior: Attachment across generations. In I. Bretherton & E. Waters (Eds.), *Growing points in attachment theory and research. Monographs of the Society for Research in Child Development,* 50 (Serial No. 209, pp. 211–230).

Rohner, R. (1980). *Handbook for the study of parental acceptance and rejection.* Storrs, CT: Center for the study of Parental Acceptance and Rejection, University of Connecticut.

Rushton, J. P., Brainerd, C. J., & Pressley, M. (1983). Behavioral development and construct validity: The principle of aggregation. *Psychological Bulletin, 94*(1), 18–38.

Sameroff, A. J., Krafchuk, E. E., & Bakow, H. A. (1978). Issues in grouping items from the Neonatal Behavioral Assessment Scale. In A. J. Sameroff (Ed.), *Organization and stability of newborn behavior: A commentary on the Brazelton Neonatal Assessment Scale. Monographs of the Society for Research in Child Development, 43*(5–6, Serial No. 177).

Sameroff, A. J., Seifer, R., & Elias, P. K. (1982). Sociocultural variability in infant temperament ratings. *Child Development, 53,* 164–173.

Soloman, J. (1982). *Marital intimacy and parent–infant relationships.*

Unpublished doctoral dissertation, University of California, Berkeley.

Sostek, A. M., & Anders, T. F. (1977). Relationships among the Brazelton Neonatal Scale, Bayley Infant Scales, and early temperament. *Child Development, 48,* 320–323.

Spieker, S. J., & Booth, C. L. (1985, April). *Family risk typologies and patterns of insecure attachment.* Paper presented at the biennial meeting of the Society for Research in Child Development, Toronto.

Sroufe, L. A. (1979a). The coherence of individual development. *American Psychologist, 34,* 834–841.

Sroufe, L. A. (1979b). Socioemotional development. In J. Osofsky (Ed.), *Handbook of infant development.* New York: Wiley.

Sroufe, L. A. (1985). Attachment classification from the perspective of infant–caregiver relationships and infant temperament. *Child Development, 56,* 1–14.

Vaughn, B. E. (1983, April). *Maternal personality variables measured prenatally predict perceptions of infant temperament.* Paper presented at the meeting of the Society for Research in Child Development, Detroit.

Waters, E., Vaughn, B. E., & Egeland, B. R. (1980). Individual differences in infant–mother attachment relationships at age one: Antecedents in neonatal behavior in an urban and ecologically disadvantaged sample. *Child Development, 51,* 208–216.

Weber, R. A., Levitt, M. J. & Clark, M. C. (in press). Individual variation in attachment security and strange situation behavior: The role of maternal and infant temperament. *Developmental Psychology.*

4

Maternal Antecedents of Attachment Quality

Susan J. Spieker
Cathryn L. Booth
Department of Parent and Child Nursing and Child Development and
Mental Retardation Center University of Washington

INTRODUCTION

Most of the seminal research on attachment in infancy has been based on low-risk samples of fairly stable, lower middle-class to upper middle-class families. Reviews of studies of predominantly middle-class American samples usually report them to be quite consistent in the proportions of secure (B), insecure-avoidant (A), and insecure-resistant (C) infants. In fact, a brief survey of several frequently cited attachment studies revealed a range in the proportions of secure and insecure (avoidant and resistant) infants. This sampling of studies of low-risk infants, summarized in Table 4.1, suggests that there is a range in the expectable proportions of avoidant, secure, and resistant classifications. Across samples, the proportion of avoidant infants ranges from 15% to 32%; the proportion of secure infants ranges from 57% to 73%; and the proportion of resistant infants ranges from 4% to 22%.

TABLE 4.1
Selected Low-Risk Samples: A, B, C, and D Attachment Classifications

Low Risk	*n*	*Age*	*A*	*B*	*C*	*D or "unclassifiable"*
Ainsworth et al. (1978)	106	12 mos	22%	66%	12%	
original Baltimore sample	23	12 mos	26%	57%	17%	
Bell (1970)	33	12 mos	15%	73%	12%	
Belsky et al. (1984)	54	12 mos	18.5%	63%	18.5%	
Main & Weston (1981)	44	12 mos	30%	52%	5%	14%

More recently, there have been a number of studies examining the impact of various types of environmental risk on attachment outcomes. The risk factors represented in these studies included low income, public assistance, maternal youth, single parenthood, low social support, parental mental illness, documented cases of child maltreatment, and inadequate parenting in the form of hostility or emotional unavailability. Frequently, several factors covaried for some, but not all subjects, and the samples were quite heterogeneous. Furthermore, the proportions of secure and insecure infants in these samples were reported in complex ways. There was generally an effort to correlate the relationships of various risk factors to the incidence of secure and insecure attachment. Tables 4.2 through 4.4 present the attachment data for some of the high-risk studies that are discussed. It is interesting to compare the incidence of secure and insecure attachment in high- and low-risk samples. There has not been, as yet, a statement in the risk literature that summarizes, in general terms, the expectable proportions in each category. Samples involving children of bipolar depressives, for example, are not comparable to samples involving children of adolescent mothers receiving Aid to Families with Dependent Children (AFDC); therefore such generalizations are not warranted.

This variation in high-risk samples raises the very real possibility that all low-risk middle-class samples may not be alike either; thus, we need to look more closely at the antecedents to attachment classifications that cut across general labels of high risk and low risk. This is the purpose of this chapter, in which we discuss early maternal and interactional antecedents and the different attachment classifications observed in a sample of high-social-risk 13-month-olds. We expand our discussion of the traditional A-B-C classification system to include the "D" category that is now being observed in several high-risk and some low-risk samples (Crittenden, 1985, this volume; Main & Solomon, in press; Radke-Yarrow, Cummings, Kuczynski, & Chapman, 1985). Before presenting our own data, however, we review various reports on attachment in high-risk samples. First, we review the proportions of A, B, and C infants reported by three sets of high-risk studies. The first set of studies deals with general high-social-risk and attachment; for some studies, the samples were screened for the presence of mental illness or child maltreatment. The second set of studies focuses on child maltreatment and attachment, and the final set focuses on parental mental illness and attachment outcomes. This review makes it clear that the presence of specific risk factors does negatively affect the incidence of secure infant attachment. Then we examine the evidence, within risk populations, for maternal and interactional antecedents of secure and insecure infant attachment. This review reveals that we know much less about why, within a risk populations, some infants are secure, some avoidant, and some resistant. The introduction of the D category, however, may eventually improve our understanding of antecedents by refining our conceptual categories. Finally, we present and discuss our own data about maternal perceptions and interactional behaviors as antecedents of attachment quality in a high-social-risk sample.

ATTACHMENT CLASSIFICATIONS IN HIGH-RISK SAMPLES

The striking conclusion of the following review of the attachment findings for two major high-social-risk studies can be briefly summarized: when known cases of child maltreatment and inadequate care are removed from high-social-risk samples, the proportions of secure and insecure attachment are very similar to those reported for middle-class samples. This is true even when risk factors like poverty and single parenthood are still present. In fact, the samples are still considered high-risk due to these factors.

TABLE 4.2
Attachment Classifications in High-Risk Samples

	n	Age	A	B	C	Unclassified
Vaughn et al. (1979)	100	12 mos	23%	55%	22%	
	100	18 mos	23%	66%	11%	
Egeland & Sroufe (1981a)						
Total sample	213	12 mos	22%	54%	21%	3%
	199	18 mos	21%	59%	15%	5%
"excellent care"	33	12 mos	15%	73%	9%	3%
	33	18 mos	18%	76%	6%	0%
"inadequate care"	31	12 mos	23%	35%	35%	6%
	31	18 mos	29%	48%	10%	13%
Egeland & Farber (1984)	212	12 mos	22%	56%	23%	
	197	18 mos	22%	61%	17%	
Lyons-Ruth et al. (1984) high-risk, maltreatment cases eliminated	15	12 mos	27%	66%	7%	
community group	23	12 mos	30%	70%	0%	

The Minnesota Mother–Infant Interaction Project involved 267 low-income mothers and their first-born infants. All families had incomes below the poverty level, and over half received some kind of public assistance. Several reports were published in the literature describing the attachment classification of different subgroups of these infants at 12 and 18 months. (Egeland & Farber, 1984; Egeland & Sroufe, 1981a; Vaughn, Egeland, Sroufe, & Waters, 1979) These findings are depicted in Table 4.2. At 12 months, the proportion of A classifications for the sample as a whole was between 22% and 23%, B classifications comprised 54% to 55% of the sample, and the C proportions ranged from 21% to 23%. At 18 months, the proportions of A classifications ranged from 21% to 23%, B classifications ranged from 59% to 66%, and C classifications consisted of 11% to 15% of the sample.

Vaughn et al. (1979) reported on only the first 100 subject recruited into the sample, but the remaining studies discussed the final sample after attrition. The slight discrepancy between these two in terms of numbers of subjects and attachment category proportions, exists because Egeland and Farber did not mention the "unclassified" subjects reported by Egeland and Sroufe (1981a). It is not clear whether Egeland and Farber "forced" these subjects into a classification or eliminated them from the analyses.

Egeland and Sroufe (1981a) divided the Minnesota sample into groups on the basis of quality of care observed in the home on several occasions in the first year of life. They identified an "excellent care" group ($n = 33$) and an "inadequate care" group ($n = 31$). At both 12 and 18 months, the excellent care group had very high proportions of B classifications: 75% and 76%, respectively. Such figures would clearly represent the very high end of the continuum of secure classification proportions for low-risk studies. At 12 months, the inadequate care group had only 38% secure infants. Even this low proportion seems high, considering that this group was selected on the basis of the presence of abuse, neglect, and extreme emotional unavailability. It is even more surprising that, by 18 months, 56% of this same group was classified as secure. Although the differences between the excellent and inadequate groups were significant, one wonders how the proportions of A-B-C classifications in the inadequate group at 18 months could be so similar to the low-risk samples reported by Ainsworth, Blehar, Waters, and Wall (1978) and Main and Weston (1981; see Table 4.1). We return to this important classification issue later in the chapter.

The second high-risk sample we consider was studied by Lyons-Ruth, Connell, Grunebaum, Botein, and Zoll (1984) as part of their Family Support Project at Cambridge Hospital in Massachusetts. This preliminary report discussed the attachment classifications of 23 infants from high-risk families and 23 controls matched on the basis of family income, mother's education, mother's ethnicity, and child's age, sex, and ordinal position. Mother's marital status was apparently not a matching variable. The high-risk families were characterized by 80% receiving AFDC, 50% being single parents, and 20% having experienced psychiatric hospitalization. Eight of the 23 high-risk mothers, and none of the low-risk controls, also had protective service involvement. For the high-risk sample, *with known cases of child maltreatment eliminated,* 27% were A, 66% were B, and 7% were C. In the matched controls, 30% were A, 70% were B, and none was C. Once again, these figures are comparable or superior to those reported for low-risk samples in Table 4.1.

MALTREATMENT AND ATTACHMENT CLASSIFICATION

In the previous section, attachment classifications in high-social-risk samples with known cases of maltreatment, both included and eliminated, were present. The present section examines the impact of maltreatment on attachment classifications in detail. More data comparing maltreatment dyads with matched, high-social-risk controls are presented, making it quite clear that lower socioeconomic status (SES), per se, is not related to a greater incidence of insecure attachment than is found in low-risk, middle-class samples. Table 4.3 presents the four maltreatment samples that are discussed later. Note that three of these four studies (Crittenden, 1985; Egeland & Sroufe, 1981b; Lyons-Ruth et al., 1985) found it necessary to identify additional patterns of insecurity, and labelled them "D," "A/C," and "unstable avoidance". These new patterns are clearly associated with maltreatment, but no consistent relationships yet emerge between the form of maltreatment and the type of newly identified insecure pattern.

Egeland and Sroufe (1981a, 1981b) reported on the relationship between child maltreatment and attachment in the Minnesota project. Recall that Egeland and Sroufe (1981a) found that only 38% of the infants of the 31 most abusive and neglectful mothers were securely attached at 12 months. In a separate report, Egeland and Sroufe (1981b) attempted to separate the effects on infant attachment of different kinds of child maltreatment. This is an extremely difficult task because multiple forms of abuse often occur in the same families. In addition, some types of abuse or combinations of abuse are rare, thus making it difficult to constitute groups of sufficient size to make meaningful comparisons. Nonetheless, Egeland and Sroufe did succeed in distinguishing six abuse types among their maltreating mothers: (a) hostility/verbal abuse; (b) psychological unavailability; and (c) neglect—each of these three with and without physical abuse. Attachment classification data for some of these maltreatment groups are presented in Table 4.3. Not all frequencies were

TABLE 4.3
Maltreatment and Attachment Classification

	n	Age	A	B	C	D or "unclassifiable"
Egeland & Sroufe (1981b)						
Psychologically unavailable,	7	12 mos	43%	57%	0%	*
no abuse		18 mos	86%	0%	0%	14%
Neglect only, no abuse	11	12 mos	*	29%	57%	*
		18 mos	50%	*	0%	*
Hostility only, no	4	12 mos	same as controls			
abuse		18 mos	*	*	*	75%
Hostility plus physical	15	12 mos	same as controls			
abuse		18 mos	15%	46%	31%	8%
Physical abuse plus other	24	12 mos	55%	27%	18%	*
forms of maltreatment		18 mos	48%	33%	19%	*
Controls	85	12 mos	18%	67%	15%	*
		18 mos	16%	71%	13%	*
Crittenden (1985)						
adequately reared	9	11-24 mos	11%	89%	0%	0%
abused	10	11-24 mos	10%	0%	20%	70%
neglected	11	11-24 mos	55%	0%	27%	18%
marginally maltreated	16	11-24 mos	31%	50%	19%	0%
Schneider-Rosen et al. (1985)						
maltreated	17	12 mos	29%	29%	41%	
	26	18 mos	46%	23%	31%	
	28	24 mos	46%	32%	21%	
high-risk comparison group	18	12 mos	11%	67%	22%	
	27	18 mos	7%	67%	26%	
	32	24 mos	9%	66%	25%	
Lyons-Ruth et al. (1984)						
maltreated	11	12 mos	46%	36%	18%	
other high-risk,						
not maltreated	15	12 mos	27%	66%	7%	
community group	23	12 mos	30%	70%	0%	
Lyons-Ruth et al. (1985)						
maltreated	10	12 mos	50%	10%	10%	30%
other high-risk,						
not maltreated	18	12 mos	28%	56%	6%	11%
community group	28	12 mos	39%	61%	0%	0%

presented by Egeland and Sroufe; thus some of the data cannot be included in the table. The maltreatment cases were compared with 85 cases from the same sample in which no abuse was suspected. About 37% of the sample was considered "questionable" in regards to possible abuse in the family; these subjects were eliminated from the comparison group.

At 18 months, the researchers found that they needed a fourth category in addition to the Ainsworth A-B-C system. They called this category "D," which was "considered anxiously attached but neither avoidant nor resistant (for example, apathetic or disorganized)" (1981b, p. 84). About 8% of the maltreated sample were classified as D in the Strange Situation. At 12 months, the children of the verbally hostile mothers, with or without physical abuse, were similar to the controls; about two-thirds were securely attached. By 18 months, 3 of the 4 infants of the hostile, nonphysically abusing mothers were in the D category, whereas 46% of the infants of the hostile and physically abusing mothers were still secure. The remaining infants were insecure, mostly resistant (31%). At 12 months, the infants of the psychologically unavailable, nonphysically abusive mothers were 57% secure and 43% avoidant. However, by 18 months, every infant was insecure: 86% were avoidant and 14% were D. At 12 months, the neglect-without-physical-abuse-group was about one-third secure; the rest were resistant. By 18 months, half of these infants were avoidant. When all of the physical abuse infants were considered as a group ($n = 24$), 55% were A, 27% were B, and 18% were C at 12 months. Essentially the same proportions were reported at 18 months.

To summarize, the D category in this study was associated with maternal verbal hostility or emotional unavailability, although most infants in the latter group were avoidant. The insecure pattern associated with neglect was avoidance, also. In general, the maltreated infants became more avoidant over time.

Crittenden (1985) examined fewer subgroups of maltreatment, as compared to Egeland and Sroufe (1981b). She assessed security of attachment for 10 adequately reared infants, 10 abused infants, 11 neglected infants, and 16 marginally maltreated infants. All families were participating in an infant stimulation program because of demographic risk (adolescent mother, limited education, low income, etc.). In addition, the abusing mothers were receiving mandatory protective services from the welfare department, and the problematic mothers were receiving voluntary services. The infants were between 11 and 24 months at the time of the assessment. Crittenden defined a resistant-avoidant (A/C) classification of Strange Situation behavior after carefully studying some discrepant classifications that "were cases of severely maltreated infants being classified as securely attached." These infants "did show the high levels of proximity-seeking and contact maintaining, which typify the secure patterns" (p. 88). But they also displayed moderate-to-high avoidance and moderate-to-high resistance. The resistance was "persistent crankiness and/or non-contextual aggression;" some infants also showed "some stereotypic or maladaptive behavior such as head cocking or huddling on the floor" (p. 89).

Seventy percent of the abused infants were classified in the new A/C category; the forced classification of most of these would have been secure. Crittenden confirmed the finding, reported by Egeland and Sroufe (1981b), that neglect was associated with avoidance, but her finding that abuse was related to a new category of insecure attachment was contrary to Egeland and Sroufe, who found that the D category was *not* related to physical abuse. Clearly, more data are needed on the relationships between types of maltreatment and types of insecure behavior in the Strange Situation (see Crittenden, this volume).

Descriptions from the Family Support Project discussed earlier (Lyons-Ruth et al., 1984) provide further evidence that maltreated infants show unusual patterns of behavior in the Strange Situation. Lyons-Ruth, Connell, Zoll, and Stahl (1985) observed a pattern of Strange Situation reunion behavior that they termed *unstable avoidance.* The pattern consisted of extreme avoidance during the first reunion, and little or no avoidance upon the second reunion. These infants would have to be classified as *secure* in the traditional Ainsworth classification scheme. However, 30% of the maltreated infants, and none of the controls, showed this pattern of behavior. Lyons-Ruth et al. argued that the maltreated infants are not organized enough to maintain a stable avoidant pattern by 12 months. The authors also pointed out that they did not code for the more subtle kinds of resistance reported by Crittenden (1985) in describing her A/C group. If recoded to include subtle resistance and other more subtle signs of disorganization, the unstable-avoidance pattern may be discovered to be yet another variant of the D or A/C Strange Situation behavior patterns.

The Harvard Child Maltreatment Project (Schneider-Rosen, Brunwald, Carlson, & Cicchetti, 1985) involved comparisons of the attachment classifications of maltreated infants at 12 ($n = 17$), 18 ($n = 26$), and 24 months ($n = 28$) with similar-sized groups of nonmaltreated infants from the same communities. All infants were lower SES. All but one maltreatment family and all comparison families were receiving welfare support in the form of AFDC. No significant differences in the number of adults in the home, maternal education, or household-prestige ratings were found between the two groups. Schneider-Rosen et al. compared the proportions of avoidant, secure, and resistant infants in the maltreatment and comparison groups, with the following expected proportions: avoidant, 20%; secure, 70%; and resistant, 10%. At every age, as Table 4.3 shows, the maltreated infants showed significantly fewer secure infants. About two thirds of the comparison infants were secure at each age, which was not significantly different from the expected values. At 18 and 24 months, however, this group had more resistant and fewer avoidant infants than expected. This intriguing finding warrants further research. In general, it would be most interesting to apply a D classification system to these samples.

It is clear from the review of studies examining the effects of maltreatment on attachment status that lower socioeconomic status, per se, is not related to a greater incidence of insecure attachment than is found in low-risk, middle-class samples. However, neglect and abuse do severely affect attachment security. Some studies of this maltreated population have found it necessary to identify additional patterns of insecurity (Crittenden, 1985; Egeland & Sroufe, 1981b; Lyons-Ruth et al., 1985). Because it seems unlikely, from the point of view of attachment theory, that maltreated infants would be securely attached, the identification of patterns of insecure attachment that are related to this risk status is very important (see Crittenden, this volume).

CAREGIVER PSYCHOPATHOLOGY AND ATTACHMENT CLASSIFICATION

This final section in a series devoted to the relationships between specific risk factors and attachment outcomes discusses three studies that focus on the risk factor of parental mental illness. The data from these studies are summarized in Table 4.4. It is clear that the results from two of the studies (Gaensbauer, Harmon, Cytryn, & McKnew, 1984; Radke-Yarrow et al., 1985) support the conclusion that parental mental illness has a negative impact on infant attachment. Methodological problems related to the Strange Situation in the third study (Sameroff, Seifer, & Zax, 1982) make its finding of no relationship between maternal mental illness and attachment less compelling.

Sameroff et al. (1982), in the Rochester Longitudinal Study, compared attachment outcomes for groups of infants whose mothers varied according to the following: diagnosis (no mental illness, schizophrenia, neurotic depression, and personality disorder), severity of illness (non, low, medium, and high), chronicity of illness (none, low, medium, and high), and socioeconomic and racial status (high SES and white, low SES and white, low SES and black). They found no differences in attachment security according to severity, chronicity, or diagnosis of mental illness. The following proportions were reported: 10% avoidant, 10% borderline avoidant, 51% secure, 15% borderline insure, 14% insecure. These

TABLE 4.4
Caregiver Psychopathology and Attachment Classifications

Sameroff et al. (1982)		$n = 232$ age = 12 mos				
avoidant		10%				
borderline avoidant		10%				
secure		51%				
borderline secure		15%				
insecure		14%				

	n	Age	A	B	C	AC
Gaensbauer et al. (1984)						
manic depressive						
parent	7	12 mos	29%	71%	0%	
	7	15 mos	57%	43%	0%	
	7	18 mos	86%	14%	0%	
matched control	7	12 mos	29%	71%	0%	
	7	15 mos	0%	86%	14%	
	7	18 mos	29%	57%	14%	
Radke-Yarrow et al. (1985)						
bipolar depression	14	30-47 mos	43%	21%	7%	29%
major unipolar						
depression	41	16-44 mos	27%	53%	2%	17%
minor depression	12	25-34 mos	17%	75%	8%	0%
no depression	31	25-39 mos	29%	71%	0%	0%

categories are different from the Ainsworth categories, and, additionally, the assessment performed by Sameroff et al. was also modified, consisting of one separation in which the child was left alone, and one reunion. SES differences in attachment security were not reported, although SES was strongly related to developmental status, mother–child interaction, and adaptive behavior at all ages. One surprising finding is that depression was the diagnosis related to greatest risk in the children at 30 months, although no depression-related differences in attachment were reported at 12 months. This result is contrary to those reported in the next two studies, which found depression to be significantly related to attachment insecurity.

Bipolar depressive illness in the family does seem to have a negative impact on the quality of the infant's relationship to the mother, whether or not she is the ill family member. Gaensbauer et al. (1984) reported on seven male infants of a manic depressive parent (in four cases the ill parent was the mother, in three cases, the father). These infants were compared with seven match controls in a modified Strange Situation at 12, 15, and 18 months.

As Table 4.4 shows, the two groups did not differ at 12 months, but probands were less likely to be secure at the older ages. The mother participated in all the Strange Situation assessments, and because she was not always the mentally ill parent, it was impossible to determine the direct effects of caregiver illness on the child's attachment to that caregiver in this study.

Radke-Yarrow et al. (1985), in the Child-rearing Study at the National Institute of Mental Health, did find a direct association between maternal depression and attachment to mothers. They studied the attachment relationships of 99 toddlers to their mothers, some of whom were depressed. The mothers had varying diagnoses: bipolar depression (n = 14), major unipolar depression (n = 42), minor depression (n = 12), and no depression (n = 31). The results showed no differences in attachment by child's age, SES, sex, or race. Also, the normal and minor depression groups did not differ from the usual low-risk figures of about 25% to 30% insecure at 12 months. However, 55% of the infants of mothers with major affective disorders were insecure; 79% were insecure if the mother was bipolar. Radke-Yarrow et al. Also reported observing an A/C attachment pattern (10% of the sample). Infants with this pattern "showed moderate-to-high avoidance and moderate-to-high resistance during reunion," and one or more of the following: "affectless or sad with signs of depression," "odd or atypical body posture or movement," and "moderate to high proximity seeking" (p. 887). Mothers of A/C infants had histories indicative of more serious depression. In contrast, the mothers of the secure infants did not differ from the mothers of infants who were simply avoidant or resistant in terms of the severity of their depression.

SUMMARY

Thus far, we have reviewed the Strange Situation behavior observed in low-risk samples and a variety of high-risk samples. It seems that low SES does not in itself constitute a risk factor for attachment. If known cases of abuse or neglect are eliminated from high-social-risk samples, proportions of secure and insecure attachment are comparable, and in some studies, superior to, the proportions reported for low-risk samples. However, the picture is dramatically different in all studies except for that by Sameroff et al. (1982), in which maltreatment or maternal affective illness characterized the high-risk sample. In addition, patterns of Strange Situation behavior, called A/C or D, that are rarely found in low-risk groups were observed in these high-risk samples.

Support for the notion that A/C or D infants are "especially insecure" is found whenever these patterns are reported in the literature on high-risk samples. This raises the questions: Are there A/C or D infants in middle class samples?, and, if so, are *they* "especially insecure"? Main and Weston (1981) reported that about 14% of their largely upper-middle-class sample (*n* = 44) in the Berkeley Social Development Project was "unclassifiable" according to the Ainsworth classification system. In a later paper, Main, Kaplan, and Cassidy (1985) studied the unclassifiable subjects from an aggregation of Berkeley studies (*N* = 189) and reported that 18% (34) could be described as "disorganized-disoriented insecure." The majority of these children classified as D had parents who "had experienced the death of an attachment figure before maturity and seemed not yet to have completed the mourning process" (p. 91). The "forced" or "imposed" classification of 68% of these D infants would have been secure. More research is needed, however, before we can conclude that the D infants of parents who have lack of resolution of mourning are as insecure as the D infants of parents who maltreat them.

The identification of patterns of Strange Situation behavior that lie outside the traditional Ainsworth A-B-C categories occurred after nearly 15 years of research in which the tripartite system dominated the literature. It is probable that forced classifications were made in every attachment study, with particularly negative effects for understanding secure infants. Based on figures reported in three recent studies in which a D category is not used, as many as 68% to 83% of disorganized-disoriented insecure infants in some samples may be given forced secure classifications (Crittenden, 1985; Lyons-Ruth et al., 1985; Main et al., 1985). It is entirely possible that *all* maltreated infants that have been classified as secure based on their Strange Situation behavior are not secure at all, but disorganized-disoriented insecure. It is quite conceivable that lack of access to such a category has obfuscated the results of many published studies that used the Strange Situation.

MATERNAL AND INTERACTIONAL ANTECEDENTS TO ATTACHMENT IN HIGH-RISK POPULATIONS

As the data are presently reported from the major projects reviewed previously, there are few compelling direct maternal personality antecedents to infant attachment classification apart from those implicitly associated with maltreatment or major depressive psychopathology. Descriptions of maternal behavior in mother–infant interaction provide, in general, stronger predictions to attachment security (but see Belsky & Isabella, this volume). There is, however, an important qualification that must be added to the above generalization, and that is that measure of maternal attitudes or personality *do* relate to the quality of parenting behavior as identified by maltreatment and inadequate care (Brunnquell, Crickton, & Egeland, 1981; Lyons-Ruth et al., 1984). We are left, then, with a confusing set of relationships: personality is related to poor parenting as measured by home observations or child protective service status (Brunnquell et al., 1981, Lyons-Ruth et al., 1984), inadequate parent–child interactions are related to insecure attachment (Egeland & Farber, 1984), and maternal personality is not related to attachment (Egeland & Farber, 1984; Lyons-Ruth et al., 1984). Perhaps the links really do exist, but the results from previous research are weakened by the particular choice of personality measures or by error variance introduced by using the A-B-C attachment classification system without a D category. We return to this issue after reviewing the personality evidence as it relates to parenting behavior, parent–infant interaction, and attachment.

Lyons-Ruth et al. (1984) compared problematic mothers with adequate mothers, from the same low-income population. Within the problematic group, some families were under protective service supervision and some were not. In a family history interview, the comparison mothers reported less major psychopathology in their families of origin, greater parental warmth, more supervision and structure, and closer relationships with peers. The problematic mothers were depressed, as measured by the Center for Epidemiologic Studies Depression Scale (Radloff, 1977). Sixty percent of the high-risk group had scores high enough to indicate a need for treatment, whereas 74% of the control group were not depressed.

Lyons-Ruth et al. (1984) found no relationship, however, between level of maternal depression and attachment classification. In addition, it was surprising that mothers of secure infants, compared to mothers of avoidant infants, reported more family conflict, less pleasure in school, and less regular attendance at school. These data are suggestive of a defensive response to the interview on the part of mothers of avoidant infants; an interpretation consistent with the findings of Main and her colleagues on adults' internal working models of attachment (Main et al., 1985).

Several reports from the Minnesota Mother–Infant Interaction Project illustrate the break in the logical connections between maternal personality, parenting behavior, and attachment. When examined as a group, they seem to suggest an explanation that perhaps the connections are only observable when extreme groups (such as excellent care and inadequate care) are examined.

Egeland and Farber (1984) reported on a battery of personality assessments administered to subjects in the Minnesota project prenatally and when the infants were 3 months old. Although the personality measures did not distinguish between the A-B-C groups, they were related to whether infants were secure at both 12 or 18 months or changed from secure to avoidant or resistant. Mothers of infants who changed classification (from secure to insecure) had higher scores on aggression and suspicion, and lower scores on social desirability (for related data, see Belsky and Isabella, this volume).

In contrast to the few significant findings relating maternal personality to infant attachment, observations of feeding and play interaction in the home at 3 and 6 months provided many more robust predictions of attachment at 12 months. At 3 months, C mothers verbalized less frequently than A and B mothers, whereas A mothers were less synchronous than B mothers, and showed less functional handling and were less responsive to crying than B and C mothers. At 6 months, B mothers were rated significantly better than A and C mothers in facility in caretaking, general sensitivity, overall cooperation and overall sensitivity. B infants in play were more satisfied than C infants and more cooperative than A infants.

An earlier report from the Minnesota project did not discuss attachment, but did show that mothers in the inadequate care group differed from the mothers in the excellent care group on four consistent factors obtained from the personality and attitude measures, as well as on five rationally derived constructs (Brunnquell et al., 1981). The four factors were labeled Impulsiveness-Anxiety, Negative Reactions to Pregnancy, Psychological Complexity, and Hostility-Suspiciousness; the constructs were Impulsiveness, General Anxiety, Level of Personal Integration, Maternal Expectations and General Personality. The factors and constructs were more useful predictors of disturbed childrearing than the traditionally conceived personality variables. Brunnquell et al. summarized the characteristics of risk as follows: "A woman who is young, lacking in understanding and awareness of her infant and her relationship to the infant, and who has negative reactions to pregnancy and her infant, should be considered at risk for abuse or neglect. When her anxiety, hostility and suspicion increase following delivery, the risk to the mother–child relationship increases" (p. 690). Applying the attachment data reported in Egeland and Sroufe (1981a), we conclude that such a mother is significantly more likely to have an insecurely attached child.

Thus far, a number of conclusions tentatively can be drawn regarding maternal antecedents of infant Strange Situation behavior in groups considered high-risk because of psychopathology, maltreatment, or problematic caregiving:

1. Structural variables are important. By and large, youth, low social support, and low education are additional risk factors for insecure attachment, mostly because they are associated with inadequate caregiving; SES does not appear to be related to attachment outcome when inadequate caregiving is controlled for.

2. Depression does seem to be related to attachment outcomes, despite the inconsistencies in findings across studies. These inconsistencies may be a result of measurement problems; a paper-and-pencil measure such as that used by Lyons-Ruth et al. (1984) is not as adequate a measure of depression as the interview-based Schedule for Affective Disorders and Schizophrenia (SADS; Spitzer & Endicott, 1977) used by Radke-Yarrow et al. (1985). If the mothers are assessed adequately, the coding of the Strange Situation may be problematic (Sameroff et al., 1982). Finally, depression may have an increasingly greater impact on many aspects of child functioning, including attachment, in the second and third years as its adverse effects accumulate. A number of studies present data that suggest this is the case (Egeland and Sroufe, 1981b; Gaensbauer et al., 1984; Sameroff et al., 1982).

3. The data indicating personality differences between mothers of avoidant versus resistant insecure infants are equivocal. There is a suggestion that A mothers are more defensive in their views of their family histories (Lyons-Ruth et al., 1984), but personality factors are unrelated to a change from secure to avoidant versus to resistant between 12 and 18 months (Egeland & Farber, 1984).

4. Behaviors of high-risk mothers can be identified that are indicative of "sensitivity" (Egeland & Farber, 1984) and "excellent care" (Egeland & Sroufe, 1981a). These behaviors are related to more positive attachment outcomes.

5. The direction of effects is from caregiver to infant. Infants may contribute to better dyadic interactions by being more satisfied and cooperative (Egeland & Farber, 1984). However, it does not seem to be the care that less cooperative infants "cause" dyadic interaction problems (Crittenden, 1985).

6. Finally, it seems that our assessments of attachment in high-risk samples, using the traditional classification systems in Ainsworth's Strange Situation, may not have captured some significant patterns of behavior. In fact, it is likely that many secure infants have been misclassified. We can only guess at the impact such misclassification has had on our understanding of the antecedents of attachment in high-risk samples. At the very least, it could well obscure differences associated with secure and insecure attachment, primarily as a result of combining the most secure and least secure subjects into the same category (consisting of "true" B's and "forced" B's). More research is needed to clarify the antecedents of the D category, and to distinguish the D category from the B category, especially in high-risk samples (see Crittenden, this volume).

In the next section, we present data from an ongoing intervention project with high-social-risk mothers and infants called, Clinical Nursing Models for Infants and Their Families. The data address a number of the issues highlighted by the preceding review.

OVERVIEW

Clinical Nursing Models for Infants and Their Families is a research project designed to determine whether fostering the social competency of pregnant women with low levels of social support increases their social competency and improves their parenting behaviors and, subsequently, the physical, mental, and social well-being of their infants. A mental health model designed to deal directly with interpersonal skills and social support, as well as information about pregnancy and parenting, is compared with a more typical public health model that provides information about pregnancy and parenting an infant.

Measures of maternal perceptions and competence are collected from pregnancy through the child's first 3 years; examples of maternal measures include: social skills, perception of life change, depression, physical and mental health, and parenting skills. Likewise, measures of child competence are gathered including mental and motor development, mastery motivation, attachment, affect, and behavioral style. Finally, dyadic competence is assessed through multiple measurements of observed parent–child interaction from 6 weeks through 3 years.

In this report we focus on the relationship between infant attachment at 13 months, and maternal perception and dyadic competence measures obtained during the prenatal period and when the infants were 6 weeks and 3 months old.

METHOD

Subjects

The subjects of the present report are 60 mother–infant pairs (of a total of 85) that were assessed in the Ainsworth Strange Situation when infants were 13 months old. Twenty-five mother–infant pairs are not included in the present analyses because we lacked confidence in their attachment classification, or because they were considered "borderline" between two or more categories. The method for eliminating these subjects is described in detail.

Assuring the Reliability of the Attachment Categories.   The Strange Situation was carried out as described by Ainsworth et al. (1978) except for two changes: our Strange Situation followed other assessments, such as infant free play and a mastery motivation assessment; and the stranger reunion before the mother's second return was omitted. We did this to save time, and because we noted that the additional stress to the infant was not necessary to code the second reunion episode. The Strange Situations were videotaped and all tapes were coded by three observers in accordance with conventions detailed in Ainsworth et al., with the addition of a D category, which was coded according to Main and Solomon (in press). D infants showed a variety of behaviors that disqualified them from an A-B-C classification, including disordered temporal sequences of behavior, out of context behavior, dazed affect, stereotypes, and moderate-to-high levels of avoidance and resistance in the same reunion episode (which we called "A/C"). When possible, the coders indicated that the forced classifications would have been. The percent agreement among each of the three coder pairs was between 78% and 79%. Disagreements were resolved by consensus among the three coders. In addition, consultation was generously provided by Mary Main for the identification of infants in the D category. Eighteen tapes, some of which were suspected of being D., were coded by both Mary Main and the University of Washington (U.W.) coders. The percent agreement between Main's judgments and the U.W. consensus classification was 89%. These reliability tapes included 1 A, 5 B's, and 12 D's.

The next steps in assuring that the attachment categories were reliable were aimed at maximizing the behavioral distinctions between the major categories. Two scales, a confidence rating and a security rating, were developed for this purpose. It has been our experience, and the experience of other investigators, that the boundaries between Strange Situation classifications are not precise. Gardner and Thompson (1983) explored the quantitative consistency of the Ainsworth system. They found that, to a certain extent, cluster analysis did not reproduce the traditional A-B-C groupings. Boundaries between A and B and between B and C were not entirely distinct. The B subgroups were quite heterogeneous, so much so, in fact, that differences within the B group often exceeded those between A and B. To some extent, then, the A-B-C trichotomy may be artificial.

Like others, we found that some Strange Situations were very difficult to code, a finding that is all too infrequently discussed in the literature. Even after consensus among coders was reached, doubts remained that the classification of some infants represented an accurate characterization of the quality of attachment security. In order to eliminate these subjects from the data analyses, we developed a 5-point "confidence rating" scale. The highest point on the scale, 5, indicated very high confidence in the classification because the child's behavior was accurately captured by the criteria for a particular category and no behaviors occurred that would disqualify the child from a particular classification. A 3 rating indicated medium confidence; most behaviors met the criteria for a particular category, but some behaviors did occur that suggested another category—for instance, a secure baby who showed some avoidance. Finally, a 1 rating indicated no confidence in the classification. Nine subjects who had a confidence rating of 2 or 1 were eliminated.

We also developed a 9-point security rating scale. This scale reflected the extent to which the child showed secure types of behaviors, such as contact seeking, contact maintaining, and distal interaction, as compared to insecure behaviors such as avoidance, resistance, and disorganization. The security rating scale was especially useful for describing the infants classified as secure because it was apparent from the variability on the Ainsworth rating scales for avoidance, resistance, contact seeking, and contact maintaining that the secure infants constituted a very heterogeneous group. Infants coded as B could receive ratings from 5 to 9 on the security scale. A 9 on this scale indicated "very secure." This rating did not necessarily correspond to the B3 "most secure" category described by Ainsworth et al. (1978). Rather, it described those infants who displayed little or not resistance or avoidance on either reunion, regardless of whether or not they also actively sought contact. Infants could be considered very secure if they only interacted with their mothers across a distance. A rating of 8 consisted of secure behavior with transitory avoidance or resistance, mostly in the first reunion. Infants in the B4 category were coded as 5 or 6, depending on the extent to which resistance was present. For the purposes of this analysis, we chose to include only those secure infants rated 8 or 9—that is, those infants considered to be more secure or highly secure, relative to the rest of the sample. This decision eliminated 16 of the 37 B infants remaining after the confidence rating restrictions were applied to the sample.

The final sample for analysis consisted of 60 infants. Thirteen were A (A1 = 5, A2 = 8), 21 were B (B1 = 1, B2 = 15, B3 = 5), 9 were C (C1 = 8, C2 = 1), and 17 were D. The distribution of the included and eliminated subjects is depicted in Figure 4.1. The eliminated subjects are represented by the darkened areas. The top half of the pie includes all of the B infants, with 17% eliminated because of high avoidance, and 8% eliminated because of high resistance. The eliminated B subjects consisted of 1 B1, 12 B2's and 7 B4's. The confidence rating procedure resulted in the elimination of 1 A2, 1 C2 and 3 D's. Note that about 65% of the D category consists of A/C infants. These infants showed moderate-to-high levels of avoidance and resistance. Of the remaining infants in the D category, 5 would have received a forced classification of A (D[A]), and one, a forced classification of B (D[B]).

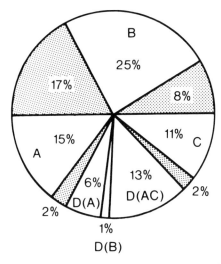

FIG. 4.1.   Proportions of subjects in each attachment category. (Excluded borderline classifications represented by darkened areas.)

The procedures previously outlined in detail eliminated "boundary" B's, that is, those B's with substantial avoidance or resistance ratings in one or both reunion episodes. The B infants that remained were *the most secure* infants in our sample. Whether they were as secure as the most secure (B3) infants in other samples is an interesting question. We also included only good exemplars of categories A, C, and D. Nevertheless, our D group was the most heterogeneous of the categories, but the subjects in this group all showed the pervasive disorganized or disoriented behavior outlined by Main and Solomon (in press). This disorganized behavior took many different forms, and we possessed no rationale for making each form a distinct category. Our first question was simply whether the D group in this particular high-social-risk population reflected especially high-risk caregiving environments, as has been reported by other studies of high-risk populations (Crittenden, 1985; Radke-Yarrow et al. 1985).

Measures

The maternal measures used in this study were selected to tap different domains of maternal perceptions regarding herself, her infant, significant others, and stressful life events. In addition, we assessed the mother's social skills in interacting with an unfamiliar adult, and her interactive competence with her infant. The assessment instruments were used at intake (when the subjects were 22 weeks pregnant or less) and 6 weeks or 3 months after the birth of the infant. The outcome variable, attachment quality, was assessed using the Strange Situation at 13 months. Table 4.5 lists the measures and their assessment points.

Maternal Perceptions Related to the Self. The Beck Depression Inventory (BDI; Beck, 1970) is a 21-item scale that assesses the severity of depression. Each item is designed to represent an overt behavioral symptom of depression. The choices within each item are intended to gauge degrees of severity of each symptom. The total score, therefore, reflects both the number and severity of symptoms. The range of possible scores extends from 0 to 63, with scores of 0 to 9 categorized by Beck as not depressed, 10 to 15 as mildly depressed, 16 to 23 as moderately depressed, and 24 to 63 as severely depressed. The Beck Depression Inventory was designed for use in psychiatric populations. However, it has been validated on nonpsychiatric populations as well (Bumberry, Oliver, &

TABLE 4.5
Assessment Instruments Clinical Nursing Models Project

Instrument		*Time*		
	Intake	*6w*	*3m*	*13m*
Beck Depression Inventory (BDI) (Beck, 1970)	x	x		
Life Experiences Survey (LES) (Sarason et al., 1978)	x		x	
Personal Resources Questionnaire (PRQ) (Brandt & Weinert, 1981)	x		x	
Social Support and Partner Involvement (SSPI)	x		x	
Symptoms	x			
Adult Conversational Skills (ACS) Scale	x		x	
Difficult Life Circumstances (DLC)	x			
Infant Temperament Questionnaire (Carey & McDevitt, 1978)			x	
Postpartum Self-Evaluation Questionnaire (Lederman et al., 1981)		x		
Nursing Child Assessment Feeding Scale (NCAFS) (Barnard et al., in press)		x		
Nursing Child Assessment Teaching Scale (NCATS) (Barnard et al., in press)			x	
Strange Situation				x

McClure, 1978). In this sample, the BDI had an internal consistency (Cronbach's alpha) of .84 at intake and .77 at 6 weeks.

The "symptoms" measure is a list of 36 physical symptoms that can occur during pregnancy. Some examples are nausea, leg cramps, frightening dreams, and hives/skin rash. Subjects indicate whether each symptom has never occurred (0 points), has occurred once or twice (1 point), or has occurred more often (2 points). Scores could range from 0 to 72. The symptoms scale had an internal consistency of .82.

The Postpartum Self-Evaluation Questionnaire (Lederman, Weingarten, & Lederman, 1981) is a Likert-type scale that measures the mother's perceptions at 6 weeks postpartum in the following areas (alpha's in parentheses): negative quality of relationship with partner (.94), partner's lack of participation in childcare (.92), lack of gratification from the labor and delivery experience (.78), dissatisfaction with life situation and circumstances (.58), lack of confidence in ability to cope with the tasks of motherhood (.78), dissatisfaction with motherhood and infant care (.82), and lack of support for the maternal role from friends and family (.88). Total scores (.92) could range from 82 to 328, with the higher scores indicating more negative perceptions. The mean total score for about 50 middle-class, childbirth-class-prepared women at 6 weeks postpartum was 110.5 (Lederman et al., 1981). In the present sample, if a woman did not have a partner, she did not receive a score for partner-related scales. However, in calculating a total score, the women without partners received scores that were appropriately augmented by their own average score.

Maternal Perceptions Related to Others. The Personal Resources Questionnaire (PRQ; Brandt, & Weinert, 1981) is a 25-item Likert-type scale designed to assess social support. It is based upon Weiss' (1974) conceptualization of the functions of social relationships and is thus designed to evaluate sharing of concerns, intimacy, opportunity for nurturance, reassurance of worth, and assistance/guidance. The PRQ had an internal consistency of .85 at intake and .90 at 3 months.

Social Support and Partner Involvement (SSPI) was a score calculated from the mothers' responses to eight questions posed by an interviewer. The questions probed the mothers' positive and negative feelings about pregnancy and childcare relative to whether they felt they were getting enough emotional support and physical help. A mothers could score higher if the person who gave the most emotional support and physical help was her partner. If a partner was not present, or not involved as much as the mother wished, she would receive a lower score. The questions were slightly different at intake and 3 months in order to reflect the different support needs for pregnancy as compared with motherhood. The scores at intake could range from 0 to 8, and at 3 months, from 0 to 9. SSPI had an internal consistency of .63 at intake and .83 at 3 months.

Maternal Perceptions of Stressful Events. The Difficult Life Circumstances Scale (28 items) assesses the presence of long-term family stressors rather than the changes in life events measured by the Life Experiences Survey. Examples of the former stressors include: having problems with a credit rating, having an abusive partner, having a household member with a long-term illness, and having trouble finding a suitable place to live.

The Life Experiences Survey (LES; Sarason, Johnson, & Siegel, 1978) is a 61-item instrument that assesses changes in life events. The subject is asked to rate each event as good or bad, and then to indicate the impact of the event on her life—no effect, some effect, moderate effect, or great effect. The LES yields a positive change score, a negative change score, and a total change score.

Maternal Perceptions of Her Infant. Mothers filled out the Infant Temperament Questionnaire (ITQ; Carey & McDevitt, 1978) when their infants were 3 months old. The ITQ has only been validated for infants 4 to 8 months old, but we chose to use it with these subjects when their infants were younger because it was the only opportunity we would have to obtain this information during the infant's first year of life. Support for the validity of this time of measurement is provided by Vaughn, Taraldson, Crichton, and Egeland (1981). Vaughn et al. administered the first version of the ITQ (Carey, 1970) to the high-social-risk sample in the Minnesota Mother–Infant Interaction Project when those infants were 3 and 6 months old. Although Vaughn et al. reported only the 6-month findings, they did say that there were no substantive differences between the 3 and 6 month assessments.

Vaughn et al. also administered the revised ITQ, which was the version used in the present study, to a pilot sample of 25 women. The authors concluded that it was too long and complicated for undereducated subjects. The mothers in our sample also had trouble completing the ITQ. However, an evaluator was available to answer mothers' questions and assist them in completing the questionnaire; as a result, these data are of high quality.

The ITQ divides temperament into nine categories: rhythmicity, approach, adaptability, intensity, mood, persistence, distractibility, and threshold. On the basis of parental responses to 95 items, 203 middle to upper middle-class infants in the Carey and McDevitt (1978) validation sample were assigned to the following clinical diagnostic groups: difficult (9.4%), slow to warm-up (5.9%), intermediate-high (difficult) (11.3%), intermediate-low (easy) (31%), and easy (42.4%). These categories were used for the present study.

Maternal Social Skills and Dyadic Competence. The Adult Conversational Skills (ACS) scale consists of 63 binary items that pertain to the following areas of adult interactive skills: greeting, nonverbal signals, speech, affect, communication, and conversation. This scale was completed by an evaluator who met with each woman in her home or in a setting of the woman's choice (e.g., clinic, coffee shop). The ACS scale had an internal consistency of .79 at intake and .83 at 3 months.

The two measures of dyadic competence used in this study were the Nursing Child Assessment Feeding (NCAFS) and Teaching (NCATS) Scales (Barnard, Hammond, Booth, Bee, Mitchell, & Spieker, in press). The scales describe with some specificity the repertoire of behaviors brought to the interaction by both members of the dyad and the contingency of their response to one another. The feeding and teaching scales comprise a set of binary items (76 for NCAFS, 73 for NCATS) that are organized into six conceptually derived subscales, four of which describe the caregiver's behavior, and two of which describe the child's behavior: parent's sensitivity to cues, parent's response to the child's distress, social-emotional growth fostering, cognitive growth fostering, child's clarity of cues, and child's responsiveness to parent. The teaching tasks that are observed are primarily derived from the motor performance items on the Bayley Scales of Infant Development. The specific tasks are designed to be slightly developmentally advanced for the child, in order to put more stress on the parent–child system. In a normative sample of 767 mothers and infants, both scales detected significant differences among mothers of differing educational backgrounds. For example, the mean score on the NCATS for mothers with less than a high school education was 36.3 (SD = 7.5); for high school graduates, 39.1 (SD = 6.4), for mothers with some college, 41.9 (SD = 4.9), and for college graduates, 42.7 (SD = 4.4).

In addition to analyzing the Mother's Total Score, the Infant's Total Score, and the combined Total Score, the NCATS was analyzed in two other ways. First, 24 items on the scale directly assessed parent or child contingent responses (e.g., "the child smiles at parent within 5 seconds after the parent's verbalization" and "the parent smiles or touches the child within 5 seconds after the child smiles or vocalizes"). The contingency scores for mother and child were analyzed separately. Second, empirically-derived variables based on the factor analysis of 404 mother–child dyads less than 1 year of age were scored and analyzed for the present sample. The eight factors were: positive parent–child mutuality, positive feedback from parent, avoidance of punishment, negative child cues, mutual eye contact, positive parental response to distress, avoidance of criticism, and cognitive growth fostering.

The 6-week NCAFS was administered in the home by a trained nurse who was also the project intervener for that family. Because of the potential for bias inherent in this procedure, we feel that the 3-month NCATS is probably more valid. The NCATS was administered by an evaluator who was blind to the subject's group membership.

RESULTS

The results are reported first in terms of the maternal measures, as obtained at the prenatal intake assessment, and at 6 weeks and 3 months infant age. The dyadic NCAFS and NCATS are also presented. In order to compare the maternal antecedents to infant A, B, C, or D behavior in the Strange Situation, the scores of mothers of infants in each category were subjected to one-way analysis of variance. Post hoc comparisons between groups were made using Duncan's Multiple Range Test.

Based on a power analysis (Cohen, 1977), an a priori significant criterion of alpha = .10 was selected to be used in comparing the four attachment groups. This procedure increases the power from .71 for an alpha of .05, to .82 for an alpha of .10, thereby decreasing the risk of failing to reject a false null hypothesis.

Prenatal Measures

Table 4.6 shows the means, standard deviations, and statistical test results for the prenatal maternal measures. No significant group differences were found for Difficult Life Circumstances, Symptoms, Personal Resources, Adult Conversational Skills, or Life Experiences. Mothers of A infants reported significantly more social support than mothers of D infants on the Social Support and Partner Involvement measure, and significantly less depression on the Beck Depression Inventory, than mothers of both D and B infants.

Six Weeks Postpartum

Table 4.7 lists the results for the two 6-week maternal measures; the Postpartum Self-Evaluation Questionnaire and the Beck Depression Inventory (BDI). Mothers of securely attached infants reported significantly less depression on the BDI, and significantly more confidence in coping with motherhood tasks (on the postpartum self-evaluation measure) than

TABLE 4.6
Means (Standard Deviations) for Maternal Intake Measures and
Analysis Results Comparing Attachment Groups

Measures	A	B	C	D	F	p	Contrast
Beck Depression Inventory	6.5 (6.8)	12.9 (7.5)	11.4 (6.3)	13.2 (7.1)	2.83	.05	A < B, D
Difficult Life Circumstances	5.6 (2.7)	5.2 (3.4)	5.8 (3.3)	5.8 (3.3)	.15	.93	
Symptoms	22.3 (7.4)	27.1 (6.7)	24.9 (9.0)	25.9(10.1)	.94	.43	
Personal Resources Questionnaire	138.0(16.2)	132.7(21.4)	122.0(20.5)	126.7(18.2)	1.4	.25	
Adult Conversational Skills Scale	51.6 (4.5)	49.7 (5.7)	49.5 (3.6)	51.0 (5.4)	.52	.67	
Social Support and Partner Involvement	5.6 (1.0)	4.7 (1.9)	4.9 (2.1)	3.6 (1.4)	3.85	.01	D < A
Life Experiences Survey (LES) Total	21.5(10.4)	30.9(16.2)	28.1(20.6)	21.2(11.4)	1.75	.17	
LES Positive	9.8 (5.0)	16.0(10.4)	16.0(13.6)	10.9 (7.7)	1.6	.19	
LES Negative	12.2(11.7)	11.0 (9.8)	12.8 (6.2)	12.7 (8.9)	.13	.94	

119

TABLE 4.7
Means (Standard Deviations) for 6-Week Maternal Measures and
Analysis Results for Comparing Attachment Groups

Measures	A	B	C	D	F	p	Contrast
Postpartum self-evaluation questionnaire total	154.2(21.1)	137.5(23.7)	158.6(35.3)	141.4(26.7)	1.94	.13	
Negative quality of relationship with partner	25.3 (10.4)	22.2(10.0)	30.8(15.3)	22.1 (8.3)	.91	.44	
Dissatisfaction with partner's participation in childcare	24.16 (9.1)	17.2 (8.1)	20.3 (6.7)	15.9 (3.0)	2.81	.05	D, B < A
Lack of gratification from birth experience	16.0 (3.5)	16.3 (6.9)	17.6 (4.9)	17.0 (5.7)	.17	.91	
Dissatisfaction with life situation & circumstances	27.3 (4.1)	24.8 (5.0)	21.6 (5.3)	24.5 (4.7)	2.40	.08	C < A
Lack of confidence coping with motherhood tasks	22.6 (5.5)	21.4 (3.9)	26.0 (3.5)	24.1 (5.2)	2.28	.09	B < C
Dissatisfaction with motherhood & infant care	17.9 (5.1)	17.4 (3.6)	20.4 (3.4)	18.3 (4.5)	.95	.42	
Lack of support for maternal role	20.9 (7.5)	16.9 (6.4)	17.4 (5.3)	18.0 (6.8)	1.04	.38	
Beck Depression Inventory (BDI)	9.0 (5.3)	6.4 (4.0)	12.3 (6.6)	10.1 (5.4)	3.04	.04	B < C

did the mothers of C infants. Of the remaining self-evaluation scores, the mothers of A infants were significantly different than the other groups on two subscales. Mothers of future avoidant infants reported, specifically, more dissatisfaction with their partner's participation in childcare, as compared to both B and D mothers, and they reported more dissatisfaction with their life situation and circumstances than C mothers.

Three-Month Measures

Table 4.8 presents the results from the 3-month analyses. At this age, there were no differences among the groups on Personal Resources and Life Experiences. However, mothers of D infants had significantly lower scores on Social Support and Partner Involvement, and were observed to have fewer adult conversational skills than mothers of B infants. The mothers' perceptions of their infants' temperament revealed patterns that varied by attachment group [x^2 (12, $N,$ = 57) = 20.9, p = .05] (see Table 4.9). More mothers in this sample perceived their infants as slow to warm-up (19.3%) and fewer mothers perceived their infants as easy (21.1%), as compared to the validation sample reported by Carey and McDevitt (1978), in which 5.9% of the infants were perceived as slow to warm-up and 42.4% were perceived as easy. In general, the C mothers had the most positive perceptions of their infants; none of them felt their infants to be difficult or slow to warm-up. About one third of the B mothers and one third of the C mothers thought that their infants were easy. None of the A mothers perceived their infants as easy, but 5 of the 12 did fall into the intermediate-low category. Finally, 13 of the 16 D infants were perceived to be difficult, slow to warm-up, or intermediate high.

Dyadic Competence.   Table 4.10 lists the results for the NCAFS at 6 weeks and the NCATS at 3 months. The contingency scores and factor scores for the NCATS are also included. There were no attachment-group differences on the NCAFS. However, there were consistent group differences on the NCATS. In general, B dyads scored significantly higher than A and D dyads. Both A and D dyads scored lower than B dyads on the Total Teaching Score, and there was a marginally significant tendency for A infants to score less than B infants. For the empirical factors, both A and D dyads scored less than B dyads on the first factor, Positive Parent–Child Mutuality. D dyads engaged in less mutual eye contact than B dyads, and the mothers of D infants were less contingent than mothers of B infants on the conceptually constructed Mother Contingency Score (see Crittenden, this volume).

TABLE 4.8

Means (Standard Deviations) for 3-Month Maternal Measures and
Analysis Results for Comparing Attachment Groups

Measures	A	B	C	D	F	p	Contrast
Personal Resources Questionnaire	137.6(20.5)	140.5(18.9)	135.2(14.5)	131.4(26.8)	.56	.64	
Adult Conversational Skills Scale	50.6 (4.0)	51.4 (4.2)	48.3 (5.9)	46.8 (5.4)	3.20	.03	D < B
Social Support and Partner Involvement	5.6 (2.5)	6.2 (2.9)	4.6 (2.3)	4.2 (2.6)	2.0	.12	D < B
Life Experiences Survey (LES) Total	25.1(19.3)	29.6(14.5)	27.0(12.0)	27.3 (2.3)	.28	.84	
LES Positive	12.9 (9.2)	18.7 (8.4)	14.2 (8.3)	14.6 (8.2)	1.43	.24	
LES Negative	12.2(11.7)	11.0 (9.8)	12.8 (6.2)	12.7 (8.9)	.13	.94	

TABLE 4.9
Comparison of Temperament Categories for CNM Sample and Carey
& McDevitt (1978) Sample

| | CNM | | | | | Carey & McDevitt |
	A	B	C	D	CNM total	
Easy	0.0%	35.0%	33%	12.5%	21.1%	42.4%
Intermediate-low	41.7%	25.0%	55.6%	6.3%	28.1%	31.0%
Difficult	16.7%	10.0%	0%	25.0%	14.0%	9.4%
Intermediate-high	8.3%	20.0%	11.1%	25.0%	17.5%	11.3%
Slow to warm-up	33.3%	10.0%	0.0%	31.3%	19.3%	5.9%

DISCUSSION

Researchers are finding that there are a variety of risk factors that are antecedents to insecure attachment. As demonstrated in the introduction to
this chapter, specific risk factors, such as maltreatment, parental depression, and early loss in the parent's life, have been identified in several
studies. however, the identification of these factors does not tell us what
mechanisms influence attachment outcomes. For instance, the interactive
behaviors of the A and D mothers in our sample were equally poor. We
have no clue from the interaction data alone as to why some of the infants
became avoidant and others disorganized. An examination of the maternal factors enables us to begin to hypothesize what mechanism are
involved. The following hypotheses we describe need to be tested in future
studies in which data reflecting a broad set of possible maternal antecedents are collected.

The data presented in the previous section suggest that, within a high-
social-risk population, there are different patterns of antecedents to
attachment classifications at 13 months. This conclusion is in accord with
data presented by Egeland and Farber (1984) and Lyons-Ruth et al.,
(1984). The data also support the idea that the new addition to the traditional Ainsworth A-B-C classification system, the D category, reflects
more problematic caregiving environments. This finding is consistent
with other studies involving high-risk samples, such as those of Crittenden
(1985, this volume; Radke-Yarrow et al. (1985).

TABLE 4.10
Means (Standard Deviations) for Mother-Infant Interaction Measures
and Analysis Results Comparing Attachment Groups

Measures	A	B	C	D	F	p	Contrast
NCAFS - Six Weeks							
Total feeding score	58.8 (8.8)	56.8 (6.7)	61.5 (3.9)	59.1 (8.0)	.86	.47	
Infant feeding score	20.0 (2.5)	18.2 (3.0)	19.4 (2.5)	18.0 (4.2)	1.19	.32	
Mother feeding score	38.8 (8.0)	38.7 (4.7)	42.1 (1.9)	41.1 (4.9)	1.24	.30	
NCATS - Three Months							
Total teaching score	41.5 (8.8)	48.8 (6.6)	46.8 (7.8)	42.6 (7.4)	3.29	.03	A, D < B
Mother teacher score	30.2 (5.6)	33.6 (3.6)	32.8 (6.4)	30.4 (4.3)	2.04	.12	
Infant teaching score	11.4 (4.6)	15.2 (4.8)	14.0 (3.0)	12.1 (4.3)	2.37	.08	A < B
Empirically Derived Factors							
Positive parent–child mutuality	1.2 (1.9)	4.1 (2.5)	2.9 (2.6)	2.3 (2.8)	3.81	.02	A, D < B
Positive feedback from parent	1.1 (1.8)	1.7 (1.7)	2.1 (2.5)	.9 (1.6)	1.2	.33	
Avoidance of punishment, criticism	8.0 (0)	7.8 (.9)	8.0 (0)	8.0 (0)	.60	.62	
Negative child cues	4.9 (3.7)	4.5 (.8)	5.8 (3.5)	5.5 (3.7)	.35	.79	
Mutual eye contact	2.8 (2.2)	4.2 (1.6)	3.3 (1.9)	2.6 (1.7)	2.49	.07	D < B
Positive parental response to distress	3.7 (1.5)	4.0 (1.3)	3.4 (1.2)	3.3 (1.5)	.87	.47	
Cognitive growth fostering	1.2 (1.5)	1.4 (1.2)	1.3 (1.6)	.8 (1.2)	.52	.67	
Conceptual Clusters							
Mother contingency score	4.5 (2.5)	6.3 (2.0)	5.9 (3.5)	4.4 (2.4)	2.25	.09	D < B
Child contingency score	14.2 (2.3)	14.6 (1.5)	14.3 (1.6)	14.6 (.9)	.22	.89	

Antecedents to the A Classification

There are few differences among the mothers of the A, B, C, and D attachment groups on the prenatal intake measures. The two differences that emerged suggest that it is the A group that is least at risk for problems in parenting. The A mothers reported significantly less depression and more partner involvement and social support prenatally (but see Belsky & Isabella, this volume, for contrasting results with a low-risk sample). Before concluding that A mothers are least at risk in this high-risk sample, it is worth considering relevant data reported by Lyons-Ruth et al. (1984), from another high-risk sample. Recall that they found that A mothers reported less family conflict and more fondness for school, as compared to B mothers. In their low-risk samples, Main et al. (1985) also reported that parents of A babies tend to idealize their past relationships with their parents, even though when probed for specific examples, they recalled memories that contradicted their rosy generalization. Thus, it is possible that both parent and child in A dyads show avoidance. In the adults the pattern would be described as a defensive strategy in attention to, or acknowledgment of, their real situation.

The data on A mothers in the present study seems to suggest that maternal perceptions of her situation are as important in evaluating risk as the presence of absence of specific structural factors, such as presence of partner. First of all, 85% of the A mothers, compared to 38% of the B's, 33% of the C's, and 24% of the D's, were living with their partners at the time of the prenatal intake   [$X^2 (3, N = 58) = 12.3, p < .01$]   These partners represented a significant source of potential support for these women. That the partners did not later provide the expected or hoped-for support is suggested by the A mothers' 6-week Postpartum Self-Evaluation scores, especially on the subscale in which they expressed dissatisfaction with their partners' participation in childcare. This interpretation is also supported by the anecdotal reports of the intervening nurses. The nurses reported that the late-postnatal through early-prenatal period was a rallying point for the mothers and their partners, and that their relationships generally strengthened at this time. However, there was a sense that by 6 weeks postpartum the "honeymoon" was over, and that relationships began to seriously deteriorate. The A mothers' high dissatisfaction at 6 weeks may reflect their extreme disappointment regarding this change. It is interesting, therefore, that their mean score on Social Support and Partner Involvement remained exactly the same. (They were, however, the only group to show a decline, although a slight one, in their mean score on the Personal Resources Questionnaire. The other groups showed some mean improvements.)

At 3 months, not one of the A mothers perceived their infants as easy. Nearly half of the A mothers scored their infants as intermediate low, which was similar to the C mothers. However, in addition, 33% of the A babies were rated slow to warm-up, and 25% were intermediate high or difficult. On the NCATS, both the mothers and infants in the avoidant dyads contributed to less optimal interaction patterns. The Infant Teaching Score was the lowest in the sample, as was the Total Teaching Score and the score on the first factor, Positive Parent–Child Mutuality. It is, of course, possible that the A infants were more difficult from birth. However, they did not differ from the rest of the sample in terms of birthweight, gestational age, or Apgar. It is more likely that a negative transaction was begun at birth, in which the A mothers' negativity impaired their capacity to be sensitive to their infants. Perhaps the infants' signals were perceived as more demanding or difficult. The infants, in turn, developed less responsive and less clear ways of interacting with their mothers. Low mutuality was observable by 3 months, and by 13 months, could have resulted in a pattern of mutual avoidance, such as was observed in the Strange Situation.

Antecedents to the C Classification

The antecedents of the resistant, or C classification were somewhat different. The mothers of the C infants did not differ from the other mothers on many measures. The exceptions, however, present an interesting set of contrasts that seem consonant with the prevailing view that C mothers possess an appropriate mothering repertoire, but are not consistent in employing it (Ainsworth et al., 1978). These exceptions involve two of the seven subscales of the Postpartum Self-Evaluation Questionnaire. The C mothers expressed the most satisfaction with their overall life situation and circumstances, but the least confidence in coping with motherhood tasks. On the Beck Depression Inventory at 6 weeks, this group had the highest mean score, and was the only group to be significantly different from the B mothers. Finally, the C mothers had quite positive perceptions of their infants' temperament at 3 months; they were the only group in which no infant was perceived as difficult or slow to warm-up. Eighty-nine percent of C infants, in fact, were perceived as easy or intermediate-low.

The data suggest, then, that A and C mothers are quite different. The C mothers perceive their lives and their infants more positively, but at the same time they are more depressed and less sure of themselves. We speculate that the C mothers showed a mixed defensive pattern characterized by their internalization of negative thoughts about the self, on the one hand, and their effort to see their external situation as positive, on the other. The A mothers viewed their lives, their partners, and their infants more negatively, but they reported fewer symptoms of depression. It may be that their negativity was directed outward, rather than being internalized. We further speculate that the differential patterns of defenses shown by the A and C mothers had differential effects on infant insecure attachment.

Antecedents to the D Classification

At intake, the mothers whose infants would later be classified in the D and B groups scored similarly on most measures. It is interesting, then, that the distinctions between the D and B groups increased over time. By 3 months, the data support the idea that the D attachment classification reflected a more problematic rearing environment. At intake, the B and D mothers had the two highest group means on the Beck Depression Inventory; both groups were significantly higher than the A group. At 6 weeks, both B and D mothers showed declines in their mean depression scores. However, the mean for the D's was still above the cutoff for mild depression, whereas the B mean, which dropped 6.5 points, was in the nondepressed range. At 6 weeks, both D and B mothers reported significantly more satisfaction than A mothers with their partner's participation in childcare, despite the fact that, overall, fewer of the D and B women had partners.

At 3 months, however, D dyads were more like A dyads in the quality of mother–infant teaching reactions. The D dyads were clearly doing less well than the B dyads, and D mothers were less competent in other ways; they scored significantly lower than B mothers on the adult conversational Skills Scale and on the Social Support and Partner Involvement measure. The Total Teaching Score was significantly lower for the D dyads as compared to B dyads, as were the D scores for Positive Parent–Child Mutuality, Mutual Eye Contact, and the Mother Contingency Score. Finally, the mothers of the B infants were more likely to perceive their infants as easy, and D mothers to perceive their infants as difficult at 3 months. Sixty percent of the B mothers, as compared to only 19% of the D mothers, perceived their infants as easy or intermediate-low.

What pattern of defensive coping do we hypothesize for the D mothers? It seems as if the D pattern could be characterized as a disorganized combination of the C and A defensive patterns. Like the C mothers, they seem to have internalized their depression while reporting mixed external perceptions; they expressed relatively high overall satisfaction on the postpartum self-evaluation scales, including the measure of their partner's participation in child care, but they also had contradictory low social support scores. And, even more so than the A mothers, they had negative evaluations of their infants' temperament.

In addition to fewer social resources, the D mothers had fewer interpersonal skills—in adult-adult conversations as well as in interactions with their infants. The D group, then, seems to encompass and surpass the risk profiles of both the A and C groups. This is especially interesting, given the most of the D's were coded A/C,—avoidant and resistant. The combination of avoidance and resistance, (A/C) is one pattern of D strange situation behavior that has been independently reported in several high-risk studies (Crittenden, 1985; Radke-Yarrow et al., 1985). In our own work the pattern was noted very early, before we become aware of documentation on D behaviors. The salience of this pattern and its association with especially high-risk groups, make it worthy of further study.

Antecedents to Secure Attachment.   The mothers whose infants would be the most securely attached at 13 months were not different from the rest of the sample at intake, except that they were more depressed than A mothers. However, the B mothers did seem to show the most *improvement* over time. We therefore hypothesize that the mother's movement in a positive direction in terms of her perceptions and social skills is a potent predictors of attachment security. The following results support this hypothesis that the B mothers improved their social support and their social skills from intake to 3 months, from lower means to the highest means for all groups. The improvement in the Social Support and Partner Involvement score is especially striking because only about a third of the B mothers had partners. Apparently the support they marshalled from other sources was enough to give them high scores on satisfaction, despite the inherent potential for subjects to score lower on this measure if a partner is not present. At 6 weeks and 3 months, B mothers had confidence in themselves as mothers, satisfaction with their partners as helpers, and positive perceptions of their infants' behaviors.

It may be that the B mothers were receiving more benefit from the intervention programs in which all of these women were participating. What might account for their receptiveness to the intervention? One factor may be that they had a tendency to view their lives and life changes less negatively than A, C, and D mothers. Perhaps the higher negativity of the mothers of insecure infants interfered with their capacity to experience satisfaction with what they did have, and actually contributed to less positive interactions with their infants and the adults in their social networks. Isabella and Belsky (in press) offered a similar interpretation of their data on mother's marital satisfaction and security of the infants' attachment. They found that mothers of insecure infants, as compared to mothers of secure infants, reported significantly greater declines in positive marital activities and sentiments, and greater increases in negative marital activities and sentiments. Mothers in both groups showed a pattern of decreased positive and increased negative marital activities and sentiments from the prenatal assessment to 3 months after birth, but the secure group maintained the same level from 3 to 9 months, although perceptions in the insecure group continued to decline. That the two groups differed in their tendency to view comparable situations in a positive or negative light is suggested by prenatal data showing that mothers of secure infants based their marital appraisals more on positive than negative aspects of the marriage, whereas the reverse was true for the mothers of insecure infants. In summary, two studies have found few differences between mothers of secure and insecure infants before the birth of the child, but discovered that mothers with apparently negative perceptions dwell on common marital and caregiving stresses, and those with less negative perceptions minimize difficulties. The two groups of mothers experience family life differently, and influence the quality of interactions to the extent that the former group fosters insecure infant attachment. What is important about the similarities of the conclusions of these two studies is that one involved a low-risk and the other a high-risk sample. The concept of *negative affectivity* may serve to organize the findings of such disparate studies.

NEGATIVE AFFECTIVITY: LINK BETWEEN LOW- AND HIGH-RISK STUDIES?

Much might be gained from interpreting our data and those of other researchers in terms of the construct of Negative Affectivity (NA). Watson and Clark (1984) reviewed the evidence in support of this construct. A number of diverse personality scales measuring trait anxiety, neuroticism, ego strength, general maladjustment, repression-sensitization, and social desirability, to name a few construct, were show by Watson and Clark to intercorrelate highly and, in fact, to all measure NA. High NA individuals "tend to dwell on the negative side of themselves and their world" (p. 465). They are more likely to feel negative at all times and across situations, even in the absence of overt stress. NA includes such affective states as "anger, scorn, revulsion, guilt, self-dissatisfaction, a sense of rejection and, to some extent, sadness" (p. 465). It is unrelated to positive emotions. That is, a high NA individual may or may not also experience joy, excitement, or enthusiasm. NA has several aspects, including negative mood and perceptions, and low self-esteem. It "centers on conscious, subjective experience rather than on an objective condition; that is, it emphasizes how people feel about themselves and their world rather than how effectively they may actually handle themselves in the world." At higher levels, however, NA is by no means separate from overt behavioral adaptation, "because self-esteem and mood are important components of adjustment" (p. 466). NA is a construct that may be appropriate across low- and high-risk samples because it is measured on a continuum. At higher levels it may, but need not necessarily, accompany maladjustment and pathology.

In general, the B mothers in our sample expressed the most positive balance of positive and negative perceptions. In addition, they seemed to have increased their positivity over time, and their positive perceptions were not contradicted by their negative perceptions, as seemed to occur for the A, C, and D mothers.

Watson and Clark stated that the behavior of low NA individuals might be "interpreted as defensive; if so, it would seem to be a healthy defensiveness that helps them to maintain a pleasant mood and a positive self-image through the mistakes, set-backs, and frustrations of life" (p. 482). The A, C, and D mothers all present different mixes of positive and negative affectivity, characterized by numerous contradictions. Watson and Clark do not discuss such contradictions, but they did describe two types of low NA individuals: "(a) those who are truly self-satisfied, well adjusted and happy, and (b) those who are not necessarily well-adjusted or happy, but who characteristically deny their unpleasant or undesirable self-perceptions" (p. 484). We hypothesize that A, C, and D mothers are all high NA individuals with different patterns of denial.

NA has been shown to correlate positively with measures of depression, anxiety, guilt, and hostility, and negatively with measures of ego strength, social desirability, and well-being. Thus, the reported links between various aspects of maternal personality and infants' insecure attachment make more sense when interpreted in terms of the NA construct. For example, Egeland and Farber (1984) reported data suggesting that mothers who were high on aggression and suspicion and low on social desirability (that is, high NA mothers), were more likely to have infants who changed from secure to insecure between 12 and 18 months. Similarly, Belsky and Isabella (this volume) report data suggesting that A mothers had less ego strength (that is, were higher on NA) than B and C mothers. Future research is needed to examine the impact of NA and different defensive strategies on the capacity to nurture an infant.

Our findings that there are significant differences among the mothers of infants in the different attachment groups in terms of their perceptions of infant temperament can also be discussed in terms of maternal NA. In the Minnesota Mother–Infant Interaction Project, Vaughn et al. (1981) reported that 9 of the 19 maternal psychological variables measured at 3 months were related to maternal perceptions of infant temperament, as measured by the ITQ (Carey, 1970) at 6 months. Mothers describing their infants as difficult had higher scores on aggression, defendence and anxiety, and lower scores on social desirability. They also had less knowledge of the reciprocal nature of mother–infant interaction, and less maternal feeling. Mothers of easy babies were generally the opposite on these measures. In general, the mothers who perceived their infants as difficult were described as more anxious, hostile and suspicious than mothers who perceived their infants as easy. Vaughn et al. (1981) felt that the ITQ was an assessment of the mother, and not the infant, and they speculated that the anxiety and hostility of these women interfered with the accurate reading of their infants' behavior, diminishing their capacity to be sensitive and appropriately responsive to infant cues.

If the mothers of insecure infants are higher on NA, as we would hypothesize, then it is surprising that Vaughn et al. (1981) found no relationships between the ITQ and attachment classifications. Perhaps such data need to be considered longitudinally, as Belsky and Isabella (this volume) did. They found that the mothers of insecure infants increased their negative perceptions of their infants' temperaments, and mothers of secure infants decreased their negative perceptions between 3 and 9 months.

CONCLUSION

In conclusion, this chapter makes several contributions to our understanding of social-risk and the antecedents to attachment quality in a high-social-risk population. This study is one of a few efforts to apply a D classification to the traditional Ainsworth A-B-C coding of the Strange Situation. The D category will enrich our understanding of the antecedents to attachment quality, in part because it functions to remove poor exemplars from the A, B, and C categories. Not all infants who are poor exemplars of the A, B, or C categories are D's, however. We view these attachment categories as existing on a continuum. In reality, some infants show behavior that is common to more than one category. We chose to eliminate these boundary cases so that we could get a clearer understanding of the meaningful differences that do exist among dyads representing the distinct categories in the Strange Situation. Finally, the findings of this study have been important in engendering the speculation that the pattern of maternal negative and positive perceptions about self and others is related to the quality of the mother's interaction with her infant and, eventually, to the quality of her infant's attachment. Although clearly not the only antecedent factor, NA may be an important one for integrating the findings from studies of low-risk and high-risk populations. Apart from the actual presence of maltreatment or severe maternal depressive illness, the number or type of family stressful life events or difficult life circumstances, as measured in this and other studies, does not seem to be related to attachment outcome at one year. The predisposition for negative affectivity, however, can cut across social class and categories of risk, and seems to be independent of actual stressful experiences. Future studies of attachment must look for explanatory links across low- and high-risk studies, and negative affectivity may provide this conceptual bridge.

ACKNOWLEDGMENTS

This research was supported by the National Institute of Mental Health, Grant No. 5 R01 MH 36894, Kathryn E. Barnard, Principal Investigator; and by a grant from the John D. and Catherine T. MacArthur Foundation, to Kathryn E. Barnard, Principal Investigator. Thanks to Jan Moser, Sandra Mitchell, Maura Costello, Charlotte Henson, Diane Majerus, Mary Main, and the members of the MacArthur Network Working Group on Attachment, for their contributions to this work.

REFERENCES

Ainsworth, M. D. S., Blehar, M. C., Waters, E., & Wall, S. (1978). *Patterns of attachment: A psychological study of the strange situation.* Hillsdale, NJ: Lawrence Erlbaum Associates.

Barnard, K. E., Hammond, M. A., Booth, C. L., Bee, H. L., Mitchell, S. K., & Spieker, S. J. (in press). Measurement and meaning of parent–child interaction. In F. J. Morrison, C. E. Lord, & D. P. Keating (Eds.), *Applied developmental psychology* (Vol. III). New York: Academic Press.

Beck, A. T. (1970). *Depression: Causes and treatment.* Philadelphia: University of Pennsylvania Press.

Bell, S. M. (1970). The development of the concept of object as related to infant–mother attachment. *Child Development, 41,* 292–311.

Belsky, J. (1984). The determinants of parenting: A process model. *Child Development, 55,* 83–96.

Belsky, J., Rovine, M., & Taylor, D. G. (1984). The Pennsylvania Infant and Family Development Project, 3: The origins of individual differences in infant–mother attachment: Maternal and infant contributions. *Child Development, 55,* 718–728.

Brandt, P. A., & Weinert, C. (1981). The PRQ—a social support measure. *Nursing Research, 30,* 277–280.

Brunnquell, D., Crichton, L., & Egeland, B. (1981). Maternal personality and attitude in disturbances of child rearing. *American Journal of Orthopsychiatry, 51,* 680–691.

Bumberry, W., Oliver, J. M., & McClure, J. N. (1978). Validation of the Beck Depression Inventory in a university population using psychiatric estimate as the criterion. *Journal of Consulting and Clinical Psychology, 46,* 150–155.

Carey, W. B. (1970). A simplified method for measuring infant temperament. *Journal of Pediatrics, 77,* 188–194.

Carey, W. B., & McDevitt, S. C. (1978). Revision of the Infant Temperament Questionnaire. *Pediatrics, 61,* 735–739.

Cohen, J. (1977). *Statistical power analysis for the behavioral sciences.* (rev. ed.). New York: Academic Press.

Crittenden, P. M. (1985). Maltreated infants: Vulnerability and resilience. *Journal of Child Psychology and Psychiatry, 26,* 85–96.

Egeland, B., & Farber, E. A. (1984). Infant–mother attachment: Factors related to its development and changes over time. *Child Development, 55,* 753–771.

Egeland, B., & Sroufe, L. A. (1981a). Attachment and early maltreatment. *Child Development, 52,* 44–52.

Egeland, B., & Sroufe, L. A. (1981b). Developmental sequelae of maltreatment in infancy. In R. Rizley & D. Cicchetti (Eds.), *Developmental perspectives in child maltreatment* (pp. 77–92). San Francisco: Jossey-Bass.

Gaensbauer, T. J., Harmon, R. J., Cytryn, L., & McKnew, D. H. (1984). Social and affective development in infants with a manic-depressive parent. *American Journal of Psychiatry, 141,* 223–229.

Gardner, W. P., & Thompson, R. A. (1983, April). *A cluster analytic evaluation of the Strange Situation Classification system.* Paper presented at the meeting of the Society for Research in Child Development, Detroit.

Lederman, R. P., Weingarten, C. G. T., & Lederman, E. (1981). Postpartum self-evaluation questionnaire: Measures of maternal adaptation. In B. S. Raff (Ed.). *Perinatal parental behavior, Vol. 17. Birth Defects: Original article series.* New York: Alan Liss.

Lyons-Ruth, K., Connell, D., Grunebaum, H., Botein, S., & Zoll, D. (1984). Maternal family history, maternal caretaking and infant attachment in multiproblem families. *Preventive Psychiatry, 2,* 403–425.

Lyons-Ruth, K., Connell, D. B., Zoll, D., & Stahl, J. (1985, April). *Infants at social risk: Relationships among infant attachment behavior, infant development and maternal behavior at home in maltreated and non-maltreated infants.* Paper presented at the meeting of the Society for Research in Child Development, Toronto.

Main, M., Kaplan, N., & Cassidy, J. (1985). Security in infancy, childhood and adulthood: A move to the level of representation. In I. Bretherton & E. Waters (Eds.), *Growing points of attachment theory and* research. *Monographs of the Society for Research in Child Development,* 50(1–2, Serial No. 209).

Main, M., & Solomon, J. (in press). Procedures for identifying insecure-disorganized/disoriented infants. In M. Greenberg, D. Cicchetti, & E. M. Cummings (Eds.), *Attachment in the preschool years: Theory, research and intervention.*

Main, M., & Weston, D. (1981). The quality of the toddler's relationship to mother and to father: Related to conflict behavior and the readiness to establish new relationships. *Child Development, 52,* 932–940.

Radke-Yarrow, M., Cummings, E. M., Kuczynski, L., & Chapman, M. (1985). Patterns of attachment in two-and three-year-olds in normal families and families with parental depression. *Child Development, 56,* 884–893.

Radloff, L. S. (1977). The CES-D scale: A self-report depression scale for research in the general population. *Applied Psychological Measurement, 1,* 385–401.

Sameroff, A. J., Seifer, R., & Zax, M. (1982). Early development of children at risk for emotional disorder. *Monographs of the Society for Research in Child Development, 47* (7, Serial No. 199).

Sarason, I., Johnson, H., & Siegel, M. (1978). Assessing the impact of life changes: Development of the life experience survey. *Journal of Consulting and Clinical Psychology, 46,* 932–946.

Schneider-Rosen, K., Braunwald, K. G., Carlson, V., & Cicchetti, D. (1985). Current perspectives in attachment theory: Illustration from the study of maltreated infants. In I. Bretherton & E. Waters (Eds.), *Growing Points of Attachment Theory and Research. Monographs of the Society for Research in Child Development, 50*(1–2, Serial No. 209).

Spitzer, R. L., & Endicott, J. (1977). *The schedule for affective disorders and schizophrenia: Lifetime version.* New York: New York State Psychiatric Institute, Biometrics Research.

Vaughn, B., Egeland, B., Sroufe, L. A., & Waters, E. (1979). Individual differences in infant–mother attachment at twelve and eighteen months: Stability and change in families under stress. *Child Development, 50,* 971–975.

Vaughn, B. E., Taraldson, B. J., Crichton, L., & Egeland, B. (1981). The assessment of infant temperament: A critique of the Carey Infant Temperament Questionnaire. *Infant Behavior and Development, 4,* 1–17.

Waters, E. (1978). The reliability and stability of individual differences in infant–mother attachment. *Child Development, 49,* 483–494.

Watson, D., & Clark, L. A. (1984). Negative affectivity: The disposition to experience aversive emotional states. *Psychological Bulletin, 96,* 465–490.

Weiss, R. (1974). The provision of social relationships. In Z. Rubin (Ed.), *Doing unto others* (pp. 17–26). Englewood Cliffs, NJ: Prentice-Hall.

5
Relationships at Risk

Patricia M. Crittenden
Mailman Center for Child Development
University of Miami

Risk status is generally attributed to individuals. However, relationships between individuals can also be at risk for deterioration or termination. This can occur when the individuals are so displeased with each other that one or both consider abandoning the relationship (either physically or emotionally). Risk to relationship is particularly evident in cases of child abuse and neglect. As the extent of maltreatment becomes greater, one may assume that the internal threat to the parent–child relationship will increase. Furthermore, at some point, if the maltreatment is severe enough, society will intervene on the child's behalf and pose the external threat of separation in the form of foster care. In such cases, not only is the child at risk of continued maltreatment, but also the parent–child relationship is at risk of dissolution. This chapter focuses on: (a) the theoretical aspects of risks to relationships; (b) the empirical evidence of such risk and its influence on child development; and (c) the process of assessing risk to relationships. The chapter includes the results of an investigation aimed specifically at these issues.

A focus on risk to relationships in maltreating dyads is of theoretical interest because of the light it sheds on the essential nature of the attachment of the child to the parent. Evidence that attachment occurs in the absence of the emotional warmth associated with the concept of love will indicate that the attachment aspect of a relationship is both functionally and behaviorally distinct from other aspects of the relationship. Evidence of atypical patterns of attachment behavior accompanying risk to relationships will expand our understanding of the evolutionary adaptiveness of attachment behavior. The focus on risk to relationships is also of practical interest because of the unique developmental patterns shown by mal-treated children. Both the clinical literature on older maltreated children, which indicates that their behavior is often atypical (Martin & Beezley, 1976; Yates, 1981), and that on maltreating parents, which indicates that they were often maltreated as children (Cicchetti & Rizley, 1981; Kempe, Silverman, Steele, Droegemueller, & Silver, 1962), suggest that the experi-ence of abuse and/or neglect has effects which may change the course of development far into the future. Therefore, the study of relationships in maltreating families has both theoretical and practical significance.

Before setting out to consider the relationship in maltreating parent–child dyads, it must be noted that relationships can be very difficult to assess. Whereas an interaction consists of observable behaviors, a rela-tionship is essentially a construct reflecting the common thread running through a series of interactions. Because relationships have no physical manifestation, they are not accessible to direct observation. Therefore, it is important to distinguish between behavior specific to an instance of interaction and aspects of that interaction that reflect the nature of the underlying relationship. The relationship aspect of a given interaction is possibly best conceptualized as behavior that reflects the expectations, based on previous interactions, of each individual regarding the other's behavior. Thus, relationships are best assessed in dyadic situations that have as few environmental influences and variations as possible and that encourage the behavioral enactment of each partner's expectations.

The difficulty of assessing relationships is compounded because relationships are not necessarily of uniform quality across all aspects of the relationship. For example, a mother may be very competent and responsible as a caregiver but at the same time be awkward or with-drawn as a playmate. Similarly, her child may be patient and cooperative when he wants his physical needs to be met, but insistent and demanding when he wants stimulation and attention. Thus, it is essential to identify, in terms of role demands, the context in which a relationship is being assessed and to recognize that only one aspect of a multifaceted relationship is being assessed.

In addition to the inherent difficulties and limitations of assessing rela-tionships, there are further issues that arise when assessment procedures (such as the Strange Situation), which were developed for normal popula-tions, are applied without revalidation to atypical samples. In such cases it is possible that the full range of behavior of atypical groups may not be encompassed by the outcome protocols of the assessment. Furthermore, it is possible that behavior that has one function for a normative population may have quite a different function in atypical populations. For example, securely attached, adequately reared infants tend to approach their moth-ers following a brief separation. Anxiously attached, adequately reared children tend to avoid their mothers or to mix approach with resistance. The same brief separation that is only mildly stressful to adequately reared children, however, may be extremely stressful to a maltreated child. Some such children may approach their mothers in the absence of overt resistance after the separation. Moreover, such approaches may be juxtaposed against earlier avoidance that preceded the separation. In such cases the interpretation of the meaning of the approach and its behavioral context may need to be reevaluated.

It is also important to consider qualitative differences in relationships as opposed to unidimensional assessment of the strength or weakness of relationships. A simple measure of the strength of the relationship may provide less information regarding *how* the relationship affects either immediate behavior or the course of the individual's development than a qualitative assessment. Ainsworth and her colleagues pioneered this approach in their differentiation of patterns of infant attachment to the mother (Ainsworth, Blehar, Waters, & Wall, 1978). Infants were found to be secure, anxious-avoidant, and anxious-ambivalent in relationships with their mothers. These differences were related to differences in both the mothers' and infants' behavior at home and to differences in the later developmental courses of the infants (Ainsworth et al., 1978; Egeland & Farber, 1984; Matas, Arhend, & Sroufe, 1978). Secure infants were better able to receive comfort from their mothers and better able to explore independently than were anxiously attached infants. Later, in the preschool years, they were more congenial with peers, cooperative with adults, and competent at problem solving. On the other hand, if the strength of the relationship had been measured by the amount of attachment behavior, many of the anxious-ambivalent children would have been found to have very "strong" attachments to their mothers and yet to be among the least competent infants or preschoolers.

Crittenden has applied such an approach to assessing the patterns of interaction of maltreating dyads (Crittenden, 1981). Crittenden's hypotheses were that maltreating mothers were less sensitive than adequate mothers, and, also, that there were differences in the type of insensitivity shown by abusing mothers as compared to neglecting mothers. Indeed, both abusing and neglecting mothers were found to be similarly low on a measure of maternal sensitivity to infant signals. When the quality of the insensitive behavior was considered, however, the groups were very different. Abusing mothers were hostile and controlling with their infants whereas neglecting mothers were withdrawn and unresponsive. Moreover, these differences in the quality of maternal interaction were related to differences in the quality of infant interaction and infant developmental quotients. On both measures the infants of neglecting mothers performed considerable more poorly than did the abused infants (Crittenden, 1985a).

The preceding discussion suggests a number of issues regarding risk to relationships that need further investigation. First, the importance of qualitative differences needs further exploration. Second, the nature of those differences across different aspects of relationships needs elaboration. Finally, the means for assessing relationships, as opposed to specific interactions, needs investigation. In particular, it is important to consider now assessment procedures developed for normal populations can be applied to special populations.

This chapter views risk to the mother–child relationship in maltreating dyads from three perspectives: mother as caregiver, mother as interactant, and mother as an attachment figure. Particular attention is paid to the function of behavior as an indication of one person's expectations of the other and to the interpretation of standard assessment procedures for a maltreating sample. In addition, the issues of developmental change in the behavioral expression of the relationship and the short- and long-term adaptiveness of such changes are considered.

ASSESSING THE MOTHER–CHILD RELATIONSHIP

Before the quality of a relationship can be assessed, decisions must be made regarding the specific aspect(s) of the relationship to be assessed. A mother has a number of possible roles relative to her young child. In all cases, she is expected to function as a caregiver and can reasonably be evaluated in terms of that basic function. Additionally, she probably serves as a social interactant to her child, thus presenting the possibility of evaluating her competence in that role. She may be playmate or a teacher. Finally, she almost certainly becomes an attachment figure to her infant. Each of these roles is separate and involves different functions for maternal behavior. For example, the mother who perceives herself as a playmate interacts with her child in a different manner from the mother who perceives herself as a teacher or from the same mother when she is trying to teach her child new skills. Any assessment procedure must, therefore, be sensitive both to the specific aspect of the relationship being assessed and also the nature of the situation used to elicit the behavior. Finally, assessments of several aspects of the mother–child relationship are necessary before one can claim to have assessed the *relationship*. Three essential aspects of the mother–child relationship are discussed in detail in this chapter: mother as caregiver, mother as interactant, and mother as attachment figure.

Mother as Caregiver

All mothers are responsible for meeting their children's life-preserving needs: their needs for adequate nutrition, for shelter, for warmth, and for protection from harm. Mothers who have the necessary physical resources and who do not meet these minimum requirements of the role of mother clearly have distorted relationships with their children. Once again, however, it is not sufficient to sum the distortion in terms of the severity of caregiving failure. There are various ways to fail and they appear to have different implications for child development (Crittenden, 1985a; Egeland, Sroufe, & Erickson, 1984).

There are a number of ways of assessing both the mother's competence as a caregiver to her infant and also the particular style of her caregiving. In the case of identified maltreating families, an evaluation of parenting competence has already been carried out by the designated state authorities in the process of substantiating the allegations of maltreatment. Thus, one can identify a mother as having an abusive relationship with her child, that is, a relationship in which needed care is generally provided but is accompanied by excessive anger, harshness, and/or hostility. In a neglectful relationship, the child does not receive sufficient normal and necessary care. In an abusing-and-neglecting relationships, the mother displays anger or harshness to the child and also withholds appropriate care. In a marginally maltreating relationship, the mother's lack of foresight and planning for her child's needs results in frequent, brief crises in which the mother shows some abusiveness and/or neglectfulness that is not as severe and pervasive as that experienced by abused and neglected children. Nonmaltreating, or adequate, mothers are generally responsive, attentive, and appropriate in their care of their youngsters. This does not mean that adequate mothers always respond appropriately; it does mean that in any given instance their children are likely to expect, and usually receive, responsive and appropriate care. Marginally maltreated children, on the other hand, generally do no know what to expect because of their mothers' inconsistency, whereas abused and neglected children can reasonably expect harsh or inadequate treatment, respectively.

Thus, it appears that two factors play a role in the evaluation of the mother as a caregiver: one involves the actual care given to the child, the other the child's expectations regarding that care. Although the child's relationship to his/her mother is probably best conceptualized in terms of his/her expectations, a procedure for directly assessing those expectations is difficult to devise. On the other hand, maternal caregiving is open to direct investigation. Because it is the basis from which the infant develops expectations, it can be used as the assessment of the mother as caregiver. Therefore, the five groupings of mothers, (abusing, neglecting, abusing-

and-neglecting, marginally maltreating, and adequate) are referred to in this chapter as *child-rearing groups* and are treated as a qualitative assessment of maternal caregiving competence.

Mother as an Interactant

Just as all mothers function in a caregiving role, all mothers are expected to interact with their young children. Moreover, the experience of this interaction appears to be a critical influence on the child's cognitive, language, and social development. Therefore, any assessment of the aspects of the mother–child relationship should consider the mother's competence as an interactant.

Numerous investigators have studied the interaction of maltreating mothers and their young children (Deitrich, Starr, & Weisfeld, 1983; Mash, Johnson, & Kovitz, 1983; Robinson & Solomon, 1979; Wasserman, Green, & Rhianon, 1983). Most, however, have attempted to identify behavioral differences in maltreating and adequate dyads rather than attempting to assess the quality of the mother–infant relationship. One tool designed specifically for the assessment of relationships is the CARE-Index (Crittenden, 1981, 1985a, 1985b). This assessment procedure uses 3 minutes of videotaped semistructured play interaction as the basis for categorizing maternal and infant patterns of interaction. Rather than being based on frequency counts of specific behaviors, this assessment device calls for categorical judgments of functionally equivalent behaviors. For example, both laughing at an infant's distress and repeating an irritating behavior can be expected to carry the same interpersonal message of hostility to the child even though one of the behaviors. laughter, is generally considered prosocial. This approach of clustering behaviors functionally reduces the influence upon the assessment of situation-specific aspects of the interaction and maximizes the influence of each interactant's generalized expectations of the other.

Each code in the CARE-Index system both identifies a category of behaviors grouped on the basis of their expectable interactional outcomes and provides one or more examples of the behavior. For example, a "responsive facial expression" is defined as "alert, actively attentive, responsive to the situation and the baby's mood, e.g., with a young infant in face-to-face interaction the adult may slowly exaggerate normal facial expressions, with an older infant engaged in toy play the adult's face may be alert with low key supportive expression changes which reflect activity changes." By defining items categorically, a large number of morphologically different, but functionally similar, interactive behaviors can be subsumed under the same category.

More specifically, the adult codes are designed to assess the mother's sensitivity to infant signals under a low stress condition; they do not assess her competence as a playmate or whether she ordinarily functions as one. There are three types of adult codes: controlling, unresponsive, and sensitive. These codes define four patterns of adult interactional behavior. The controlling pattern identifies behaviors that are either overtly hostile, (e.g., glaring at the infant, muttering profanity, jerking the infant's body) or covertly hostile (i.e., pseudo-sensitive behaviors that appear playful but are irritating to the infant—inappropriate laughter, teasing, and abrupt cutting off of the infant's activity by the offer of another). The unresponsive pattern consists of items describing forms of facial, vocal, and physical withdrawal, e.g., extended looking away from the interaction, silence, and sitting at a distance from the infant. The items defining the sensitive pattern are tied to the mother's accommodation to her infant's behavior, e.g., timing adult turns on the basis of infant signals, or rhythmic voice tone that is adjusted for the baby's age and mood. The inept pattern consists of a mixture of items from at least two patterns including a substantial proportion of sensitive items.

In a similar manner, the infant codes differentiate difficult, passive, and cooperative patterns of infant behavior. The items associated with the difficult pattern describe overt forms of resistance to maternal behavior, e.g., turning away, grimacing, crying, wincing, or pushing offered toys away. The passive pattern consists of behaviors that function to reduce contact with the mother, e.g., a vacant facial expression, ignoring of adult overtures, or lack of play. The cooperative pattern identifies behaviors associated with the expression of pleasure and facilitation of turn-taking, e.g., bright or attentive facial expressions, initiation of contact with the adult, or acceptance of adult overtures. Each item is constructed so that the categorical portion of the definition is suitable across a wide age range. The items do not require that the coder consider the infant's "intention" or the appropriateness of the response in the context of the mother's behavior.

In three separate samples of low-income mothers whose children ranged from birth to 24-months old, the controlling interaction pattern was associated with abusing mothers, the unresponsive pattern with neglecting mothers, the inept pattern with marginally maltreating mothers, and the sensitive pattern with adequate mothers (Crittenden, 1981, 1985a). Moreover, the infants of these mothers behaved in predictable ways: abused children were generally difficult, neglected children passive, and both marginally maltreated and adequately reared children cooperative. In other words, abusing mothers seemed to expect a dominant role in a coercive relationship; their infants seemed to expect the need for overt resistance to that control. Neglecting mothers appeared not to expect that a relationship with their babies be established, and their infants' passivity suggested similar expectations. Marginally maltreating and adequate mothers were generally sensitively responsive to infant signals, suggesting that they expected engaging, noncoercive, reciprocal relationships. Their infants' cooperativeness, in turn, suggested that they expected their mothers to be responsive to their needs and wishes. It should be pointed out, however, that the inept mothers' play was less smooth and attentive than the sensitive mothers' and that their infants often had to repeat and intensify signals before their mothers noticed and responded.

Although all three studies confirmed the finding that maternal and infant behavior tended to mesh predictably and to differ by quality of caregiving, in the third sample there was a sizable group of infants whose behavior was discrepant with that hypothesis (Crittenden, 1985a). These were 16 maltreated children who were unusually accommodating and whose behavior could only be classified as cooperative in spite of maternal insensitivity and a disturbing lack of positive affect in the children. It was decided that exploration of the behavior of these infants might prove informative. Seven of the 16 appeared distinctly anxious to please their mothers and this seemed to override their interest in the toys. One cried violently until his mother put him down and then was superficially cooperative while still subtly ignoring as many of her overtures as possible. Five others seemed both ecstatic at and terrified by their mothers' vigorous teasing, kissing, and roughhousing.

A review of the family history data on these children indicated that they tended to differ from the remainder of the maltreated children in three ways. First, these children were older than the others. They tended to cluster in age around 18 months; in contrast, 20 of the 22 passive or difficult children were less than 15 months old. Possibly, the older children had learned that it was dangerous to be passive or difficult with their mothers and thus had modified their behavior accordingly. Second, these anxious-to-please toddlers tended to have experienced more severe or pervasive maltreatment than the passive or difficult children. Finally, they tended to have experienced more major mother–infant separations than the other infants; nine of the 16 had been placed in foster care, hospitalized, left with relatives, or separated from a hospitalized mother.

None of these explanations completely accounted for the data and all were post hoc attempts to explain an unexpected finding. Nevertheless, all these patterns of covariation raised the possibility that increased stress and helplessness may result in anxious cooperation in older infants. These children had experienced maltreatment longer, possibly recognized its dangers better, and, conceivably, had not found protest or withdrawal to be successful strategies for changing it. They were anxious to please, resentful, and fearful. They tried not to make themselves the focus of their mothers' anger. Compliant responses seemed to function to maximize the possibility of obtaining their mothers' attentions and goodwill. Their anxiety is easily understood in terms of the danger inherent in a relationship with a maltreating mother as well as their inability to modify their mothers' behaviors through direct, negative signals. These observations suggested that an additional pattern of behavior, compulsive compliance, might be identified and used to discriminate truly cooperative children from inhibited, wary, and compliant ones. This hypothesis was tested in the following investigation.

Mother as Attachment Figure

According to Bowlby (1969), attachment behavior functions to keep the child close enough to the mother so that, in moments of perceived danger, the infant can increase the likelihood that he/she will be protected. In the absence of danger, the child uses the mother as a secure base from which to explore the environment. Because such a pattern of behavior has obvious survival value, Bowlby hypothesized that it was selected during the period of human evolution and is, therefore, essentially universal among children. Because maltreatment poses so painful a threat to children and because maltreating parents are not sensitively responsive to their infants' signals, some theorists have assumed that maltreated children do not become attached to a maltreating parent (Lamb, 1976; Rajecki, Lamb, & Obmascher, 1978). Although such conclusions are plausible, the evidence is to the contrary. Maltreated children do become attached to their mothers although the quality of the relationship may be suboptimal (Crittenden, 1985a; Egeland & Sroufe, 1981; Gaensbauer & Harmon, 1982). Moreover, such attachments clearly have survival value because instances of abuse are brief and infrequent compared to the infant's constant need for protection and nurturance. An infant who does not seek a parent, even a maltreating parent, might avoid parental mistreatment but only at the cost of lost succor.

Ainsworth has identified several qualitatively different patterns of attachment which are described throughout this volume. These qualitative differences represent modifications of the genetically preselected behaviors as a result of the child's experience with a specific attachment figure. Because samples of maltreated children differ from Ainsworth's sample not only in terms of parental adequacy, but also in terms of SES and racial composition, it is possible that the meaning or function of their behavior may be different from that described by Ainsworth.

Assessments of attachment have largely relied on the Ainsworth Strange Situation. The very ease with which the Strange Situation procedure can be implemented, however, has resulted in a paucity of research, particularly research with atypical samples, that attempts to replicate the original relationships that Ainsworth found between daily home behaviu̇ и and Strange Situation behavior. The Strange Situation patterns are often thought of as the pattern of the relationship, even though the original interpretation of Strange Situation behavior was entirely dependent upon extensive observation of the dyads' behavior at home under ordinary conditions (Ainsworth et al., 1978). When interpretations of Strange Situation behavior have not been tied to home observations, the meaning of the behavior may be misunderstood and new variations in the patterning of behavior more easily overlooked. Several studies have reported that a substantial proportion of maltreated infants were classified as securely attached (Egeland & Sroufe, 1981; Schneider-Rosen, Braunwald, Carlson, & Cicchetti, 1985)—a startling finding that demands an explanation. The findings of other studies regarding the home behavior of maltreating dyads suggest the possibility that the meaning or organization of the maltreated infant's behavior in the Strange Situation may differ from that of the adequately reared infant and, thus, distort the meaning of Ainsworth's classification procedures (Burgess & Conger, 1978; Crittenden, 1981, 1985a, 1985b).

If so, it may be that the classificatory system needs to be expanded. In this regard, some investigators have identified children who are unclassifiable using the A-B-C categories developed by Ainsworth (Main & Weston, 1981). Others are developing classification criteria for children who do not fit the A-B-C patterns (Crittenden, 1985a, 1985b; Main & Solomon, in press; Radke-Yarrow, Cummings, Kuczynski, & Chapman, in press). Main and her colleagues have identified a disorganized D pattern for extremely anxious children from apparently "normal" families. Both Crittenden and Radke-Yarrow and her colleagues have identified an avoidant-ambivalent (A/C) pattern for maltreated children and the children of depressed mothers, respectively. Because of the importance to this chapter of alternative patterns, and of the A/C pattern in particular, its development in Crittenden's third sample (1985a) is considered in detail.

The Strange Situation tapes of the children in Crittenden's third sample were coded and classified twice. The first time the standard Ainsworth A-B-C classificatory system was used yielding relationships between abuse and secure attachment, neglect and anxious/avoidant attachment, marginal maltreatment and borderline secure attachment (i.e., B_1, B_2, B_4, A_2, C_1), and adequate childrearing and secure attachment. The substantial number of abused children classified as secure in the Strange Situation (wen forced classification into the original Ainsworth A-B-C categories was used) was both unexpected and unexplainable. The unusual behavior of these children suggested, however, that the classificatory system might be inadequate to describe the form or meaning of the behavior of children reared in extremely deviant environments. Therefore, the tapes and the ratings were reviewed by the investigator with full knowledge of the mother's child-rearing group status. This review yielded several differences in the behavior of securely attached maltreated infants and securely attached adequately reared children. First, the proximity seeking of the maltreated children often was not carried out with the positive affect displayed by the adequately reared children. The behavior of the maltreated children appeared to maintain the semblance of interaction in the absence of intimacy. For example, a child might repeatedly approach the mother and systematically offer her toys without ever looking at her or touching her. Second, the maltreated children's approaches were accompanied by moderately strong avoidance often consisting of oblique or backwards approaches such as have been previously associated with abuse (George & Main, 1979). Third, there was also moderate to high resistance. The resistance was more often discernible as whiney petulance than overtly angry behavior. It was frequently accompanied by noncontextual aggression, i.e., aggression directed at aspects of the inanimate environment and indicative of anger. And finally, 8 of the abused-and-neglected children displayed clinical indicators of stress such as face covering, head cocking, huddling on the floor and rocking, and wetting.

On the basis of this review, the classificatory system was modified to emphasize indirect approaches as both, proximity seeking and moderate avoidance, and crankiness and noncontextual aggression as resistance. Furthermore, a new classification, avoidant-ambivalent (A/C), was defined as consisting of extremely anxious infants whose scores on Ainsworth's scales combined: (a) moderate to high proximity seeking; (b) moderate to high avoidance; and (c) moderate to high resistance. In addition, these infants often displayed unusual, stress-related, maladaptive behaviors.

Using these four major attachment patterns, A, B, C, and A/C, the tapes were recoded and reclassified by raters blind to the child-rearing group of the mothers as well as the original attachment classifications of the children. The results of this classification indicated that all of the children could be classified in one of the patterns and all, therefore, could be considered attached. Moreover, none of the severely maltreated children was classified as securely attached now that the alternative A/C classification was available. Most of the abused children were A/C's, most of the neglected children were A's, the marginally maltreated children were split evenly between the secure and anxious classifications but had no A/C's, and all but one adequately reared child was securely attached. These results were considerably more in line with predictions drawn from attachment theory. Because the A/C classification was created using knowledge of the same sample to which it was then applied, the results must be considered exploratory. Combined with replication on a new sample, however, this method using clinical observations, theory based interpretation, and experimental procedures maximizes the information that can be gained from a single sample.

The results of an investigation on a larger sample with a broader age range is reported in the next section. In this study, specific attention was directed to the mother's roles as caregiver, interactant, and attachment figure. In addition, evidence was sought regarding the possibility of a compulsive compliant pattern of interaction and an avoidant-ambivalent (A/C) pattern of attachment for children.

DEVELOPMENTAL CHANGE AND ADAPTATION

The possibility of a compulsive-compliant pattern of interaction suggests two separate but related issues. First, compliance, as observed in Crittenden's third sample, was a behavioral pattern common only to older children who had experienced abuse; young abused infants did not show the pattern. A developmental change is implied. Second, the reason for such a change needs to be explored. If it only occurs under the condition of mistreatment, it may represent an adaptation to the demands of an unusual environment.

Developmental Change

Another issue concerning the organization of behavior in maltreated infants has to do with developmental changes. In the previous discussion of mother–child interaction, it was suggested that over time children who have experienced abuse may become less difficult and more compliant and inhibited. Such a developmental trend differs from that of adequately reared children who are expected to show increased initiation, reciprocity, and positive affect as a function of age. Similarly, securely attached, adequately reared children and their mothers gradually increase their proximity set-goal, the degree of distance and time from the attachment figure that can be tolerated under nonthreatening conditions (Bowlby, 1969). This increase is dependent in part on the infants' increasing competence and self-reliance and in part on their ability to negotiate with their mothers satisfactory conditions for separation that permit their freedom and also ensure their mothers' availability should the need arise (Marvin, 1977). It may be that very anxiously attached maltreated children follow a different course. This issue is also explored further in the investigation discussed later.

Adaptation

The findings concerning maternal behavior during interaction as well as the mothers' quality of caregiving make it very clear that there are a number of very different interpersonal environments with which individual infants have to cope. Moreover, the infants' interactional behaviors and patterns of attachment indicate that there are a variety of coping strategies they can display. Specifically, infants of sensitively responsive mothers tend to cooperate with and trust their mothers. Infants of mothers who are sometimes inattentive or insensitive provide a mixture of positive and negative feedback to their mothers and develop mild to moderate anxiety regarding their mothers' availability when needed. Most of these children take the direct approach of seeking their mothers and protesting unpleasant situations. Some infants of mothers whose pseudo-sensitive behavior is covertly hostile and controlling protest their treatment whereas others, particularly the older ones, appear to inhibit their protests in spite of obvious discomfort. Some of these children control their anxiety through the use of avoidance following a separation from their mothers; others show a combination of approach, avoidance, and resistance. Infants of withdrawn, unresponsive mothers show yet another pattern with infant passivity giving way in older infants to difficult behavior in interaction and avoidance under the stress of separation. Of interest here is the adaptiveness of these strategies (cf. Ainsworth, 1984).

Both Bowlby (1980) and Main (1979) have interpreted the use of avoidance in infants of insensitive mothers as a defense mechanism, a cognitive disconnection of some classes of information, particularly those that might result in the activation of the attachment system. Such a response is believed to reduce the pain resulting from unmet emotional needs at the cost of loss of the opportunity for the individual to remain responsive to incoming information. Thus, a person using a defense mechanism would experience reduced stress at the unresponsiveness of an attachment figure (through exclusion of that information from conscious thought.) He or she would also exclude indications of increased responsiveness of the attachment figure, as well as the attachment-related signals of a new, and potentially more satisfying, attachment figure. Because the exclusion of such information can be detrimental to the individual, such defensive behavior is considered maladaptive.

Therefore, it is important to know if the coping strategies used by maltreated infants are defensive. That is, do they permit the infants to maximize the responsiveness of their present environment but only at the cost of an inability to accommodate change? The behavioral patterns of maltreated infants just described would tend to maximize the likelihood of the infants' receiving whatever positive maternal attention was available while at the same time reducing the likelihood that the infant would become a source of irritation. This is probably adaptive in the proximate or immediate sense (Ainsworth, 1984). On the other hand, if such behavior prevents the infant from attending or responding to new information, then the response can be considered defensive or maladaptive in the ultimate sense. An initial investigation of the infants' behaviors suggested that infants below 30 months of age retain behavioral flexibility and responsiveness under at least some conditions (Crittenden, 1985a; Crittenden & DiLalla, 1984). This leads to the possibility that the behavioral accommodations shown by some infants to the deviant behavior of their mothers may be adaptive rather than defensive. The data on this sample give no indication of whether such adaptiveness remains as the children grow older, i.e., whether it is adaptive in the ultimate sense. The investigation discussed later explored the issue of adaptation across a wider age range of children than the Crittenden and DiLalla study.

Summary and Overview

The preceding discussion has focused on the nature of the mother–child relationship in maltreating dyads and on the problems surrounding assessment of it. The studies reviewed suggest that the mother–child relationship in maltreating dyads is atypical from the perspectives of mother as caregiver, interactant, and attachment figure; that the nature of the relationship varies with both the perspective on the relationship and the type of maltreatment; and that children develop response patterns to atypical environments that may enable them to cope more effectively with their immediate situation. Furthermore, with regard to the process of assessment, it appears necessary to assess separately each aspect of a relationship; to devise assessments that evoke, as much as possible, a behavioral enactment of each person's expectations of the other and that result in a functional evaluation of those behaviors; and to validate the usefulness of both standardized assessments as a whole and also the specific diagnostic categories before applying them to special populations.

These conclusions form the rational for the study to be reported here. The goals of this study were to replicate the finding that different qualities of childrearing were related to different qualities of relationship; to seek evidence of a compulsive compliant pattern of child interaction; to validate the expansion of the Strange Situation classificatory system; to seek developmental trends in the children's response to a maltreating environment; and to consider the immediate and long term significance of those trends.

METHOD

Subjects

The families studied were referred to the research director by five Protective Service Units of the Department of Social Services or, if the family was not maltreating, by a health provider, which in most cases was the Public Health Department. Because all of the referrals of maltreating families were for very low-income families, the adequate families were chosen to be at or below the income level for eligibility for public assistance; not all families were receiving such assistance, however. The families were grouped into five child-rearing groups based on protective service status. There were 22 abusing families, 31 abusing-and-neglecting families, 20 neglecting families, 22 marginally maltreating families, and 29 adequate families. The subjects were 121 mother–child dyads drawn from a sample of 124 families. (Three families were omitted because the child had not participated in the Strange Situation assessment.) In each case, the youngest child with complete data was chosen for inclusion in this study.

The children ranged in age from 2 to 48 months (mean = 24 months) and in every case the chosen child had experienced the type of childrearing implied by the mother's child-rearing group. Of the children, 72 were white and 49 were black. Sixty were female; 61 were male. Thirty percent were first-born; 36% second-born; 15% third-born; 19% fourth- through sixth-born. Their mothers ranged in age from 15 to 38 years (mean = 23.7 years). One third of the mothers were married with half of the abusing and adequate mothers having a husband, as compared to only 11% of the neglecting mothers. The mothers averaged a tenth-grade education with the adequate mothers having completed 11 years of schooling on the average and the neglecting mothers only 8 years. A fifth of the mothers were mentally retarded; these included 5% of abusing mothers, 23% of abusing-and-neglecting mothers, 72% of neglecting mothers, 18% of marginally maltreating mothers, and 6% of adequate mothers. The families had a mean of 2.6 children per family with the abusing-and-neglecting mothers have the most (3.0), and the abusing families the fewest (2.0).

Procedures

Each family was seen four times with additional visits if there was more than one child under the age of 4 years. The first visit was devoted to gathering family history data and to assessing the home environment. The second visit consisted of a developmental assessment of the child(ren). The third visit involved an extended observation of the children at home and videotaping of their interaction with their mothers. The final visit was carried out in the laboratory and consisted of each child's participation in a videotaped Strange Situation followed by a family interview. The data for this report were drawn from the first, third, and fourth meetings.

Mother as a Caregiver.   Previous samples reported by this investigator have been distributed among only three maltreatment groups: abuse, neglect, and marginal maltreatment (problematic). In reality, however, some of the children had experienced both abuse and neglect. In the past, these cases have been forced into either the abuse or the neglect group depending on which type of maltreatment was predominant. In most cases, this resulted in an abuse classification. The present sample was large enough to create a separate category, called abuse-and-neglect, for these children. Although no categorical system exactly reflects reality, the use of categories of maltreatment both highlights different developmental patterns and facilitates the clustering of information in ways that are useful to direct service personnel.

Mother as an Interactant.   Three-minute videotapes of mother–child interaction were made at the family's home (with the exception of a few which were made in the lab for the families' convenience.) In each case a small blanket was spread on the floor with a standardized box of toys nearby. Each mother was asked to play with her child as she ordinarily would and given no further instructions.

The videotapes were coded using the third revision of the CARE-Index (see Appendix). This revision differed from the previous ones in two ways. First and most important, it contained items describing a fourth child pattern of interaction, compulsive compliance. The compulsive-compliant pattern was developed from indications in the third Crittenden sample (1985a) that some maltreated cooperative children were wary and inhibited rather than genuinely engaged and happy. The compulsive-compliant pattern identified the behavioral aspects of this compliance. Second, this revision clustered the behavioral items around seven aspects of interactional behavior: facial expression, vocal expression, position and body contact, expression of affection, pacing of turns, control, and choice of activity. Each of the seven aspects had one item describing each of the three adult patterns, i.e., sensitive, controlling, and unresponsive, and one item for each of the four child patterns, i.e., cooperative, compulsively compliant, difficult, and passive. Each item consisted of a general description followed by one or more behavioral examples. In addition, each of the patterns was described functionally.

The coding process involved viewing the full 3-minute videotape and then making categorical judgments, worth 2 points each in scoring, amongst the three adult items for each of the seven aspects and, separately, amongst the four items describing child behavior. The tape was viewed a minimum of four times, each time viewing for different aspects of behavior. In cases where the observed behavior was partially described by two different items, the 2-point score could be split between them: only two-way splits were permitted. The scoring, thus, resulted in the allocation of 14 points among three adult patterns and, separately, 14 points among the four child patterns. These scale scores were the data used in the analyses reported below.

The interaction tapes were coded by five trained undergraduate coders. The coders were blind to both the hypotheses being tested and the mothers' child-rearing group status. Unlike previous studies using earlier versions of this assessment, each coder evaluated both mother and child behavior. This was done for two reasons. First, the three previous studies using separate mother and infant coders had already established the expected relationship between mother and infant behavior. Second, trial coding using this revision of the coding system indicated no differences in the codings carried out by separate coders as opposed to those produced by single coders. This probably resulted from the emphasis in the coding system on functional interpretation of behavior in the context of the interactant as opposed to quantitative identification of specific and discrete behaviors. The only difference resulting from the use of one versus two coders was a reduction in coding time from nearly an hour per dyad to less than one-half hour. This saving may make the device more feasible for use in nonresearch settings. The percentage of agreement was computed on a conservative item-by-item basis rather than on the more generous scale score that was used for analysis. The mean percentage of agreement on one third of the tapes for the five coders was 82%.

Mother as Attachment Figure. The Strange Situation was used as the assessment of mother as attachment figure. The avoidant-ambivalent (A/C) classification developed by Crittenden (1985a) was used in the present study as one of four basic patterns. With subgroups, this produced 10 possible classifications: A_{1-2}, B_{1-4}, C_{1-2}, A/C_{1-2}. The four main patterns were used for the analyses with the subgroups used for descriptive purposes only.

All of the children in the sample were assessed using the Strange Situation. In the 12 cases in which an infant was first seen at less than 11 months of age, the administration of the Strange Situation was delayed until the infant was 11 months old. Children over 24 months of age also participated in the Strange Situation even though previous research has shown that the Strange Situation is not sufficiently stressful to elicit attachment behavior in adequately reared, middle-class 2- and 3-year-old (Maccoby & Feldman, 1972; Marvin, 1977). The decision to include older children in this sample was made for two reasons. First, attachment theory predicts that securely attached children would, by 2 to 3 years of age, be able to use their mothers as a secure base from which they could explore extensively. The increased language and cognitive competence of these older children would facilitate their negotiation with their mothers of the conditions for safe exploration. Under such conditions, the brief separations encountered in the Strange Situation would not lead to anxiety and the activation of attachment behavior. Attachment theory does not, however, assert that anxiously attached 2- and 3-year-olds necessarily will develop the same confidence and autonomy; their developmental course may either be delayed or different, hypotheses that could best be tested by including older children in the Strange Situation procedure. Second, pilot work with some of the preschool-aged siblings of the children in the third Crittenden sample indicated that the brief separations in the Strange Situation did, in fact, arouse both considerable anxiety and also observable attachment behavior in these older maltreated children. Consequently, it was decided to systematically employ the Strange Situation with 24 through 48-month-old children. The scoring system was modified slightly to include verbal contact, as well as smiling and greeting, and to permit scoring a full approach and the maintenance of physical contact when the older child leaned on, held, or otherwise touched the mother without actually clambering on her.

Three trained undergraduate research rated and classified the Strange Situation videotapes. The raters were blind to both the hypotheses and the child-rearing group of the dyads. The percentage of agreement on the four major patterns was 90% on the 42 tapes classified by more than one rater.

RESULTS AND DISCUSSION

The results of this study were consistent with those of previous studies; maternal patterns of interaction varied as a function of child-rearing group as did child pattern of attachment to the mother. In addition, maternal pattern of interaction was related to child pattern of interaction as well as to child pattern of attachment to the mother. This study also validated the creation of the two new patterns of behavior: a compulsive compliant pattern of interaction and an avoidant-ambivalent pattern of attachment. Both patterns were associated with abuse or abuse-and-neglect of the child. In addition, developmental trends were identified for abused and neglected children that were distinct from the patterns shown by adequately reared children. In the sections that follow the results of this investigation with a fourth sample are presented in detail and discussed in terms of the relation between the three aspects of the mother–child relationship: mother as caregiver, interactant, and attachment figure. Concurrently, the evidence regarding the existence of the child compulsive compliant and avoidant-ambivalent (A/C) patterns are presented. Finally, the results of the analysis of developmental trends are considered.

Quality of Childrearing and Mother–Child Interaction

The results of the analysis of the videotapes of play interaction between the mother and child at home were consistent with those from previous studies using the CARE-Index within the same age range, (1 through 24 months). An analysis of variance indicated that abusing mothers tended to be controlling; abusing-and-neglecting mothers, both controlling and unresponsive; neglecting mothers, unresponsive; marginally maltreating mothers, somewhat sensitive; and adequate mothers very sensitive (see Table 5.1). Similarly, children of adequate mothers tended to be cooperative; those of abusing or abusing-and-neglecting mothers, compliant; and those of neglecting mothers, passive (see Table 5.2). Again, there was a relationship between maternal interactive behavior and child interactive behavior: maternal sensitivity was correlated .72 with child cooperation; maternal control .50 with child compulsive compliance and .50 with child difficultness; and maternal unresponsiveness .69 with child passivity (all correlations were significant at $p < .001$).

The findings for the older (25 through 48-month-old) maltreated children in this sample were similar to those for the younger ones, but expressed somewhat differently. The association between quality of childrearing and maternal pattern of interaction was significant only for maternal control (See Table 5.1). The data on child behavior, however, were more pronounced than for the younger children. Older children in all groups were more cooperative than younger children. In addition, older abused and abused-and-neglected children were more compliant and less difficult or passive than younger children. Overall, adequately reared children were the most cooperative, abused and abused-and-neglected the most compliant, neglected children the most difficult and the most passive (see Table 5.2). The correlations between maternal and child interaction scale scores were similar to those for the younger children with the exception that maternal control was correlated more strongly with child compliance and less strongly with child difficultness: maternal sensitivity was correlated with child cooperation (.74, $p < .001$), maternal control with child compliance (.72, $p < .001$) and with child difficultness (.24, $p < .044$), and maternal unresponsiveness with child passivity (.74, $p < .001$).

It could be argued that the interaction coding systems developed for dyads with an infant under 24 months of age neither adequately captured the salient aspects of the mothers' behavior with older children nor

TABLE 5.1
Maternal Interaction Scales By Child-rearing Group

Group Means and Percentages

Maternal Interaction	Abusing	Abusing/ Neglecting	Neglecting	Marginally Maltreating	Adequate	F	p <
Children < 25 mo.							
Sensitivity	4.20	3.95	4.11	5.33	8.46	4.99	.001[1]
Control	6.90	6.70	2.94	3.55	3.33	4.45	.003[1]
Unresponsiveness	2.80	3.35	6.83	5.11	2.13	5.87	.000[1]
Children > 24 mo.							
Sensitivity	7.25	6.36	5.00	7.07	8.50	.69	.597[2]
Control	4.41	4.54	1.50	4.38	1.57	2.40	.062[2]
Unresponsiveness	2.33	3.09	7.50	2.53	3.92	1.42	.240[2]

[1] F with 3 and 68 degrees of freedom.
[2] F with 3 and 48 degrees of freedom.

TABLE 5.2
Child Interaction Scales By Child-rearing Group

Child Interaction	Group Means					F	p <
	Abusing	Abusing/ Neglecting	Neglecting	Marginally Maltreating	Adequate		
Children < 25 mo.							
Cooperation	2.20	1.90	3.89	5.44	7.73	7.19	.0001[1]
Compulsive compliance	4.10	4.50	1.67	1.22	.87	5.81	.0001[1]
Difficultness	3.60	3.40	2.22	2.00	2.80	.56	.693[1]
Passivity	4.10	4.20	6.28	5.33	2.60	2.20	.078[1]
Children > 24 mo.							
Cooperation	5.50	5.80	1.00	8.77	8.71	3.35	.017[2]
Compulsive compliance	4.33	4.72	.50	2.54	1.14	3.13	.023[2]
Difficultness	2.08	.63	4.50	1.23	.28	2.48	.056[2]
Passivity	2.08	2.81	8.00	1.46	3.85	2.84	.034[2]

[1]F with 3 and 68 degrees of freedom.
[2]F with 3 and 48 degrees of freedom.

detected the negative affect in those children. It is certainly possible that another coding system would capture more of the age-specific aspects of the behavior of mothers and their older children. On the other hand, many of the coding items used here are relevant across the lifespan. These include turn-taking, voice tone, gaze behavior, facial expression, and attentiveness. What is surprising is that many maltreated children cease to use universally understood negative signals, e.g., scowling, turning away, refusing to comply, or protesting vocally.

A partial explanation for the apparent harmony of some of the maltreating dyads may result from a change in the demands of the interactional situation. Most mothers of the older maltreated children did not indulge in unstructured play. Instead, they chose a repetitive directive or teaching task. Moreover, the lessened salience of intimate dyadic play to older children may be relevant. Physical contact with the child was no longer necessary as it had been during early infancy. The aversion to close bodily contact shown by mothers of avoidant children (Ainsworth et al., 1978) would be likely to apply to many maltreating mothers of avoidant or avoidant-ambivalent children and to make interactions without contact more comfortable to the mothers. If, in addition, the older maltreated children had learned to inhibit negative signals and to become more compliant, the mother's job as a sensitive interactant would be considerably eased. To the extent that these children appear vigilant, affectless, and anxious to please, an additional pattern of child behavior, compulsive compliance, may be useful. The developmental change to the use of a compulsive compliant pattern could help to account for the improvement seen in both the maternal and child patterns of interaction. The question to be raised is whether such a behavioral change reflects an improvement in the quality of the underlying relationship between mother and child or whether it masks the feelings between them.

Quality of Childrearing and Pattern of Attachment

There was a significant relationship between maternal quality of childrearing and child pattern of attachment as assessed in the Strange Situation (∇ PRE = .43, $p < .001$) (see Table 5.3). The new avoidant-ambivalent (A/C) classification was associated with older and more severely maltreated children, particularly those who had been both abused and neglected. Children classified as A/C_2 had more often experienced serious neglect (87% of all A/C_2's) than serious abuse. The neglect group was most strongly associated with the avoidant pattern (50% of all neglected children), although all child-rearing groups had some A's; the A's in the adequate group tended to be A_2's. The anxious/ambivalent pattern (C) was

TABLE 5.3
Child Pattern of Attachment by Child-Rearing Group

Child Pattern of Attachment	Child-Rearing Group				
	Abuse	Abuse/ Neglect	Neglect	Marginal Maltreatment	Adequate
Secure (B)	5%	13%	10%	36%	59%
Anxious-avoidant (A)	36%	26%	50%	41%	31%
Anxious-ambivalent (C)	9%	3%	20%	14%	3%
Avoidant-ambivalent (A/C)	50%	58%	20%	9%	7%

split with the C_1 subclassification being associated with marginal maltreatment and the C_2 subcategory associated with neglect. The secure pattern (B) was associated with adequate childrearing. About half of the marginally maltreated children were classified as B_1, B_2, or B_4; most of the remainder were classified A_2 or C_1. With the exception of one abused-and-neglected child, all children classified as B_3 were adequately reared.

In terms of the assessment of quality of attachment, there was evidence that older maltreated children did not progress by 48 months of age to the goal-corrected partnership proposed by Bowlby (1969) for preschool-aged children. Instead, unlike adequately reared children, they remained disturbed by the mothers' brief departures in the Strange Situation. Although this could be considered a delay, it is quite possible that the nature of the relationship, i.e., the lack of security and mutual trust, did not change with development and represents a qualitative rather than developmental difference. The issue is whether older maltreated children were unable to venture away from their mothers because they were immature (behaving in a way that is normal for younger children and that is outgrown eventually) or because they were following a different developmental path. The lack of affect shown by maltreated children is not similar to the behavior of young adequately reared children. Likewise, older maltreated children showed ambivalence about seeking contact and derived little or no comfort from it whereas the contact seeking of young adequately reared children lead to their feeling comforted and able to venture forth from their mother to explore the environment. Because the behavior of older maltreated children was typical of very insecure children and not of younger adequately reared children, it seems inappropriate to consider them immature. Instead, further exploration of the nature of this alternative developmental path seems warranted.

Mother–Child Interaction and Pattern of Attachment

Finally, the mother's pattern of interaction during the play session was related to the child's pattern of attachment for both the younger and older children. Securely attached (B) children tended to have sensitive mothers, anxious-ambivalent (C) children tended to have unresponsive mothers, anxious-avoidant (A) children tended to have mothers who were both controlling and unresponsive, and avoidant-ambivalent (A/C) children had mothers who were highly controlling (see Table 5.4).

Some of the subpatterns were associated with particular adult patterns of interaction; of greatest interest are those subpatterns that are rarely seen in sufficient numbers in normative samples in order to provide a basis for generalization. The B_1 pattern was associated with older children of sensitive mothers. The B_4 pattern was associated with inconsistent mothers whose responsiveness could not be controlled or even predicted by their children regardless of the intensity of the child's behavior. These children appeared to have no strategy for engaging their mothers' protection other than to maintain body contact and no strategy for obtaining a feeling of security. In this context, the B_4 pattern appeared more similar to the anxious patterns than to the other B patterns. The C_1 pattern was associated with interfering mothers who tended not to attend to child behavior unless it was greatly intensified. These mothers did, however, tend to respond eventually and to be able to provide their children with some comfort and also to permit the development of a child strategy for obtaining the mother's attention. The C_2 pattern was associated with very withdrawn, unresponsive mothers who seemed unable to respond in any way to their child's distress. These children sensed their ultimate isolation and made no effort to seek any comfort from adults.

Mother–Child Interaction as a Function of Child Age

The results of previous work suggested that older abused children became more compliant and that their mothers were less controlling than those of younger abused children. Developmental trends in the interaction scales were, therefore, tested in this investigation. There were no linear or quadratic trends in any of the scales for marginally maltreating or adequate mothers or their children. On the other hand, in the two groups in which the children had experienced abuse, there was a significant (unique) linear relationship between greater child age and increased maternal sensitivity ($F_{1,45} = 5.70, p < .02$) and child cooperativeness ($F_{1,45} = 13.53, p < .001$, and a marginally significant (unique) linear trend for decreased child difficultness ($F_{1,45} = 3.85, p < .05$) and passivity ($F_{1,45} = 3.65, p < .06$). Thus, the interactions of older abused and abused-and-neglected children

TABLE 5.4
Maternal Interaction Scales By Child Pattern of Attachment

Maternal Interaction Scale	Child Pattern of Attachment					
	Secure (B)	Anxious/ Avoidant (A)	Anxious/ Ambivalent (C)	Avoidant/ Ambivalent (A/C)	F	p <
Children < 25 mo.						
Sensitivity	7.5	4.9	5.5	3.7	3.60	.01[1]
Control	4.7	4.2	2.5	6.3	2.86	.04[1]
Unresponsiveness	1.7	4.7	6.0	4.0	3.98	.01[1]
Children > 24 mo.						
Sensitivity	10.0	6.2	8.4	6.4	2.79	.05[2]
Control	1.5	3.5	4.0	4.5	1.69	.18[2]
Unresponsiveness	2.4	4.2	1.6	3.0	1.44	.24[2]

[1] F with 3 and 68 degrees of freedom.
[2] F with 3 and 48 degrees of freedom.

and their mothers appeared less angry and more smooth than those of younger children. Similarly, there was a nonsignificant trend for the passivity of the neglected infants to give way to increased difficultness in older neglected children, suggesting a change in their means of coping with an unresponsive environment.

These date reflected developmental trends suggesting directions for further research. Maltreating mothers with 2- and 3-year-old children appeared more likely to be sensitively responsive than maltreating mothers with younger children. Their children appeared to be more cooperative and less difficult and passive. Significantly, child compliance began increasing at 12 to 18 months, whereas maternal sensitivity and child cooperation did not increase until 18 to 24 months. This suggests that child compliance (and reduced difficultness and passivity) may lead to less need for overt maternal control and the apparent increase in maternal sensitivity. It is even possible that, in the context of less difficult child behavior, the abusive mothers learned how to respond more sensitively to their children.

In addition, infant passivity in the face of maternal unresponsiveness appeared to change in older children to a more aggressive approach to dealing with maternal behavior. These data do not indicate whether older neglected children demand more of their mothers or merely protest their lack of responsiveness more. In either case, the behavior may change the nature of the mother–child relationship considerably. As they become less passive, neglected children's behavior may either push their very depleted mothers too far, thus incurring a hostile response, or it may function to engage their withdrawn mothers in interaction. Such a change in strategy may be adaptive in reducing the children's helplessness and maximizing the potential responsiveness of their mothers. It may also be dangerous if it results in maternal anger and abuse. The suggestion from the birth order and child age data is that where neglected toddlers live in homes with several other children, increased difficultness leads to the family's moving from the neglect group to abuse-and-neglect group as the intellectually limited neglecting mothers try to cope with increasing numbers of competing demands. When few other children are in the family, the mother may, under the pressure a limited number of increased demands, be able to respond to some of her child's needs. In that case, the young child is less likely to experience abuse and the strategy may be more consistently adaptive.

CONCLUSION

This chapter represents an attempt to expand our knowledge of attachment in cases where the relationship itself is at risk. The major conclusions are: (a) that assessment procedures applied to atypical populations must be carefully validated on those populations and possibly modified before being employed in applied settings; (b) that different types of child-rearing environments are related to different patterns of mother–child interaction and different patterns of child attachment to the mother; and (c) that some of these patterns change as a function of child development, thus, possibly, changing the nature of both the child-rearing environment and the mother–child relationship.

Expanding Classificatory Systems

The proposal of a new pattern of attachment brings up issues regarding the universality and comprehensiveness of the patterns. The original three major patterns and their eight variations identified by Ainsworth and her colleagues were based on observations of 56 white, middle-class infants and have served well in identifying patterns of attachment in other similar samples. As Ainsworth pointed out (Ainsworth et al., 1978), however, it is unrealistic to expect than these 56 infants would embody all possible patterns. Without extensive studies of other cultures, ethnic groups, social classes, and child-rearing styles, it is premature to speculate about the total number of patterns that best describe the behavior of infants. What may be more important is the universality of the underlying dimensions, i.e., proximity seeking and contact maintaining, resistance, and avoidance, which Ainsworth has identified. Although the eight original patterns were not sufficient to account for the range of behavioral organization in the low SES maltreated samples reported here, the underlying dimensions were. This type of validation of the applicability of the dimensions to a variety of ecological situations may prove more useful in the long run than attempts to specify fully the variations in the patterns, i.e., the behavioral organizations of the dimensions, which are applicable to all infants.

It seems fairly clear from data presented here and in other studies that both maltreated children and maltreating adults show atypical behavior (Burgess & Conger, 1978; Crittenden, 1981; Egeland & Sroufe, 1981; George & Main, 1979). Furthermore, both parents and children appear to experience unusually high levels of stress on a daily basis. This stress is seen as contributing to the anger, hostility, and/or withdrawal of the parents. Their children tend to respond with negative signals, passivity, avoidance, and/or resistance. At least this is how it generally appeared. Now it seems that under sufficiently greater stress, that is, risk to the relationship itself, all of the responses listed above, except extreme hostility and withdrawal, tend to be replaced by desperate, anxiety-ridden approximations of normal behavior. This is true of both mothers and infants. The most severely abusing mothers were not openly hostile; they were pseudo-sensitive. The most severely abused children were not difficult; they were compulsively compliant. The children most stressed in the home showed proximity seeking in the Strange Situation.

Adaptation and Development

The developmental trends in the data suggest a changing pattern of behavior in maltreated children's adjustment to their environment. All of the very young infants in this investigation gave direct, universally understood, and genetically based signals regarding their state and needs. Similarly, all the children formed attachments with their mothers. Such behavior is adaptive in the context of a sensitive and available mother. When the infants' actual experiences were of maltreatment, however, they appeared to learn to modify their behavior to fit the constraints of their actual situation. Accommodation to reality is also adaptive at least in the sense of increasing the probability that the children will survive to reproduce. Thus, two points are suggested. First, adaptive behavior changes as a result of the interaction between genetic predispositions, development, and environment; it is not necessarily the same from one age to another nor across all situations. Second, it is not clear whether, having adapted to unfavorable circumstances, maltreated children can remain sufficiently flexible to modify their behavior further if conditions improve.

Of particular concern is the abused child's tendency to inhibit universally understood signals of displeasure even in situations that clearly warrant protest. Such inhibition may reduce the likelihood of the child's threatening her/his mother's security and incurring her wrath, but it does so at a potentially high cost. The child's internal feelings are consistently denied by her/his behavior. Moreover, the child is rewarded for this deception. Because the pattern begins when the child is very young, certainly too young to be aware of this process, the outcome for the child may be confusion regarding her/his actual feelings and the source of those feelings as well as a sense of impotence regarding the resolution of them. This may be maladaptive for the individual's long-term development and relationships with others.

Attachment theory proposed that the maintenance of affectional bonds, particularly the bond between a mother and her young child, is essential to the survival of the human species and a compelling individual need. The data from this study suggest that those people who are most at risk for destroying their love relationships altogether devote the most intense effort toward maintaining the semblance of bonds; inept mothers and their children scrap and feud; mildly abusing mothers and their infants are hostile and difficult, but many severely maltreating mothers and their children do not dare to challenge the durability of their relationships. Rather, they struggle to hide from themselves and from each other the tenuous nature of their bonds; it is as though they fear that a simple dispute could become an uncontrollable attack on the relationship. Such disasters cannot be risked often. This suggests that the pseudo-sensitive behavior of maltreating mothers and the pseudo-cooperative behavior of maltreated children are not false fronts offered to the prying observer, but rather reflect an armed peace protecting the interactants from themselves. Only those who have completely given up, who are totally depressed or angry beyond control, can withdraw from relationships entirely. These are the most tragic casualties a family can produce.

If this is so, procedures for assessing the quality of relationships need to be modified to include these more extreme form of behavior. The creation of an A/C category for the Strange Situation has been suggested as has the modification of the infant codes to differentiate a compulsively compliant pattern of interaction and to better describe the behavior of older maltreated children. Finally, the older children should be assessed in situations that neither force them into close proximity with their mothers nor threaten them with separation. It may be that, in these less dangerous situations, the older children express more negative emotions. Whatever the changes, they should be clearly tied to the functional meaning of behavior and to ecologically valid information. Without such external validation, it is possible that behaviors alone may guide our research rather than the function and meaning of behavior.

ACKNOWLEDGMENTS

This research was supported, in part, by the National Center on Child Abuse and Neglect, Administration for Children, Youth, and Families, DHHS Grant # 90-CA-844. Additional support was received from the Charlottesville-Albermarle Association for Retarded Citizens and the Departments of Social Services in Charlottesville, VA and the counties of Albemarle, Fluvanna, Greene, Louisa, and Nelson.

REFERENCES

Ainsworth, M. D. S. (1984, April). *Attachment, adaptation, and continuity.* Paper presented at the International Conference on Infant Studies, New York.

Ainsworth, M. D., Blehar, M. C., Waters, E., & Wall, S. (1978). *Patterns of attachment: A psychological study of the strange situation.* Hillsdale, NJ: Lawrence Erlbaum Associates.

Bowlby, J. (1969). *Attachment and loss,* Vol. 1: *Attachment.* New York: Basic Books.

Bowlby, J. (1980). *Attachment and loss,* Vol. 3: *Loss.* New York: Basic Books.

Burgess, R. L., & Conger, R. D. (1978). Family interaction in abusive, neglectful, and normal families. *Child Development, 49,* 1163–1173.

Cicchetti, D., & Rizley, R. (1981). Developmental perspectives on the etiology, intergenerational transmission, and sequellae of child maltreatment. In R. Rizley & D. Cicchetti (Eds.), *New directions for child development: Developmental perspectives on child maltreatment* (Vol. 11, pp. 31–57). San Francisco: Jossey-Bass.

Crittenden, P. M. (1981). Abusing, neglecting, problematic, and adequate dyads: Differentiating by patterns of interaction. *Merrill-Palmer Quarterly, 27,* 1–18.

Crittenden, P. M. (1985a). Maltreated infants: Vulnerability and resilience. *Journal of Child Psychology and Psychiatry, 26,* 85–96.

Crittenden, P. M. (1985b). Social networks, quality of child-rearing, and child development. *Child Development, 56,* 1299–1313.

Crittenden, P. M., & Bonvillian, J. D. (1984). The effect of maternal risk status on maternal sensitivity to infant cues. *American Journal of Orthopsychiatry, 54,* 250–262.

Crittenden, P. M., & DiLalla, D. L. (1984, April). *Compulsive compliance: The development of an inhibitory coping strategy in infancy.* Paper presented at the meeting of the International Conference on Infant Studies, New York.

Deitrich, K. N., Starr, R., & Weisfeld, G. D. (1983). Infant maltreatment: Caretaker–infant interaction and developmental consequences at different levels of parenting failure. *Pediatrics, 72,* 532–540.

Egeland, B., & Farber, E. A. (1984). Infant–mother attachment: Factors related to its development and changes over time. *Child Development, 55,* 753–771.

Egeland, B., & Sroufe, A. (1981). Developmental sequellae of maltreatment in infancy. In R. Rizley & D. Cicchetti (Eds.), *New directions for child development: Developmental perspectives on child maltreatment* (Vol. 11, pp. 77–92). San Francisco: Jossey-Bass.

Egeland, B., Sroufe, L. A., & Erickson, M. (1984). The developmental consequence of different patterns of maltreatment. *Journal of Child Abuse and Neglect, 7,* 459–469.

Gaensbauer, T. J., & Harmon, R. J. (1982). Attachment behavior in abused/neglected and premature infants: Implications for the concept of attachment. In R. N. Emde & R. J. Harmon (Eds.), *The development of attachment and affiliative systems* (pp. 263–280). New York: Plenum Press.

George, C., & Main, M. (1979). Social interactions of young abused children. *Child Development, 50,* 306–318.

Kempe, C. H., Silverman, F. N., Steele, B. B., Droegemueller, W., & Silver, H. K. (1962). The battered child syndrome. *Journal of the American Medical Association, 181,* 17–24.

Lamb, M. E. (1976). The role of the father: An overview. In M. E. Lamb (Ed.), *The role of the father in child development* (pp. 1–63). New York: Wiley.

Maccoby, E. E., & Feldman, S. S. (1972). Mother-attachment and stranger-reactions in the third year of life. *Monographs for the Society for Research in Child Development, 37*(1, Serial No. 146).

Main, M. (1979). The "ultimate" causation of some infant attachment phenomena: Further answers, further phenomena, and further questions. Commentary on Rajecki, D. W., Lamb, M. E., & Obmascher, P. Toward a general theory of infantile attachment: A comparative review of aspects of the social bond. *Brain and Behavioral Sciences, 2,* 640–643.

Main, M. & Solomon, J. (in press). *Discovery of an insecure-disorganized/disoriented attachment pattern: Procedures, findings, and implications for the classification of behavior.* In M. Greenberg, D. Cicchetti, & M. Cummings (Eds.), *Procedures for assessing attachment in the preschool years.* Chicago: University of Chicago Press.

Main, M., & Weston, D. (1981). The quality of the toddler's relationship to mother and to father: Related to conflict behavior and the readiness to establish new relationships. *Child Development, 52,* 932–940.

Martin, H. P., & Beezley, P. (1976). Personality of abused children. In H. P. Martin (Ed.), *The abused child: A multidisciplinary approach to developmental issues and treatment* (pp. 105–111). Cambridge, MA: Ballinger.

Marvin, R. S. (1977). An ethological-cognitive model for the attenuation mother–child attachment behavior. In T. M. Alloway, L. Krames, & P. Pliner (Eds.), *Advances in the study of communication and affect. Vol. 3. The development of social attachment* (pp. 25–60). New York: Plenum.

Mash, E. J., Johnson, C., & Kovitz, K. (1983). A comparison of the mother–child interactions of physically abused and non-abused children during play and task situations. *Journal of Clinical Child Psychology, 12,* 337–346.

Matas, L., Arhend, R. A., & Sroufe, L. A. (1978). Continuity and adaptation in the second year: The relationship between quality of attachment and later competence. *Child Development, 49,* 547–556.

Radke-Yarrow, M., Cummings, M., Kuczynski, L., & Chapman, M. (in press). Patterns of attachment in two- and three-year olds in normal families and families with parental depression. *Child Development.*

Rajecki, D. W., Lamb, M. E., & Obmascher, P. (1978). Toward a general theory of infantile attachment: A comparative review of aspects of the social bond. *Brain and Behavioral Sciences, 2,* 640–643.

Robinson, E., & Solomon, F. (1979). Some further findings on the treatment of the mother–child dyad in child abuse. *Child Abuse and Neglect, 3,* 247–251.

Schneider-Rosen, K., Braunwald, K., Carlson, V., & Cicchetti, D. (1985). Current perspectives in attachment theory: Illustrations from the study of maltreated infants. In I. Bretherton & E. Waters (Eds.), *Growing points in attachment theory. Monographs of the Society for Research in Child Development* (pp. 194–210).

Wasserman, G. A., Green, A., & Rhianon, A. (1983). Going beyond abuse: Maladaptive patterns of interaction in abusing mother–infant pairs. *Journal of the American Academy of Child Psychiatry, 22,* 245–252.

Yates, A. (1981). Narcissistic traits in certain abused children. *American Journal of Orthopsychiatry, 51,* 55–62.

APPENDIX: CHILD–ADULT RELATIONSHIP
EXPERIMENTAL INDEX (CARE-INDEX)

This coding system is being developed for research purposes only. It has not been examined for its suitability for applied use and, because very highly trained coders are required, may give results that are easily misinterpreted. In particular, the items marked "a" are often confused with the preceding items. Diagnostic statement based on this assessment are unwarranted at this time because investigations of the reliability and validity of this assessment in applied settings have not been carried out and because many different conditions are associated with lower sensitivity as assessed on the device (Crittenden & Bonvillian, 1984).

The behavioral items listed below cover seven aspects of interactional behavior. For each there are three types of adult descriptions: (S)ensitive, (C)ontrolling, and (U)nresponsive. Following them are four types of infant items: (C)ooperative, (D)ifficult, (P)assive, and (C)ompulsive (C)ompliant. Items marked "a" are pseudo-sensitive controlling items; items marked "b" are openly angry controlling items.

Facial Expression

1. *Responsive*—alert, actively attentive, responsive to the situation and the baby's mood, i.e., with a young infant in face-to-face interaction the adult may slowly exaggerate normal facial expressions, with an older infant engaged in toy play the adult's face may be alert with low key supportive expression changes that reflect activity changes (nods, slight smiles, etc.);

   Functions to attract or maintain the infant's attention either to the adult or to the activity;

   Infants generally attend to the activity and show no avoidance of eye contact with the mother; their facial expression range from alert, serious concentration to playfulness (C);

   Score 1–2a if the adult has an unchanging omitting or self-conscious face but genuinely brightens during eye contact; score 1–3 for adults showing steady attention with a pleasant or neutral but unchanging expression (any eye contact must involve at least brightening to be considered sensitive).

2a. *Incongruous*—apparently happy but unchanging in spite of situational change, incongruous with the baby's affect or rigid, i.e., increasing smiling when the baby is distressed, laughing *at* a solemn or unhappy baby, alert but rigid, unceasing smiling when the baby is not smiling, ignoring the baby until cued to begin and then suddenly performing what appears to be a pseudo-engaged interaction for the observer;

   Functions to make the interaction appear happy and congenial when, in fact, the baby is not pleased with, and may even be in opposition to, the adult;

   The infants have rigid or masked expressions which are sometimes interrupted by sudden, full-blown "peak" expression that seem overdone, lack natural rhythm, and appear briefly at full intensity before disappearing equally quickly; these infants tend to avoid eye contact but to monitor the adult peripherally (CC).

2b. *Hostile or Angry*—angry, frowning, or disgusted, i.e., grimaces that occur whenever the child doesn't comply or succeed at a task set by the adult, glaring at the infant;

   Functions to openly acknowledge the adult's disappointment in or anger at the child to either the infant or the viewer;

   Some infants look angry or alternate grimaces at the adult with interest in the activity; the infants tend to actively avoid eye contact with the adult and appear wary and fearful when they do have eye contact (D);

3. *Impassive*—dull, inattentive, blank, or expressionless, e.g., looking away, glazed and unchanging expression;

Functions to reduce the infant's interest in the adult and the activity while concurrently signalling the adult's lack of involvement in the interaction;

Young infants generally appear inattentive and bored (vacant expression, eyes wide open but unseeing and unblinking or downcast and dull, glazed)—there is often a subtle evasion of eye contact in which the eyes drift just out of a direct line of gaze such that the infant appears available but consistently eludes contact (P);

Scores 2–3 for anger or pseudo-pleasure combined with boredom.

Vocal Expression

4. *Warm*—slow, gentle, and rhythmic; adjusted for the baby's age and state or mood, e.g., a higher than usual lilting or melodic voice with alert babies, a soothing voice with distressed babies, a voice with rhythmic "surprises" as in peek-a-boo! with playful babies;
   Functions to attract or maintain the baby's attention;
   Infants generally respond with increased attention, vocalization, and sometimes excitement (C);
   Score 4–5 for speech which sounds nervous or "silly" laughter and score 4–6 for gentle, well-paced speech which lack intonation.

5a. *Strained*—intonation and rhythm are exaggerated, overdone, or artificial sounding and often have a forced, too sweet quality, i.e., adult laughter when the infant refuses to cooperate or is distressed, cajoling, sugary voice in the absence of infant responsiveness;
   Functions to create a discrepancy between the apparent pleasantness of the adult's behavior and the resistance or distress of the infant;
   Infants may comply with adult demands for speech with rote answering or repeating of the adult's words in a flat, expressionless voice; other infants show inconsistencies in vocal expression (strained voice tone, displeasure at apparently pleasant activities and the reverse, a flat voice tone in spite of apparent involvement in the activity) (CC);

5b. *Angry*—openly hostile, irritated, or disgusted, e.g., shouting, muttering profanity, insults, or disparaging comments;
   Functions to inhibit the child or express adult displeasure;
   Some infants respond with angry fussing and vocalizing (D).

6. *Flat*—expressionless tone (lack of intonation change), low volume, slow or whispered speech, little or no vocalization, e.g., adult silence, monotone speech;
   Functions to reduce infant involvement with the activity and, especially, with the adult;
   Infants generally do not vocalize to such adults, their toy play is gen-

erally silent also; any vocalizations which they do make tend to be uninterpretable (P);
Score 5–6 when adults use a harsh voice that lacks intonation.

Position and Body Contact

7. *Comfortable and Accessible*—both adult and infant are seated comfortably, both have physical access to each other and the toys, and at least the adult can see the infant's face, e.g., holding the baby against the adult's body in order that the adult can look down at the baby's face and the baby can reach the toys and/or easily look at the adult for face-to-face play, sitting on the floor facing the baby with the toys between the adult and baby;
   Functions to facilitate involvement with the toys and with each other;
   Infants generally use at least their access to the toys; their position is comfortable and they respond with at least acceptance if not pleasure to adult contact (C);
   Score 7–8 for accessible positions accompanied by two or three nonintense intrusions or for appropriately positioned adults who cannot get access to a noncompulsive compliant child's face because the child holds his/her head down or away in active avoidance of the adult; score 7–9 for a behind positioned adult who holds the child especially tenderly or otherwise signals active involvement in a way that the infant could perceive.

8. *Intrusive*—either the infant is placed too close to the adult (especially in terms of face to face distance) or the adult suddenly and unexpectedly moves in the infant's space, e.g., poking infant, manipulating his body against his will, grabbing toys;
   Functions to create a general physical wariness and/or instances of infant distress or discomfort in reaction to the adult's behavior either because the infant is being made to comply physically with adult demands or because the infant is not able to predict and prepare for sudden instances of adult closeness;
   Infants usually respond with a wince, startle, or withdrawal resisting awkward positioning or intrusions (D); older infants, in particular, may inhibit resistance in a situation in which most people would feel uncomfortable; others appear to prevent intrusions by lowering their heads or turning away so as to achieve distance from the adult; they may appear excessively alert and still to the extent that an awkward body or limb position may be held unnecessarily (CC).

9. *Awkward*—adult and/or infant are positioned uncomfortably, with toys or infant's face inaccessible, or at a distance form one another or the toys, i. e., adult seated behind child, adult holding child in lap but

away from adult's body or suspending child from armpits, adult kneeling or bending over awkwardly rather than seated comfortably, placing infant so far from the toys that they are inaccessible;

Functions to reduce activity, especially interaction or contact between the adult and child;

Infants generally respond to adult distance by not seeking either visual or physical contact; to awkward placement with passivity or intermittent, mild fussing; and to distant toy placement by inactivity (P);

Score 8–9 for distant or awkward positioning accompanied by at least intermittent intrusions.

Expression of Affection

10. *Affectionate*—vocal, visual, or kinesthetic warmth of any type (because most adults are fond of infants and most adults do not show strong, overtly affectionate behavior in a brief play interaction, this item should be assumed unless there is evidence of items 11 or 12), e.g., gentle patting or stroking, tender holding, murmuring, smiling, joint laughter;

    Functions to express the adult's pleasure in the infant to him/her in a way that the infant could perceive;

    Infants generally respond by appearing happy and initiating or prolonging contact, such as eye contact, touching, or vocalizing, with the adult (C);

    Score 10–11 when the affectionate behavior seems awkward and forced but not hostile or unpleasant to the baby; Score 10–12 when the adult seems pleasant and attentive, but there is no overt expression of affection and little or no interaction between the adult and child.

11a. *Covertly Angry*—similar in morphology to affectionate or playful behavior but sharper and out of synchrony with the infant's behavior, e.g., physical contact which looks playful but is more like poking, jabbing, or pinching, teasing;

    Functions to permit the adult to irritate the infant or take pleasure in his/her distress without overtly appearing to do so;

    Infants tend to withdraw in this situation but some display ambivalence (both liking the playful attention and fearing the intrusiveness of the adult); approaches tend to be indirect (tentative, aborted, sideways or backwards, without eye contact) (CC).

11b. *Overtly Hostile*—openly angry or disgusted, e.g., shouting, jerking, rough handling, disparaging remarks to the infant, angry facial expression, glaring eye contact;

    Functions to express the adult's displeasure in the baby in a way that both baby and observers can recognize;

Infants generally respond with clear avoidance or anger and frustration (D).

12. *Uncaring*—conspicuous lack of emotion or affection, e.g., sitting silently behind or away from the infant, looking away from the interaction, showing no warmth, attention, or touching;

Functions to inhibit infant overtures to the adult;

Infants generally ignore the adult or, if they make an overture, it is partial and does not include eye contact, e.g. reaching toward the adult while turned away (P);

Score 11–12 if the adult seems both, annoyed with the baby or to be showing pseudo-affection, and inattentive or uncaring, i.e., holding a baby away from the adult's body, losing track of the activity, etc.;

Pacing of Turns

13. *Contingent*—timing adult turns on the basis of signals or cues from the infant in a clear effort to create a turn-taking dialog, e.g., giving a baby time to mobilize a response before stimulating him/her further, actively supporting a child's play by talking, nodding, etc. (even though only the child may actually handle the toys), playing take-turn games, conversing;

Functions to keep the adult and infant in an interaction with smoothly alternating turns each related to the other's behavior;

Infants respond by accepting adult overtures, initiating turns by offering toys, vocalizing, or attending to adult turns with expectation (C);

Score 13–14 for adults who offer a number of toys at reasonably paced intervals but who receive no signals from a noncompulsive compliant baby suggesting when another toy might be wanted or if something else is wanted; score 13–15 if adult offers toys or assistance infrequently but does so on cue from baby.

14. *Noncontingent*—adult turns seem to depend more upon adult inclination than any infant signals, e.g., repeatedly and rapidly offering toys before the baby has finished with the last, active involvement which interferes with the infant's activity, cutting off infant responses;

Functions to cause interruptions in infant activity and to prevent smooth turn-taking;

Most infants find it difficult to settle on an activity; instead many activity changes are made without smooth transitions from one to the next (the cause of the abrupt changes may be either the infant himself or the adult); often the infants spend more time in reactive avoidance of the adult than in an activity (D); other infants accept abrupt changes without any behavioral disorganization—them immediately switch to the adult's new interest (CC).

15. *Uninvolved*—lack of active adult involvement in the infant's play, e.g., long, empty pauses between instances of adult involvement or stimulation, parallel infant and adult play, no adult talking or activity;
Functions to prevent turns of adult and child interaction;
Some infants play alone without attention to, or active avoidance of, the adult; other infants do no play at all; any infant play that does occur is of very low intensity (P);
Score 14–15 for adults who interact only intermittently but whose acts are noncontingent.

Control

16. *Joint*—either or both partners may choose the activity but both are clearly enjoying it and taking turns playing together, e.g., coacting as in give-and-take games, observer/actor combinations in which one partner's turns consist of observation and encouragement for the other to continue;
Functions such that no obvious use of control is apparent, so that the wishes of both partners affect the process of the play;
Infants respond with willing involvement and a lack of resistance to adult suggestions (C);
Score 16–17 for cases in which the adult directs the play and the (noncompulsive compliant) infant accepts it but without clear pleasure and invitations for the adult to continue; score 16–18 if the adult seems attentive but offers very little to the play or seems pleased with the infant's play but reluctant to take a turn.

17. *Adult*—the adult controls the choice and duration of the activity in spite of clear signals that it is not liked by the infant, has been continued too long (or should be continued longer), or is too difficult, e.g., forcing an eager baby to sit through a demonstration, refusing to let a child play with a desired toy or to use it as he/she wishes;
Functions to impose the adult's will upon the child;
Some infants fuss, physically resist, refuse to play, or even throw toys away or at the adult (D) although others comply without any display of active interest and with mere rote involvement in the activity— some will even continue with an activity of their own choosing while at the same time meeting the adult's demands (CC).

18. *Infant*—infant play without the involvement of the adult, e.g., adult involvement only to refocus an inactive infant back on the toys, parallel play, no play at all (if the infant ignores an interfering adult and plays his/her own way, score 17);

Functions to give the infant full choice over the activity but only because the adult does not choose to be involved;

Infants either do not play at all (out of boredom) or play in a subdued manner (P);

Score 17–18 for intermittant, but controlling, involvement.

Choice of Activity

19. *Developmentally Appropriate*—the activity is both feasible and enjoyable as presented, e.g., offering sufficient assistance with a difficult toy to make it feasible without taking over the activity, offering a toy with highlighting that suggests an enjoyable way to use it;

    Functions to maximize the acceptance of the activity by the infant (all activities are deemed to be the adult's choice because the adult could change an inappropriate activity);

    Infants respond with acceptance of the activity and prolonged interest (C);

    Score 19–20 if the adult offers a difficult activity but the (noncompulsive compliant) infant either is not frustrated or uses the activity in some more satisfying way without adult disapproval; score 19–21 if the adult offers appropriate toys which the child plays with but which the adult does not highlight at all.

20. *Too Demanding*—the activity is too advanced, intense, or complex as presented, i.e., giving a small baby a toy to hold and not letting him/her put it in the mouth, offering an appropriate toy but being so structured about its use that the infant cannot enjoy exploring it, offering too many activities at once, offering overly intense interpersonal play;

    Functions to frustrate the infant;

    Infants respond with anger to the adult, fussing, and rejection of the toy (D); others persist without complaint in the face of clearly impossible demands (CC).

21. *Understimulating*—the activity is too boring, repetitive, or simple to hold the infant's interest, i.e., no activity offered, offered toys not highlighted and not encouraged once the infant uses them;

    Functions to leave the infant on his own to amuse himself;

    Infants become bored and vacant looking, play listlessly with an object without exploring its potential, or become involved in something outside of the interaction (P);

    Score 20–21 if the activity can be construed as both too difficult and not interesting to the infant or if periods of too intense involvement alternate with periods of little activity.

III

CONSEQUENCES OF ATTACHMENT SECURITY AND INSECURITY

6
Attachment and the Ontogeny of Conduct Problems

Mark T. Greenberg
Matthew L. Speltz
University of Washington

INTRODUCTION

The conduct problems of young children have become a focus of recent research within child clinical psychology, perhaps because of their potential to predict future maladjustment. Although the relationship between early conduct and later adjustment is complex and mediated by a variety of developmental and situational variables (Loeber, 1982), the notion that chronic problem behavior in early childhood portends future problem behavior, emotional instability, and delinquency in adolescence and adulthood is supported by several longitudinal studies (e.g., Olweus, 1979; Robins, 1966). The term *conduct problem* has not been defined with great precision for young children but is generally used to summarize a collection of antisocial behaviors including aggressiveness, chronic noncompliance, intense and immature emotional responses to limits (e.g., tantrums) and early forms of delinquency (e.g., stealing and lying). Although the summary labels for these behaviors vary considerably among researchers and clinicians (see Quay, 1979; Robinson, 1985), all refer to a behavioral pattern of strong child opposition to the rules of family, school, and/or community, a pattern that is often first observed clinically during the preschool years within parent–child dyads.

The apparent predictive power of early conduct problems has led clinicians to develop a variety of treatment regimens for use with the preschool child, and in some cases with his or her parent. This focus on secondary prevention stems from the hope that interventions with incipient forms of antisocial behavior during the preschool years may prove more effective

177

than interventions with the less malleable preadolescent or adolescent. Thus, clinicians from a variety of theoretical backgrounds have employed such divergent strategies as play therapy, social skills training, special pre-school curricula, and parent training in their efforts to improve the conduct and social competencies of young, oppositional children.

Of these different approaches, parent training based on principles of operant reinforcement and punishment has been the most commonly applied and the most frequently investigated treatment for child conduct problems during the past decade. The operant parenting model holds that a child's misbehavior is primarily a function of parental behavioral ante-cedents and consequences, and that the most effective and efficient way to change this behavior is by teaching parents to modify their interactions with their child. Among behavior therapists there is a strong belief in the efficacy of parent training for conduct problems (Forehand & McMahon, 1981) and much confidence in the power of operant learning variables to explain the development of child misbehavior in the parent–child dyad or family group (Patterson, 1976).

Although initial reports and enthusiasm by researchers and clinicians alike appeared to validate the operant parent training approach, it has been criticized on both philosophic and empirical grounds. First, despite the number of parent training studies showing short-term improvements in parent skills (with corresponding reductions in child deviance), a care-ful examination of long-term maintenance and immediate and subse-quent generalization of child behavior change reveals a less optimistic assessment of efficacy. Thus, the empirical results, which we subsequently review, lead us to question the belief that operant parent training effec-tively promotes generalized social competence in the majority of cases. Second, some behavior therapists have questioned the degree of one-sided control held over the child by the successfully trained parent and the effects of such strong parental control on the child's attributions and feel-ings of self-efficacy (Corson, 1976; Peterson, 1976).

Further, as developmental psychopathologists, we have been struck by two glaring deficiencies of the operant model, as presently formulated. First, there has been little or no attention devoted to understanding either the emotional or social-cognitive delays or deficits in either parent or child (or both) that may be an important part of the etiological puzzle that underlies the "conduct problem." Second, there have been few or no link-ages in the operant model between basic developmental research on early parent–child relationships and emotional development and the etiology of such problems (Maccoby, 1984; Robinson, 1985). Thus, presently there is a gulf between developmental understanding and clinical intervention that leads to treatment of the symptom (surface structure) rather than its fundamental basis.

We believe that attachment theory and its underlying developmental model as delineated by Bowlby (1969, 1973, 1980) can provide a more encompassing theoretical framework in which to embed previous explanatory models of some childhood behavior disorders. Bowlby's model of the development of attachment is particularly cogent because it synthesizes ideas from evolutionary theory, psychoanalytic and neo-analytic models (Ego Psychology, Object Relations Theory), learning theory, control systems theory, and cognitive-developmental psychology. Importantly, it provides an explanatory framework that carefully elaborates the developmental changes both in the infant and in the dyadic interaction. These developmental changes involve progression through hierarchically-organized levels from: (a) behavioral interaction (attachment behaviors); to (b) the organization of behavior systems; to (c) the development of representational models of both the self and other and the manner in which such models both influence and are influenced by observable behavior.

Further, we believe that attachment theory can provide not only an etiological framework, but also lead to a new model(s) for treating conduct disorders during the preschool years. One model (Speltz, in press) draws from attachment constructs associated with the developing partnership between the parent and preschooler (Bowlby, 1969, 1980; Marvin & Greenberg, 1982). These ideas are then integrated into a revised model of dyadic skills training which recognizes the influence of parental "operants" in maintaining child misbehavior within the context of their entire relationship.

In this chapter, we first describe the prevailing operant learning formulation of child misconduct and the standard parent training procedures that reflect this formulation. Then, we briefly review the research on parent training efficacy with respect to immediate outcome, maintenance and generalization. We then review attachment theory and research relevant to the development of conduct problems in young children and propose a multipathway model of parent–child conflict that reflects the developmental changes in the child, the parent, and the attachment relationship. Finally, we outline some of the clinical implications of this approach. We are hopeful that an integrated review and discussion of both the behavioral parent training literature and attachment theory and its formulations will: (a) highlight both the critical differences and potential points of congruence between these approaches; and (b) emphasize the potential for comparative treatment outcomes studies that would test the relative efficacy of such models.

OPERANT FORMULATION OF CONDUCT PROBLEMS

Operant conceptualizations of oppositional child behavior focus on the relatively immediate interpersonal antecedents and consequences of a specific child behavior. Patterson has offered the best articulated formulation of this process which focuses on the effects of negative social reinforcement on the parent–child dyad (Patterson, 1976; Patterson & Reid, 1973). Called an S-R-C paradigm (parent aversive stimulus-child response-parental consequence), the escalation of conflict is viewed as follows: the parent places a limit on the child's behavior (e.g., gives a command to put toys away), the child responds with behaviors highly aversive to the parent (e.g., whining, crying, aggressiveness) that persist until the parent responds further by withdrawing or terminating the original limit (i.e., the parent "gives up"). The child's aversive behaviors are negatively reinforced and the probability of their future occurrence is enhanced.

An important second part of Patterson's formulation concerns the further escalation of coercive behavior in the dyad. Going back to the preceding example, instead of withdrawing the limit, the parent may respond to aversive child behavior with aversive behaviors of his/her own, for example, repeating the command in a loud, angry voice, coupled with verbal threats, criticism of the child, and so on. The child, in turn, may increase his/her aversive behavior, leading to a further increase in parental coercive behavior until the child complies, thus negatively reinforcing the parent's use of increasingly more aversive tactics. Whether the child "wins" by getting the parent to give up, or the parent "wins" by getting the child to comply, each party's coercive behavior is reinforced strongly by the other in reciprocal fashion, with each member of the dyad essentially "training" the other to use coercive behaviors as the primary strategy for social influence. This is a process that Patterson has called the "negative reinforcement trap."

Wahler (1976) adds to Patterson's formulation the role of positive reinforcement in maintaining child misconduct. An example often given by behavior therapists is the child who exhibits tantrum behavior when told to go to bed. Rather than responding to the tantrum as proposed in the S-R-C paradigm (i.e., with withdrawal of the limit or an increase in coercive behavior), the parent in Wahler's "positive reinforcement trap" responds with behaviors potentially pleasing to the child, for example, explaining to the child the rationale for bedtime, asking the child why she/he is upset, making attempts to confront the child or talk her/him "out of" the tantrum. These sources of positive verbal and possibly physical attention are believed to serve as rewarding consequences for the child behavior that precipitated them. The effects of a positive reinforcement trap might be particularly evident in a relationship in which parental verbal or nonverbal attention to the child is relatively infrequent and obtained most reliably when the child challenges parental limits.

The operant viewpoint thus conceptualizes oppositional child behavior as a product of observable parent–child interactional patterns that are characterized primarily by the reciprocal reinforcement of coercive behaviors. Although inadvertent positive parental reinforcement of oppositional behavior is considered, behavior therapists generally assume that negative reinforcement is the more influential process in generating problem behavior (Forehand & McMahon, 1981). Empirical support for the coercion hypothesis has come from studies that have compared the family interactions of children referred for clinical treatment of aggressive or oppositional behavior with the family interactions of nonproblem children (Delfini, Bernal, & Rosen, 1976; Patterson, 1976).

Role of Developmental and Cognitive Variables

The formulation presented thus far has focused on immediate interactional variables associated with current manifestations of child problem behavior. This formulation does not explain the long-term development of these maladaptive parent–child interactions; nor does it explain clearly why some dyads develop high rates of coercive control although others do not. Behavior therapists, with their change-oriented emphasis on variables that maintain current behavior—rather than variables of historical importance—generally have had little to say in this regard. An exception is Patterson (1976) who has offered a "developmental viewpoint" on the coercive child. According to this analysis, infants have certain unconditioned "pain control" techniques for eliciting maternal attention, caregiving, and so on. For example, the infant's screaming when he/she is cold or hungry is an aversive stimulus that influences parent's attentional behaviors by negatively reinforcing the maternal behaviors that terminate the stimulus. Patterson (1976) assumes that by age 2 most children have learned a wide range of behavioral alternatives to these primitive coercive responses of infancy. However, Patterson believes that some parenting behaviors encourage the retention of the child's primitive responses, e.g., a failure to teach and reinforce prosocial behaviors; positive reinforcement, or inconsistent punishment of coercive behaviors. Thus, Patterson's developmental analysis of coercive behavior suggests that: (a) parent–infant relationships are characterized, in part, by a coercive cycle of interaction in which the parent's satisfaction of the infant's needs are negatively reinforced by a cessation of "aversive" infant behaviors; and (b) in most parent–child relationships, this cycle is replaced by more socially appropriate patterns of interaction as the child matures and acquires less coercive ways of eliciting attention and care.

In operant formulations of coercive behavior no causal significance is given to child or parent cognitive variables. Such variables are recognized, however, but primarily as *consequences* of the coercive patterns noted. Patterson (1976) briefly alluded to "alterations" in parent and child self-esteem that accompany the presence of chronic coercive cycles in the family system. However, such alterations were not specified and it is unclear how cognitive variables within this model might further influence the maintenance of coercion.

PROCEDURAL CHARACTERISTICS OF OPERANT PARENT TRAINING

The operant formulation of oppositional behavior leads naturally to an intervention that teaches parents to avoid positive and negative reinforcement traps and to replace these maladaptive interactions with behavioral contingencies that promote prosocial behavior or punish undesirable behavior. In one of the major, research-oriented parent training programs, Forehand and his colleagues developed a two-phase training model that is intended to meet these objectives (Forehand & McMahon, 1981). The goal of the first stage is to train the parent to attend to different contingences during play interaction, deliberately giving or withholding attention (e.g., looking, touching, talking, shouting, praising) as they continuously evaluate the desirability of the child's behavior. Well-trained parents, then, have learned to praise and look at their children periodically as they play quietly and carefully, abruptly turn away when inappropriate behavior is first noticed and quickly turn back to praise their children when they return to acceptable behavior. Techniques and procedures for enhancing the impact of both the delivery and withholding of parent attention are emphasized. Parents are taught, for example, to use *labeled* praise that specifically labels the appropriate child behaviors that preceded the praise (e.g., "good job of playing quietly and carefully with the blocks"), and to increase the saliency of the praise by adding physical affection and direct eye contact. Some behavior therapists also teach the parent to use on occasion a verbal, "when/then" prompt that tells the child under what immediately following conditions parent attention can be obtained (e.g., "when you ask politely, then I will listen"). Phase 1 in the Forehand model thus encourages parents to view their attention as if it were something tangible, something to be given and withheld in a deliberate, systematic fashion, depending on a quick appraisal of child behavior.

Forehand and McMahon call the second phase of their intervention "compliance training." Parents are first taught how to modify the antecedents of noncompliant behavior, primarily interactions having to do with the giving of commands and instructions to the child. They are encouraged to give concise, direct, and specific commands (e.g., "put the blocks away on the shelf") rather than indirect commands (e.g., "let's put the blocks away"); vague commands (e.g., "be a good girl"); or question commands (e.g., "would you like to put the blocks away now?").

Once a command is given, the parent is instructed to give the child a 5-second opportunity to comply. If the child does so, specific verbal praise is given. Any child behavior within the 5-second interval that does not follow the parent's command is regarded as noncompliance, including an outright refusal, ignoring of the parent, asking the parent for a rationale, attempts to negotiate the specifics of the requested task, and so on. After 5 seconds have elapsed, the parent is taught to give a single warning for a time-out consequence: "If you don't put the toys away, then you will need to sit in the chair." If the child continues to be noncompliant for another 5 seconds after the warning, time-out is used. After the time-out is over, the parent is trained to repeat the direction and to follow through with the same procedures until the child eventually complies. Throughout all of this, the parent is encouraged to be as calm and matter-of-fact as possible, moving quickly through the command-warning-punishment sequence in an efficient and business-like manner. It is believed that when the parent behaves in this way, the potential for coercive escalation is reduced as well as attentional rewards for the child's noncompliance.

One important extension of the standard training model is a child-directed play activity with parent called, "Child's Game," by the Forehand group. Originally developed by Hanf (1969), Child's Game is a play situation that enables the parent to rehearse Phase 1 skills directly with the child as the therapist observes and coaches. Age-appropriate toys are made available to the child and the parent is told to allow the child to lead whatever play activity results, occasionally describing to the child what he/she is going ("you're stacking the blocks"), praising frequently, and above all, refraining from giving the child commands or making critical statements. Among the several research groups that have studied child-directed play, there have been some important variations in the intended purpose of the play as well as specific procedures. Whereas Forehand and McMahon (1981) view child-directed play primarily as an opportunity for parents to rehearse specific operant skills in the clinic, other therapists (Eyberg & Robinson, 1982; Speltz, Beilke, Cantor, & Wiltuner, 1985; Wimberger & Kogan, 1974) emphasize more the potential effects of the play on the quality of the parent–child relationship, the child's self-esteem, sense of autonomy, or perceptions of control over parent caregiving.

Evidence for the Effectiveness of Operant
Parent Training

There are many factors that cannot be reviewed within the scope of this chapter that preclude a simple, dichotomous evaluation of parent training efficacy. These include the many procedural variations in method and context of training, the different ages of the children served, differing severity of presenting problems, length of treatment, therapist experience, and so on. The evaluation of this field is also complicated by the relatively narrow measures of overt interaction that have been used as the primary assessment of outcome. Although these measures provide good informa- tion about the parent's acquisition of specific skills (e.g., praising, giving commands) and the child's compliance to the parent, they provide very lit- tle information about *typical* parent–child interaction, the child's social relations with others, or change in child cognitive variables (self-esteem, social problem-solving) or affect. Despite these problems, 20 years of par- ent training research have produced findings of sufficient number to permit several conclusive statements about overall effectiveness (for more detailed and comprehensive reviews, refer to Graziano, 1977; Moreland, Schwebel, Beck, & Wells, 1982).

Immediate Treatment Effects.   There is ample evidence in support of immediate posttreatment changes in specific parenting behaviors and child deportment with the parent. The strength of this conclusion is based primarily on the consistency of positive results from early single-subject studies in which parents were taught a few simple strategies for responding to a child "target" behavior (Johnson & Brown, 1969; Patterson & Brodsky, 1966; Patterson, McNeal, Hawkins, & Phelps, 1967; Wahler, Winkle, Peterson, & Morrison, 1965: Zeilberger, Sampen, & Sloane, 1968). These studies were unanimous in reporting positive change, although this degree of success may in part reflect the fact that case studies with negative or no effects are rarely published. Nevertheless, the opti- mism that followed from these findings led to the development of more extensive, standardized treatment packages that were evaluated in quasi- experimental group studies. These investigations produced mixed results with some finding that both observational measures and parent question- naire data indicated desirable change (Forehand & King, 1974; Patterson, 1976), although others found improvement only in parents' questionnaire responses (Eyberg & Johnson, 1974; Ferber, Keeley, & Shemberg, 1974).

Efforts to employ comparisons with random assignment of families to control and treatment groups began to appear in the mid-1970s. The results of these studies also varied, with some reporting significant differ- ences between treatment and control groups in the expected direction

(Patterson, Chamberlain, & Reid, 1982; Peed, Roberts, & Forehand, 1977; Webster-Stratton, 1984) and others finding no differences using the same or highly similar training procedures (Anchor & Thomason, 1977; Bernal, Klinnert, & Schultz, 1980; Fleischman, 1981). Patterson (1987), in his review of these findings, suggested that the studies with negative results may have suffered from a time-limited format and the use of inexperienced student therapists. Nevertheless it is striking that a sizeable proportion of the controlled outcome studies in this area have not found immediate treatment effects using measures that are highly sensitive to the content of training.

Maintenance of Treatment Effects. Most investigations reporting immediate treatment effects found that these changes persisted over time, as indicated by follow-up assessments ranging from 12 months (Forehand, et al., 1979; Patterson & Fleischman, 1979) to 54 months after treatment (Baum & Forehand, 1981). These results suggest "good maintenance" but it is important to consider family drop-out rates (as high as 55% in the Baum & Forehand, 1981 study) and the fact that some "deviant" preschool behaviors (e.g., crying, whining, tantrumming) may occur less frequently as the result of maturation (replaced, perhaps, by more "mature" forms of problem behavior not captured by follow-up measures). Because there have been no follow-up comparisons with untreated control groups identified at the time of treatment, the influence of this factor is unknown. Moreover, the focus on observable interaction during these follow-up assessments again does not provide a clear picture of how the child is doing generally. A parent–child dyad may "look good" during a brief therapist observation of interaction despite continuing problems in generalized child adjustment. This possibility is suggested by a 1-year follow-up study by Charlop, Parrish, Fenton, and Cataldo (1983) who found that over 90% of trained parents were satisfied with what they had learned from the program, but 49% reported that their child's presenting problem still existed and 77% reported that their child was currently receiving treatment services elsewhere.

Generalization of Treatment Effects. As operant procedures focus on a limited set of behaviors and usually on only one dyadic relationship, the generalization of effects across persons, settings, and behaviors is a crucial index of effectiveness. For parent training to be considered a successful intervention, the child's behavior change with parent should generalize to other social relationships. This is a critical issue, as the nature of operant training may limit some forms of generalization. For example, the very structured, inflexible nature of the trained parent's response to misbehavior (one command, one warning, and time-out) or very consistent reward of good behavior, may depart so thoroughly from the responses of most adults that the child easily discriminates this special disciplinary situation and will behave well only when these conditions are clearly in effect.

Research on the generalization of parent training effects has produced both positive and negative findings. Humphreys, Forehand, McMahon, and Roberts (1978) found that parents' acquisition of new skills within the context of intervention with identified problem children generalized to transactions with siblings. Wells, Forehand, and Greist (1980) reported positive generalization in a sample of children treated successfully for one targeted behavior who showed desirable posttreatment changes in other behaviors not specifically targeted for change (tantrums, crying, aggressiveness).

Generalization of improved child behavior across untreated settings and social relationships has not been found, and some research suggests that negative transfer, or "behavioral contrast" (Johnson, Bolstad, & Lobitz, 1976), can occur in some cases. Johnson et al. (1976) studied this possibility in a sample of 12 children who displayed behavioral problems in either their home *or* school environments. These children were observed in both settings but participated in a behavioral treatment intervention (parent training or classroom-behavior management) only in the environment in which their problem behavior was evident. These investigators found that out of 7 children who responded favorably to the classroom intervention, 6 showed an *increase* in deviant behavior in the home from baseline to postclassroom intervention. Likewise, 4 of 5 children showing a positive response at home to parent training manifested more frequent inappropriate behavior in their classroom from baseline to termination.

Responding directly to this research, Forehand and colleagues added pre–post observational measures of child deviant behavior at school to their standard home evaluations of parent training outcome. School data reported on 24 treatment children and their nontreated peers (Breiner & Forehand, 1981; Forehand et al., 1979) revealed no evidence of either positive generalization or behavioral contrast.

Conclusions.   Although there is some empirical evidence to support the effective use of operant parent training, its status as the preferential treatment for preschool conduct problems is not justified, given the lack of evidence thus far for generalized change in child adjustment. We believe that the lack of generalization may be due to the strong focus in this training model on parent control and child compliance, as well as an extreme adherence to a reductionist view of personality (see Reese & Overton, 1970; Robinson, 1985; Sroufe, 1983). This view of personality is characterized by: (a) an ahistorical perspective that ignores questions of ontogeny and almost exclusively addresses questions of immediate causation; (b) little recognition of biological, species–specific propensities that affect both the structure and patterning of survival-focused behavior systems; (c) a failure to incorporate critical developmental maturational changes in the child's competencies (language, symbolic representation and cognitive structures, locomotor skills, etc.) and how these capabilities influence behavior; and (d) little recognition of the interface between the child's changing developmental skills and the transactional manner in which these changes are affected by and influence complementary changes in the child's surrounding ecology (including parental behavior systems).

Operant parent training formulations and intervention have targeted children during a period of rapid developmental change, i.e., toddlerhood and the preschool years, but have not been influenced significantly by the broad knowledge base regarding the effects of both cognitive and social development on the behavioral competencies of preschool children (Harris & Ferrari, 1983). Although operant approaches to childhood behavioral disorders are theoretically parsimonious, this has been accomplished at significant cost. On the other hand, it is important to acknowledge the advantages of the behavioral training model, including the existence of a researchable technology for the reduction of parent–child conflict and a treatment approach that lends itself easily to dyadic skills training procedures. Perhaps, by adding components to this model that reflect a broader conceptualization of child development and the parent–child relationship, the generalization of treatment effects can be enhanced.

ATTACHMENT THEORY AND RESEARCH

In elaborating our own approach that integrates developmental and behavioral formulations of preschool conduct problems, we have been strongly influenced by attachment theory. However, it is obvious that there have been theoretical additions and extensions as well as empirical explorations of these ideas by numerous researchers and theorists (Ainsworth, Blehar, Waters, & Wall, 1978; Bretherton, 1985; Main, Kaplan, & Cassidy, 1985; Marvin, 1977; Sroufe, 1979, 1983; Sroufe & Waters, 1977). Further, concepts are also drawn from concordant models of parent–child relations and personality development (Kegan, 1982; Mahler, Pine, & Bergman, 1975; Pine, 1985; Sander, 1975). We first review aspects of the theory itself. A review of empirical findings on the predictive relationship of early attachment and later behavior follows. Finally, we then contrast several developmental models that might explain such findings.

Bowlby (1969) proposed a developmental model of attachment that includes four phases during early childhood. Phases I and II occur in early infancy and are characterized by increasing differentiation of specific caregivers. During the second half of the first year, Phase III begins. This phase is linked to Piaget's Stage 4 of the sensorimotor period in which the child first shows primitive forms of object permanency, the differentiation of means and ends, and intentionality. Given suitable conditions of caregiving, the infant now develops a "set-goal" of a variable, but specified, degree of proximity or contact with specific attachment figures. Over the ensuing months children develop a wide variety of behavioral plans to achieve this set-goal (Bishof, 1975). Having been provided with sensitive caregiving, a child is able to balance her/his desire to explore the environment and fear of novelty by intermittently directing attachment behavior to her/his "secure base" (the attachment figure). One way to characterize the child's trust in the accessibility of her/his attachment figure(s) is by observing the balance of these various behavior systems (Bretherton, 1985).

Phase IV, which begins somewhere after the third birthday, is characterized by a new level of dyadic relationship termed *the goal-corrected partnership*. In this phase, the child and mother become increasingly able to construct and maintain joint plans for proximity and the attachment relationship is thus increasingly regulated by communicative and other symbolic processes (language, social inference) as well as by behavioral interactions.

In reviewing the contribution of attachment research, we primarily focus on Phase III of attachment because it has been studied in greatest detail. Later, we discuss the development of Phase IV and its implications for behavioral/personality disorders. However, it should be noted that attachment is a life-span concept, and it can be clearly distinguished from trait-life concepts such as dependency (Sroufe, Fox, & Pancake, 1983).

One of the major empirical contributions of attachment research has been the description of reliable and valid patterns of individual differences during infancy (Ainsworth, 1982; Ainsworth et al., 1978). Although these patterns of security (insecure-avoidant, secure, insecure-resistant) and a more recently noted fourth pattern (Crittenden, this volume; Main & Solomon, in press; Radke-Yarrow, Cummings, Kuczynski, & Chapman, 1985; Spieker & Booth, this volume) have been assessed through the use of the Strange Situation, Ainsworth's independent validation of these patterns by assessment of concurrent home behavior demonstrates their trans-contextual validity (Ainsworth et al., 1978; Main & Weston, 1982). Further, a series of independent replications with a variety of populations have now confirmed Ainsworth's original formulations that sensitive and responsive caregiving throughout the first year of life are predictive of secure attachment (Bates, Maslin, & Frankel, 1985; Belsky, Rovine, & Taylor, 1984; Egeland & Sroufe, 1981; Grossmann, Grossmann, Spangler, Suess, & Unzner, 1985).

ATTACHMENT STABILITY AND ITS CONSEQUENCES

Of particular important in attempting to establish a connection between infant attachment and later behavioral problems is the demonstration of: (1) the cross-time stability of attachment classification itself; and (2) the predictive validity of attachment security in infancy to later functioning. The stability of attachment classifications from 12 to 18 months has been reported in a number of projects. Stability estimates across this 6-month period have ranged from approximately 60% in high-risk samples to approximately 70% to 90% in stable middle-class samples (Owen, Easterbrooks, Chase-Lansdale, & Goldberg, 1984; Thompson, Lamb, & Estes, 1982; Vaughn, Egeland, Sroufe, & Waters, 1979; Waters, 1978). Further, instability in classification has been directly related to changes in family life stress and caregiving arrangements. At present there are no studies that have assessed the stability of individual classification past 24 months of age. Given the passage of time, one would expect lower rates of stability with longer intervals of measurement. Main et al. (1985), studying a carefully chosen middle-class sample, reported a high correlation ($r = .79$) between infant attachment classification and a 9-point rating scale of attachment security when children were 6 years of age.

Although the stability of attachment classifications has only been explored in the toddler period, a number of studies have examined the predictive validity of early attachment to later parent–child interaction and personality in a variety of samples. Matas, Arend, and Sroufe (1978) found that 2-year-olds who had been secure (B) as infants showed more persistence, enthusiasm, and positive affect in attempting to solve a series of increasingly difficult problem-solving tasks than did insecure children. The secure children also were more effective at seeking their mothers' assistance in the most difficult tasks. In contrast, resistant (C) children were whiney, negativistic, and easily frustrated by the task; and avoidant (A) toddlers were less compliant and less cooperative. Similarly, Main (1973) found that compared to toddlers earlier classified as insecure, secure toddlers showed more positive affect, more cognitively mature toy exploration, and longer attention spans in a free-play context.

Two recent longitudinal studies have examined the relationship between attachment security and toddler–parent interaction. Maslin and Bates (1982) examined the relationship between attachment security at 13 months and home observations of parent–child interaction at 24 months. They found that toddlers earlier classified as secure had lower levels of conflictive interaction with their mothers at 24 months than did avoidant or resistant children. Avoidant children showed particularly high conflict in the two interaction patterns that involved maternal physical restraint/contact. An examination of maternal control tactics indicated that mothers of avoidant and resistant toddlers were rated higher on restriction in control and thus lower on mutual, reciprocal control However, no differences were found on ratings of affection, consistency of maternal control, or maternal nonpunitiveness. High contact-maintenance in the Strange Situation at 13 months was also related to increased compliance at 24 months.

Erikson and Farber (1983) examined 2 and 4-year observations of parent–child interaction from the Minnesota High-Risk Study. This report followed children who had been classified as secure or insecure at *both* 12 and 18 months of age (approximately 60% of the total sample). Replicating the findings of Matas et al. (1978), they found that secure infants were more compliant, more enthusiastic and persistent in the problem-solving attempts, and expressed less anger and frustration than did the insecure toddlers. Gove (1982, as reported in Sroufe, 1983), using profile and cluster analysis to examine differential patterns of these infants at 24 months, found that resistant infants showed more mother-directed anger, whereas avoidant infants showed more object-related aggression and subtle forms of noncompliance. However, at 42 months, secure and avoidant infants looked quite similar in parent–child teaching interactions, whereas resistant infants showed significantly lower compliance, enthusiasm, persistence, and more reliance on their mothers for assistance. Finally, a number of studies have indicated a relationship between insecure attachment at 12 months and lower sociability and higher avoidance in later interactions with other adults (Londerville & Main, 1981; Thompson & Lamb, 1983).

Recently, the Minnesota High-Risk Study reported a number of findings concerning the quality of preschool behavior, peer relations, and measures of personality organization. Once again, in these reports only children who maintained a stable attachment classification from 12 to 18 months were examined. Sroufe (1983) reported that children classified as insecure as infants now showed higher negative and lower positive affect ratings in the preschool and that teachers rated these children as more compliant. The secure group showed less whining, and were higher in positive social engagement. Secure preschoolers also showed higher ego resiliency as assessed by teacher Q-sorts. Finally, Sroufe, Fox, and Pancake (1983) utilized a number of scales to examine preschool measures of dependency and its relationship to earlier attachment security. Results indicated that the secure group showed greater positive attention-seeking, whereas both avoidant and resistant groups showed greater negative attention-seeking as well as greater dependence on the teacher in self and social management contexts.

In summary, a number of independent projects have demonstrated that infant attachment security is related to optimal parent–child interaction, interaction with other adults, measures of personality functioning, and pre-school social behavior. Furthermore, the quality of early attachment has been specifically related to behaviors that are later associated with clinic referrals for treatment (whining, noncompliance, and negative attention-seeking) and that often serve as target behaviors in operant parent training programs. Thus, insecure infants may be more at risk for behavior disorders in the preschool years. This idea has recently received some support from two studies that directly address the relationship between early attachment and behavioral problems in 3- to 6-year-olds.

Lewis, Feiring, McGuffog, and Jaskir (1984) examined mothers' reports of psychopathology in their 6-year-olds using the Child Behavior Profile (CBP; Achenbach & Edlebrock, 1981) and related these findings to attachment classifications derived from a modified separation situation at age 1. Strong negative relationships were found for boys between early security of attachment and both internalizing and externalizing types of behavioral problems. Examining only those boys who scored above the 90th percentile on the CBP total score, it was found that 40% of the insecure group did so as compared to only 6% of the secure group. Further, infants who had been classified as resistant were most likely to show serious behavioral problems (60%), whereas infants who were avoidant were significantly, but less likely to do so (33%). However, no such effects were found for girls. A parsimonious explanation for this major sex difference was not obvious.

Bates et al. (1985), studied 120 children longitudinally from early infancy to age 3 years and examined the multiple factors that contributed to behavioral problems as measured by maternal report using the Pre-school Behavior Questionnaire (Behar & Stingfield, 1974). Previous reports had indicated that infant attachment was related to compliance and degree of parent–child conflict in parent–child interaction at 24 months. At age 3, using a multiple regression model, 1-year attachment ratings significantly predicted anxiety problems and showed a moderate relationship to mothers' ratings of hostility. However, no relationships were found between teachers' ratings of behavioral problems and earlier attachment status. Thus, although providing partial support for the hypothesis, the relationships were not highly predictive. Sex by attachment classification analyses were not reported. Finally, although the analyses presented were quite complex, no path analyses were reported that might have further elucidated both the direct and indirect effects (via 24 month parent–child interactions) of this complex phenomenon.

DEVELOPMENTAL MODELS: LINKAGES BETWEEN
INFANT ATTACHMENT AND LATER BEHAVIOR

The preceding review has provided some evidence of the relationship between infant attachment and preschool-age behavioral problems and competencies as well as characteristic child and parent behaviors associated with conduct disorders. However, findings on the prediction of behavioral problems are moderate at best and it is unclear how these effects are to be understood. At least four explanatory models should be considered.

The first model postulates that there is a direct causal effect between the infant's attachment and later behavior. This child attribute (Lewis et al., 1984) or "template" model (Main et al., 1985) asserts that the child acquires a trait or disposition to act in certain ways and that this trait directs future behavior. Such models also have been proposed to account for the effects of temperament on the developing child (Sroufe, 1985). However, this model appears inadequate for at least two reasons. First, it has been demonstrated that attachment is not a trait, as is evidenced by the independence of attachment classification to mothers and fathers (Sroufe, 1985). Second, the fact that changes in attachment classification are predictably related to environmental/family stress suggests continuing environmental influence (Lewis et al., 1984).

The second model attempts to explain continuity of relationships as a function of continuity of environmental influences at both points in time (Brim & Kagan, 1980). This model would predict that instability in classification, or in predictions to outcome, would be explained by changes in the environment, e.g., parent and familial stresses and supports that directly and/or indirectly affect the child. Although aspects of this model have received partial support from the preceding review of research, its simplicity belies the complexity of developmental transformations. As Main et al. (1985) have noted, this model portrays the child as only a reactive participant, rather than an active organizer of his/her own world. This passive view of the developing child is inconsistent with current models of development that emphasize the child's active behavioral and cognitive roles in influencing its environment and outcomes. Further, such a position would be incompatible with the belief that any intrinsic child variables (e.g., cognitive expectancies, temperament) influence development.

A number of theorists have recently proposed a third model in which these developmental continuities are mediated by the child's cognitive/affective schema(s) derived from his/her early relationship(s) (Bretherton, 1985; Main et al., 1985; Sroufe & Fleeson, in press). These "working models" of the self and other that the child constructs result from the behavioral and communicative transactions he/she experiences beginning in infancy. As Bretherton states:

Because the internal working models of self and attachment figures are constructed out of dyadic experience, they may at first be closely intertwined.
Indeed, in early development it may be preferable to speak of an internal
working model of the relationship (Main, Kaplan, & Cassidy, 1985). However, even when the models of self and other have become distinct, they
represent obverse aspects of the same relationship and cannot be understood
without reference to each other. For example, if an attachment figure frequently rejects or ridicules the child's bids for comfort in stressful situations,
the child may come to develop not only an internal working model of the parent as rejecting but also one of himself or herself as not worthy of help or
comfort. Conversely, if the attachment figure gives help and comfort when
needed, the child will tend to develop a working model of the parent as loving and of himself or herself as a person worthy of such support. (Bowlby,
1973, p. 12)

As the child's representational skills and understanding of affective
states become increasingly complex, these models undergo further speci-
fication and differentiation. Main et al. (1985) define the *internal
working model* "as a set of conscious and/or unconscious rules for the
organization of information relevant to attachment, and for obtaining
and limiting access to that information, i.e., to information regarding
attachment related experiences, feelings, ideations" (pp. 66–67). Thus,
individual differences in attachment behavior patterns are viewed as
manifestations of individual differences in the child's internal working
models of specific relationships.

Although the assertion that the child develops cognitive-affective representations of social relationships has been central to neo-analytic thought
(Fairbairn, 1952; Mahler et al., 1975; Sullivan, 1953), there has been little
empirical investigation of the development of these representations. Some
theorists propose that primitive working models exist by 12 months (Main
et al., 1985; Sroufe & Fleeson, in press), whereas other theorists, such as
Mahler, propose that partial models, e.g., of the "good" or "bad" object
(attachment figure), slowly develop and only become integrated in the
third year of life during the beginnings of the development of object constancy. Further, at present there is little understanding of how resistant
these working models are to revision given change in the quality of one's
relationships, or if there are any specific ages/stages during childhood in
which such models may become very resistant to revision. This seems
especially important in light of the empirical findings that changes in the
family environment are related to changes in attachment classifications.
As Bowlby (1980) makes clear, an individual may (and often does) hold
conflicting internal models of certain relationships. Moreover, the individual may have limited or no conscious access to one or more of these
models however strongly they may affect behavior and personality.

Given the complexity of these issues (Bretherton, 1985), it is not surprising that it is difficult at present to posit specific empirical predictions concerning the conditions that might lead to qualitative change in the child's working models at different developmental stages. Related to this issue of the stability of working models and their effect on later personality, Bowlby (1973) states:

> Yet it is not only environmental pressures that tend to maintain development on a particular pathway. Structural features of personality, once developed, have their own means of self-regulation that tend also to maintain the current direction of development. For example, present cognitive and behavioral structures determine what is perceived and what ignored, how a situation is construed, and what plan of action is likely to be constructed to deal with it. Current structures, moreover, determine what sorts of person and situation are sought after and what sorts are shunned. In this way an individual comes to influence the selection of his own environment; and so the wheel comes full circle. (pp. 368–369)

A strong version of this third model would propose that during late infancy the child develops cognitive-affective representations of self and other that reflect the nature of attachment interactions and that tend to resist revision. Further, these expectancies direct attention and behavior and lead to conscious and unconscious processes (such as cognitive distortions) that influence memory, attention, and affect (Main et al., 1985). Thus, given relative stability in caregiving, the child's working models will be self-perpetuating and mediate between early relationships and later personality and behavior. However, Bowlby has also stated that even though working models become increasingly resistant to change during childhood, they are continually being revised throughout childhood and adolescence.

We propose a fourth model that is an extension of the transactional model developed by Lewis and his colleagues (1984). We believe that a multipathway model is necessary that recognizes: (a) the transactional nature of developmental processes (Sameroff & Chandler, 1975); (b) the increasing role of the child's working models in directing behavior and thought; (c) the importance of developmental changes in the child and parent and the structure and process of their relationship during the period of infancy to the preschool years; and (d) the influence of changes in the parent–child relationship on the child's working models.

This model integrates certain aspects of models two and three that are based on two central assumptions. First, it is necessary to recognize that the continuity of caregiving across the preschool years has a significant influence on later functioning and that it is critical for models of continuity to explain the effects of discontinuity (Cicchetti, 1984). This is critically important in attachment research where stability is only moderately high across 6-month periods. Further, as stability has been found to be lower in high-risk populations that are more likely to show psychopathology later, it is especially important to account for factors that might produce discontinuities when attempting to use infant attachment classification to predict later problems.

A recent report of the Minnesota High-Risk sample (Erikson, Sroufe, & Egeland, 1985) provides support for this proposed fourth model. At 4½ to 5 years, 96 of the original 267 children were assessed by teachers' ratings of behavior on the Preschool Behavior Questionnaire and a new behavioral problem scale. Results indicated that infants classified as avoidant (A) showed greater withdrawal, less ability to persist, more impulsiveness and hostility, as well as higher total behavioral problem scores. The resistant group was not found to be different than the secure group. A subanalysis examining the effects of attachment stability between 12 and 18 months on later behavioral problems indicated that 85% of those infants with stable insecure attachments, 60% of these with unstable attachments (secure at one time, insecure at another), and 29% with stable secure attachments, showed significant later behavioral problems.

In order to examine what factors might lead securely attached infants to show later behavioral problems and insecurely attached infants to not do so, analyses of 24 and 42 month parent–child interaction, parental anxiety, quality of the home environment, life stress, and child developmental factors were conducted. Compared to the secure group without behavioral problems, the secure infants with later behavioral problems had mothers who were less supportive and encouraging at both 24 and 42 months, and at the later assessment were less effective teachers who provided little support, unclear expectations, and inconsistent limits. Further, at 30 months these homes had fewer play materials and less maternal involvement. These mothers also reported more confusion and disorganized moods states than did mothers of secure infants who did not later show behavioral problems.

Compared to anxiously attached infants with later behavioral problems, those without such problems had mothers who were warmer, more supportive, and more appropriate at limit setting at 42 months. The children were also more positive in their affect, and more compliant and affectionate with their mothers at 42 months. There were no differences at 24 months. The home environment of insecure infants without later problems contained more appropriate play materials and were characterized by higher maternal involvement. Thus, although the quality of early attachment was related in a predictable manner to preschool measures of behavioral problems, this association was in some cases mediated by later aspects of the parent–child relationship. As stated in Erikson et al. (1985):

In cases where the outcome changes (that is, the quality of the child's adaptation or behavioral organization does not fit the predicted pattern), we expect that there were changes in the quality of care and support. The findings here provide some evidence to support that expectation. Where securely attached children developed behavior problems, there was a pattern of inadequate maternal care and support at subsequent stages of development. And where anxiously attached children became well-functioning by preschool, their mothers were sensitive and responsive to the special needs of their children at later stages. (p. 165)

The findings of this study clearly support a multipathway model by demonstrating that information about early security of attachment in a stable environment *and* the effects of later parent–child relationships are necessary to predict later behavioral problems accurately.

A second assumption of this model is that the infant and toddler are continually attempting to interpret or "make meaning" (Kegan, 1982) of his/her experience in close relationships and that these developing cognitive models of self and other: (a) have an increasingly strong effect on behavior and personality; and (b) become increasingly resistant to change. However, we also propose that the child's working models are quite resilient and that in the early years of life may undergo significant change. Although attachment researchers have focused almost exclusively on the 12 to 18 month period, it may very well be that the child's working models are equally influenced by changes that occur between 18 months and age 3 to 4, in which significant structural and functional changes occur in the child, parent, and the parent–child relationship (Lieberman & Pawl, in press). This assumption necessitates incorporation of specific hypotheses into the model regarding developmental phase changes between infancy and the preschool years. Furthermore, in order to develop appropriate treatment recommendations that are derived from attachment theory, it is necessary to examine changes in the structure of attachment relations in the preschool years. It is to these issues that we now turn.

DEVELOPMENTAL CHANGES IN THE CHILD, PARENT, AND THEIR RELATIONSHIP

The Child

Although developmental psychology has been revolutionized by new knowledge regarding the previously unknown competencies of infants, it is during the period beginning at around 18 months that new and critical aspects of the development of "personhood" emerge. Maccoby (1984) presented an eloquent critique of the state of research on socialization and its relationship to the study of development. A central point of her thesis was that developmentalists studying socialization have almost exclusively focused on individual differences. In doing so there has been the implicit assumption that similar processes occur across stages of development. Moreover, this focus on individual differences has taken place at the expense of exploring the *developmental* changes in socialization. Maccoby elaborates on seven areas of developmental change in the child that have profound effects on parenting and subsequent personality development: physical and locomotor growth, language, impulsiveness, social-cognitive understanding, conception of the self, cognitive executive processes, and autonomy. We highlight some of these changes as they relate to attachment and the child's working models.

Using an object relations perspective, Mahler and her colleagues (Mahler et al., 1975) emphasized the importance of the transition to toddlerhood for personality formation. They described the process of separation-individuation, and the specific subphase of rapprochement that ushers in a significant structural change in the child and his or her social relationships. The toddler has an increasing desire for self-determination and control that co-occur with the realization of his/her individuality and sense of separateness. The child's newly acquired skills of locomotion, increased interest in exploration, the beginnings of both symbolic play and representation, the use of language, and the developing recognition of the self, all play important roles in the resolution of the child's separation-individuation crisis. Separation can be characterized as the intrapsychic achievement of a sense of separateness from the attachment figure(s) that leads to the child beginning to represent the self as distinct from the child's objects. This process of separation is dynamically interrelated to the development of the previously mentioned skills that constitute individuation. During this period that surrounds the second birthday, the child asserts control (sphincter control, toilet training, saying "no"), but also requires guidance and support from caregivers in order to develop a sense of autonomy (Erikson, 1963). Temper tantrums, which are ubiquitous at this stage, can be seen as an expression of the child's ambitendency, e.g., desire for control and yet need for the parent.

Although the foregoing description captures aspects of the second year of life that might affect attachment relations and security, a number of critical changes also occur during the third and fourth years (Marvin, 1977; Marvin & Greenberg, 1982). First, as cognitive/representational abilities increase, the child is increasingly able to anticipate and to plan longer and more complex sequences of behavior. Second, as language develops, the child is now able to represent the external world symbolically, discuss and consider nonpresent events, utilize internal talk to begin to control impulses, and begin to communicate and understand the feelings, attitudes, and desires of self and others. A critical development here is the child's ability to differentiate and discuss his/her internal states (Bretherton, Fritz, & Zahn-Waxler, in press; Pine, 1985). Third, the development of social-cognitive skills such as perspective-taking allow the child to begin to differentiate his/her own feelings and plans from those of the attachment figure(s). This last development is obviously predicated on the recognition of one's sense of self.

The Parent

The role of the parent also shifts in the second year from one characterized primarily by sensitivity and nurturance mediated by close physical contact to sensitivity that is characterized not only by warmth and affection, but also by providing appropriate limit-setting while simultaneously supporting the child's growing sense of independence and autonomous action. Further, the parent is now confronted by a more willful child with a separate sense of self, as well as a bundle of impulses, that need to be both accepted and guided. Optimal parenting in this stage might be characterized by a "relaxed-firmness" in which the parent allows the child to express his/her emotions fully, and also socializes the child by making important norms for behavior salient and by providing appropriate limit-setting when necessary.

   During this age range parenting includes a diversity of roles and behaviors that may appear conflicting or incompatible. Extending the ideas of Winnicott and Mahler, Kegan (1982) elaborated on three functions served by the embeddedness culture at each stage in development; holding on, letting go, and remaining in place. In this model, Kegan has borrowed concepts from different stages of development that powerfully illustrate the dynamic tension between agency (individuality) and communion (relationship) that characterizes the dialectic of development across the lifespan. The embeddedness culture at each stage of development is defined as that part of the social environment and/or self with which one is currently fused; subject–object distinctions have not yet been achieved. The embeddedness culture of toddlerhood is one's attachment figure(s). The first function provided by the caregivers is a "holding on" or nurturing function that supplies the child with the warmth and stimulation that is necessary for self-growth. The second function, letting go, lays the foundation for separation and recognizes the child's motion toward increasing differentiation of subject–object relationships, i.e., in this case, self versus others. Thus, letting go is the process of encouraging the person, at any stage, to further differentiate him/herself in both cognitive and affective domains. The development of a symbiotic relationship during toddlerhood would be an example of dysfunction in this process. Third, the culture of embededness functions to "remain in place" or "stay with" the person during the period of transition, when it is necessary for the child to repudiate the former self and reach a new equilibrium in which a new level of "meaning-making" occurs. In the toddler period an example of a difficulty in this function is when parents are not able to control their own affect when the child begins to attempt to assert his or her own needs in primitive ways such as temper tantrums.

These functions point to the complex nature of parenting during toddlerhood. It is important that the caregiver(s), in providing the holding environment, allow their children to express their ambivalence and anger while "remaining in place." Thus, the attachment figures' abilities to adjust to their children's growth and tolerate these direct expressions of ambivalence call for qualities that may not be as critical in infancy. We believe that the parents' own ego development, i.e., their ability to tolerate ambivalence and separation, are related to: (a) their ability to tolerate their children's struggle for separateness; and (b) their interest in, and ability to, appropriately express and label both their own and their children's emotions. Of course, both of these factors should be related to parents' own working models that, in turn, result from their own attachment-related experiences during development (Belsky, 1984).

The Parent–Child Relationship

As conflict between parent and child is inevitable in the preschool years, what is of crucial importance to the quality of their relationship is the manner in which the dyad handles such conflict. Further, we believe that conflicts regarding attachment-related interactions should be especially salient to the development of a wide range of competencies. An important goal of the parent–child relationship in this period is the development of strategies that both assist the child and parent in: (a) promoting autonomy; and (b) moving toward more mutual and reciprocal regulation of aspects of their relationship. Through this process, the child's autonomy is supported by assisting her/him in gaining more awareness of self and other, and by the increasing power of communication strategies that develop joint goals and plans.

As the child comes to differentiate his/her own plans, goals, and feelings from those of others, and becomes able to make inferences about and anticipate the behavior of others, a new structural level emerges in the relationship with the caregiver. When the child is able to recognize the degree of match between his/her own and the caregiver's desires/plans, both members of the dyad can begin intentionally to construct mutually agreed-upon plans for coaction. For Bowlby (1969), the hallmark of Phase IV of attachment, "the goal-corrected partnership," is the developmental achievement of joint planning between parent and child.

Although these "partnership skills" are general purpose skills that form the foundation for negotiation in a variety of later relationships (Marvin, 1977; Marvin & Greenberg, 1982), we believe that they have a major influence on the course of the attachment relationship for the following reasons. First, the development of the ability to develop such plans mutually alters both the structure (set-goal) and process of attachment interactions. Second, the manner in which plans are developed directly affects the child's sense of felt security and working models. Third, individual differences in attachment patterns should be reflected in the dyad's willingness and ability to develop such plans.

Marvin (1977) developed operational definitions of the goal-corrected partnership and utilized data gathered in the Strange Situation to examine strategies of negotiation prior to separation as well as at the child–parent reunion. He found that 25% of the 3-year-olds and 75% of the 4-year-olds attempted to construct or agreed to a plan regarding the separation. Further, those that did show such agreement responded to their mothers' return with relaxed, sociable patterns, without seeking their mothers' proximity. If a joint plan had not been reached prior to separation, upon reunion the children acted in a angry, controlling fashion, Neither pattern of partnership was found in 2-year-olds. Greenberg and Marvin (1979), in studying the developmental changes in attachment in profoundly deaf children, demonstrated the relationship between specific communication skills and the development of Phase IV.

Thus, in early childhood children build more complex and differentiated representational models of the self, the inanimate environment, and others. Accompanying the developmental shift to Phase IV, children's feelings of security are related to both the degree of match between the cognitive representations of their plans and goals and those of their attachment figures, as well as their actual behaviors in gaining, maintaining, and regulating physical proximity. Thus, although the parent's sensitivity to their baby's signals is a critical feature leading to secure attachments during infancy, in a similar manner, parents' abilities to mesh their goals and plans with those of their preschoolers by including children's desires and affects in the planning process will relate to children's security and trust in the preschool years. If parents share jointly in the development of plans for regulating those separations and reunions, children now come to realize that the relationship with the parent continues even when they are separated and thus promotes children's feelings of security and confidence upon separation.

This notion shares similarities with Mahler's ideas regarding the attainment of a certain degree of object constancy in which mental representations of the parent may substitute for his/her physical presence. However, as Van Leewuen and Tuma (1972) noted, at the beginnings of object constancy children react quite differently to separations that are under their initiation and control versus those that are initiated by their attachment figures. Moreover, even in children and adults with healthy attachments and object relations, a variety of temporary conditions or stressors (illness, long separations, parental insensitivity) may lead to regressive behaviors dominated by tantrums, extreme fear, and controllability that are characteristic of the rapprochement phase.

This change in the structure of the parent–child relationship is not punctuated, but rather is the result of interactions during the preceding year(s). Marvin (1972, 1977) proposed a phase termed the *emergent partnership* prior to the *goal-corrected partnership*. During the emergent partnership, the caregiver presents the overall structure of negotiation and joint-planning for the child and scaffolds these interactions in a manner similar to that described in the origins of parent–infant conversations (Bruner, 1975; Stern, 1977). That is, in early infancy the parent often takes both roles in the dialogue process, speaking both for herself and her infant. At this later age, a similar process occurs in which the parent teaches the child the use and structure of dyadic planning. That is, by initially supplying plans for both themselves and their child as well as making explicit both their internal state and that of their child, the parent assists the child in recognizing salient cues of the need for planning. Thus, the parent initially provides both structure and control for the child while helping the child learn how to make choices. As the child becomes increasingly able to take over these skills, more mutual regulation occurs. Importantly, this process allows the child both increasing control and a sense of effectiveness, but *within the structure that the parent creates.* That is, the child has input in the decision process, but seldom to the highest levels of decision in the hierarchy of the overall plan. For example, rather than asking the child if the parent can separate, the parent might ask the child if she/he wants to play with the blocks or color during her absence. Or, in a similar situation, rather than negotiating the ability to separate, the parent might both fill in the child's plan by providing information regarding the separation, the reunion, what the child might do in the interim, and what the dyad might do on her return. During this process the parent can solicit and utilize the child's input where appropriate. Thus, the parent both makes the child's world (especially around separation issues) less arbitrary and more predictable while giving the child some direct control over the course of their interaction.

Self-control is an important achievement of the preschool years. The ability to control impulses is greatly aided by children's developing abilities to use language to label and communicate their emotions. This developmental achievement has received scant attention in attachment theory, but has been emphasized by psychoanalytic theorists (Katan, 1961) and has recently been elaborated by Pine (1985). Through the naming of emotional states, the control function is aided. As Pine states, "words provide a moment of recognition and delay in which discomfort over a feeling might have a chance of being handled in other ways than through denial or imme-diate discharge through actions" (p. 139).

Clearly, the parent plays a crucial role in this developmental achieve-ment. Stern (1985) has eloquently discussed how the sensitive and responsive parent attunes to the child's affect at a nonverbal level during infancy. By doing so, the infant learns what affective states are sharable and allowable in social relationships. Similarly, one aspect of parental sen-sitivity and responsiveness during the preschool years is the ability to attune to and *discuss* the child's affective states. As Pine (1983) states, "the parent who labels feelings and inner states for the child brings them into the region of social communication–they are shared, the child is not unique and alone with them, they are capable of being understood, the power of words and the psychological achievements words facilitate can be applied to them" (p. 169). Thus, through the use of emotion language, the child develops greater affect tolerance and self-control, as well as a new way to cope with his/her needs and desires.

As the constructs of sensitivity and responsiveness are central to attachment theory (Ainsworth et al., 1978), it is surprising that there has been scant attention to the behavioral patterns that reflect these con-structs after infancy. In infancy, such optimal parenting leads the child to develop expectancies (primitive working model) that he/she will be cared for and responded to when necessary. This trust in the accessibility of one's attachment figure(s) leads the young child to feel secure and self-confident in explorations and to develop a working model of self as loveable and valuable. This process is brought about through countless daily behavioral responses of the parents and is reflected in the nature of the child's reactions to separations and reunions. We believe that during the preschool years nonverbal aspects of responsiveness and sensitivity are still very important to the child's working model. However, these con-struct will also be reflected in the communicative nature of the parent–child relationship as evidenced by: (a) the use of empathic emo-tion language by the parent; and (b) the nature of joint planning regarding separations and reunions.

As Marvin and Greenberg (1982) noted, the development of the child's social-cognitive and communicative skills and the parent's adaptation to the possibilities it presents may resolve the paradox of how it is that although the child is separating and individuating in both a psychic and physical sense, in other ways the relationship between parent and child moves to a new level of intimacy. That is, mesh of the relationship is dependent not only on the behavior of self and other but also on the thoughts, feelings, and projections of each other and the joint goals or plans that are constructed. Further, by examining both the dyad's ability to develop and maintain joint plans and the process by which they do so (including the moment-to-moment monitoring of each other), one should be able to infer the desired outcomes (goal-states) and the underlying working models of each individual (Marvin, 1977). However, certain aspects of attachment security may only be revealed in situations that are at least moderately stressful to the dyad such as when conflicting goals of each partner must be resolved in order to reach an acceptable joint plan (Greenberg, 1984).

Thus, the goal-corrected partnership can be viewed as a dyadic structuralization that regulates the needs/gratifications between parent and child as separate selves. The process of joint planning helps to strengthen the child's coping/defenses, and thus reduce the child's anxiety regarding separation by providing a cognitive-affective map or short-term, situational-based working model of his/her relationship. In this way, it assists in the control of anxiety during separations and increases the child's autonomy by providing a reality-based intersubjective plan of action. The nature of joint planning both affects and is affected by the child's current working model of the relationship. Further, the partnership is obviously affected both by earlier experiences and affects associated with the parent as well as earlier modes of defense in response to separation.

PATHWAYS LEADING TO PARENT–CHILD CONFLICT AND CONDUCT DISORDERS

As discussed previously, we believe that there are multiple pathways that might lead either to later competence or behavioral problems and psychopathology. A discussion of some of these possible pathways and their relationship to attachment security follows.

Although there may be other deficits shown by parents of children with serious conduct disorders, we believe that critical difficulties lie in the absence of appropriate sharing of joint goals and plans as well as the related skill of sharing and tolerating affective states in both the self and other. We separately discuss these two skills and how the quality of attachment relationships affects and is affected by their expression.

Issues in Joint Planning

This "deficiency in planning" hypothesis reframes the meaning of certain symptoms of conduct disorder and can account for both the effects of authoritarian or overcontrolling parenting, as well as for laissez-faire or undercontrolled, permissive parenting. For example, the aggressive and highly controlling behavior of some 4-year-olds can be seen as a futile or desperate attempt to gain control, i.e., affecting parent's internal plans and goals and thus future events. These patterns of coercion (Patterson, 1976) may in some cases be a disordered or protracted extension of attempts/efforts that arose during the individuation process and were met with overcontrolling patterns by parents (Campbell, Breavz, Ewing, & Szunowski, 1985; Mahler et al., 1975). Often these patterns escalate when the child is not able to secure the parent's attention and may be chronic patterns for eliciting attention or care in some children (Schneider-Rosen & Cicchetti, 1984). From an attachment theory perspective, these patterns of negative attention-seeking may be seen as the child's only successful way to elicit proximity and contact. Thus, although they may be well adapted to the child's ecology, they may also lead to later incompetence in close interpersonal relationships (Cicchetti, 1984; Crittenden, this volume).

However, the same or similar patterns of aggression and control might arise from situations in which parents are undercontrolling or extremely laissez-faire in their parenting (Baumrind, 1973). In such a situation, the parent does not require the child to consider the parent's plan in making his/her own plan. Thus, the parent is allowing the child to carry out his/her own plans without developing an awareness of the perspectives, needs, and feelings of others. As a result, the child is "unsocialized" and develops patterns of aggression or avoidance when thwarted by the parents. The lack of early limit setting and the attendant absence of the process of joint planning and sharing of internal states has led to a child who finds limit setting unacceptable.

A variant of this schema, which is probably more frequent, is a parent who is usually laissez faire but is occasionally (and probably unpredictably from the child's point of view) very overcontrolling or punitive. This is likely to lead to conduct problems because the child who does not have limits may unknowingly cause considerable damage or violate critical family prohibitions or sociocultural norms. This type of disordered structure of communication and limit-setting in the preschool years may be isomorphic to the characteristics of the parenting in infancy that lead to the anxious-resistant pattern (c), i.e., the parent is unpredictable or inconsistent with the child. The findings that anxious-resistant infants are more likely to show mother-directed anger at age 2 is consistent with this hypothesis (Maslin & Bates, 1982). A similar pattern in the child's attachment is often seen in certain families with deaf children where communication is particularly impoverished (Greenberg & Kusche, in press).

However, reaching agreement per se should not be interpreted as a measure of security or of the quality of the relationship. as stated earlier the *manner* in which the goal is reached may be of more importance than the actual outcome. Two counter-examples are as follows. An extremely compliant and fearful child may easily "give in" to the parents' demands for fear of stating her/his own position. Rather, such an anxious child instead "copes" by following the parent's plan (see Crittenden, this volume, in her discussion of compulsive compliance). This may be an indication of a very insecure attachment, a prototypical example of Winnicott's notion of the "false self" (Winnicott, 1965). In contrast, a securely attached child may easily accept the mother's plan even though it is contrary to her/his own, under the expectation that given the basic trust in their relationship, a positive outcome will ensue. This may be one example of how the development of security in infancy may lead to greater contextual flexibility and tolerance at later ages (Sroufe, 1979).

Thus, if acceptance of the plan is used as the sole criterion, trust and security may be confused with compliance. In the same light, not coming to an agreement would not always connote insecurity. A secure, but self-assured and feisty child may strongly disagree with the parent's solution and not give in. Thus, a full characterization of the communicative process, affective atmosphere, and style of the dyad is critical information in understanding their relationship.

Language and Affective Communication

Language serves the child's behavior and emotional control in at least two ways. First, its serves the internal executive function of mediating between intention and behavioral action. Deficiencies in this "second signal system," often termed *verbal self-control* (Vygotsky, 1978), have been clearly related to impulsiveness and behavioral problems (Kendall & Braswell, 1985). The second function of language is its use interpersonally to communicate one's internal state. Greenspan and Greenspan (1985) have described the toddler's progression from "being their affect" to representing their affective states symbolically and thus becoming able to work through affective conflict with the use of fantasy and pretend play, as well as through conversation.

As during infancy, the parent's ability to be responsive to the child's needs during situations of high emotional arousal (fear, anger, sadness), such as separation and reunions, is quite important. As all children, regardless of degree of attachment security, experience these emotions, it is the parent's ability to be responsive to its expression with empathy and labeling that helps show the child both that his/her emotional expressions will not overwhelm the parent and that these affects are sharable and tolerable experiences. Thus, the optimal parent is able to accept the child's expression of conflicting or negative affect, while also modeling for the child new ways to express these affects.

In relationships characterized by conduct-disorder there is often expression of negative affect, but these expressions are seen by the parent as intolerable and are often stimuli for the elicitation of coercive cycles. Thus, a maladaptive pattern is established in which the parent indicates to the child that her/his negative or conflicting affects are intolerable or "bad", but they do not assist the child to develop internalized control or more mature forms of emotional expression. A variety of maladaptive patterns may result. For example, the development of the false self, previously described, may eventuate from the child learning that indications of emotional needs are not sharable. Such a child learns to cope either by denying or repressing such affect and by developing a working model of the self and other in which need states are not expressed. A quite different pattern may result in relationships where the parents, themselves, have poor ability to control their affects, rarely communicate these affects verbally, and show an absence of joint planning. In this case, childhood impulse disorders are the likely scenario.

The study of deaf children, some of whom have received very poor early communication training, vividly illustrates the effects of the absence of emotional labeling and joint planning in families in which parental pathology is not a factor. In such cases, even with responsive parenting, the inability to discuss plans for future behavior delays the development of the goal-corrected partnership phase of attachment (Greenberg & Marvin, 1979). Additionally, the lack of communication and understanding regarding the labeling of emotional states during early childhood is related to impulsiveness and behavioral problems (Greenberg, Kusche, Gustafson, & Calderon, in press).

Summary

It is our belief that preschoolers who have developed cognitive-affective models of insecure attachment relationships are more likely to show behavioral problems than children with secure models of attachment. This is primarily due to insensitive, nonresponsive caregiving, which in turn leads to the child's acquisition of maladaptive patterns of emotional control and interpersonal communication. In many cases, *behaviors commonly labeled as "conduct problems" can be viewed as strategies for gaining the attention or proximity of caregivers who are unresponsive to the child's other signals.* In other words, the child may resort to conflict producing behaviors as his/her primary means of regulating caretaking. Given the preschooler's drive for self-control and self-reliance, conduct problems can also be understood as part of the child's affective reaction (often a mixture of fear, anger, sadness, and frustration) to his/her inability to otherwise regulate or have accessibility to attachment figure(s). Thus, the link between joint planning, emotional regulation and overt problem behavior is that all are critically involved in the regulation of the attachment relationship postinfancy. Just as nonverbal, proximal interactions are the mediators of attachment processes in infancy, these distal, and primarily verbal, behaviors serve the maintenance or development of attachment security and the child's sense of self and others in early childhood.

From the transactional viewpoint, the early quality of attachment does not directly affect later security or behavioral disorders. Rather, because sensitive and responsive caregiving is critical at both stages of development, it influences not only early security but also later planning and affective expression. However, both biological factors (temperament, developmental problems) in the child, as well as the child's earlier working model(s) also affect later attachment security. Thus, a child who has a secure attachment in infancy may be more likely to manage successfully stressors that may cause temporary perturbations in parenting and his/her social milieu (e.g., parent illness, family difficulties, divorce).

In many cases there will be continuity that is the result of the dynamic interplay of the self-perpetuating effects of the child's working model and the consistency in parenting across the stages of early childhood. However, there are certainly many cases of instability within these processes and a lack of continuity. In certain cases parents may be very sensitive during infancy and the infant develops a secure attachment, but begin to experience difficulty in negotiating the stage of autonomy and its attendant changes in parenting (Greenspan, 1981). A variety of clinicians have noted the damaging effects of maternal overprotection and the desire to maintain symbiosis during toddlerhood and beyond (Levy, 1943; Mahler, 1968). Mahler, as well as others, have presented case studies of (a) positive and responsive early parenting that later manifested serious difficulties during the subphase of rapproachement and beyond; and (b) mothers who had grave difficulties in infancy but who recovered and were more easily able to parent during the preschool years.

A related issue is our present lack of understanding of the different etiological factors that may account for certain pathways (Maccoby, 1984; Sroufe, 1985). For example, both the adaptation of the child who develops an extremely compliant pattern and that of a child who becomes aggressive and defiant are relatively incompetent. However, it is unclear if the divergence in these two maladaptive patterns is due to differences in caretaking, temperament, or other biological factors; reinforcement strategies by the parent; differences in early attachment; or some complex combinations of these factors that we might expect would be different for different individuals. Surely, there must be multiple factors interacting in such outcomes.

CLINICAL IMPLICATIONS

As the working model of the 4-year-old is becoming more stable and increasingly resistant to change, i.e., some degree of object constancy has been attained, it should be more difficult to alter the child's working model of both self and others. This aspect of cognitive/affective development may explain the lack of generalization in operant parent training programs. These approaches may temporarily, or possibly even permanently, improve the compliance of preschoolers, but they may do so at the cost of further reinforcing the child's working model that other's will be unresponsive to her/his own needs and feelings and that the modus operandi is to do what she/he is told. Such experiences are likely to reinforce the child's external locus of control and decrease her/his ability and/or desire to either monitor her/his own feelings or make them directly evident to others.

Thus, whereas in many instances an insecure attachment may be a critical precursor of later conduct disorders, the most commonly researched and well-known intervention (operant parent training) has as its goal to produce surface change, although it does not attempt to impact the "deep structure" of either the child's working model of relationships or of the parents' view of the child (i.e., "my child only complies because I learned new techniques, not because we have a warm, loving relationship"). In this sense, this approach may also undermine the parents' own abilities. This is not to say that behavioral techniques are not important or effective. They can be both; parents with harmonious relationships with their children use them continuously. The concern here is that their use in disjointed, disharmonious relationships is likely to do little to influence the organization of affect, personality, and sense of self and others. We should also note that the use of these techniques may be especially damaging in cases in which the child has been previously abused (Crittenden, 1985; Schneider-Rosen & Cicchetti, 1984), which is probably a considerable percentage of referrals for conduct disorders. Our concern lies with the belief that behavioral techniques give the parents a strong tool by which they can continue, or even escalate, their overcontrolling position in the relationship.

How would the formulation presented here add to, or modify, existing parent training programs? Speltz (in press) has described a dyadic skills training program that has evolved from Forehand and McMahon's (1981) model, but differs from this approach in several important ways: (a) the emphasis on child-directed play has been expanded with the primary goal of giving the child daily opportunities for the regulation (control) of parental caregiving; (b) child-directed play is used as a context within which the parents examine and are helped to modify cognitive attributions/expectations of specific child behaviors (Dix & Grusec, 1985); (c) parent–child separation/reunion situations are used to assist the parents to model and encourage specific negotiating and joint planning skills (e.g., constructing a plan, filling in child's part of the plan, helping the child to anticipate reunion); (d) the parents are shown how to discuss their own affects appropriately as well as to help their children to identify and label a variety of internal states; and (e) in order to enhance children's attributions of change to themselves as well as their parents, the children are included in discussions of parent "homework" assignments and are given assigned roles in these parent–child transactions. Further, we believe that in many cases there is a need to explore the parents' own attitudes and fears regarding their children's growing independence (Greenspan, 1981), as well as issues in their own working models regarding intimacy (Lieberman & Pawl, in press; Main & Goldwyn, 1984; Morris, 1980; Ricks, 1985).

In this model, then, important operant parenting skills (praising, limit-setting) are combined with skills that reflect the attachment-based cognitive and affectual variables presented in our formulation. This approach offers the advantage of including the child actively in the learning process; child and parent both learn to use negotiating skills that should have more global applicability in interpersonal conflict situations than teaching the parent simply to give directions and requiring the child to comply without recourse.

We believe that the proposed treatment model, which incorporates both behavioral and attachment-related constructs, leads to a number of empirically testable hypotheses. First, parent–child dyads containing a conduct problem preschooler should evidence less competent joint planning skills and fewer verbal communications regarding affect than dyads containing a well-adjusted child. Second, the dyadic training model described here should produce more generalized, cross-setting change in child overt behavior, cognitive functioning, and affective development than the standard operant approach. We are excited about these research possibilities and hopeful that this work will produce treatment models that bridge the existing gap between child behavioral therapy and developmental psychopathology.

ACKNOWLEDGMENTS

We would like to thank Drs. Geraldine Dawson, Robert S. Marvin, and Jay Belsky for the insightful critiques of earlier versions of this chapter. We would also like to thank the MacArthur Foundation Working Group on Attachment for their encouragement to explore the concept of attachment post-infancy.

REFERENCES

Achenbach, T. M., & Edlebrock, C. S. (1981). Behavior problems and competencies reported by parents of normal and disturbed children aged four through sixteen. *Monographs of the Society for Research in Child Development, 46* (1, Serial No. 188).

Ainsworth, M. D. S. (1982). Attachment: Retrospect and prospect. In C. M. Parkes & J. Stevenson-Hinde (Eds.), *The place of attachment in human behavior* (pp. 3–30). New York: Basic Books.

Ainsworth, M. D. S., Blehar, M. C., Waters, E., & Wall, S. (1978). *Patterns of attachment.* Hillsdale, NJ: Lawrence Erlbaum Associates.

Anchor, K. N., & Thomason, T. C. (1977). A comparison of two parent-training models with educated parents. *Journal of Community Psychology, 5,* 134–141.

Bates, J. E., Maslin, C. A., & Frankel, K. A. (1985). Attachment security, mother–child interaction, and temperament as predictors of behavior-problem ratings at age three years. In I. Bretherton & E. Waters (Eds.), *Growing points of attachment theory and research. Monographs of the Society for Research in Child Development, 50* (1–2, Serial No. 209).

Baum, C., & Forehand, R. (1981). Long-term assessment of parent training by use of multiple outcome measures. *Behavior Therapy, 12,* 643–652.

Baumrind, D. (1973). The development of instrumental competence through socialization. In A. D. Pick (Ed.), *Minnesota Symposium on Child Psychology* (Vol. 7). Minneapolis, MN: University of Minnesota Press.

Behar, L. B., & Stingfield, S. (1974). A behavior rating scale for the preschool child. *Developmental Psychology, 10,* 601–610.

Belsky, J. (1984). The determinants of parenting: A process model. *Child Development, 58,* 83–96.

Belsky, J., Rovine, M., & Taylor, D. (1984). The Pennsylvania infant and family development project II: Origins of individual differences in infant–mother attachment: Maternal and infant contributions. *Child Development, 55,* 706–717.

Bernal, M. E., Klinnert, M. D., & Schultz, L. A. (1980). Outcome evaluations of behavioral parent training and client centered parent counseling for children with conduct problems. *Journal of Applied Behavioral Analysis, 13,* 677–691.

Bischof, N. (1975). A systems approach toward the functional connections of attachment and fear. *Child Development, 46,* 801–817.

Bowlby, J. (1969). *Attachment and loss:* Vol. 1. *Attachment.* New York: Basic.

Bowlby, J. (1973). *Attachment and loss:* Vol. 2. *Separation.* New York: Basic.

Bowlby, J. (1980). *Attachment and loss:* Vol. 3. *Loss, sadness and depression.* New York: Basic.

Bretherton, I. (1985). Attachment theory: Retrospect and prospect. In I. Bretherton & E. Waters (Eds.), *Growing points in attachment theory and research. Monographs of the Society for Research in Child Development, 50* (1–2, Serial No. 209).

Bretherton, I., Fritz, J., & Zahn-Waxler, C. (in press). Emotions in the context of events: The acquisition and development of affect language. *Child Development.*

Brim, O. G., Jr., & Kagan, J. (1980). Constancy and change: A view of the issues. In O. G. Brim, Jr. & J. Kagan (Eds.), *Constancy and change in human development* (pp. 1–25) Cambridge, MA: Harvard University Press.

Bruner, J. (1975). The ontogenesis of speech acts. *Journal of Child Language, 2,* 1–19.

Breiner, J., & Forehand, R. (1981). An assessment of the effects of parent training on clinic-referred children's school behavior. *Behavioral Assessment, 3,* 31–42.

Campbell, S., Breauz, A. M., Ewing, L. J., & Szumowski, E. K. (1985). *Family characteristics as precursors of externalizing symptamology at school entry.* Paper presented at the Society for Research in Child Development, Toronto, Canada.

Charlop, M. H., Parrish, J. M., Fenton, L. R., & Cataldo, M. F. (1983). *Long-term follow-up of a large scale parent training program.* Paper presented at the American Psychological Association Convention, Anaheim, CA.

Cicchetti, D. (1984). The emergence of developmental psychopathology. *Child Development, 55,* 1–8.

Corson, J. A. (1976). Families as mutual control systems: Optimization by systematization of reinforcement. In E. J. Mash, L. A. Hamerlynck, & L. C. Handy (Eds.), *Behavior modification and families* (pp. 317–330). New York: Brunner/Mazel.

Crittenden, P. M. (1985). Maltreated infants: Vulnerability and resilience. *Journal of Child Psychology and Psychiatry, 26,* 85–96.

Delfini, L. F., Bernal, M. E., & Rosen, R. M. (1976). Comparison of deviant and normal boys in natural settings. In E. J. Mash, L. A. Hamerlynck, & L. C. Handy (Eds.), *Behavior modification and families* (pp. 228–248) New York: Brunner/Mazel.

Dix, T. H., & Grusec, J. E. (1985). Parent attribution processes in the socialization of children. In I. E. Sigel (Ed.), *Parental belief systems: The psychological consequences for children* (pp. 201–233). Hillsdale, NJ: Lawrence Erlbaum Associates.

Egeland, B., & Sroufe, L. A. (1981). Developmental sequelae of maltreatment in infancy. In R. Rizley & D. Cicchetti (Eds.), *Developmental perspectives on maltreatment* (pp. 77–92). San Francisco: Jossey-Bass.

Erikson, E. H. (1963). *Childhood and society.* New York: Norton.

Erikson, M. F., & Farber, E. A. (1983). *Infancy to preschool: Continuity of adaptation in high-risk children.* Paper presented at the Society for Research in Child development, Detroit.

Erikson, M. F., Sroufe, L. A., & Egeland, B. (1985). The relationship between quality of attachment and behavior problems in preschool in a high-risk sample. In I. Bretherton & E. Waters (Eds.), *Growing points of attachment theory and research. Monographs of the Society for Research in Child Development, 50* (1–2, Serial No. 209).

Eyberg, S. M., & Johnson, S. M. (1974). Multiple assessment of behavior modification with families: Effects of contingency contracting and order of treated problems. *Journal of Consulting and Clinician Psychology, 42,* 594–606.

Eyberg, S. M., & Robinson E. A. (1982). Parent–child interaction training: Effects on family functioning. *Journal of Clinical Child Psychology, 11,* 130–137.

Fairbairn, W. R. D. (1952). *An object-relations theory of personality.* New York: Basic Books.

Ferber, H., Keeley, S. M., & Shemberg, K. M. (1974). Training parents in behavior modification: Outcome of the problems encountered in a program after Patterson's work. *Behavior Therapy, 5,* 415–419.

Fleischman, J. J. (1981). A replication of Patterson's "intervention for boys with conduct problems." *Journal of Consulting and Clinical Psychology, 49,* 342–351.

Forehand, R., & King, H. E. (1974). Pre-school children's noncompliance: Effects of short term therapy. *Journal of Community Psychology, 7,* 229–242.

Forehand, R. L., & McMahon, R. J. (1981). *Helping the noncompliant child: A clinician's guide to parent training.* New York: Guilford.

Forehand, R., Sturgis, E. T., McMahon, R., Auger, D., Green, K., Wells, K., & Breiner, J. (1979). Parent behavioral training to modify child noncompliance: Treatment generalization across time and from home to school. *Behavior Modification, 5,* 3–25.

Graziano, A. M. (1977). Parents as behavior therapists. In M. Hersen, R. M. Eisler, & P. M. Miller (Eds.), *Progress in behavior modification* (Vol. 4, pp. 251–298). New York: Academic Press.

Greenberg, M. T. (1984). *Working paper on the measurement of attachment during the preschool years.* Unpublished manuscript, Department of Psychology, University of Washington.

Greenberg, M. T., & Kusche, C. A. (in press). Cognitive, personal and social development of deaf children and adolescents. In M. C. Wang, H. J. Walberg, & M. C. Reynolds (Eds.), *The handbook of special education: Research and practice* (Vol. 1–3). Oxford, England: Pergamon Press.

Greenberg, M. T., Kusche, C. A., Gustafson, R., & Calderon, R. (in press). *The PATHS curriculum.* Seattle, WA: University of Washington Press.

Greenberg, M. T., & Marvin, R. S. (1979). Attachment patterns in profoundly deaf preschool children. *Merrill-Palmer Quarterly, 25,* 4, 265–279.

Greenspan, S. I. (1981). *Psychopathology and adaption in infancy and early childhood: Principles of clinical diagnosis and preventive intervention.* New York: International Universities Press, Inc.

Greenspan, S. I., & Greenspan, N. T. (1985). *First feelings.* New York: Viking.

Grossmann, K., Grossmann, K. E., Spangler, G., Suess, G., & Unzner, L. (1985). Maternal sensitivity and newborns' orientation responses as related to quality of attachment in northern Germany. In I. Bretherton & E. Waters (Eds.), *Growing points of attachment theory and research. Monographs of the Society for Research in Child Development, 50* (1–2, Serial No. 209).

Hanf, C. (1969). *A two-stage program for modifying maternal controlling during mother–child interaction.* Paper presented at the meeting of the Western Psychological Association, Vancouver, B.C.

Harris, S. L., & Ferrari, M. (1983). Developmental factors in child behavior therapy. *Behavior Therapy, 14,* 54–72.

Humphreys, L., Forehand, R., McMahon, R., & Roberts, M. (1978). Parent behavioral training to modify child noncompliance: Effects on untreated siblings. *Journal of Behavior Therapy and Experimental Psychiatry, 9,* 235–238.

Johnson, S. M., Bolstad, O. D., & Lobitz, G. K. (1976). Generalization and contrast phenomena in behavior modification with children. In E. J. Mash, L. A. Hamerlynck, & L. C. Handy (Eds.), *Behavior modification and families* (pp. 160–188). New York: Brunner/Mazel.

Johnson, S. M., & Brown, R. A. (1969). Producing behavior change in parents of disturbed children. *Journal of Child Psychology and Psychiatry, 10,* 107–121.

Katan, A. (1961). Some thoughts about the role of verbalization in early childhood. *Psychoanalytic Study of the Child, 16,* 184–188.

Kegan, R. (1982). *The evolving self.* Cambridge, MA: Harvard University Press.

Kendall, P. C., & Braswell, L. (1985). *Cognitive behavior therapy for impulsive children.* New York: Guilford.

Levy, M. (1943). *Maternal overprotection.* New York: Columbia University Press.

Lewis, M., Feiring, C., McGuffog, C., & Jaskir, J. (1984). Predicting psychopathology in six-year-olds from early social relations. *Child Development, 55,* 123–136.

Lieberman, A., & Pawl, J. (in press). Working with disordered parent–child attachments: Issues in the preschool years. In M. T. Greenberg, D. Cicchetti, & M. Cummings (Eds.), *Attachment in the preschool years: Theory, Research and Intervention.*

Loeber, R. (1982). The stability of anti-social and delinquent child behavior: A review. *Child Development, 53,* 1431–1446.

Londerville, S., & Main, M. (1981). Security of attachment, compliance, and maternal training methods in the second year of life. *Developmental Psychology, 17,* 289–299.

Maccoby, E. E. (1984). Socialization and developmental change. *Child Development, 55,* 317–328.

Mahler, M. S. (1968). *On human symbiosis and the vicissitudes of individuation.* New York: Internations University Press.

Mahler, M. S., Pine, F., & Bergman, A. (1975). *The psychological birth of the child.* New York: Basic Books.

Main, M. (1973). *Play, exploration and competence as related to child–adult attachment.* Unpublished doctoral dissertation, Johns Hopkins University, MD.

Main, M., & Goldwyn, R. (1984). Predicting rejection of her infant from mother's representation of her own experience: Implications for the abused-abusing intergenerational cycle. *Child Abuse and Neglect, 8,* 203–217.

Main, M., Kaplan, N., & Cassidy, J. (1985). Security in infancy, childhood, and adulthood: A move to the level of representation. In I. Bretherton & E. Waters (Eds.), *Growing points of attachment theory and research. Monographs of the Society for Research in Child Development, 50* (1–2, Serial No. 209).

Main, M., & Solomon, J. (in press). Discovery of an insecure disorganized/disoriented attachment pattern: Procedures, findings, and implications for the classification of behavior. In M. Yogman & T. B. Brazelton (Eds.), *Affective development in infancy.* Norwood, NJ: Ablex.

Main, M., & Weston, D. R. (1982). Avoidance of the attachment figure in infancy: Descriptions and interpretations. In C. M. Parkes & J. Stevenson-Hinde (Eds.), *The place of attachment in human behavior* (pp. 31–59). New York: Basic Books.

Marvin, R. S. (1972). *Attachment-, exploratory- and communicative behavior in 2, 3, and 4-year-old children.* Unpublished doctoral dissertation, University of Chicago.

Marvin, R. S. (1977). An ethological-cognitive model for the attenuation of mother–child attachment behavior. In T. M. Alloway, L. Krames, & P. Pliner (Eds.), *Advances in the study of communication and affect: Vol. 3. The development of social attachments* (pp. 25–60). New York: Plenum.

Marvin, R. S., & Greenberg, M. T. (1982). Preschooler's changing conception of their mothers: A social-cognitive study of mother-child attachment. In D. Forbes & M. T. Greenberg (Eds.), *Children's planning strategies, No. 18, New directions in child development.* San Francisco: Jossey-Bass.

Maslin, C. A., & Bates, J. E. (1982). *Anxious attachment as a predictor of disharmony in the mother–toddler relationship.* Paper presented at the International Conference on Infant Studies, Austin, TX.

Matas, L., Arend, R., & Sroufe, L. A. (1978). Continuity of adaptation in the second year: The relationship between quality of attachment and later competence. *Child Development, 49,* 547–556.

Moreland, J. R., Schwebel, A. I., Beck, S., & Wells, R. T. (1982). Parents as therapists: A review of the behavior therapy parent training literature 1975 to 1981. *Behavior Modification, 6,* 250–276.

Morris, D. (1980). Attachment and intimacy. In G. Stricker (Ed.), *Intimacy* (pp. 305–323). New York: Plenum.

Olweus, D. (1979). Stability of aggressive reaction patterns in males: A review. *Psychological Bulletin, 86,* 852–875.

Owen, M. T., Easterbrooks, M. A., Chase-Lansdale, L., & Goldberg, W. A. (1984). The relation between maternal employment status and stability of attachments to mother and to father. *Child Development, 55,* 1894–1901.

Patterson, G. R. (1976). The aggressive child: Victim and architect of a coercive system. In E. J. Mash, L. A. Hamerlynck & L. C. Handy (Eds.), *Behavioral modification and families* (pp. 267–315). New York: Brunner/Mazel.

Patterson, G. R. (1985). Beyond technology: The next stage in the development of parent training. In L. L'Abate (Ed.), *Handbook of family psychology and psychotherapy* (pp. 1344–1379). Homewood, IL: Dorsey.

Patterson, G. R., & Brodsky, G. (1966). A behavior modification program for a child with multiple problem behaviors. *Journal of Child Psychology and Psychiatry, 7,* 277–295.

Patterson, G. R., Chamberlain, P., & Reid, J. B. (1982). A comparative evaluation of a parent training program. *Behavior Therapy, 13,* 638–650.

Patterson, G. R., & Fleischman, M. J. (1979). Maintenance of treatment effects: Some considerations concerning family systems and follow-up data. *Behavior Therapy, 10,* 168–185.

Patterson, G. R., McNeal, S., Hawkins, N., & Phelps, R. (1967). Reprogramming the social environment. *Journal of Child Psychology and Psychiatry, 8,* 181–194.

Patterson, G. R., & Reid, J. B. (1973). Intervention for families of aggressive boys: A replication study. *Behavior Research and Therapy, 11,* 383–394.

Peed, S., Roberts, M., & Forehand, R. (1977). Evaluation of the effectiveness of standardized parent training program in altering the interaction between mothers and their noncompliant children. *Behavior Modification, 1*(3), 323–350.

Peterson, R. F. (1976). Power, programming, and punishment: Could we be overcontrolling our children? In E. J. Mash, L. A. Hamerlynck, & L. C. Handy (Eds.), *Behavior modification and families* (pp. 338–352). New York: Brunner/Mazel.

Pine, F. (1985). *Developmental theory and clinical process.* New Haven: Yale University Press.

Quay, H. C. (1979). Classification. In H. C. Quay & J. S. Werry (Eds.), *Psychopathological disorders of childhood* (2nd ed., pp. 1–42). New York: Wiley.

Radke-Yarrow, M., Cummings, E. M., Kuczynski, L., & Chapman, M. (1985). Patterns of attachment in two-and three-year olds in normal families and families with parental depression. *Child Development, 56,* 884–893.

Reese, H. W., & Overton, W. F. (1970). Models of development and theories of development. In L. R. Goulet & P. B. Baltes (Eds.), *Life-span developmental psychology: Research and theory* (pp. 116–144). New York: Academic Press.

Ricks, M. H. (1985). The social transmission of parental behavior: Attachment across generations. In I. Bretherton & E. Waters (Eds.), *Growing points of attachment theory and research. Monographs of the Society for Research in Child Development, 50* (1-2, Serial No. 209).

Robins, L. N. (1966). *Deviant children grow up: A sociological and psychiatric study of sociopathic personality.* Baltimore: Williams & Wilkins.

Robinson, E. A. (1985). Coercion theory revisited: Toward a new theoretical perspective on the etiology of conduct disorders. *Clinical Psychology Review, 5,* 577–626.

Sameroff, A. J., & Chandler, M. J. (1975). Reproductive risk and the continuum of caretaking casualty. In F. D. Horowitz, M. Hetherington, S. Scarr-Salapatek, & G. Siegel (Eds.), *Review of child development research* (Vol. 4, pp. 187–244). Chicago: University of Chicago Press.

Sander, L. (1975). Infant and caretaking environment. In E. J. Anthony (Ed.), *Explorations in child psychiatry* (pp. 129–166). New York: Plenum.

Schneider-Rosen, K., & Cicchetti, D. (1984). The relationship between affect and cognition in maltreated infants: Quality of attachment and the development of visual self-recognition. *Child Development, 55,* 648–658.

Speltz, M. L. (in press). Dyadic skills training for parent-child conflict during the preschool years: A working synthesis of attachment and social learning constructs. In M. T. Greenberg, D. Cicchetti, & M. Cummings (Eds.), *Attachment in the preschool years: Theory, research and intervention.*

Speltz, M. L., Beilke, B., Cantor, J., & Wiltuner, L. (1985). *A comparison of four methods of teaching child-directed play to the parents of conduct problem preschoolers.* Unpublished manuscript, Children's Orthopedic Hospital & Medical Center, Seattle, Washington.

Sroufe, L. A. (1979). The coherence of individual development. *American Psychologist, 34,* 834–841.

Sroufe, L. A. (1983). Infant-caregiver attachment and patterns of adaptation in preschool: The roots of maladaptation and competence. In M. Perlmutter (Ed.), *Minnesota symposia in child psychology* (Vol. 16, pp. 41–81). Hillsdale, NJ: Lawrence Erlbaum Associates.

Sroufe, L. A. (1985). Attachment classification from the perspective of infant-caregiver relationship and infant temperment. *Child Development, 56,* 1–14.

Sroufe, L. A., & Fleeson, J. (in press). Attachment and the construction of relationships. In W. Hartup & Z. Rubin (Eds.), *Relationships and development.* Hillsdale, NJ: Lawrence Erlbaum Associates.

Sroufe, L. A., Fox, N. E., & Pancake, V. R. (1983). Attachment and dependency in developmental perspective. *Child Development, 54,* 1335–1354.

Sroufe, L. A., & Waters, E. (1977). Attachment as an organizational construct. *Child Development, 48,* 1184–1199.

Stern, D. (1977). *The first relationship.* Cambridge, MA: Harvard University Press.

Stern, D. (1985). *The interpersonal world of the infant.* New York: Basic Books.

Sullivan, H. S. (1953). *The interpersonal theory of psychiatry.* New York: Norton.

Thompson, R. A., & Lamb, M. E. (1983). Security of attachment and stranger sociability in infancy. *Developmental Psychology, 19,* 184–191.

Thompson, R. A., Lamb, M. E., & Estes, D. (1982). Stability of infant-mother attachment and its relationship to changing life circumstances in an unselected middle-class sample. *Child Development, 53,* 144–148.

Van Leewuen, K., & Tuma, J. M. (1972). Attachment and exploration. *Journal of American Academy of Child Psychiatry, 11,* 314–340.

Vaughn, B. E., Egeland, B., Sroufe, L. A., & Waters, E. (1979). Individual difference in infant-mother attachment at 12 and 18 months: Stability and change in families under stress. *Child Development, 50,* 971–975.

Vygotsky, L. S. (1978). *Mind in society.* Cambridge, MA: Harvard University Press.

Wahler, R. G. (1976). Deviant child behavior within the family: Developmental speculations and behavior change strategies. In H. Leitenberg (Ed.), *Handbook of behavior modification and behavior therapy* (pp. 516–543). Englewood Cliffs, NJ: Prentice-Hall.

Wahler, R. G., Winkle, G. H., Peterson, R. F., & Morrison, D. C. (1965). Mothers as behavior therapists for their own children. *Behavior Research and Therapy, 3,* 113–124.

Waters, E. (1978). The reliability and stability of individual differences in infant-mother attachment. *Child Development, 49,* 483–494.

Winnicott, D. W. (1965). *The maturational processes and the facilitating environment.* New York: International University Press.

Webster-Stratton, C. (1984). Randomized trial of two parent training programs for families with conduct disorder children. *Journal of Consulting and Clinical Psychology, 52*(4), 666–678.

Wells, K., Forehand, R., & Griest, D. (1980). Generality of treatment effects from treated and untreated behaviors resulting from a parent training program. *Journal of Clinical Child Psychology, 9,* 217–219.

Wimberger, H. C., & Kogan, K. L. (1974). A direct approach to altering mother-child interaction in disturbed children. *Archives of General Psychiatry, 30,* 636–639.

Zeilberger, J., Sampen, J., & Sloane, H. (1968). Modification of a child's problem behavior in the home with the mother as therapist. *Journal of Applied Behavior Analysis, 1,* 47–58.

7

Origins and Consequences of Social Withdrawal

Kenneth H. Rubin
Susan P. Lollis
University of Waterloo

The scientific study of developmental psychopathology represents one of the more significant new growth areas in psychology. According to Sroufe and Rutter (1984), developmental psychopathology weds the two traditional disciplines of developmental and clinical psychology. As such, it may be defined as "the study of the origins and course of individual patterns of behavioral maladaptation whatever the age of onset, whatever the causes, whatever the transformations in behavioral manifestation and however complex the course of the developmental pattern may be" (p.18).

Our own interests in this new field of inquiry have been driven by theoretical concerns, the absence of data relative to these concerns, and the pragmatic implications of this heretofore, nonexistent evidence. More specifically, we are guided by theoretical contentions concerning the role and significance of peer relations for normal development. These theories (described below) may be taken to suggest that children who lack opportunities for normal peer interactive experiences are at risk for later social, cognitive, and socio-emotional difficulties. Our own data base consists of information regarding the concurrent and predictive correlates of social withdrawal in childhood. Our practical concerns derive from the relevant theories and our data base; i.e., how, when, and why should one intervene in the lives of children observed to be extremely withdrawn?

In this chapter we describe briefly some of the extant theoretical rationales for examining peer interaction, and the lack thereof, in children. We also indicate, from the traditional clinical perspective, why social withdrawal in childhood represents an applied concern. These brief introductory statements are followed by an extensive description of our own model of socioemotional, developmental continuities. This model enables us to consider the possible origins and course of extreme social withdrawal in childhood. We examine, too, the possible consequences of this behavior for later development. This focus binds us to the other contributions in this volume, as we are of the opinion that familial relationships and constructs such as "felt security" play causal roles in determining which children become socially competent and which children become isolated from their community of peers.

After outlining our theory, we describe data from the Waterloo Longitudinal Project—a study designed to examine selected points in our developmental framework. Given our data base, we conclude with some suggestions for preventing or ameliorating problems associated with social withdrawal in childhood.

DEVELOPMENTAL AND CLINICAL REASONS FOR STUDYING SOCIAL WITHDRAWAL IN CHILDHOOD

Piaget (1926, 1932) offered one of the earliest statements concerning the significance of peer relations in determining normal social and social-cognitive growth. In his writings on communicative and moral development, Piaget indicated that peer play fostered opportunities for cooperation, negotiation, conflict and mutuality within the context of egalitarian social relationships. He further posited that such opportunities play major roles in the development of social-cognitive competencies and in the decline of egocentric thought (Shantz, 1983). Empirical support for these theoretical contentions is found in evidence linking peer communication, conflict, and role-playing with: (1) advances in perspective-taking skills and prosocial behaviors; and (2) declines in aggressive behaviors (e.g., Burns & Brainerd, 1979; Chandler, 1973; Iannotti, 1978).

A second theorist to implicate peer relations as causal agents in development was Sullivan (1953). In his writings on personality development, Sullivan argued that, during the elementary school years, children's peers played significant roles in the development of personality as well as in the growth of understanding social-cognitive rules of cooperation and competition. Sullivan posited further that during preadolescence, children's *chumships* fostered understandings of equality, mutuality, and reciprocity; these he believed to be critical factors definitive of intimate relationships. Clearly, peer relations were deemed developmentally significant. Finally, social learning theorists and researchers have demonstrated that peers serve as control agents and as models that reinforce or punish, directly and indirectly, such social behaviors as helping and sharing, aggression, and gender-appropriate acts (Hartup, 1983).

These theoretical perspectives, and the data generated by them, lead to the conclusion that peers are important causal agents in child development. Adopting a slightly different perspective, one might conclude from the aforementioned theoretical premises that children who do not interact with their peers may (inadvertently) deny themselves opportunities that routinely maintain, promote, and enhance normal growth and development. This line of reasoning leads to the hypothesis that socially withdrawn, isolated children are "at risk" for problems in the social-cognitive (Piaget), personality (Sullivan), and social-behavioral (learning theorists) domains.

In addition to this theoretical foundation, the notion that withdrawn children are at risk comes from the status of such children as a clinical group. That is, social withdrawal is viewed clinically as a problem in and of itself. It is implicated in, at least, three DSM-III (Diagnostic and Statistical Manual of Mental Disorders-III; Spitzer & Sheehy, 1976) categories of disturbance: shyness disorder, adjustment disorder with withdrawal, and introverted disorder. Moreover, social withdrawal is included as a "symptom" of internalizing disorders in childhood on the basis that it is a concomitant of anxiety disorders and depression (e.g., Achenbach & Edelbrock, 1981; Hetherington & Martin, 1979; Quay, 1979).

Given this theoretical and clinical background, one would have reason to presume that children whose rate of interaction with peers significantly deviates from the norm for their age group are likely to evidence developmental problems and, consequently, should be targeted for intervention programs. Furthermore, it is easy to see why applied psychologists have developed, in recent years, many varieties of intervention programs to deal with the correlates and consequences of social withdrawal (see Conger & Keane, 1981; Wanlass & Prinz, 1982, for recent reviews of the intervention research). What is surprising to note, in view of the aforementioned, is that there is a dearth of data supportive of these theoretical assertions and clinical assumptions. It remains, unfortunately, the case that the correlates and consequences of childhood social isolation are virtually unknown. Moreover, the limited evidence that is available fails to demonstrate that childhood social withdrawal is predictive (via retrospective and follow-through data analyses) of major psychiatric disorders in adolescence or adulthood (e.g., Michael, Morris, & Soroker, 1957; Robins, 1966).

The questions that this discrepancy between theory and data raise are obvious. First, is social withdrawal in childhood a risk factor? On the basis of cognitive and social-personality developmental theory one would expect to observe problems in the social-cognitive and interpersonal domains for withdrawn children. From the clinical research extant, the consistent loading of withdrawal on scaled factors of anxiety and depres-

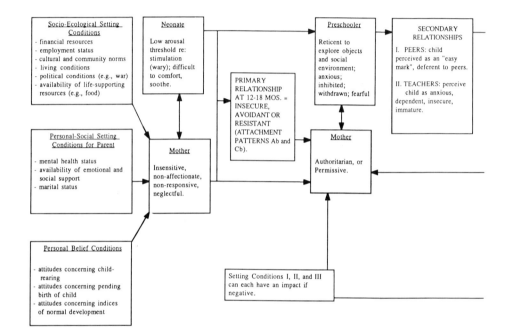

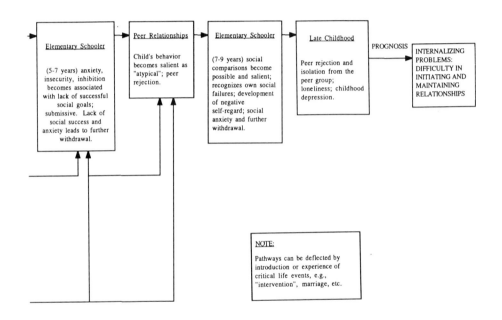

FIG. 7.1.   A possible developmental pathway to internalizing disorders.

223

sion might suggest a predictive outcome of internalizing problems (Achenbach & Edelbrock, 1981; Quay, 1979).

Other relevant questions include why is it that children become withdrawn to begin with? Is the phenomenon explained by dispositional characteristics of children, early familial relationships, socio-ecological factors, or an interaction of all three? Finally, what might one do to prevent or ameliorate the problems (if there are any) associated with social withdrawal in childhood?

Consideration of these interrelated issues underscores the need for a developmental framework. In what follows, we offer such a framework before proceeding to explicitly consider the possible causes and consequences of childhood social withdrawal. An illustration of this developmental pathway appears in Fig. 7.1 (see also Rubin, LeMare, & Lollis, in press). When reading our description of this continuities model one should keep in mind that we are making conceptual (and not necessarily empirical) links between many disparate areas of inquiry. Our goal is to develop a set of conceptually based questions that are subject to empirical analysis.

A DEVELOPMENTAL MODEL FOR THE STUDY OF
SOCIAL WITHDRAWAL IN CHILDREN

Why is it that some children are observed to be extremely withdrawn relative to their age-mates? What phenomena or circumstances predict social withdrawal in childhood? What might extremely withdrawn youngsters be at risk for during the later years of childhood and adolescence? These and other related questions guided us in the development of the causal model described as follows.

The Significance of Setting Conditions

We begin by drawing attention to those contextual variables within which relationships are formed, maintained and generalized. Drawing liberally from Bronfenbrenner (1979; Bronfenbrenner & Crouter, 1983), we posit that there are some situations and environments that can have a deleterious impact on the ways that mothers interact initially with their infants. Being impecunious, living in crowded quarters, and not having access to desired and necessary goods may well result in maternal feelings of stress and frustration that can affect the emerging parent–infant relationship (Belsky, Robins, & Gamble, 1983). Needless to say, these negative *socio-ecological* conditions impact on familial relationships *throughout* the course of childhood. Thus, loss of income and employment, domestic resettlement, and loss of life-supporting resources may all negatively influence marital and parent-child relations even though these relationships may have, at one time, been positive (e.g., Belsky, 1980; Elder, 1974; Kemper & Reichler, 1976).

Interacting with these setting conditions and conceivably resulting from them are *personal-social* characteristics of family members, especially parents. Parental mental health (depression, schizophrenia) and the availability of familial and extra-familial support systems (friends, community agencies) may exacerbate or inhibit the negative impact of socio-ecological settings. It is certainly the case that the presence of personal-social stressors, in and of themselves, exact tolls from the parent–child relationship. Researchers who have examined the consequences of divorce, separation, and marital hostility (e.g., Hetherington, 1979) and those who have studied parental mental health status (Zahn-Waxler, Cummings, McKnew, & Radke-Yarrow, 1984) have found that such conditions negatively affect the course of child development. Given these data, it is probably safe to suggest that the presence of both negative socio-ecological *and* negative personal-social conditions would have a stronger and more devastating impact on parent–child and other familial relationships than the presence of negative conditions of only one sort (Belsky, 1984). For example, it has been found that impoverished mothers who received socioemotional support from their husbands/boyfriends, friends, and relatives were less punitive and authoritarian with their children than those who lack social support (Colletta, 1979).

A third condition that likely influences the early establishment and maintenance of parent–child relationships emanates from those beliefs that parents carry with them concerning children, in general, and socialization practices in particular. Parents who do not want a baby to begin with may be neglectful or hostile from the infant's moment of birth. This negative attitudinal set and its concomitant behavioral reactions are likely to undermine the parent–child relationship and the child's development. Thus, parental beliefs concerning how children should be reared are likely to affect parent–child interactions and, thereby, the child's socioemotional development. Although researchers have only begun to examine the relations between parental attitudes/beliefs, socialization practices, and child functioning (e.g., Sigel, 1985), it seems reasonable to suggest that when negative attitudes and beliefs interact with negative socio-ecological and personal-social setting conditions, the familial environment will be less than optimal for the healthy development of children.

In summary, we suggest that certain setting conditions influence the development of parent–child relationships from the infant's moment of birth and throughout childhood. When setting conditions are predominately negative, familial relationships are likely to suffer. As family relationships suffer, it is likely that the members of the family unit will evidence personal and relationship difficulties. We describe some of the difficulties for children in the section that follows.

Finally, is important to note that changes in setting conditions, if positive, may serve to alter negative developments in interpersonal relationships and individual skills. Alternately, negative changes in setting conditions may result in undesired alterations in familial circumstances and individual development. Despite the dearth of data concerning the impact of setting conditions on child and interpersonal development, it is imperative to remain open to the possibility that the precursors and consequences of social withdrawal in childhood may be related to negative socio-ecological, personal-social, and parental belief conditions.

Infant Dispositions

What are the precursors of social withdrawal in childhood? One possibility is that some infants bring with them, from birth, a temperamental disposition to react cautiously to unfamiliar social and nonsocial stimulation. Primary advocates for a biological basis of shy, withdrawn, inhibited behavioral patterns include Kagan and his colleagues (Garcia-Coll, Kagan, & Reznick, 1984; Kagan & Moss, 1962; Kagan, Reznick, Clarke, Snidman, & Garcia-Coll, 1984; Reznick, Kagan, & Snidman, 1985) and Plomin and his colleagues (Buss & Plomin, 1984; Buss, Plomin, & Willerman, 1973; Daniels & Plomin, 1985; Plomin, 1974; Plomin & Rowe, 1979). Kagan, in particular, has long been an ardent advocate of a biological basis for "passive-dependent" (Kagan & Moss, 1962) or "inhibited" behavioral patterns. In the classic Fels Longitudinal Study, Kagan and Moss found that early ratings of passive-dependent behavior, that is, retreat and withdrawal from social stimulation between birth and 3 years, significantly predicted similar ratings between 3 to 6 years, 6 to 9 years, and 10 to 14 years. Furthermore, one "outcome" for these passive dependent infants and children appeared to be social interaction anxiety when they were adolescents and adults.

More recently, Kagan and his colleagues have reported that a behavioral constellation comprised of irritability, withdrawal, and clinging to the mother when faced with unfamiliar people or novel objects, is a highly recognizable, individual differences phenomenon in toddlerhood (Garcia-Coll et al., 1984). This pattern of behavior appeared quite stable from 21 months to 4 years (Kagan et al., 1984). Furthermore, Kagan et al. (1984) have found that at 4 years, toddlers rated as behaviorally inhibited at 21 months demonstrated at 4 years, longer latencies to initiate play with an unfamiliar child, made fewer approaches to an unfamiliar child, and spent more time than uninhibited children near their mothers watching (onlooking) the unfamiliar child at play.

These data indicate that an identifiable and stable inhibition/ withdrawal trait may exist as early as the toddler years. Clearly, though, their data do not provide evidence for or against the biological basis of the trait. Indeed, the major source of evidence in support of biological or genetic origins of inhibition/withdrawal is found in Plomin's research. Plomin and Rowe (1979) reported, for example, that behavioral indices of social inhibition/apprehension toward strangers are more similar for identical twins than for fraternal twins. Earlier work had shown that the sociability items of the EASI Temperament Survey were considerably more similar for identical than fraternal twins (Buss et al., 1973; Plomin, 1974). More recently, Daniels and Plomin (1985) found that parental ratings of infant shyness (i.e., inhibition, withdrawal, and fear responses to novel situations) were related to maternal self-reports of shyness, low sociability, and introversion. Furthermore, these relations were significantly stronger in nonadoptive than in adoptive homes, thereby suggesting the possibility of genetic influences. Finally, Daniels and Plomin indicated that significant correlations existed between biological mothers' self-reported shyness and sociability prior to the birth of the infant and the infants' shyness scores at 24 months of age.

Taken together, these data and those of Kagan are suggestive of the existence of a rather stable temperamental disposition toward withdrawal/ sociability that is linked to familial factors. However, caution must be exercised before assuming a biological basis for anxious, withdrawn behavior in childhood. First, it is obvious that the initial work of Plomin and Kagan must be replicated in other research settings. Second, it is most likely that if a temperamental disposition vis-á-vis "shyness" or inhibition does exist, then the responses of parents to these behavioral traits will play a significant role in the ultimate development of either positive or negative outcomes in these children. This relation between parental behavior and early childhood dispositions is certainly recognized by most of the primary figures in the study of infant temperament (e.g., Thomas, Chess, & Birch, 1968). In the words of Buss and Plomin (1984), "Temperaments are not immutable" and "genetic factors cannot account for all the variance" in individual differences in children's behavior.

Socialization of the Inhibited Infant

What is known about parental responses to infantile inhibition? Unfortunately, programatic research in his area is practically nonexistent. Kagan et al. (1984) reported that mothers were more distressed by an inhibited than an uninhibited child and that infantile inhibition was likely to lead mothers to make conscious efforts to change the child's behavior. These data are hardly surprising in view of the facts that behaviorally inhibited babies become extremely upset when confronted with novelty and uncertainty and, subsequently, are difficult to soothe. Thus, it *may* be that parental reaction to behaviorally inhibited infants is more likely to be comprised of hostility, insensitivity, lack of affection and/or nonresponsitivity than parental reaction to noninhibited infants. These reactions may be exacerbated by the presence of negative setting conditions. Thus, a baby who is difficult to soothe and who is inhibited in the face of novel circumstances may be an aversive stimulus to the parent at the best of times; if one adds to these dispositional characteristics the presence of difficult like circumstances and the absence of maternal social support, then parental reaction may take on all the possible characteristics previously described.

Interestingly, because it appears as if behavioral inhibition is a somewhat stable trait, it may be that parental efforts to alter the infant's behaviors will sometimes fall short. Under these circumstances, the parent may become increasingly unresponsive and insensitive. Needless to say, it is presently unknown whether the stability of inhibition is caused, in part, by parental responses to the infant and whether the imutability of the trait itself leads to increased parental hostility, alienation, and/or neglect.

A Conceptual Link Between Dispositional Inhibition and Insecure Attachment

The lack of knowledge concerning the socialization of dispositionally inhibited babies has led us to search elsewhere for relevant, related information. In our examination of the socialization literature, we discovered a group of infants who, on the fact of it, appeared to resemble those children whom Kagan and his colleagues label "behaviorally inhibited." We are referring to a subset of *insecurely attached* babies who were reticent to explore objects and responded negatively to strangers when they were brought into novel settings with their mothers. Their reticence to explore and interact with objects and people was heightened when their mothers left during the Strange Situation. Indeed, the typical reaction of these infants in the mothers' absences was wariness and a tendency to be easily upset; when the mothers returned, the babies were extremely difficult to settle. The composite of behaviors just described, of course, is one that fits the description of the *anxious-resistant* (C) attachment classification (Ainsworth, Blehar, Waters, & Wall, 1978; Sroufe, 1983). Thus, in the face of novelty, it appears as if some 12-month-old, anxious-resistant babies (particularly Cb babies; Sroufe, 1983) behave similarly to behaviorally inhibited toddlers.

What then do we know about the precursors and concomitants of insecure-resistant attachments in infancy? Mothers of insecure-resistant 12-month-old infants were less responsive to their children than mothers of securely attached infants when their babies are 3 and 9 months of age

(Belsky, Rovine, & Taylor, 1984). Furthermore, mothers of insecure-resistant 12-month-old and 18-month-old infants have been found to be unskilled, insensitive as caregivers, and less accepting of, cooperative with, and accessible to their infants (Egeland & Farber, 1984; Egeland & Sroufe, 1981).

The Developmental Model in Infancy

Given these data, we offer the following developmental scenario. It is possible that babies who are temperamentally inhibited and wary may, *in some cases*, have mothers who respond insensitively and incompetently to them. This interplay between endogenous characteristics and material socialization behaviors may be mediated strongly by the setting conditions described earlier (e.g., poverty, single parenthood, lack of social support; see also Belsky & Isabella, this volume; Crockenberg, 1981; Egeland & Farber, 1984; Erickson, Sroufe, & Egeland, 1985). The convergence of temperamental, socialization and socio-ecological forces may produce an insecure attachment relationship by the end of the baby's first year of life (see Fig. 7.1). Indirect support for this perspective stems from the recent research of Water, Vaughn, and Egeland (1980) and Egeland and Farber (1984). Collectively, these researchers have reported that infants later classified as resistant were rated, shortly after birth, as having lower scores on the Brazelton Neonatal Behavioral Assessment Scale (Brazelton, 1973) and as being less alert, active, and socially engaging than securely attached infants. Egeland and Farber (1984) have concluded from these data that resistantly attached babies may have some initial physiological difficulty in coping with stress—a statement that is strikingly similar to that offered by Kagan and his colleagues (Garcia-Coll et al., 1984; Kagan et al., 1984) in their description of the roots of behavioral inhibition. Moreover, it is also from Egeland and Farber (1984) that we find mothers of resistant babies to be unresponsive, insensitive, and inaccessible.

Our developmental model is certainly not unique. Sroufe (1985), for example, suggested the possibility that security/insecurity of attachment may be most heavily influenced by socialization factors; however, the particular form that insecurity takes may be determined by endogenous characteristics. Specifically, one suggested pathway described by Sroufe (1985, and attributed originally to G. Bronson) is that when the nonoptimally functioning infant encounters insensitive care, insecure-resistant attachment may result.

We are extremely sympathetic with Sroufe's recent writings. As such, we suggest that it is the notion of insecure attachment and its allied construct of "felt insecurity" that is one of the most significant driving forces underlying the development of future social relationships and social skills deficits. We, thus, find ourselves in agreement with the classical attachment theory perspective that mother–child attachment can play a significant causal role in the development of children's social skills and social relationships (Ainsworth, 1973).

Our support for the premises of attachment theory does not negate our earlier suggestions that dispositional wariness and inhibition may play critical roles in the development of withdrawn behavior in childhood. We have already described data that indicate moderate stability of behavioral inhibition from infancy throughout the childhood years. We believe, however, that dispositionally inhibited babies may vary with regard to the degree to which they are at risk for later social and socio-emotional problems. This variation is likely caused by early socialization experiences and setting conditions that determine that quality of attachment.

For example, an infant who is endogenously inhibited but living in a warm, supportive family is likely not to develop an insecure relationship with his/her mother (Sroufe, 1985). Perhaps when this child enters preschool, parents and teachers may indicate that he/she is a little shy or prefers to play with objects rather than peers (Wachs, 1985). We would not predict that this child would be at severe risk for later difficulties. On the other hand, the dispositionally inhibited baby who is reared in an unsupportive, unresponsive family, which, itself, may be experiencing stressful circumstances may well develop feelings of insecurity vis-á-vis his/her primary caregiver(s). These feelings of insecurity may serve to place the child at risk for later social and socioemotional problems. In this *untested* model of risk, we might predict further that the temperamentally inhibited baby whose parents are unresponsive and insensitive would be more likely to develop an insecure relationship with his/her primary caregiver than the infant who is temperamentally "average" and yet experiences negative and/or negligent parental care. Alternately, from G. Bronson (see Sroufe, 1985) the dispositionally "average" baby being reared by unresponsive, insensitive parents may develop an insecure-avoidant (A) rather than an insecure-resistant (C) attachment. Needless to say, these statements reflect conjecture and are not borne out by any extant data. What appears to be called for is a multiple regression-type analysis in which the relative independent *and* interactive contributions of temperament, socialization patterns, and setting conditions are examined in a prediction of the various attachment categories.

Infant Attachment and Social Withdrawal in Early Childhood

We have indicated that inhibited toddlers appear to display shy, withdrawn patterns of behavior when they are 3 to 6 years of age (Kagan & Moss, 1962;

Kagan et al., 1984). We have noted also that, in many ways, these children resemble insecure-resistant infants when they encounter novelty in their environments. As already noted, we do not mean to imply that dispositionally inhibited infants *necessarily* develop insecure primary relationships; rather, we would argue forcefully that when an inhibited infant does become involved in an insecure and resistant primary relationship, he/she may be considered at risk for later social and socioemotional problems. Moreover, we would predict that one of the *early* childhood consequences for such infants would be extreme social withdrawal.

Is there any reason to believe that insecure (and in particular, resistant) babies are extremely withdrawn as preschoolers? Conceptually, the connection between felt insecurity and social withdrawal makes sense. If a young child is wary of novelty and if she/he feels insecure in her/his primary relationship, it seems reasonable that the child may avoid the peer milieu when first entering school. After all, not only would the school be a new experience for the child, but so too would the presence of a large network of age-mates.

Consistent with this line of thinking is Sroufe's (1983) finding that anxious-resistant babies were rated, as preschoolers, as impulsive, tense and/or helpless, and fearful by their teachers. Sroufe also reported that these C babies were more dependent at 4 years than their security attached age-mates. LaFreniere and Sroufe (1985) indicated that C babies are more withdrawn and less dominant as preschoolers than children classified as A's or B's in their attachments as infants.

In keeping with the above findings, Marvinney (1985) has recently discovered that passive-withdrawn behavior patterns at 4-years were predicted from insecure attachment status at 12 months. Marvinney did not find, however, that C status prevailed over A status in forecasting subsequent passive withdrawal. Erickson et al. (1985) did find, though, that resistant babies were less confident and assertive (i.e., less agentic) in preschool and less socially skilled than their secure counterparts. Furthermore, as in Marvinney, insecure attachment status at 12 and 18 months, regardless of category, significantly predicted ratings of behavioral withdrawal at 4 years. Erickson et al. were thus led to conclude that the "resistant children's withdrawal would stem from passivity, wariness, and fearfulness" (p. 163); all characteristics that we believe had, as their roots, socialization, socio-ecological and possibly endogenous factors.

Despite the promising support for the assumption that anxious-resistant children appear to become inhibited and withdrawn, extreme caution should be exercised in interpreting the data extant. First, all of the findings emanate from a single, coordinated group of studies carried out at a single locale—the University of Minnesota. It would be useful to see this seminal research replicated by other investigators. Second, the number of insecure-resistant children studied in these investigations is rather small; thus, once again, replication with larger numbers of children is called for.

One non-Minnesota study that is relevant to our line of reasoning was reported recently by Lewis, Feiring, McGuffog, and Jaskir (1984). These researchers examined the link between attachment status at 12 months and indices of psychopathology at 6 years. Somewhat consistent with the data described above, anxious-resistant 12-month old males (but not females) were described as more withdrawn, depressed and uncommunicative than securely attached males at age 6 years. The sex differences found by Lewis et al. certainly attests to the importance of replicating and extending the original work of the Minnesota group, since these investigators rarely discuss major sex differences in their continuity data. Indeed, in the only report concerning sex differences, LaFreniere and Sroufe (1985) reported that C girls, not boys, were subsequently found to be passive, withdrawn, submissive and neglected by their peers. These findings directly contradict those of Lewis et al. (1984); however, the measures used to assess sociability-withdrawal-inhibition in the two studies varied considerably.

In summary, we believe that the roots of social withdrawal in childhood may be found in the interaction between infant endogeny, socio-ecological setting conditions, and the socialization practices of the parent(s). These factors may conspire to produce an anxious, insecure, and resistant primary relationship. It is this relationship that we believe plays *the* critical role in the development of fearful, withdrawn behavior in early childhood. That is, each of the three contributing variables (endogeny, socialization, ecology) may be considered more or less necessary, but insufficient, in and of themselves, to generate negative social outcomes for children. However, when taken together, these forces may produce a heightened sense of "felt insecurity" which could be considered necessary and sufficient for predicting extreme forms of social withdrawal in childhood. Having considered the possible developmental antecedents of social withdrawal we now turn attention to the concomitants and consequences of withdrawal during the childhood years.

Social Withdrawal in Early Childhood

In Fig. 7.1, and in the preceding discussions, we have suggested that withdrawal from the peer culture may be preceded and, in part, caused by feelings of insecurity in one's primary relationship. Our developmental model suggests further that during the early childhood years, the extremely withdrawn child should still evidence feelings of anxiety, insecurity, and fear of the social milieu. This constellation of withdrawal and anxiety we contend, is recognized by peers and teachers alike and, as a result, has ramifications for the child.

Are there any data to support these conjectures? As noted earlier, basic research concerning concurrent and predictive correlates of the phenomenon are virtually nonexistent. The most extensive program of research in the area is the Waterloo Longitudinal Project (WLP) in which the concurrent and predictive correlates of extreme withdrawal are being examined from the early to later childhood years. Unfortunately, infancy data, which would permit the testing of our notions of early antecedents, were not gathered in this sample, as the children in the study were first observed at 5 years of age.

The data from the WLP are informative in that they have enabled us not only to think carefully about possible antecedents of withdrawal, but also to go beyond the preceding theory building and more fully characterize the extremely withdrawn preschooler and kindergartener. It is our contention that such characterization is essential if developmental antecedents are to be examined. Indeed, one reason for some of the inconsistency between the data of Sroufe (1983) and Lewis et al. (1984) may be differences in the measurement of behavior problems in early childhood. In our work, we have found that *extremely* withdrawn preschoolers and kindergarteners play in less cognitively mature ways than their more sociable age-mates (Rubin, 1982a). In fact, the nonsocial play of these withdrawn children is *more* likely to involve sensorimotor actions, and their group-interactive play is *less* likely to include dramatic and games-with-rules components (Rubin, 1982a). Because these latter forms of group activities have been suggested to play causal roles in the development of social-cognitive skills (see Rubin, Fein, & Vandenberg, 1983, for a review), it may follow that withdrawn youngsters evidence difficulties in the latter mentioned domain. Accordingly, we have found that observed withdrawal in preschoolers and kindergarteners *is* associated with poor social-cognitive problem solving skills. For example, when asked what one cartoon character might say or do to obtain an attractive object from a second character, withdrawn children produce fewer alternative solutions than their more sociable age-mates (Rubin, Daniels-Bierness, & Bream, 1984). Furthermore, when informed that their solutions would not work, withdrawn youngsters are less able to produce a flexible second response; instead, they are more likely to persevere and suggest the re-use of the first strategy or to give up (Rubin et al., 1984). Furthermore, a qualitative analysis of the strategies suggested by these withdrawn children reveals that they are more likely than more sociable children to suggest that an adult intervene on the part of the cartoon protagonists to aid in the solution of the problem (Rubin, 1982a; Rubin et al., 1984; Rubin & Krasnor, 1986).

Socially withdrawn preschool and kindergarten children differ also from their more sociable age-mates in the ways they communicate during free play. Examinations of the videotaped dyadic free play of isolate and nonisolate children show that when paired with children of average sociability, withdrawn children emit more nonsocial, egocentric speech. The bulk of this egocentric speech, it should be noted, is not directed to the self in the form of self-guiding utterances to aid in construction or impersonal problem-solving (Rubin, 1979, 1982a). Instead, isolated children's nonsocial speech is distinguished from that of their more sociable playmates by its direction to nonpresent or inanimate objects (Rubin, 1982a). That is, during dyadic free play, withdrawn youngsters appear to direct utterances, not only to their social partners, but also to toys or to make-believe friends. The latter form of egocentric speech is rarely observed in more sociable children. The above described characteristics suggest that the withdrawn 4- and 5-year-old is less cognitively mature, perhaps more adult reliant, and more egocentric than his/her more sociable age-mates.

Our videotaped analyses of dyadic free play reveal a number of other interesting findings as well. First, the socially directed requests of isolated children are less assertive and direct than those of their more sociable counterparts; that is, their requests are less likely to be spoken in the imperative. Furthermore, the goals of their verbal requests appear to be less "costly"; withdrawn youngsters are most likely to use requests to gain their playmate's attention and less likely to try to gain access to objects or to elicit active behaviors from their play partners. The latter two request bids require greater effort and mobility from the targets than the first requestive goal. Most significant, perhaps, is the finding that the requests of isolate preschool and kindergarten children are more likely to result in failure despite the fact that their overtures are less direct and less costly to their social partners. Finally, withdrawn children are much more compliant with the more assertive demands of their play partners (Rubin & Borwick, 1984).

The picture we have painted of the extremely withdrawn young child is one of solitude, deference, submissiveness, and immaturity. We have also found that teachers rate an anxious and fearful those youngsters who display a high frequency of quiescent, nonsocial behavior (Rubin & Clark, 1983). All of these data are clearly supportive of our pathways description of the withdrawn young child (Fig. 7.1). Interestingly, despite our data suggesting that the withdrawn child's peers perceive him/her to be an "easy target," we have found that the extremely withdrawn youngster is not rejected by the peer group (Rubin, 1982a). These data concerning the lack of a relation between rate of social interaction and peer rejection have led some psychologists to conclude that the withdrawn child is not at risk for later difficulties (e.g., Asher, Markell, & Hymel, 1981). However, given the description of the withdrawn youngster offered previously, we would argue against accepting this conclusion. Indeed, we counter by suggesting that during the early years of childhood, solitary or nonsocial activity is actually quite normal (Rubin et al., 1983); consequently, there is little reason for nonsocial players to be singled out by their peers as displaying deviant, unlikeable behaviors. In fact, withdrawn youngsters are extremely compliant and responsive to the social overtures of their peers (Rubin & Borwick, 1984); these are behaviors that are probably quite attractive to young children.

We do know, however, that children become increasingly sociable with age (Greenwood, Todd, Hops, & Walker, 1982; Parten, 1932). Thus, it is likely that individuals who continue to remain on the periphery of the peer group during the middle and later years of childhood and who are anxious and insecure may become increasingly salient to their age-mates. As such, their deviance from age-group socioemotional norms may result in the development of negative peer reputations. We describe data relevant to these suggestions in the section that follows.

Finally, as we have indicated, teachers perceive the highly withdrawn preschooler as anxious and fearful. It may be that if the preschooler does not become more positively integrated into the peer interactive milieu, over time the teacher may reveal her/his perceptions of the child to her/his parents. Such disclosures may prime the initially insensitive and/or unresponsive parent to take one of several possible courses of action. For example, the parent may view the child as socially (and perhaps, *generally*) incompetent. Such a perception might motivate the parent to teach autocratically those skills deemed deficient in the child's repertoire. In short, the parent may become increasingly authoritarian (Baumrind, 1967) and she/he might rely heavily on "low distancing" strategies to directly teach the child academic and social skills (Sigel, 1985).

Another alternative parental response might be to become detached and thus adopt a laissez-faire, permissive attitude (Baumrind, 1967). Such a response may be mediated by parental efforts to place the "blame" for the child's purported failures on sources external to the parent. Thus, the parent may attribute the child's difficulties to characteristics that he/she believes are inalterable and endogenous. One possible consequence of such an attribution could be increased neglect of the child; for example, parents might distance themselves psychologically as well as physically from their children.

We have offered the above described parental responses as conjecture. At this time, little is known concerning parental attributions for and responses to their children's successful and unsuccessful development of social skills and interpersonal relationships (one relevant study has been published by Dix & Grusec, 1985). Consequently, support for this aspect of our pathways model is, as yet, unavailable. However, Baumrind's (1967, 1971, 1977) own extensive research program has shed some light on the socialization concomitants of childhood withdrawal. During the preschool years, parents of withdrawn children made fewer independence demands and were less warm and supportive of their children than parents of competent preschoolers. Although the reasons (attributional or other) for the parental adoption of particular socialization practices were not examined by Baumrind, her data are in keeping with our pathways model described earlier.

Finally, we know very little about how stressors beyond the parent–child relationship, both within and external to the family, affect the development of social behaviors in childhood. More specifically, we know virtually nothing about the relation between setting conditions like marital conflict and social network embeddedness, and the development of anxiety and social withdrawal in children.

Social Withdrawal in the Early Elementary School Years

In the middle and later years of childhood the "costs" of extreme social withdrawal are likely to become diversified. For example, in our model (Fig. 7.1), we suggest that the anxious, withdrawn preschooler who maintains these characteristics as a student in elementary school becomes increasingly salient to the peer group. Furthermore, if the child continues to experience negative peer responses to his/her bids for social compliance, if he/she remains deferent and anxious in the company of peers, and if his/her withdrawal becomes salient to the peer group, we predict a number of negative outcomes.

First, in middle childhood the cognitive ability to make social comparisons is firmly established (Hymel & Franke, 1985). Thus, children are able to compare their own feelings, thoughts and abilities with those of their age-mates/peers. As a function of comparing the self to others around him/her, the anxious-withdrawn child may come to believe that he/she is not as successful in the peer culture as his/her age-mates. Moreover, given these beliefs, the child may assume that he/she is disliked by the peer group and that he/she is socially (and, perhaps, otherwise) incompetent. These responses may lead to, still yet, further withdrawal from the peer group and to increased social anxiety.

Data supportive of these predictions are found in recent reports from the WLP. For example, second grade peers perceived children (especially males) who displayed high frequencies of nonsocial activity as isolated and sensitive (Rubin & Cohen, 1986). Interestingly, despite their emerging visibility, behaviorally withdrawn second graders were not rejected by their peers (Rubin, 1985). Furthermore, children identified as consistently withdrawn from kindergarten to Grade 2 did not evidence difficulties in their abilities to *think about* solving relatively common social dilemmas like acquiring desired objects from others or initiating friendships. From these data, it is easy to conclude that, in middle childhood, extremely withdrawn youngsters do not appear to have major social difficulties; they are able to competently think about solutions to interpersonal dilemmas (Rubin & Krasnor, 1986) and they are not unpopular among their peers (Rubin, 1985).

Yet, despite these seemingly positive characteristics, extremely and continuously withdrawn Grade 2 children did appear to have difficulties. First, when observed during dyadic play with a same-sex, same-age partner, withdrawn children were likely to adopt deferent and submissive roles rather than dominant ones. For example, they were often the targets of their peers' managerial/dominating and teaching efforts. Furthermore, when they did attempt to assert themselves, their efforts were more likely to be rebuffed; alternately, the dominating efforts of their social partners were very often complied with (Rubin, 1985).

In many respects, these data concerning the role relationships of grade two social isolates mirror the aforementioned communicative and naturalistic social problem-solving behaviors of kindergarten isolates. The picture painted in both scenarios is one of a child who is submissive and compliant and whose own efforts to dominate or maneuvre her/his social partners often results in failure or rebuff. Thus, some continuity appears to exist in the general social "styles" of withdrawn children when they are observed during dyadic free play.

These patterns of relationship functioning are particularly interesting in light of our discovery that withdrawn children do not evidence difficulties in thinking about interpersonal dilemmas. Despite being able to produce competent and relevant responses to an interviewer's set of questions about hypothetical social dilemmas, children in second grade who are withdrawn cannot manage their real social worlds as effectively as more sociable children. As such, there appears to be somewhat of a social competence-performance distinction for withdrawn elementary schoolers.

From our perspective, this discrepancy between thinking about solutions to social dilemmas and being able to manage the social world effectively may well be mediated by affect (see also Rubin & Krasnor, 1985; Rubin et al., in press). Specifically, it may be that social anxiety and insecurity is the critical factor that leads to withdrawal in the first place and, furthermore, that this felt anxiety-insecurity in the world of peers is what inhibits the utilization of productive strategies known to be in the child's social-cognitive repertoire. In lay terminology, the anxious, withdrawn child, when faced with real-life interpersonal dilemmas, may "choke." When appropriately assertive or sociable strategies are called for, the withdrawn child may be inappropriately unassertive or avoidant. One consequence of this competence-performance discontinuity may be the experience of a good deal of social failure. These failure experiences may, in turn, lead anxious-withdrawn children to develop negative *self-perceptions* of their social competencies.

This latter speculation, which follows from our pathways model, has been supported by WLP data. Continuously identified (from kindergarten) and extremely withdrawn Grade 2 children think more negatively than more sociable children, not only about their own *social* competencies, but also about their cognitive and physical skills and their general self-worth (Rubin, 1985).

In summary, the results of the WLP indicate that by the mid-years of childhood, the costs of social withdrawal include a disproportionate (relative to the norm) number of social failure experiences and an emerging sense of personal incompetence. These are certainly areas that require attention by social skills intervention advocates. Interestingly, specific costs in the domains of hypothetical-reflective social problem-solving skills (Rubin & Krasnor, 1986) and peer rejection (Rubin, 1985) do not appear evident during this period. We believe that the nonsignificant differences between withdrawn children and their sociable counterparts with regard to social cognition and popularity are largely a function of developmental phenomena. First, the lack of a relation between social isolation and social-cognition may be explained by reference to the original theoretical writings of Piaget (1926) and Sullivan (1953). These theorists argued that peer interaction would not have its greatest impact on social-cognitive and personality development until the middle years of childhood. Yet, we did find a relation between social withdrawal and hypothetical-reflective social reasoning for preschool and kindergarten-age children. An alternative explanation may thus be that the dilemmas we posed to assess social problem solving in Grade 2 children were simply too easy for this age-group. As such, the data could be interpreted as representing a measurement-specific ceiling effect.

At any rate, we have indicated two possible explanations for the nonsignificant relation between withdrawal and hypothetical-reflective social problem solving in our Grade 2 sample. Interestingly, in a recent analysis of complex perspective-taking skills, we found a nonsignificant difference between the competencies of withdrawn and more sociable *kindergarten* children; yet, in Grade 3 a significant difference did emerge, thereby supporting the theoretical, developmental premises cited previously (LeMare & Rubin, 1987).

The lack of a relation between social withdrawal and peer rejection may be a function of its nondisruptive character. Although peers are able to identify those Grade 2 children who play alone with high frequency (Rubin & Cohen, 1986), the solitary nature of this activity does not impinge on the activities of others. As such, social withdrawal may not be particularly salient as a nonnormative form of behavior when children are

6 and 7 years of age. During this age period, the best predictors of peer rejection include disruptive, nonnormative behaviors and highly immature forms of cognitive play (e.g., Rubin & Daniels-Beirness, 1983). Perhaps then, as anxiety-mediated social withdrawal becomes increasingly salient as "abnormal," it emerges as a correlate of peer rejection.

Social Withdrawal in the Middle and Late Elementary School Years

We have, heretofore, described preschool and kindergarten withdrawn children as socially deferent, somewhat immature and yet socially responsive to the overtures of peers. By Grade 2, despite their abilities to think about optimal solutions to social dilemmas, they nevertheless experience a proportionally greater number of social failure experiences than their more sociable age-mates. We have suggested that these failure experiences, which first appear evident in the dyadic play of withdrawn *preschoolers* (Rubin & Borwick, 1984), may lead to the development of negative self-perceptions of social competence. Indeed, our longitudinal data provide support for this premise (e.g., Rubin, 1985).

It is now possible to extend our developmental conceptualizations into the mid- and late-childhood years. Children who perceive themselves as deficient in social and other skills may dispose themselves to heightened feelings of anxiety (e.g., Cicchetti & Schneider-Rosen, 1985). Indeed, negative self-perceptions have long been considered criterial for the development of anxiety disorders and depression (e.g., Beck, 1967). Thus, one possible developmental sequence may be that the negative self-perceptions of young withdrawn children may provoke, within them, an even greater sense of insecurity and anxiety. This combination of negative self-perceptions and heightened anxiety may be associated with continued withdrawal in the peer milieu. By the mid- and late-elementary school years, extreme levels of social withdrawal may not only be salient, but also viewed as nonnormative. Consequently, one result may be peer rejection. The concurrent experience of social anxiety, negative self-perceptions, and peer rejection may interact to exacerbate each of these problems. Furthermore, interactions between these phenomena may "pull for" the subsequent development of major anxiety disorders and depression (see Cicchetti & Schneider-Rosen, 1985, for a similar developmental perspective).

At this time, the scenario described in the previous paragraph, and in Fig. 7.1, has not been subjected to explicit empirical testing. There do exist, however, some empirical links between some of the variables described in the preceding paragraphs. For example, Sacco and Graves (1984) recently reported that depressed fourth and fifth grade children had lower perceptions of their own social skills than did their nondepressed counterparts.

A more thorough examination of relations between social withdrawal, peer rejection, social anxiety, self-perceptions, and depression is being carried out in the WLP. First, we have recently discovered a developmental change in the sociometric correlates of social withdrawal. In years prior to Grade 2, we found a nonsignificant association between social isolation and peer rejection. From Grades 2 to 5 peer-rated isolation and sensitivity becomes increasingly correlated with peer rejection (Hymel & Rubin, 1985). In fact, as Hymel and Rubin observed, these peer ratings of isolation and sensitivity become more highly correlated with sociometric status than ratings of aggressive-disruptive behaviors by the time children are in the fourth grade. Second, in a recent analysis of the Grade 4 WLP data, we discovered a significant negative correlation between the most frequent form of sedentary, solitary activity (solitary-constructive play) and peer popularity, $r(81) = -.36, p < .001$. The frequency of all types of solitary play (not simply solitary-contructive play) was also negatively related to peer popularity, $r(81) = -.29, p < .008$. Considered together, these data indicate that, with age and development, children who engage in high frequencies of solitary behavior become increasingly likely candidates for peer rejection.

Preliminary analysis of our Grade 4 data (Rubin & Hymel, 1986) also reveal that children observed to be socially withdrawn: (a) perceive *themselves* as lacking social skills; (b) report being desirous of avoiding peer interactions; (c) are perceived by teachers as highly anxious and fearful; and finally, (d) tend to report that they are feeling depressed on the Children's Depression Inventory (Kovaks, 1983). Furthermore, we have recently discovered that children who engage in high frequencies of solitary-quiescent play in Grade 2 are more likely to be socially withdrawn, lonely and depressed in Grade 4 than their more sociable Grade 2 counterparts; these data are clearly supportive of our developmental pathways model (Rubin & Hymel, 1987).

In conclusion, we have described a model of developmental continuities that begins with possible precursors of childhood withdrawal and that ends with possible consequences of withdrawal. Needless to say, no one research program has tracked the possible pathway that we have described herein. We have simply attempted to provide some meaningful conceptual links between numerous emerging areas of research inquiry. In so doing, we are hoping to stimulate further research on developmental psychopathology concerning those features of children, parents, and setting conditions that cause or inhibit the development of social isolation, peer rejection, negative self-perceptions, and depression in childhood.

SUMMARY AND CONCLUSIONS

The purpose of this chapter has been to examine the possible precursors, concomitants, and consequences of social withdrawal in childhood, a phenomenon that has attracted much attention in child clinical research and practice. Drawing from a conceptual model of developmental continuities and from extant empirical data, we have shown that withdrawal is a fairly stable phenomenon during the years of childhood. From here we went on to consider why and how social withdrawal emerges as a salient psychological phenomenon. Our analysis led us to focus on recent research concerning dispositional traits in infancy (e.g., behavioral inhibition), the quality of infant–parent relationships (e.g., attachment) and the existence of negative setting conditions such as poverty and the lack of support networks. These literatures enabled us to draw conceptual and empirical connections to our working construct of childhood social withdrawal.

More specifically, we described one possible developmental pathway that might lead to social withdrawal and peer rejection in childhood. Our conceptualization of an insecurely attached (C) infant who remained on the periphery of the childhood peer group only to later become rejected, led to the suggestion that this child might develop extremely negative self-perceptions of his/her own abilities and worth. Our prognosis for this child was the development of anxiety related disorders and/or depression in late childhood and/or adolescence.

There are several questions that emerge from our examination of insecure infant attachment, dispositional traits of inhibition, and childhood withdrawal. In the remainder of this chapter we consider these in turn:

1. *Are all resistantly attached (C) infants at risk for later problems?* Although researchers have yet to address this question directly with specific reference to the C group of babies, the answer is undoubtedly "no." Instances in which insecurely attached infants (A's and C's combined) later showed no behavioral problems in preschool have been documented (Erickson et al., 1985). From this research, those factors that appear to be important for a problem-free prognosis include those relating to mother–infant interaction and to socio-ecological setting conditions. For example, mothers of insecure infants who did not evidence difficulties as preschoolers were more respectful of their children's autonomy, less hostile, used consistent limits, and were more confident than mothers of insecure infants who demonstrated problematic behavior (Erickson et al., 1985). Furthermore, changes from infant insecurity to normalcy at preschool age were associated with greater maternal support from family and friends and qualitatively better home stimulation.

The implications of these data seem obvious. It would appear desirable to identify parents who are insensitive and unresponsive toward their infants. Needless to say, the exact means by which such identifications can be made require some working out. At any rate, once identified, these parents might then be offered educational and support group opportunities. The goals of these opportunities might include: (a) altering parental beliefs, attitudes, and behaviors vis-a-vis socialization and child development; and (b) providing parents with supportive resources. Given participation in such programs, parents and educators may deflect an insecure infant from a dysfunctional developmental pathway (see Barnard, Hammond, Mitchell, Booth, Spietz, Snyder, & Elsas, in press, for a description of a relevant intervention project). In addition to parent-intervention experiences, sensitive preschool teachers and a responsive peer group also may play a role in the post-infancy/toddler years in directing the insecure baby toward a developmental pathway of normalcy.

2. *Are all behaviorally inhibited infants at risk for later problems?* Assuredly not. A major mediator is, no doubt, how the infant's parents respond to his/her low threshold for arousal. Sensitive, responsive parenting will, most likely, divert the inhibited or otherwise temperamentally difficult child from our negative pathway (e.g., Buss & Plomin, 1984). Moreover, living under nonstressful socio-ecological circumstances will likely play a diversionary role, as well (Belsky, 1984).

3. *Are all securely attached infants or sociable children not at risk for later problems?* There are obviously events in any individual's life that can change a prognosis of normalcy to one of risk. Critical life events such as *parental* death, unstable marital relationships or divorce, sudden unemployment, the birth of a new sibling, etc., may all conspire to place a secure infant or sociable child onto a negative developmental pathway. If the child's responses (often regressive or hostile) to these critical life events are reacted to insensitively or inappropriately by an adult who is also coping with the same stressful event, the prognosis for the child may be negative. For example, a common childhood response to the birth of a sibling is one of jealous and regressive behavior; a common familial accompaniment to this critical life event is the decreased availability of the mother to the older child. If familial support and responsivity to the older child is available, then she/he will remain on a "normal" pathway. If familial support, for whatever reason, is unavailable, the child's regressive behavior may become increasingly aversive to the mother. If the mother responds with hostility, a negative cycle of family coercion may result that places the once normal child into a "risk" category. Therefore, secure attachment in infancy or sociability in early childhood does not guarantee a positive outcome. Familial circumstance and socio-ecological factors will likely affect a child at all points in childhood.

4. *Are all withdrawn children at risk for later problems?* Although researchers have yet to address this question, the answer is probably "no."

In the Waterloo Longitudinal Project our risk group is one that is not only extremely withdrawn, but also anxious, insecure, submissive, and adult-dependent in childhood. However, it is conceivable that there are other withdrawn children who *choose* to remain distant from the peer group and who appear to be more object than person oriented (e.g., Wachs, 1985). Such children may be very constructive in their preschool activities (Rubin, 1982b) and academically oriented in elementary school. In short, the quiet but academically astute child who parents reinforce impersonal rather than social competencies may be characterized as withdrawn but not at risk. Needless to say, we are describing a child who exists only from our everyday observations as teachers and parents; longitudinal outcome data concerning our nonrisk isolate have yet to be gathered.

5. *Are the causes, correlates, and consequences of social withdrawal identical for all socially isolated children?* The primary focus of this chapter (and of the WLP) has been on the child who appears early in life to evidence timidity, insecurity, anxiety, and social withdrawal. We have speculated that if the child's behaviors and feelings remain stable, perhaps until the mid to late years of childhood, then she/he may be at risk for becoming rejected by peers and for developing negative perceptions of her/his own competencies.

At this time, we would like to present, very briefly, an alternate pathways model that results in a child being identified as socially isolated and rejected by her/his peer group. Our intention in providing this alternative model is to focus the reader's attention on the possibility that different children may demonstrate similar difficulties at a given point in time, but that they may have very different developmental histories that antedate these difficulties. Furthermore, we suggest that the ultimate outcomes for socially isolated, rejected children may vary given differences in developmental histories.

The developmental scenario we described is taken liberally from Rubin et al. (in press). We begin with an infant who is perceived as being fussy, overactive, and in general, temperamentally difficult. If the setting conditions described earlier are somewhat negative, it may be that the infant will be responded to with parental aggression, rejection and nonnurturance (Booth, 1985; Vaughn, Taraldson, Crichton, & Egeland, 1981). Interestingly, these parental behaviors have been associated with the development of anxious-avoidant (A) attachment status in infancy (Ainsworth, Bell, & Stayton, 1971; Egeland & Farber, 1984).

The importance of setting conditions is indicated by recent research of Bates, Maslin, & Frankel (1985) and Crockenberg (1981). Bates et al. studied a *middle-class* sample of infants and parents and did not find a relation between infant difficult temperament and subsequent attachment status. Crockenberg found that when social support was available to *lower class*

mothers, then irritable infants were less likely to develop insecure attachments than those whose mothers who experienced familial stress and the
lack of social support.

We, thus, argue that anxious-avoidant attachment status may be a function of the interaction between difficult, overactive/fussy infant
temperament, maternal hostility and rejection, and stressful socio-
ecological experiences. In recent years, psychologists have suggested that
anxious-avoidant (A) babies harbor hostile feelings toward their primary
caregivers (Main, 1981; Sroufe, 1983). Their felt insecurity and hostility is
demonstrated by avoiding the mother and acting independently in novel
settings, and by their lack of affect and proximity seeking when their
mothers leave them in the Strange Situation (Ainsworth et al., 1978).

Sroufe (1983) has suggested that the felt anger and hostility of A babies
is carried with them into later years when they enter the social environment of peers. In support of Sroufe, researchers have shown that A babies
do demonstrate hostile, aggressive behavioral patterns in the company of
their toddler and preschool age-mates (e.g., Jacobson, Tianen, Wille, &
Aytch, 1986; Pancake & Sroufe, 1985; Pastor, 1981; Sroufe, 1983).

One thing that we know about aggressive behavior in early and middle
childhood is that it is salient and aversive to the peer group. Furthermore,
researchers have demonstrated that aggressive behavior in early and mid-
childhood is a major cause and predictor of subsequent peer rejection
(e.g., Coie & Kupersmidt, 1983; Rubin & Daniels-Beirness, 1983). Since
aggressive behavior is often met with peer rejection, it follows that those
children who do persist in directing hostility toward their age-mates will
be isolated from the social community by their peers (Coie, 1985). In
short, anxious-avoidant babies who demonstrate hostility in their preschool peer encounters may, in turn, be rejected by their age-mates and
ultimately be isolated from them. Consequently, we have provided the
reader with another possible pathway to observed withdrawal in early
childhood (a pathway that is consistent with Sroufe's, 1983, finding that
avoidant babies are not only aggressive, but also withdrawn relative to B
babies).

Following this scenario forward, it may be that aggressive-rejected children will be singled out by their teachers as problematic and disruptive
(e.g., Rubin & Clarke, 1983). These teachers might communicate their
concerns to the children's parents, who themselves have provided an
in-home experience of hostile caretaking. One likely result of such negative feedback from the schools is an increase in parental control efforts in
order to keep in check the child's oppositional, coercive, and aggressive
behaviors (Baumrind, 1967). These authoritarian parents might use many
imperatives that focus on direct control and they may eschew the use of
"distancing" techniques that focus on both previous and future conse-

quences of behaving in aggressive, hostile manners (e.g., "When you've hit someone in the past, what happened next?" or "If you hit someone, what might happen next?"). Direct parental control and low distancing strategies have recently been found associated with impoverished problem-solving skills in children (Sigel, 1985). Thus, high parental control may foster poor social problem-solving skills that may, in turn, engender hostile, aggressive (and unthinking, impulsive) children's behaviors (Dodge, 1986). This cycle is likely to exacerbate difficulties not only for the family at home (Patterson, 1982) but also for the child in school and in the neighborhood.

Given the previous description, we would suggest that this second possible pathway to social isolation and peer rejection would lead to a very different prognosis from the first pathway; in this latter case we predict that psychopathological outcomes of an "externalizing" nature (Achenbach & Edelbrock, 1981) might develop during late childhood and adolescence.

6. *What can be done for the insecure, anxious, and withdrawn young child?* We have suggested that parent education may prove worthwhile for mothers (or fathers) of infants who are identified as insecurely attached. In the case of anxious, fearful, withdrawn children, we advocate intervention procedures drawn from an original paradigm developed to restore social behavior in withdrawn rhesus monkeys (Suomi & Harlow, 1972) and later used successfully in a preschool intervention program by Furman, Rahe, and Hartup (1979). If withdrawn children are unsuccessful in managing their social lives, are submissive and deferent to peers, and if they feel negatively about their own competencies, then it may be appropriate to advocate confidence boosting, social experiences for them. Furman et al., for example, paired preschool-age, withdrawn children with either same-age or younger dyadic playmates for 10 sessions of free play. The results indicated that those social isolates who had opportunities to interact with *younger* playmates became more sociable, following "treatment," in their classrooms than those who were in the same-age pairing and control groups. Ostensibly, by interacting with younger children, the isolates had opportunities to assert themselves and to play dominant and successful social roles during dyadic interaction. Given the success of Furman et al.'s intervention, in the next phase of the WLP we will be examining the efficacy of the peer pairing procedure with older, second grade social isolates. Moreover, we will explore the processes by which such free play, pairing procedures work.

In conclusion, we have offered the reader some theoretically and empirically informed explanations concerning how and why children become withdrawn from and rejected by their peer groups. Furthermore, we have posed some significant questions regarding the risk status of temperamentally inhibited, insecurely attached, and/or socially withdrawn children.

Our developmental framework and our answers to the risk status questions are based primarily on conceptual, rather than empirical analyses. We encourage others to join us in examining the linkages proposed in our frameworks and in answering the questions regarding risk status posed in this chapter.

ACKNOWLEDGMENTS

Preparation of this chapter and the collection of the data reported herein were supported, in part, by grants from Health and Welfare Canada and the Ontario Mental Health Foundation. We would like to thank Jay Belsky and Al Cheyne for their helpful comments on an earlier draft.

REFERENCES

Achenbach, T.M., & Edelbrock, C.S. (1981). Behavioral problems and competencies reported by parents of normal and disturbed children aged four through sixteen. *Monographs of the Society for Research in Child Development, 46*, (Serial No. 188).

Ainsworth, M.D.S. (1973). The development of infant-mother attachment. In B.M. Caldwell & H.N. Ricciuti (Eds.), *Review of child development research* (Vol.3, 1–99). Chicago: University Press.

Ainsworth, M.D.S., Bell, S., & Stayton, D. (1971). Individual differences in strange-situation behavior of one-year-olds. In H.R. Schaffer (Ed.), *The origins of human social relations* (pp. 17–57). New York: Academic Press.

Ainsworth, M.D.S., Blehar, M., Waters. E., & Wall, S. (1978). *Patterns of attachment.* Hillsdale, NJ: Lawrence Erlbaum Associates.

Asher, S.P., Markell, R.A., & Hymel, S. (1981). Identifying children at risk in peer relations: A critique of the rate-of-interaction approach to assessment. *Child Development, 52*, 1239–1245.

Barnard, K.E., Hammond, M., Mitchell, S.K., Booth, C.L., Spietz, A.L., Snyder, C., & Elsas, T. (in press). Caring for high risk infants and their parents. In M. Green (Ed.), *The psychosocial aspects of the family.* Lexington, MA: D.C. Heath.

Bates, J.E., Maslin, C.A., & Frankel, K.A. (1985). Attachment security, mother-child interaction and temperament as predictors of behavior-problem ratings at age three years. In I. Bretherton & E. Waters (Eds.), *Growing points of attachment theory and research. Monographs of the Society for Research in Child Development, 50*, (Serial No. 209).

Baumrind, D. (1967). Child care practices anteceding three patterns of preschool behavior. *Genetic Psychology Monographs, 75,* 43–88.

Baumrind, D. (1971). Current patterns of parental authority. *Developmental Psychology Monograph,* 4.

Baumrind, D. (1977). *Socialization determinants of personal agency.* Paper presented at the biennial meeting of the Society for Research in Child Development, New Orleans.

Beck, A.T. (1967). *Depression: Clinical, experimental, and theoretical aspects.* New York: Harper & Row.

Belsky, J. (1980). Child maltreatment: An ecological integration. *American Psychologist, 35,* 320–335.

Belsky, J. (1984). The determinants of parenting: A process model. *Child Development, 55,* 83–96.

Belsky, J., Robins, E., & Gamble, W. (1983). The determinants of parental competence. In M. Lewis & L. Rosenblum (Eds.), *Social connections: Beyond the dyad.* New York: Plenum.

Belsky, J., Rovine, M., & Taylor, D.G. (1984). The Pennsylvania infant and family development project, III: The origins of individual differences in infant-mother attachment: Maternal and infant contribution. *Child Development, 55,* 718–728.

Booth, C.R. (1985, April). *New and old predictors of cognitive and social outcomes in high-social-risk toddlers.* Paper presented at the Biennial Meeting of the Society for Research in Child Development, Toronto.

Brazelton, T.B. (1973). *Neonatal Behavioral Assessment Scale.* Philadelphia: Lippincott.

Bronfenbrenner, U. (1979). *The ecology of human development: Experiments by nature and design.* Cambridge, MA: Harvard University Press.

Bronfenbrenner, U., & Crouter, A.C. (1983). The evolution of environmental models in developmental research. In W. Kessen (Ed.), *Handbook of child psychology, Vol. 1. History, theory, and methods* (pp. 357–414). New York: Wiley.

Burns, S., & Brainerd, C. (1979). Effects of constructive and dramatic play on perspective-taking in very young children. *Developmental Psychology, 15,* 512–521.

Buss, A.H., & Plomin, R.A. (1984). *Temperament: Early developing personality traits.* Hillsdale, NJ: Lawrence Erlbaum Associates.

Buss, A., Plomin, R., & Willerman, L. (1973). The inheritance of temperaments. *Journal of Personality, 41,* 513–524.

Chandler, M. (1973). Egocentrism and antisocial behavior: The assessment and training of perspective-taking skills. *Developmental Psychology, 9,* 326–332.

Cicchetti, D., & Schneider-Rosen, K. (1985). An organizational approach to childhood depression. In M. Rutter, C. Izard, & P. Read (Eds.),

Depression in children: Developmental perspectives (pp. 71-134). New York: Guilford.

Coie, J.D. (1985). Fitting social skills intervention to the target group. In B. Schneider, K.H. Rubin, & J. Ledingham (Eds.), *Children's peer relations: Issues in assessment and intervention* (pp. 141-156). New York: Springer-Verlag.

Coie, J.D., & Kupersmidt, J. (1983). A behavioral analysis of emerging social status in boys' groups. *Child Development, 54,* 1400–1416.

Colletta, N. (1979). Support systems after divorce: Incidence and impact. *Journal of Marriage and the Family, 41,* 837–846.

Conger, J., & Keane, S. (1981). Social skills intervention in the treatment of isolated or withdrawn children. *Psychological Bulletin, 90,* 478–495.

Crockenberg, S.B. (1981). Infant irritability, mother responsiveness, and social support influences on the security of infant-mother attachment. *Child Development, 52,* 857–865.

Daniels, D., & Plomin, R. (1985). Origins of individual differences in infant shyness. *Developmental Psychology, 21,* 118–121.

Dix, T.H., & Grusec, J.E. (1985). Parent attribution processes in the socialization of children. In I.E. Sigel (Ed.), *Parental belief systems* (pp. 201-233). Hillsdale, NJ: Lawrence Erlbaum Associates.

Dodge, K.A. (1986). A social information processing model of social competence in children. In M. Perlmutter (Ed.), *The Minnesota symposia on child psychology* (Vol. 16 pp. 77-125). Hillsdale, NJ: Lawrence Erlbaum Associates.

Egeland, B., & Farber, E.A. (1984). Infant-mother attachment: Factors related to its development and changes over time. *Child Development, 55,* 753–771.

Egeland, B., & Sroufe, L.A. (1981). Attachment and early maltreatment. *Child Development, 52,* 44–52.

Elder, G.H. (1974). *Children of the great depression.* Chicago: University of Chicago Press.

Erickson, M., Sroufe, A., & Egeland, B. (1985). The relationship of quality of attachment and behavior problems in preschool children from a high risk sample. *Monographs of the Society for Research in Child Development, 50,* (Serial No. 209).

Furman, W., Rahe, D.F., & Hartup, W.W. (1979). Rehabilitation of socially withdrawn preschool children through mixed-age and same-age socialization. *Child Development, 50,* 915–922.

Garcia-Coll, C., Kagan, J., & Reznick, J.S. (1984). Behavioral inhibition in young children. *Child Development, 55,* 1005–1019.

Greenwood, C.R., Todd, N.M., Hops, H., & Walker, H.M. (1982). Behavior change targets in the assessment and treatment of socially withdrawn preschool children. *Behavioral Assessment, 4,* 273–297.

Hartup, W.W. (1983). Peer relations. In E.M. Hetherington (Ed.), *Handbook of child psychology: Socialization, personality, and social development* (pp. 103–196). New York: Wiley.

Hetherington, E.M. (1979). Divorce: A child's perspective. *American Psychologist, 34,* 851–858.

Hetherington, E.M., & Martin, B. (1979). Family interaction. In H.C. Quay & J.S. Werry (Eds.), *Psychopathological disorders of childhood.* New York: Wiley.

Hymel, S., & Franke, S. (1985). Children's peer relations. Assessing self-perceptions. In B.H. Schneider, K.H. Rubin, & J.E. Ledingham (Eds.), *Children's peer relations: Issues in assessment and intervention* (pp. 75-92). New York: Springer-Verlag.

Hymel, S., & Rubin, K.H. (1985). Children with peer relationship and social skills problems: Conceptual, methodological, and developmental issues. In G.J. Whitehurst (Ed.), *Annals of child development* (Vol. 2, pp. 251-297). Greenwich, CT: JAI Press.

Iannotti, R. (1978). Effects of role-taking experiences on role-taking, empathy, altruism, and aggression. *Developmental Psychology, 14,* 119–124.

Jacobson, J.L., Tianen, R.L., Wille, D.E., & Aytch, D.M. (1986). Infant-mother attachment and early peer relations: The assessment of behavior in an interactive context. In E. Mueller & C. Cooper (Eds.), *Process and outcome in peer relations* (pp. 57-78). New York: Academic Press.

Kagan, J., & Moss, H.A. (1962). *Birth to maturity.* New York: Wiley.

Kagan, J., Reznick, S., Clarke, C., Snidman, N., & Garcia-Coll, C. (1984). Behavioral inhibition to the unfamiliar. *Child Development, 55,* 2212-2225.

Kemper, T., & Reichler, M. (1976). Fathers' work integration and frequencies of rewards and punishments administered by fathers and mothers to adolescent sons and daughters. *Journal of Genetic Psychology, 129,* 207–219.

Kovaks, M. (1983). *The children's depression inventory: A self-rated depression scale for school-aged youngsters.* Unpublished manuscript, University of Pittsburgh.

LaFreniere, P.J., & Sroufe, L.A. (1985). Profiles of peer competence in the preschool: Interrelations between measures, influence of social ecology, and relation to attachment history. *Developmental Psychology, 21,* 56–69.

LeMare, L., & Rubin, K.H. (1987). Perspective taking in peer interaction: Structural and developmental analyses. *Child Development, 58,* 306–315.

Lewis, M., Feiring, C., McGuffog, C., & Jaskir, J. (1984). Predicting psychopathology in six-year-olds from early social relations. *Child Development, 55,* 123–136.

Main, M. (1981). Avoidance in the service of attachment: A working paper. In K. Immelmann, G. Barlow, L. Petrinovich, & M. Main (Eds.), *Behavioral development: The Bielefeld interdisciplinary program* (pp. 651-693). Cambridge: Cambridge University Press.

Marvinney, D.A. (1985, April). *Passive-withdrawal in high-risk children: A study of continuity and change in adaptation.* Paper presented at the Biennial Meeting of the Society for Research in Child Development, Toronto.

Michael, C.M., Morris, C.P., & Soroker, E. (1957). Follow-up studies of shy, withdrawn children. 2: Relative incidence of schizophrenia. *American Journal of Orthopsychiatry, 27,* 331–337.

Pancake, V.R., & Sroufe, L.A. (1985, April). *Qualitative assessment of dyadic peer relationships in preschool.* Paper presented at the Biennial Meeting of the Society of Research in Child Development, Toronto.

Parten, M.B. (1932). Social participation among preschool children. *Journal of Abnormal Psychology, 27,* 243–269.

Pastor, D.L. (1981). The quality of mother-infant attachment and its relationship to toddlers' initial sociability with peers. *Developmental Psychology, 17,* 326–335.

Patterson, G.R. (1982). *Coercive family processes.* Eugene, OR: Castilia Press.

Piaget, J. (1926). *The language and thought of the child.* London: Routlege & Kegan Paul.

Piaget, J. (1932). *The moral judgement of the child.* Glencoe: Free Press.

Plomin, R. (1974). *A temperament theory of personality development: Parent-child interactions.* Unpublished doctoral dissertation, University of Texas.

Plomin, R., & Rowe, D.C. (1979) Genetic and environmental etiology of social behavior in infancy. *Developmental Psychology, 15,* 61–72.

Quay, H.C. (1979). Classification. In H.C. Quay & J.S. Werry (Eds.), *Psychopathological disorders of childhood.* New York: Wiley.

Reznick, J.S., Kagan, J., & Snidman, N.C. (1985, April). *The stability of behavioral inhibition in children.* Paper presented at the biennial meeting of the Society for Research in Child Development, Toronto.

Robins, L.N. (1966). *Deviant children grow up: A sociological and psychiatric study of sociopathic personality.* Baltimore: Williams & Wilkins.

Rubin, K.H. (1979). The impact of the natural setting on speech for self. In G. Zivin (Ed.), *Development of self regulation through speech* (pp. 265-294). New York: Wiley.

Rubin, K.H. (1982a). Social and social-cognitive developmental characteristics of young, isolate, normal and sociable children. In K.H. Rubin

& H.S. Ross (Eds.), *Peer relationships and social skills in childhood* (pp. 353-374). New York: Springer-Verlag.

Rubin, K.H. (1982b). Non-social play in childhood: Necessarily evil? *Child Development, 53,* 651–657.

Rubin, K.H. (1985). Socially withdrawn children: An "at risk" population. In B. Schneider, K.H. Rubin, & J. Ledingham (Eds.), *Children's peer relations: Issues in assessment and intervention* (pp. 125-140). New York: Springer-Verlag.

Rubin, K.H., & Borwick, D. (1984). Communication skills and sociability. In H. Sypher & J. Applegate (Eds.), *Communication by children and adults* (pp. 152-170). Beverly Hills, CA: Sage Publications.

Rubin, K.H., & Clarke, M.L. (1983). Preschool teachers' ratings of behavioral problems: Observational, sociometric, and social-cognitive correlates. *Journal of Abnormal Child Psychology, 11,* 273–286.

Rubin, K.H., & Cohen, J. (1986). Predicting peer ratings of aggression and withdrawal in middle childhood years. In R. Prinz (Ed.), *Advances in behavioral assessment of children and families* (pp. 179-206). Greenwich, CT: JAI Press.

Rubin, K.H., & Daniels-Beirness, T. (1983). Concurrent and predictive correlates of sociometric status in kindergarten and grade one children. *Merrill-Palmer Quarterly, 29,* 337–351.

Rubin, K.H., Daniels-Beirness, T., & Bream, L. (1984). Social isolation and social problem solving: A longitudinal study. *Journal of Consulting and Clinical Psychology, 52,* 17–25.

Rubin, K.H., Fein, G., & Vandenberg, B. (1983). Play. In E.M. Hetherington (Ed.), *Handbook of child psychology: Socialization, personality, and social development* (pp. 693-774). New York: Wiley.

Rubin, K.H., & Hymel, S. (1986, April). *Anxious and withdrawn children: Another group "at risk" for peer rejection?* Paper presented at the annual meeting of the American Educational Research Association, San Francisco.

Rubin, K.H., & Hymel, S. (1987, April). *Predicting childhood depression: A longitudinal investigation.* Presented in symposium, 'Recent perspectives on the study of developmental psychopathology', Biennial Meeting of the Society for Research in Child Development, Baltimore, MD.

Rubin, K.H., & Krasnor, L.R. (1986). Social cognition and social behavioral perspectives on problem-solving. In M. Perlmutter (Ed.), *Minnesota symposia on child psychology* (Vol. 16, pp. 1-68). Hillsdale, NJ: Lawrence Erlbaum Associates.

Rubin, K.H., LeMare, L., & Lollis, S.P. (in press). Social withdrawal in childhood: Developmental pathways to peer rejection. In S.R. Asher &

J.D. Cole (Eds.), *Children's status in the peer group*. New York: Cambridge University Press.

Sacco, W.P., & Graves, D.J. (1984). Childhood depression, interpersonal problem-solving, and self-ratings of performance. *Journal of Clinical Child Psychology, 13*, 10–15.

Shantz, C.U. (1983). Social cognition. In J.H. Flavell & E. Markman (Eds.), *Handbook of child psychology, Vol. 3, Cognitive development* (pp. 495-555). New York: Wiley.

Sigel, I. (1985). *Parental belief systems*. Hillsdale, NJ: Lawrence Erlbaum Associates.

Spitzer, R., & Sheehy, M. (1976). DSM III: A classification system in development. *Psychiatric Annals, 6*, 9–15.

Sroufe, L.A. (1983). Infant-caregiver attachment and patterns of adaptation in preschool: The roots of maladaption and competence. In M. Perlmutter (Ed.), *The Minnesota symposia on child psychology* (Vol. 16, pp. 41–83). Hillsdale, NJ: Lawrence Erlbaum Associates.

Sroufe, L.A. (1985). Attachment classification from the perspective of infant-caregiver relationships and infant temperament. *Child Development, 56*, 1–14.

Sroufe, L.A., & Rutter, M. (1984). The domain of developmental psychopathology. *Child Development, 55*, 17–29.

Sullivan, H.S. (1953). *The interpersonal theory of psychiatry*. New York: Norton.

Suomi, S.J., & Harlow, H.F. (1972). Social rehabilitation of isolate-reared monkeys. *Developmental Psychology, 6*, 487–496.

Thomas, A., Chess, S., & Birch, H.G. (1968). *Temperament and behavior disorders in children*. New York: New York University Press.

Vaughn, B.E., Taraldson, B.J., Crichton, L., & Egeland, B. (1981). The assessment of infant temperament: A critique of the Carey Infant Temperament Questionnaire. *Infant Behavior and Development, 4*, 1–17.

Wachs, T.D. (1985). Home stimulation and cognitive development. In C.C. Brown & A.W. Cottfried (Eds.), *Play interactions: The role of toys and parental involvement in children's development* (pp. 142-151). Skillman, NJ: Johnson & Johnson Publications.

Wanlass, R.L., & Prinz, R.J. (1982). Methodological issues in conceptualizing and treating social isolation. *Psychological Bulletin, 92*, 39–55.

Waters, E., Vaughn, B.E., & Egeland, B.R. (1980). Individual differences in infant-mother attachment relationships at age one: Antecedents in neonatal behavior in an urban, economically disadvantaged sample. *Child Development, 51*, 208–216.

Zahn-Waxler, C., Cummings, M., McKnew, D.H., & Radke-Yarrow, M. (1984). Altruism, aggression, and social interactions in young children with a manic-depressive parent. *Child Development, 55*, 112–122.

8
Attachment and the Development of Behavior Problems

John E. Bates
Kathryn Bayles
Indiana University

Some children do well in their social relationships; they enjoy others and are enjoyed, and they develop a wide range of adaptive skills. However, as many as 15% of children do not develop as well; they show problem behaviors and signs of internal and interpersonal disturbance. It is not apparent how these major variations in children's adaptations come about, even when we have the benefit of hindsight. How do some children attain a wealth of socially valued roles, whereas others are comparatively poverty-stricken, and still others attain notoriety, with a wealth of negative roles? Our major goal is greater understanding of how children's behavior problems develop. Attachment concepts are increasingly relevant to this goal, and we use them as one way of examining the paths individual children follow toward differing social adaptations.

There has been an impressive accumulation of research in the past 15 years on attachment security; the literature has been suggesting it as a major factor in children's social competence and emotional adjustment outcomes (e.g., Belsky & Isabella, this volume; Lamb, Thompson, Gardner, & Charnov, 1985; Sroufe, 1983). The attachment literature leads toward a rich model of how personality develops, registering impressive gains in empirical support for the claim that there are coherent patterns of psychosocial development. The data generally support the argument that early characteristics of the child in a basic relationship, especially the infant-mother one, predict socially meaningful characteristics at later times, even ones observed in relationships with peers and teachers. How it may be that attachment security research has been able to predict developmental outcomes is discussed later. We also discuss recent attachment concepts and data, including data from our own longitudinal research project. In both the literature review and in our own study, we focus on the interconnections between four major concepts: pathology outcome, family process, attachment security, and child temperament.

ATTACHMENT AND PSYCHOPATHOLOGY

Child psychopathology is a large network of constructs. It can represent many different dimensions of child functioning, and each of its dimensions can be operationalized in many ways. We are particularly interested in child psychopathology in the sense of parents', teachers', and clinicians' evaluations that the child's behavior deviates from the norms for social development. This essentially represents the perception that the child's behavior causes more problems than usual for both the child and the social network. (Also of interest, though less crucial as operational definitions, are peers' evaluations, deviations from the norm in response to theoretically relevant, experimental tasks, e.g. problem-solving cognitions in a hypothetical situation, and the child's own perceptions of his/her social situation and self.) The two major dimensions of childhood psychopathology that have been identified, especially in questionnaire measures, are: (a) externalizing, with excesses in aggression and exploitation; and (b) internalizing, with excess negative emotion, inhibition, and avoidance.

What role might attachment security play in the development of behavior problems? Toward an answer to this, we consider three interacting influences of the complex system represented by a child's level of attachment security. The first kind of influence we discuss, ethological, is envisioned on a more fundamentally biological level than the more symbolic and social influences we discuss subsequently.

Ethological

We have not found it easy to imagine how the more biological aspects of attachment play a role in development of behavior problems; ordinarily we focus on more social aspects of that process, as have other writers (e.g., Sroufe, 1983; Lamb et al., 1985). Moreover, we have little of an empirical nature to contribute to the discussion of ethological factors. However, we share the belief of Hinde (1982) and Lamb et al. that conceptual discussions of basic biological factors ultimately aid the attempt to understand how child-environment transactions produce personality. Therefore, we speculate briefly on ways in which evolutionary factors may be operating in the hypothesized link between attachment security and personality development.

At the level of the psychobiological system, attachment is thought to reflect an evolutionary adaptation of the species, a way to enhance the survival of the young (Bowlby, 1969). The adaptiveness of the secure attachment pattern (Ainsworth, Blehar, Waters, & Wall, 1978) appears clear, in that a well-attached pair might be more closely coordinated in times of danger. However, why this pattern is not even more numerically dominant than it is, i.e. why there is such a substantial minority of insecure or anxious attachment, is not clear. It may be that the environment of human evolution selected for secure attachment, but the current environment does not, and this allows substantial numbers of anxiously attached children to survive. However, it seems more likely that evolution supported both insecure and secure patterns. Atypical attachment patterns could be adaptations to particular constitutional and environmental characteristics (see Lamb et al., 1985).

Main and Weston (1982) suggest that avoidance of the caregiver under conditions of arousal of the attachment need, which appears at first to be counter-adaptive, could in fact be adaptive (see also Crittenden, this volume). Under conditions of extreme anger at the mother, for example, avoidance may be used by the young child as a means of maintaining organization in behavior. It is assumed that such means are needed in relationships where the attachment object frustrates the infant's affectional needs; some research suggests that mothers of avoidant infants are indeed frustrating (Main & Weston, 1982). Thus, the infant's avoidance in the face of an attachment need helps him/her to avoid the stress and disorganization of frustration and the high levels of anger that are directed toward someone the child is dependent on. In Main's scenario, the adaptiveness of the avoidant pattern of attachment could be seen as primarily a learned adaptation, and not necessarily relevant to the ultimate reproductive success of the individual. However, it is also possible that Ainsworth's three major categories have strong, direct roots in constitutionally prepared reaction patterns to the range of environments. Perhaps the avoidant pattern makes the caregiver less likely to abandon or abuse the infant, which enhances survival and eventual reproduction; a caregiver confronted with rage in a young child responding to frustration about their interaction might be more likely to dangerously mistreat the child than is a caregiver who is met with coolness (Schneider-Rosen, Braunwald, Carlson, & Cicchetti, 1985; Young, 1975).

It is plausible that the moderate levels of ambivalent resistance and anger shown directly by C babies in the attachment situation could reflect a similar, though less tightly controlled, effort to manage similar feelings. The anxious-resistant child's mixture of anger and dependency might, like the A child's coolness, mitigate the probability of maltreatment of an angry child.

We are arguing that there may be a survival pattern to be seen in the large minority of anxiously attached children. As Hinde (1982) and Lamb et al. (1985) emphasize, there are sound reasons to expect that parents will sometimes be unresponsive to a given child. The modern emphasis in ethological writings seems to be on "inclusive fitness," the proliferation of the maximal amount of one's genetic material. This suggests that sometimes parents need to attend to their own needs or those of other offspring. Evolution, therefore, would have prepared a child to respond to a range of caregiving environments, rather than just to the sensitive, responsive kind (Hinde, 1982).

The child who experiences neglect and rejection would apparently have more occasions for anger at her/his parent than the one who experiences accepting, sensitive care. The adoption of conflicted or misdirected expressions of such anger could, in at least some cases, prevent the moderately maltreated child from contributing to a compounding of the maltreatment. We are not saying here that avoidant and resistant behavior may not also be maladaptive in the sense that neurotic conflicts are maladaptive. They can become parts of rigid personality dynamics, insensitive to changing environmental conditions. However, proximal adaptation is not necessarily the same as adaptation in the sense of reproductive success, and there are also proximal maladaptive aspects to variations in aggressiveness and many other ethologically significant behavioral systems. The presence of a biological substrate may channel the development of behavioral variations, but it would certainly not preclude psychological and social adaptations. The neurotic aspects of attachment security variations are explored later.

The aforementioned adaptiveness scenario for anxious attachment patterns is not the only one possible. For example, Belsky (personal communication, September, 1985) suggests that the C baby is the most neglected of children, and the anger that is seen represents a "last ditch effort" to get needs met. The A child is less severely deprived, according to Belsky, and thus perhaps less desperate in the Strange Situation. It is not adequately established that the C baby is indeed the most neglected (see Lamb et al., 1985), but if this were to be better established, Belsky's interpretation would be quite plausible. We are not able to decide here whether the "anger-mitigation" function applies to both A and C babies or whether anger mitigation applies to only the A's and the "nurturance-seeking" function applies to the C's.

The important point of the foregoing discussion is that the positive adaptive significance of insecure attachment patterns is being considered, as Sroufe (1983) encouraged. Behavior that at first appears maladaptive may on closer consideration be psychobiologically appropriate to the situations in which a particular child is developing. Anxious attachment does not necessarily mark the beginning of a poor track of development. Sroufe (1983) and others have emphasized that positive environmental changes can reroute a child who is initially anxiously attached. Nevertheless, the ethological perspective enables us to consider the possibility that even where there are not major changes in the environmental qualities that produced the anxious attachment, the child still might develop well. The anxious attachment may reflect in some cases a relatively limited, ethologically adaptive response to a moderate conflict between infant and parent needs, and not signal subsequent failures in developmental tasks. In other cases, the anxious attachment may be a byproduct of a more serious disturbance in the caregiver-child relationship, and thus would forecast future problems (see Crittenden, this volume; and Schneider-Rosen et al., 1985, for similar arguments).

Cognitive/Affective

At the second level of theoretical meaning, the child's pattern of behavior in the Ainsworth-type attachment situation is seen as an index of fundamental, cognitive/affective attitudes of the child toward the mother or other attachment figure. An important source for the outward variations in attachment behavior is the child's "internal working model" of the social world, i.e., the child's expectancy that the caregiver will meet needs for comfort in stressful situations and the inference that the child draws concerning his/her social value (see Bretherton, 1985, for discussion of this Bowlby concept). These notions spring in part from neoanalytic concepts. Since early in our reading of the attachment literature, we have been especially intrigued by the complementarity of Ainsworth's attachment ideas and Horney's ego-analytic ideas. For Horney, neurotic functioning begins with "the basic anxiety," the sense of being alone and helpless in a hostile world (Horney, 1945). Horney suggested that the basic anxiety develops as a result of inadequacies in early caregiving, although she left these largely unspecified. She went on to describe how such a core conflict would be defensively resolved by the three basic strategies of moving toward people (roughly corresponding to compliance), moving against people (aggression), and moving away from people (withdrawal).

Ainsworth (Ainsworth et al., 1978; Bretherton, 1985) suggests a fair analog of Horney's model. Under the stress of brief separation from the caregiver in an unfamiliar environment, children reveal the security or anxiety that they feel. If they are indeed stressed by the situation, they will have need of emotional support. Those children who have been supported inadequately in prior stresses would experience negative cognitions and affect in the current situation. These thoughts and feelings would interfere, paradoxically, with the ability of reunion with the caregiver to resolve the child's distress.

Feiring (1983) has suggested one way in which infants' attachment patterns might correspond to neurotic trends in Horney's terms: The securely attached group, particularly the B4 subgroup, might be predisposed to use the moving-toward style of dealing with the basic anxiety, whereas the anxious-avoidant (group A) would tend to use the moving-away style, and the anxious-resistant (group C), the moving against style.

Another way of collating the two theoretical systems, based on our own clinical experience and interpretation of the literature (particularly Sroufe, 1983), differs from Feiring's. We consider the possibility that a given type of attachment could signal the beginnings of more than one kind of neurotic solution to the basic anxiety. This consideration may eventually be important in predicting links between attachment security and childhood behavior problems. Horney said that there is usually a mixture of the different approaches to resolving the basic conflict/anxiety, although a person may make one of the trends more salient than the others.

In our interpretation, the avoidant pattern does clearly correspond to the moving-away solution to the basic anxiety, as Fiering noted. However, the avoidant pattern also has the seeds of a second neurotic trend— moving against people. If a child is distressed at being left alone, and yet does not trust her/his attachment figure to effectively relieve the distress on return through affection and soothing, she/he could experience a conflicted anger. This conflict could be resolved by turning a cold shoulder to the attachment figure (Ainsworth et al., 1978). However, we must recall the Main and Weston (1982) finding that the child who avoids the mother in situations where the attachment need has been aroused expresses anger relatively often toward the mother in other situations. It appears, thus, that anxious-avoidant infants can best be characterized by a combination of moving away and moving against. In contrast, the anxious-resistant group, with a pattern of overtly expressed anger, plus need for reassurance, appears better characterized by the combination of moving toward and moving against. According to Ainsworth and her colleagues (1978), the mothers of the anxious-resistant babies are not sensitive, but they are also not as rejecting as the mothers of anxious-avoidant babies. This may provide enough support for the child's moving toward response to anxiety, even if the child also has feelings of aggression. However, we must be tentative on this point, since the existing research is ambiguous on mothering antecedents of the two insecure attachment patterns (Lamb et al., 1985).

Aside from possible parenting antecedents of the contrasting mix of neurotic trends in A versus C infants, there is also the possibility of constitutional differences between the groups. Most intriguing are the hints in reviews of the literature (Ainsworth et al., 1978; Belsky & Isabella, this volume; Lamb et al., 1985) that more of the anxious-resistant infants have mild neurological impairments as neonates than the other attachment groups. Perhaps these or other health problems predispose the infant toward relatively disorganized responses to stress. Further research is needed to establish more definitely whether there are such physical differences between the attachment groups. Such differences might influence the development of behavior problems both through their effects on child–caregiver relations, and also through placing continuing limits on the child's abilities to deal with the normative stresses of development, such as age-related demands for increasing symbol use, compliance, independence, internal control of impulses, bonding with peers, and assertive pursuit of individual and group goals.

To predict which of the neurotic trends might be most salient in the later adaptations of the child, one would ideally need to predict the challenges and choices available to the individual child. Sroufe (1983) recommends considering both the developmental tasks that are central to definitions of competence at a given age and the qualities of the social environment within which the adaptation is measured. For example, child communication skills and teacher warmth might have much to do with whether neurotic trends would emerge at a given time. Ideally, we should consider the functions of behavior as an ethologist would, not merely check for gross normative standards of competence.

However, because we cannot now predict such particular circumstances with confidence, for the present, we must make predictions for a given phase of development based on a general concept of the social environment, one with considerable support, but also with some indifference, rejection, and aggressive challenge. On the basis of Horney (1945), we assume that the neurotic trends develop as ways of dealing with negative expectations acquired in the child's early transactions with caregivers. We further assume that, if these neurotic trends operate in the development of behavior problems, they do so via continuity (with age-relevant transformations in the specific patterns of expression) of the child's expectations of and transactions with parents, teachers, and peers.

In making predictions for the two anxious attachment groups, we followed a somewhat different conceptual route than Sroufe (1983), but end up in nearly the same place: The anxiously attached, avoidant children should be especially likely to develop behavior problems in which they are seen as angry, coercive (Patterson, 1982), and also interpersonally cool and aloof. The anxiously attached, resistant children should develop problems in which they are seen as angry, but in a more disorganized, ambivalent way than the group A children. Their aggression, as Sroufe (1983) puts it, would be more a response to frustration than a systematic interpersonal strategy. These children, using the moving-toward strategy, would also show problems of immature dependency. Perhaps ultimately they might get into trouble by too readily following other children, if they fall into a deviant group of peers. The group C children might also show some patterns of withdrawal, but these should be clearly traceable to stress and anxiety in particular situations, e.g., the classroom, rather than a general personality style, as in the group A children.

Although the securely attached children should be less likely to develop behavior problems stemming from early cognitive/affective learning because their basic anxiety should be less intense than the A and C children's, they might still develop problems, and the problems should pertain to their attachment subgroup. Ainsworth et al. (1978) suggest that the B1 and B2 children's behavior in the Strange Situation resembles that of the A children, and thus perhaps they might be at a slightly elevated risk for the moving-away and against pattern that A children would hypothetically develop. On the other hand, the B4 children's attachment behavior more closely resembles the C group's, and perhaps their social adjustment pattern would partly resemble the hypothetical moving-toward and against of the C group. The B3 children, to the extent that the attachment relationship and its correlates are important in the etiology of behavior problems, should be the least likely to develop problems.

The foregoing hypotheses seem reasonable guesses as to how attachment and neurotic strategies in core relationships may forecast personality. However, operationalizing the hypotheses for empirical testing is quite complicated. First, the behavior problem outcomes could be operationalized in many different ways. As indicated before, child psychopathology is far from a unitary concept. Second, the three-level nature of the attachment security concept also adds complications. The fact that we were able to form such specific hypotheses based on the cognitive/affective level reflects the relatively high state of conceptual development of this aspect of the concept. However, the other two levels, and integration among the three levels, are not as highly developed.

If it is to be useful to speculate (as we have done) that in some cases insecure attachment classification represents a psychobiologically positive adaptation to a moderate conflict in parent and child needs, rather than a failure to develop trusting bonds with an attachment object and the inculcation of a persistently maladaptive internal working model of the social world, then there must be some way of distinguishing such cases. How can we separate the two types? Perhaps such distinctions involve a multidimensional consideration of the individual child's characteristic needs for attention and affection, the availability and competition for such resources in the child's environment, and the presence of possible compensatory characteristics of the environment (e.g., a safe, interesting, and conflict-free environment, even if the mother is not inclined to provide the amount of responsive warmth the infant needs).

The final level of the concept of attachment security, the developing social system, also provides for possible complications in predictions based on the core, cognitive/affective level. The speculation on how one might distinguish an ethologically adaptive pattern of infant avoidance and resistance from a neurotic one considers child constitution in relation to the social environment. It may also be important to keep in mind that the social environment is a developing system. There are many ways in which a child's family, neighborhood, school, etc., may change. These could further complicate predictions based on the cognitive/affective level alone. We consider in more detail the social system level.

Social System

The third level of meaning of infants' patterns of behavior in the Strange Situation is the social system. Even though the child's behavior is the main focus of attachment assessments, it is fundamentally assumed that attachment behavior reflects the child's relationships, and not simply the child as a separate entity. The two previously discussed levels of meaning in the concept of attachment security must be included in the social systems level of the concept. Behavior patterns inherited from evolution can only be inferred in relation to the context of particular environments, and neurotic versus secure cognitive/affective patterns can only be inferred from social behavior in a social context. Sroufe's theoretical descriptions of the process (1979, 1985) suggest that the parent-child relationship functions as a sort of crucible, melding the child's constitutional dispositions with the products of experience. We would emphasize the systems theory principle (e.g., Bell, 1979) that the child's parents are to some extent in the crucible with the child. In this bidirectional influence process, hypothetical child tendencies, such as temperament, influence the transactions from the outset, and the child's evolving personality grows increasingly stronger in the role it plays in the social system.

Even so, we agree with the view that the parent would in general be the one with the far greater influence on the transactions, and thus on the adaptiveness of the relationship (see Belsky & Isabella, this volume). To be more exact, we would argue that child constitutional and environmental factors may operate in dynamic equilibrium with one another. As child constitutional characteristics are more and more extreme and pervasively relevant for adaptation, e.g., as in cases of congenitally retarded versus gifted children, one would expect parent influence to shrink and child influence to grow. We would also make the converse proposition: As major preexisting environmental qualities are more extreme, e.g., economic situation or parental social competencies, then the developmental implications of the child's predispositions would be more limited. Evidence reviewed by a number of writers (e.g., Rutter, 1981; Sameroff & Chandler, 1975; Werner & Smith, 1982) is generally consistent with the aforementioned assumption. The data suggest the outlines of an additive pattern in the levels of adjustment that are predicted by extreme traits in the child or the environment. For example, the most numerous and the more extreme the positive characteristics of the environment, as indexed by socioeconomic status, the more likely a family is to overcome the potentially harmful effects of premature birth.

With this very general framework for understanding the developmental system, we now can ask a more specific question. How might the social system dimensions involved in the development of attachment security affect the development of behavior problems? For the first attempt to answer, we cite again suggestions that the child is shaped by the caregiving environment. As the result of transactions with caregivers, the child learns attitudes about self and others, habits for dealing with important situations, and roles to play in society. Attachment security is thought to represent a wide section of the parent-child relationship, and thus a wide section of the child's attitudes and competencies.

Toward a more particular answer, there could be several kinds of links between the environmental characteristics influencing insecure attachment and those influencing behavior problems. One is that the environmental effects produce the attitudes and competencies, such as basic trust versus mistrust or language acquisition rate, and these traits are translated into what we diagnose as behavior problems when the child faces preschool and middle-childhood demands for social development. Another is that the insecure attachment directly interferes with the child's mastering subsequent developmental steps, e.g., anxious attachment restrains exploration of the environment. A third is that the family that stumbles in helping the child over one developmental step will continue to stumble on subsequent steps.

This child-shaping process has important clinical implications, but it is only part of the picture. The child contributes to the relationship from the outset, and the characteristics the child acquires in building attachments may become a force for continuity in the child's transactions with the environment. For example, the aggressive, coercive behavioral pattern seems to be likely to elicit the kind of response that maintains both the behavior pattern and its fundamental attitude (see Kelley & Stahelski, 1970; Patterson, 1982). Some have also suggested that inborn child characteristics could influence the transactions that produce the attachment security, and perhaps even also, in direct fashion, the transactions that produce the later behavior problems. In a separate section to follow, we consider in detail the hypothesis that temperament is involved in attachment security.

Appreciation of such systems principles opens the way to attempts to make more precise predictions than attachment security by itself could yield. However, for the current time, although research attempts to improve the scope and efficacy of operationalizations of the system concepts, the picture becomes more complicated. Even if we allow the assumption that attachment security does predict behavior problems, there could be a number of complications in how the social system affects predictions from attachment security to behavior problems. We see two major areas in which we can suggest approaches toward refining hypotheses.

Fit between child and parent predispositions (Lerner & Lerner, 1983), is the first area to consider. It is possible to envision some families where there is a high degree of complementarity between child and parent characteristics, and some where the fit is poor. For example, we have already mentioned fit between child need for warmth and parent disposition to provide it as a possible determinant of attachment security. This type of fit may also be involved in the development of behavior problems. Many other dimensions of fit could be hypothesized. Furthermore, there could be complex blends of areas in which parent and child do and do not fit, providing a range of possible problem factors versus compensating factors. There is some overlap among the dimensions within the domains of parent and child behavior (e.g., Bates, Olson, Pettit, & Bayles, 1982), but the overlap is limited enough that there is considerable room within each domain for variability in profiles of characteristics. The principle of fit is theoretically important as a guide for systems-based research (Lerner & Lerner, 1983); however, empirical methods for demonstrating the possible operation of such a process are not well developed.

The second area to consider in refining hypotheses about attachment and behavior problems is possible discontinuities in the social system. We can discuss three ways in which change might have implications for links between attachment security and later behavior problems. First, the social system can change, in ways to be specified, which produces a change in the attachment security, which, in turn, affects the development of behavior problems versus adjustment. Second, social system changes can affect adjustment directly, without the intervening effects of changes in attachment-related cognitions. And third, there is also the theoretical possibility of children themselves making individual choices deflecting them from the path predicted by attachment security alone (cf. Kagan, Kearsley, & Zelazo, 1978; Tyler, 1978). Research distinguishing between these three general scenarios for change might ultimately improve clinicians' preventive intervention choices. The distinction could be of a normative type, (i.e., findings that one of the paths is the most common) or of an individual differences type, (i.e., findings identifying patterns of child, family, and community characteristics that predict which kind of path will most likely operate).

There are two major ways that change might affect the relationship between attachment security and behavior problems: (a) Inherent forces of development would produce various opportunities for deflection from the basic attachment-predicted path. An anxiously attached child may grow (e.g., by developing language ability), which might either allow the child to compensate for environmental deficits with his/her own increasing powers, or allow a better fit between child and parent characteristics (e.g. the parent is more responsive to a child who walks, talks, and uses the toilet than to an infant). On the other hand, a securely attached child could run into difficulties, e.g., independent of the attachment relationship, the child's language abilities could be poor relative to peers', leading to problems in school, which in turn lead to behavior problems. Or, the child's increasing maturity could produce a rift or tension in the parent-child relationship, e.g., in the case of a parent, especially a single one, who is fond of babies, but is relatively rejecting of older children and unable to deal effectively with autonomy issues. (b) Social force toward change is the second way deflections might occur. When there are problems in adaptation, there is some tendency to continue in the poor adaptation, but there also appear to be corrective forces. In fact, poor adaptations in children and their families are notably less stable than positive adaptations (Kohlberg, Ricks, & Snarey, 1984). Instigations for changing a poor pattern can come from both within the family and from outside, e.g., relatives, teachers, or social service agents. Furthermore, not all positive adaptations continue, despite generally strong tendencies to do so. Families sometimes face stresses, such as illness, death, and economic setbacks, to which they are not able to adapt quickly.

The previous discussion represents an attempt to organize the multitude of factors that could be seen as affecting the relationship between attachment security and the development of behavior problems. The precise outlines of the systemic process are far from clear. It is clear, however, that we need to keep trying to conceptualize and measure the phenomena of social development in systems terms. Cicchetti and his colleagues, in the context of trying to understand the relationship between attachment security and child abuse, have made similar efforts to consider the compensating and augmenting effects of multiple variables on developmental outcomes, even going so far as sorting them into the four categories of enduring and transient influences promoting and preventing disorders (Belsky & Isabella, this volume; Schneider-Rosen et al., 1985).

Conceptually, at least, the distant goal of the research area appears to be the attempt to find combinations of variables from many facets of the child's system that form a coherent developmental gestalt. The complications in such an attempt are daunting at times, but there seems not to be, even with the comparative success of the attachment security variable, a serious trend toward searching for a single variable, a "silver bullet," that will solve our problems in predicting developmental outcomes.

Prior Empirical Data

We now focus more sharply on the empirical results of the few, most relevant studies on links between attachment security and psychopathology. Given the clinically interesting, generalizable patterns of behavior in the Ainsworth procedure, do these patterns have theoretically appropriate implications for what will be seen in other situations and at different points in time?

Mother–Infant Antecedents.   In order to understand the ways in which attachment might be an origin of psychopathology, we must consider, at least briefly, the origins of attachment itself. Maternal sensitivity and responsiveness during the first months of life, as opposed to rejection and inept or inconsistent care, have been empirically established as antecedents to secure attachment at one year of age (Ainsworth et al., 1978). Replication studies have supported this finding (e.g., see Bates, Maslin, & Frankel, 1985; Belsky & Isabella, this volume; Kiser, Bates, Maslin, & Bayles, 1986; Lamb et al., 1985). It is possible that through having an insensitive, undependable, or frustrating attachment object, the child is learning that his/her social worth is low and is failing to learn communication and empathy skills that would help the child resolve conflicts and gain the benefits of society. These characteristics are hallmarks of clinical behavior problems.

However, as Goldsmith, Bradshaw, and Rieser-Danner (1986) graphically pointed out, the mother-behavior measures actually account for only modest portions of the variance in attachment. Furthermore, studies have not yet adequately addressed the question of whether it is maternal responsiveness per se that produces a secure attachment, or whether it might also be due to other aspects of the package of socially valued characteristics, e.g., stimulation of cognitive growth, which tend to co-occur with maternal responsiveness (Bates et al., 1982).

Preschool Competency Consequences.   There have been several studies showing that secure attachment in infancy predicts a variety of social competencies in toddlerhood and the preschool years, including 2-year-olds' solving tool problems in the company of the mother (Matas, Arend, & Sroufe, 1978; Frankel & Bates, 1984) and positive social and task orientation in nursery school and kindergarten (Arend, Gove, & Sroufe, 1979; Erickson, Sroufe, & Egeland, 1985; Sroufe, 1983; Waters, Wippman, & Sroufe, 1979). In that such competencies are often related to emotional/behavioral adjustment versus problems, the studies suggest that attachment security might promote adjustment in general

However, important question do remain about how the observed continuities between attachment and later competencies come about. Is it something about the early attachment per se, or is it the continuing quality of the parent-child relationship that accounts for the predictiveness of attachment? Attachment research has not yet adequately assessed continuity in relationship (Lamb et al., 1985). Another possible limitation in the meaning of the follow-up research is in the characteristics of the samples in the relevant studies. In the Sroufe (1983) and Erickson et al. studies, the sample was extremely disadvantaged socioeconomically. In the Sroufe (1983) study, about 66% of the children of the preschool class had been anxiously attached. This could create an unusual social climate in the classroom. Furthermore, in both the Sroufe (1983) and Erickson et al. studies, the subjects in the key comparisons were ones who had shown stability of attachment from 12 to 18 months of age. Although these choices were made for good reasons, they could limit generalizability. We assume that extreme samples might be atypical in multiple aspects of life adjustment, not just attachment security, even when controlling for possible moderating variables, such as SES, on a gross level. Thus, when attachment effects are obtained, they might be due to either continuity of parent-child relations or due to general environmental and constitutional forces that characterize a particular sample, rather than to attachment by itself. These considerations make follow-up studies on different kinds of samples, such as the current one (discussed later) especially crucial.

Behavior Problem Consequences.   Behavior problems are usually considered relevant to the general concept of social competence, but are not necessarily rooted in the same developmental processes. According to Sroufe (1983) and Erickson et al. (1985), teachers of the socioeconomically disadvantaged children in their sample rated the insecurely attached groups as having more problem behavior than the secure group, although in the more inclusive sample of Erickson et al., it was only the avoidant group who were comparatively high on behavior problems, not the resistant group.

Consistent with the earlier discussion of factors that might mediate the hypothetical link between attachment security and behavior problem outcomes, the Erickson et al. study provides general support for such factors operating from 24 to 42 months of age. Those children who were securely attached at 18 months but who did develop behavior problems in preschool, and those who were anxiously attached but did not develop problems, tended to have more positive indicators in their social systems. Their interactions with their mothers were more positive and supportive, and the children showed faster cognitive and language development. Because of their strong assumption that the insecure attachment resulted from inadequacies of maternal caregiving, Erickson et al. interpret these findings as showing that improvements in the quality of care produce deflections from the predicted problem outcomes. However, their analyses did not actually demonstrate change per se. It is possible that secure dyads that did and insecure dyads that did not develop behavior problems were functioning better even in the first year, while the attachment security was forming. The presence of cognitive test differences between the outcome groups at 24 months of age supports the latter interpretation. As Olson, Bates, and Bayles (1984) showed, mothers' tendencies to provide the warmth and stimulation that predict cognitive/language development at 24 months show strong continuity from 6 to 24 months.

A second project that assessed attachment origins of behavior problems is that of Lewis, Feiring, McGuffog, and Jaskir (1984). This study assessed attachment in an abbreviated, but valid version of the Ainsworth procedure. Lewis et al. used an unusually large group of 12-month olds from 113 normal, middle-class families. The families were followed-up when the children were 6 years via mother report on the Achenbach Child Behavior Checklist, an increasingly used instrument for assessing children's behavior problems. The results partially replicate Sroufe's (1983) findings. Anxiously attached boys had significantly more behavior problems of internalizing type (e.g. fears, worries, depression) compared to the securely attached boys, and nonsignificantly more externalizing problems (e.g. fighting, defiance to authority). For girls, however, attachment security made a significant difference on externalizing, and not internalizing. Lewis et al. also suggested that the predictions of attachment security were moderated by other variables. They concluded that insecurely attached boys with negative environmental features, especially being an unplanned, second child and experiencing stressful events in the family, were at elevated risk for behavior problems.

Our own research is a third, relevant entry in the literature. We followed-up at age 3 years 52 children from a normal sample of middle and lower class families whose attachment security had been assessed at 13 months (Bates, et al., 1985). Mothers and secondary caregivers (preschool teachers, daycare workers, regular babysitters) completed the Behar Preschool Behavior Questionnaire. Neither internalizing nor externalizing problems as rated by either mothers or secondary caregivers were predicted by attachment security. Given the important differences between this study and Sroufe's (1983) in sample selection and in outcome criteria, this study's nonreplication of Sroufe's results is not crucial. However, it does further raise the issue of how general the links between attachment and behavior problems are.

Our nonreplication of the Lewis et al. (1984) study is more puzzling, but perhaps the explanation has to do with the 3-year difference in age at this mothers' reports were collected. This latter attribution can be checked in the present study—further follow-up results from our longitudinal study are reported later. The Lewis et al. study comes closer to replicating the Sroufe and Egeland study results, but there are still discrepancies. The Lewis et al. group found attachment effects that differed according to sex of child and internalizing versus externalizing dimension of behavior problems, whereas Sroufe (1983) and Erickson et al. (1985) found attachment effects that differed according to the type of insecure attachment. The Bates et al. (1985) study considered possible contributors to behavior problems besides attachment, finding that perceived temperament and social class related differences in verbal development predicted behavior problems at 3 years in a pattern that depended on the specific nature of the behavior problem outcome and whether the outcome rating was by the mother or secondary caregiver. This study also checked for conceptually interesting interactive effects, e.g., attachment security by marital stress or difficult temperament. No significant interaction effects were found; therefore this study sheds no direct light on possible mediators of the hypothetical link between attachment and behavior problems.

ATTACHMENT AND TEMPERAMENT

Even if there were a large body of data showing links between attachment security and later behavior problems, it would be important to consider the meaning of the links. One argument is that the hypothetical links could be due to the influence of the temperament of the child. Several writers have argued recently that temperament must play a role in the security of an infant's attachment (Goldsmith & Campos, 1982; Goldsmith et al., 1986; Kagan, 1982). Furthermore, there is a longstanding hypothesis (Thomas, Chess, & Birch, 1968) that temperament, particularly difficult temperament, is involved in the formation of behavior problems. Kagan's argument is the key one; he noted that there are early-appearing and stable individual differences in infants' fear of new people and situations. He also noted that this temperamental trait would directly influence the infant's level of distress and the likelihood that the infant would need comfort from the attachment figure in the strange situation. We accept the logic of these points.

However, Kagan's conclusion that the level of the infant's distress would thus influence the attachment security classification is not so easily accepted (Belsky & Isabella, this volume; Sroufe, 1985). We would not deny that a complex, clinical rating such as attachment security could in practice be influenced by the infant's level of distress. However, as Sroufe has repeatedly pointed out, the classification should not rest on this variable. Sroufe (1983, 1985) argued that a good caregiver compensates for a temperamentally fearful or difficult infant, finding a way to meet the infant's basic needs. When attachment security is scored, the level of the infant's distress is explicitly considered as context for understanding the meaning of the attachment behaviors. So far, the evidence we are aware of supports Sroufe's position that temperament and attachment security are independent.

In both our own study (Bates et al., 1985) and in Sroufe and Egeland's study (Sroufe, 1985), early parent ratings of temperament on standard questionnaires did not predict attachment classification. Belsky and Isabella (this volume) report the same, although they did observe that babies destined to be secure showed decreases from age 3 to 9 months in perceived unpredictability of biological functioning and fearfulness in new situations, whereas those who became insecurely attached showed increases on these variables. However, Belsky and Isabella point out that this interaction between attachment and time of measurement is not equivalent to saying that temperament per se relates to attachment; indeed, it runs directly counter to such a contention, because it was secure infants who initially showed greater unadaptability and unpredictability. Using a novel method, Stevenson-Hinde and Simpson (1985) did show direct links between temperament and attachment. They reported that mother and father ratings of several toddler temperament dimensions, especially mood, correlated with a mother Q-sort measure of attachment security. However, even if the Q-sort method turns out to converge well with the standard behavioral assessment procedure, the parent-report nature of the Q-sort may influence the correlation with perceived temperament.

Do observational measures of temperament predict attachment better than parent reports? According to our own analyses, home and laboratory observation measures of temperament do not predict attachment security (Bates et al., 1985). Belsky and Isabella (this volume) review several studies showing a variety of connections between neonatal infant characteristics and later attachment. These studies are sometimes cited in the literature as support for the role of temperament in attachment security. However, the data consist of a variety of rather poorly convergent links between neonatal assessments and attachment. Aside from this, we argue that there is insufficient basis for regarding the neonatal measures as temperament. The neonatal measures do not show the stability/continuity that we regard as essential for calling a characteristic temperament (Bates, in press). Furthermore, it is not hard to imagine ways in which a link with attachment could be mediated by social environment qualities. For example, a mother who is not health conscious during her pregnancy might have an infant who scores nonoptimally on the Brazelton neonatal test. The same mother might produce insecure attachment in her infant by being relatively unresponsive, manifesting another version of the same attitudes that led to poor prenatal care.

We do not reject the possibility of eventual discovery of links between temperament and attachment security, but expect that if a coherent pattern is found it will be a complex, interactive one, such as the one of Belsky and Isabella (this volume) or one similar to that which Sroufe (1985) envisions, where the child's constitution influences the type of anxious attachment resulting from poor caregiving. Goldsmith et al. (1986) have a similar expectation, although they also argue that there already is some evidence that temperament does predict an infant's interactive behavior in the Strange Situation (e.g., Bates et al., 1985). Goldsmith et al. argue that proneness to distress predicts resistant behavior, and suggest that this may sometimes result in a classification of C. They also argue that tendencies toward interest, persistence, and pleasure predict avoidant behavior, perhaps leading to an A classification. Goldsmith et al.'s review serves to keep the question of temperament's role in attachment open. However, for the present, we would emphasize that not only are there good reasons for not expecting direct links between temperament and attachment classification, but also that the empirical results on the issue are generally null. Furthermore, the current evidence also suggests that there are no deleterious effects of temperamental difficultness on the mothering qualities of warmth and responsiveness, which are regarded as crucial in attachment security (Bates, in press).

TEMPERAMENT AND PSYCHOPATHOLOGY

Until recently, contrary to the impression of many writers, there has not been direct evidence that temperament assessed in infancy is predictive of behavior problems in later childhood. Recently, however, both Wolkind and Desalis (1982) and Bates et al. (1985) have found direct support for the Thomas et al. (1968) hypothesis that difficult infants are at elevated risk for behavior problems. Both studies found that early temperament predicts problems in the preschool years. Wolkind and Desalis observed that children described by their mothers at 4 months of age as negative in mood and irregular scored significantly higher on the Behavioural Screening Questionnaire (mother report) at age 42 months than the more positive and regular children. In cases where mothers were depressed at 42 months and had had negative infants, the children were especially likely to have marked behavior problems. Bates et al. (1985) also found that infancy-era mother reports of difficult temperament (defined by questionnaire ratings primarily of frequent and intense negative emotion) predicted mother questionnaire ratings of both externalizing and internalizing behavior problems on the Preschool Behavior Questionnaire. Infancy-age reports of unadaptability, referring to negative reactions to new people and situations, and probably analogous to fear reactions to novelty (Bates, in press), predicted 3-year anxiety problems, but not acting-out problems. The reverse was true for reports of difficult-to-manage activity in the second year (i.e., forecasting externalizing problems but not anxiety). Thus, two studies support the hypothesis that infant temperament may be involved in the development of behavior problems in the preschool era.

However, the evidence on the issue of temperament origins of behavior problems is far from complete. For one thing, more follow-ups are needed to see how general the effects of difficult temperament are. For another, assuming that the link is widely generalizable, work is needed on the issue of how it is that temperament predicts behavior problems. We have offered some speculations on what happens (Bates, in press), but the relevant empirical efforts are just underway (Bates, Miller, & Bayles 1984). We consider the link between early temperament and later behavior problems attributable at least in part to stable features of the child in interaction with the family. However, even if the link is merely one of maternal perceptual bias, the bias would have to be an impressively well-differentiated rather than a global one; this is because, along with evidence for general validity in maternal perceptions, we have also found consistent differentiation between markers of anxiety and resistance to management in maternal perceptions across 3 years of development and across varied questionnaires (Bates & Bayles, 1984). However, whatever the ultimate perceptual bias versus child characteristics conclusion, we note that the perceptions of the parent are crucial in the diagnosis of behavior problems. Further, even if the early measures are more reflective of the parent-child relationship history than of constitution, it is still remarkable that the roots of behavior problems can be seen empirically within the first 2 years of life.

Having reviewed the relevant conceptual material, we now detail some recent findings from our longitudinal study. We consider not only how attachment security relates to behavior problems at ages 5 and 6, but also how early mother-child interactions and child temperament predict these developmental outcomes, as well.

METHOD

Subjects

Our original sample, formed when the infants were approximately 6 months of age, numbered 168, with 57% male and 51% firstborn children. We also selected our sample such that 31% were perceived by their mothers as easy on the Infant Characteristics Questionnaire (ICQ; Bates, Freeland, & Lounsbury, 1979), 40% average, and 29% difficult. We did not select for SES, but found that our sample is a representative cross-section of our locale, with 14% upper-middle, 68% middle, and 18% working class. All marriages were intact at the time of initial assessment (6 months). In follow-ups at succeeding ages, we have collected information from as much of the sample as possible. The continuing participants are described next. Like most longitudinal researchers, our initial tendency in describing the changes in N of subjects over the 6 years of the study was to speak in terms of sample attrition. However, when we examined more carefully the pattern of attrition, we found that we did not have a simple pattern of subject attrition versus retention.

Of the original 168 families, at this writing we still have at least minimal contact with 145. Of the 145, about 50 live more than 50 miles from our city. We lost contact with 23 families between the 6 and 13 month assessments, but have not had further drop-outs of this sort since 13 months. We found through the years that about 66% of the sample were able to participate in the assessments. Out-of-town families usually contributed only questionnaires. The group of families participating at a given age had a solid core of about 70 who participated each time, and a fluctuating subgroup of about 20 to 40. This fluctuating sample is something we must be aware of, but so far it has not had detectable effects on the generalizability of our findings at a given age. Of the families who returned questionnaires at 3 ($N = 132$), 5 ($N = 98$), and 6 years ($N = 90$), the range of males is 54% to 60%; firstborns 43% to 51%; and the SES distribution is also relatively constant: 14% to 16% upper-middle, 64% to 68% middle, and 18% to 20% working class. These figures are practically identical to those at the onset of the study. We also compared the families who had unambiguously dropped out of the study with those who continued in full and those who continued in partial cooperation. We compared these groups on both demographic variables and measures of child temperament and cognitive competencies, and discerned no significant differences, except a tendency for the partial continuity subgroup to have higher SES and child developmental quotients. This is because some of this subsample had been students at the University when recruited for the study. Although the sample is stable in major characteristics of families, the fact that different individuals participate caused us, when we did multivariate analyses, to include only subjects who had all the relevant variables, rather than substitute average scores for missing subjects.

Another area of fluctuation in our sample has been marital status, with 35 families having experienced divorce, and 2 families the death of the father.

Procedures

The child and family assessments we conducted over the first 3 years have been documented elsewhere, and are briefly described here. The variables used in the present analyses are listed in Table 8.1, and the procedures used to obtain those indexes are summarized in the following paragraphs.

TABLE 8.1
Summary of Assessments at Each Age

I. Home Observation, Molecular Composites

Age 6 Months

1. Baby Happy and Active (smile + positive vocalization + activity burst + manipulative activity)
2. Baby Fussy (fuss/cry frequency + fuss/cry duration)
3. Baby Look and Reach (look at mother + reach toward mother)
4. Maternal Affectionate Contact (proximal vocalization, special quality + affectionate touch + bounce/jiggle/rock + put to shoulder + smile at infant + hold)
5. Mother Object Stimulation (offer toy + offer and demonstrate toy + return object to baby)
6. Mother Look and Tickle (look at infant + tickle/poke)
7. Mother Nonaffectionate Speech (distal vocalization + proximal vocalization normal quality + negative vocalization)
8. Mother Come and Go (mother approach infant + mother leave infant view)

Age 13 Months

1. Baby Socially Demanding (reach toward mother + fuss/whine + go to mother + follow mother + cry)
2. Baby Object Communication (bring object to mother + comply with request + point)
3. Baby Persists (persist after verbal prohibition + touch or play with nontoy object)
4. Baby Speech Sounds and Independent Play (speech-type position vocalization + independent toy play)
5. Mother Teaching (question + offer object + offer and demonstrate object + accept baby action + naming + draw attention to object)

6. Mother Management (prohibit/scold + direct nonverbal behavior + remove object)
7. Mother Response to Infant Speech (acceptance of infant speech + nonacceptance of infant speech)
8. Mother Affection and Caregiving (affection + social-expressive speech + caregiving)

Age 24 Months

1. Child Speech (verbal request + declarative statement + answer question + question)
2. Child Trouble (threaten mildly forbidden act + perform mildly forbidden act + violate nonobvious prohibition)
3. Child Negative Emotion (fuss/whine + cry)
4. Child Compliance (comply with positive request + laugh/smile + naming).
5. Child Mastery (self-help or mastery attempt + brings object)
6. Child Disengaged (empty time + watch – follow mother)
7. Mother Verbal Stimulation (refuse request + request information + nonacceptance of child speech + answer question + ignore request + comply with request + praise + maturity demand)
8. Mother Restrictive (prohibit + repeat prohibition + restrain + punish + scold + remove object)
9. Mother Affection (laugh/smile at child + playful conversation + affection + praise + pickup/hold + play game)
10. Mother Positive Control (suggest activity + give child choice)

II. Home Observation, Observer Ratings

Age 6 months

1. HOME Scale, Emotional and Verbal Responsivity of the Mother (is verbally expressive and shows a positive attitude re: baby)
2. HOME Scale, Mother's Involvement with the Child (gives direct cognitive stimulation and shows general interest in the baby)

Age 13 months

1. HOME Scale, Emotional and Verbal Responsivity of Mother (see above)
2. HOME Scale, Mother's Involvement with the Child (see above)

Age 24 months

1. Post Observation Questionnaire (POQ). Child Mature Communication (maturity of language development, how well needs, ideas and reactions are communicated)
2. POQ, Pleasant, Nonirritating Child (positive expression of demands, rare frustration when demands not met, rare irritating behavior)
3. POQ, Mother-Child Independence (child independent for age, mother promotes mastery, uses mild control, accepts child exploration, has own business—does not hover around child, mother and child jointly contribute to interactions)
4. POQ, Clear Consistent Mother Control (communicates demands clearly, consistent rule enforcement, sensitive to child needs and communications)
5. POQ Mutual Affection and Fun (child affectionate to mother, mother affectionate to child, spontaneous, "fun" interactions)
6. POQ, Mother Nonpunitiveness (infrequent scold or punish, mild punishment)

III. Mother's Perceptions

Age 6 months

1. Infant Characteristics Questionnaire (ICQ), Fussy-Difficult (frequent irritability, hard to soothe)
2. ICQ, Unadaptable (negative reaction to new things and people)

Age 13 months

1. ICQ Fussy-Difficult-Demanding (irritable, hard to soothe, doesn't like to be left alone)
2. ICQ Unsociable (doesn't like to play with people)
3. ICQ Unadaptable (negative reaction to new things and people)
4. ICQ Persistence (continues activity after prohibition, upset when forbidden object is removed)
5. Maternal Perceptions Questionnaire (MPQ), Unsociable (shy and fearful, negative reaction to new people)

Age 24 months

1. ICQ Difficult (irritable, hard to soothe)
2. ICQ Negative Adaptation (negative reaction to new people and things)
3. ICQ Unstoppable and Noncuddly (continues activity after prohibition, doesn't like to cuddle or be held)
4. MPQ Unsociable (shy and fearful, doesn't approach new people, upset when left with sitter)

Age 3 years

1. Preschool Behavior Questionnaire (PBQ) Anxiety (unhappy, worrisome, fearful, speech difficulty)
2. PBQ Hostility (irritable, disobedient, destructive, aggressive)
3. PBQ Hyperactivity (can't sit still, can't concentrate, inattentive)

IV. Other assessments

Age 6 months

1. Bayley Mental Development Index (MDI)
2. Mother Interview (closeness of husband and wife, supportiveness and helpfulness of husband)
3. Occupational status

Age 13 months

1. Bayley MDI
2. Attachment Security

Age 24 months

1. Bayley MDI
2. Peabody Picture Vocabulary test (number of words passed) (PPVT)

Age 3 Years

1. Mother Personality (MMPI)
2. Mother's years of education
3. Spanier Dyadic Adjustment Scale

Age 6 Months.   (a) Mother-child interaction: We sent trained, women observers into the homes for 2 3-hour visits. They encoded behaviors on electronic event recorders and gave more global impressions via Caldwell's HOME scales (e.g., see Bradley, Caldwell, & Elardo, 1979). In the present instance we focus on the mothering qualities of the HOME scales Emotional and Verbal Responsivity (Responsivity) and Maternal Involvement with Child (Involvement).

Frequencies of the coded behaviors were factor analyzed, as detailed in Bates et al. (1982). The factor names and constituent molecular codes are listed in Table 8.1. Our prior work has led us to interpret the mother factors Object Stimulation and Affectionate Contact as indicators of the mother's educative, teaching orientation, as well as HOME Involvement (Bates et al., 1982; Olson, Bates, & Bayles, 1984; Pettit & Bates, 1984). The Affectionate Contact factor, however, also has a more purely affective, warm, and responsive component, as do the factor Look and Tickle and the HOME scale, Responsivity (Bates et al., 1982). The infant factors Happy and Active and Look and Reach are indicative of the infant's emotional tone, activity level, and alertness (Bates et al., 1982). The infant Fussy factor appears to relate to difficult temperament (Bates et al., 1982; Pettit & Bates, 1984).

(b) Mothers' perceptions: The mothers were given the 6-month version of the ICQ at the time of the observation. In the current analyses we used the well-validated Fussy-Difficult factor of the ICQ, which indexes the mother's perception of the infant as irritable, hard to soothe, and difficult. We also used the Unadaptable factor, which indexes the infant's reactions to new situations.

(c) Other 6-month measures: We brought the mother and infant to the laboratory, where we gave the Bayley test of mental development and interviewed the mother about the challenges and changes faced since the baby's arrival. We also used family occupation status at this age as our main SES index.

Age 13 Months.   (a) Mother-child interactions: The observers went to each home for one 3-hour visit, with procedures very similar to those at 6 months. The factor composites derived from the coded behaviors (Pettit & Bates, 1984) are listed in Table 8.1. The factors mother Teach, mother Respond to Speech, and baby Object Communication, and the HOME Involvement scale are all seen as reflecting the educative, cognitively stimulating aspects of the dyad's interaction (Pettit & Bates, 1984; Olson et al., 1984). The factor Affection and Caregiving and the HOME Responsivity scale index the responsive, warm dimension. Also at this age, we found factors describing the mother's attempts to control the child's activity/exploration of limits, mother Management and a corresponding baby factor, Persists. Management consists of behaviors such as prohibit, direct, or remove object. Persists concerns nonresponse to maternal prohibitions and playing with nontoy objects. Other mother-child interaction factors are baby Socially Demanding, which concerns proximity and attention demanding behaviors directed to the mother and the expression of negative emotion. Baby Independent Play indexes frequency of playing alone, but also speech-type vocalizations.

(b) Mother perceptions: The mothers completed the 13-month version of the ICQ and the Maternal Perceptions Questionnaire (MPQ; Olson, Bates, & Bayles, 1982). We used all of the ICQ factors (Fussy, Difficult and Demanding, Persistent, Unadaptable, and Unsociable) and the MPQ factor Unsociable (reacts negatively to new people).

(c) Other 13 month measures: The mother and child came to the laboratory for a Bayley test. On another visit, to a different part of the building, the mother and infant participated in the Ainsworth et al. (1978) Strange Situation to assess attachment security. This second procedure was carried out on the second half of our sample only ($N = 74$). L. A. Sroufe and B. Vaughn provided us with training and checks of the reliability of our classifications. Details are in Bates et al. (1985) and Maslin (1983). Approximately 66% of our sample were described as securely attached, 13% anxious-avoidant, 16% anxious-resistant, and 5% mixed avoidant and resistant.

Age 24 Months.   (a) Mother-child interaction: The observers made two 3-hour home visits, with procedures similar to those at 6 and 13 months. The 10 factors in the coded behaviors are listed in Table 8.1 (see Lee & Bates, 1985, for details). We also used the behavior codes to form three-step sequences of various child trouble actions followed by various mother control actions and then either compliance or conflict in response to the control effort (Lee & Bates, 1985). We reduced these sequential indexes to five relatively independent factor composites indexing rate of conflict in the context of (1) mother power assertion (mother action precludes child making a choice); (2) prohibition/warning; (3) scold (harsh/angry tone) without an obvious child trouble act preceding the scold; (4) mild or nonobvious trouble which was followed by mild control; and (5) physically removing or punishing child. The sequences and their reliability are described in Lee & Bates. In addition to coding the behavior stream in molecular codes, observers also recorded their more global impressions on the Post Observation Questionnaire (POQ; Olson et al., 1982; Olson et al., 1984). The six factors from the questionnaire are listed in Table 8.1.

The molecular code factors, mother Verbal Stimulation, mother Positive Control, and child Speech, and the POQ factor, Mature Child

Communication, represent the educative aspects of the dyad (Olson et al., 1984). Positive affect qualities are indexed with the mother Affection and Play factor and the POQ factor, Mutual Affection and Fun. Trouble and control aspects of the interaction are indexed by the behavioral factors, mother Restrictive (reactive, negative control), child Trouble, and child Compliance, the conflict sequences (listed earlier), and the POQ factors, Clear, Consistent Mother Control and mother Nonrestrictive, Nonpunitive.

(b) Mother perceptions: Mothers completed the 24-month versions of the ICQ and MPQ. From the ICQ we used the factors Fussy-Difficult, Negative Adaptation, and Unstoppable (persistent in the face of prohibition). From the MPQ we used the Unsociable factor (reacts negatively to people).

(c) Other 24-month measures; As measures of the child's verbal and cognitive competence we administered the Peabody Picture Vocabulary Test at the end of the second home observation, and had the mother bring the child to the laboratory for the Bayley test.

Reliability of 6 to 24 Month Measures

Reliability information has been reported in our earlier work (see especially Bates et al., 1982; Lee & Bates, 1985; Olson et al., 1982, 1984; Pettit & Bates, 1984). We summarize the information here:

1. Molecular behaviors. Interobserver reliability was computed using the correlation between total frequency counts of a given code across visits where two observers were present. Day to day stability was computed by correlating total frequency of the codes on the first visit with the frequency on the second visit. As a rule, we did not include low frequency, low reliability codes in analyses, but in some instances we did consider a variable important enough to use despite low reliability. Codes retained despite low reliability are specified later. Codes with low stability were used if interobserver reliability was adequate. At 6 months, the average interobserver reliability correlation (over 25 visits) was .85, ranging from .54 to .97. The day to day stability across the first 84 subjects averaged .51, ranging from .23 to .80. The least stable code ($r = .23$) was included in factor analysis, but not in the factor composite scores used here. At 13 months, the average interobserver r (25 visits) was .85, ranging from .62 to .97, with the exception of one code, baby smile at mother ($r = .26$), which was retained despite low reliability. At 24 months, the average r (31 visits) was .81, ranging from .38 (for the code mother remove object) to .99. The day to day stability across the first 59 subjects at this age averaged .51 and ranged from .08 (mother initiates game) to .85. These reliabilities and stabilities are within the expected range for molecularly coded behaviors,

especially when such comprehensive lists of behaviors are being coded naturalistically. We also computed coefficient alpha internal consistency reliabilities of the factor composites we used. The average alpha at 6 months was .60, range .43 to .76; at 13 months the average was .64, ranging from .53 to .76; and at 24 months the average was .50, range .18 to .76. The composites with fewer items generally had lower internal consistencies, as would be expected. The composites with the lowest internal consistencies, 24-month mother Positive Control (.18) and child Disengaged (.19), were used in analyses, but must be interpreted with caution.

2. Questionnaires. For the HOME scale and Post Observation Questionnaire, we computed interobserver agreement percentages. HOME Responsivity items were agreed on at a 92% rate at 6 months (25 visits) and 95% at 13 months (25 visits). HOME Involvement items were agreed on at 84% at 6 months and 80% at 13 months. On the POQ, we counted as agreement ratings within one point on the 5-point rating scales. Over the 30 items of the instrument, the average agreement was 80%, ranging from 67% to 95%, across 22 visits.

For the mother questionnaires, the ICQ and MPQ, we computed test–retest correlations, across a span of about two weeks. The 6 month ICQ correlations were .70 for Difficult, .54 for Unadaptable, .57 for Dull, and .47 for Unpredictable. We have assumed, based on these results and results of other temperament questionnaires at later points of development, that test–retest reliabilities are comparable for the other forms of the ICQ. Results were similar for the MPQ, tested at 13 months. The 13 month MPQ factor used here, Unsociability, had a test–retest correlation of .68 across 51 subjects.

Age 3 Years. Shortly after the children turned 3 years of age, we sent the mothers a set of questionnaires that included the Behar (1977) Preschool Behavior Questionnaire (PBQ), which indexes hostile, hyperactive, and anxious behavior problems of the child; the Faschingbauer (1974) short form of the MMPI, a standard measure of self-reported psychopathology; and the Spanier (1976) Dyadic Adjustment Scale, a measure of marital satisfaction. Mothers also reported their years of education at this assessment.

Age 5 and 6 Years. When the children were 5 and 6 years old, their mothers were sent Achenbach's (1979) Child Behavior Checklist (CBCL). This questionnaire has been extensively used as a measure of child behavior problems. Its subscales (8 at age 5, 9 at 6 years) can be summarized by more global dimensions of externalizing (aggressive, destructive, etc.) and internalizing (anxious, withdrawn, etc.) problems. Furthermore, the norms on the subscales allow the user of the CBCL to examine a behavior problem profile. We generally did analyses on the 5 and 6 years CBCL's separately. However, for the correlations and regressions described as follows, we averaged scores for ages 5 and 6 where they were both available, and used only one year's scores if the other was missing.

RESULTS

We searched for the origins of mother-reported problem behavior at ages 5 and 6 years in several ways. First, we checked for a simple, direct relationship between attachment security and problem behaviors using analysis of variance and chi-square tests. Next, we moved to a more intuitive examination of the characteristics of the attachment sample, trying to see how the social system might affect the attachment relationship and the subsequent processes. Finally, we examined nonattachment predictors of behavior problems through correlations and multiple regressions.

Attachment Classification and Behavior Problem Scores

ANOVAs.   We used the A, B, and C attachment classifications as the independent variable and the Achenbach CBCL subscales, as well as the externalizing, internalizing, and total problems summary scores as dependent variables. We predicted that the anxiously attached, avoidant children would show problems concerning anger, coerciveness, and interpersonal aloofness; that the anxiously attached, resistant children would show anger, low frustration tolerance, immature dependency, and specific anxieties; and that the securely attached children would show lower behavior problem scores than the insecurely attached children.

Contrary to our predictions, none of the ANOVA comparisons revealed significant differences between attachment groups. Group means for boys and girls on the age 5-year Achenbach subscales and summary scores are shown in Table 8.2. Results for analysis of the 6-year scores were similar. As can be seen in the table, not only were the group differences generally small, but in many cases the means suggest that, if there was any difference between the groups, the securely attached children were seen as having more problem behavior than either insecure group.

CBCL Profile Comparison.   We also analyzed the hypothetical attachment-behavior problem relationship using a chi-square test of association. For this analysis, the 5-year CBCL's eight scores were standardized and profiled. On the basis of clinical knowledge and experience, we sorted the individual profiles into groups according to their similarity. This resulted in 8 "pathology groups" (for both boys and girls).

TABLE 8.2
Five-Year Achenbach Scores by Attachment Classification

Boys	A (N=4)		B (N=18)		C (N=6)	
	$\overline{X}$	SD	$\overline{X}$	SD	$\overline{X}$	SD
1. Social Withdrawal	1.5	2.4	2.1	1.7	1.0	1.3
2. Somatic Complaints	1.0	0.0	0.8	1.2	0.8	0.8
3. Depressed	5.8	4.8	4.9	5.1	3.3	2.7
4. Immature	3.0	2.2	3.2	2.4	2.5	2.1
5. Sex Problems	0.0	0.0	0.3	0.6	0.2	0.4
6. Schizoid	1.0	0.8	0.7	1.0	0.2	0.4
7. Aggressive	15.2	5.7	12.2	6.4	7.2	6.6
8. Delinquent	0.3	0.5	1.3	1.6	1.5	1.5
9. Total	28.8	13.3	27.8	16.0	18.2	12.5
10. Internalizing (1 + 2 + 3 + 4)	11.2	8.8	11.0	9.0	7.7	5.6
11. Externalizing (7 + 8)	15.5	5.5	13.4	7.4	8.7	8.0

Girls	A (N=5)		B (N=19)		C (N=3)	
	$\overline{X}$	SD	$\overline{X}$	SD	$\overline{X}$	SD
1. Depressed	2.0	2.3	3.4	2.8	4.3	3.5
2. Somatic Complaints	2.8	1.5	4.0	2.6	3.7	3.0
3. Schizoid	4.2	1.3	5.6	2.9	6.0	3.5
4. Social Withdrawal	2.0	1.9	3.3	2.0	2.7	2.1
5. Sex Problems	0.2	0.4	0.9	1.2	1.3	1.2
6. Obese	1.2	1.1	1.8	1.3	2.7	1.2
7. Aggressive	9.2	3.8	10.4	7.3	4.7	5.5
8. Hyperactive	3.6	0.9	4.1	2.6	3.0	3.5
9. Total	21.6	5.7	31.4	16.4	24.3	17.2
10. Internalizing (1 + 2 + 3 + 4)	11.0	3.5	16.3	8.5	16.7	11.5
11. Externalizing (7 + 8)	12.8	3.6	14.5	9.2	7.7	9.0

The groups ranged from normal, with all or nearly all scale scores within the normal range, to a group with most scale scores beyond the 90th percentile. Intermediate groups, with low to moderate levels of psychopathology, were divided according to the dominant kind of problem shown—internalizing, externalizing, or mixed. Chi-square tests, with cases sorted into the three attachment groups by eight pathology groups, showed that the distributions did not closely covary (chi-square for boys [df = 10) = 12.9, p = .23; for girls chi-square (14) = 14.3, p = .42]. Neither extreme nor moderate problem CBCL profiles were more likely to be found in children who had been anxiously attached than in those who had been securely attached. Thus, we conclude that there is no linear relationship between attachment security and mother-reported behavior problems in our longitudinal sample. There are both methodological and substantive interpretations of these unpredicted, null results. The power of the analyses to detect small differences could have been low due to small N's. On the other hand, as speculated previously, there might be an appreciable number of instances where insecure attachment does not represent a pervasive parent-child relationship/developmental problem, especially in a fundamentally normal sample such as the present one. However, the possibility of more complex, interactive effects still remains.

Case History Profiles

Our next data analysis strategy involved a partly qualitative examination of the child and family data from age 6 months to 6 years in the form of matrixes of Z-scores. Here we can present only the most relevant results. (Other findings and details of the analytic procedures will be sent on request.)

We were especially interested in the possible role of attachment subgroups in behavior problems. The chi-square analysis on the subgroups showed that the observed frequency of behavior problems (see Table 8.3) differed from the expected frequency at a probability of about .15, not conventionally significant, but worth mention. As seen in Table 8.3, among the boys there were two subgroups that appeared to have more than their share of high behavior problem scores. Of 5 A1 boys, 4 were scored as having high behavior problems at one or more ages. These boys tended to show either externalizing or both externalizing and internalizing problems rather than internalizing alone. The complete Z-matrix did not confirm the neglect and rejection in A1 mothers that we might have expected to see. The A1 males were the only A group children in our sample who were exceptionally likely to show behavior problems. The single A2 boy did not show any problems, nor did any of the 5 A2 girls with follow-up data on behavior problems. There were no A1 girls in the sample. Perhaps this A1 versus A2 difference is due to the fact that the A1 category indicates an unconflicted avoidance of the mother in reunion episodes, whereas A2 indicates a more ambivalent mixture of approach and avoidance (Ainsworth et al., 1978). Perhaps A2 children, especially girls, have a stronger need for attention and approval than A1 children, and this makes them easier for their mothers to control, and thus less likely to be seen as having behavior problems. We did not detect factors in the case history profiles, such as low levels of positive mother-infant involvement and early child resistance to control, which would more precisely account for the A1 boys' differences from other children in problem outcomes.

TABLE 8.3
Number of Children Showing Problems by Attachment Subgroups[a]

Boys[b]	A_1	A_2	B_1	B_2	B_3	B_4	C_1	C_2
Any Problems	4	0	2	7	2	0	2	1
No Problems	1	1	1	1	1	4	1	2
Girls[b]								
Any Problems	—	0	1	7	1	3	2	1
No Problems	—	5	3	4	1	2	0	0
Boys and Girls[b]								
Any Problems	4	0	3	14	3	3	4	2
No Problems	1	6	4	5	2	6	1	2

[a]Subjects with any behavior problems at age 3, 5 or 6 years were counted as having problems. Subjects missing data at all three ages (3, 5, 6 years) are excluded.
[b]Chi-square for boys (df = 7) = 11.4,ns; for girls, chi-square (6) = 10.0,ns; for boys and girls, chi-square (7) = 11.9,ns.

The second subgroup of boys that appeared to have more than their share of high behavior problem scores was B2, where 7 of 8 with follow-up data showed such problems at one age or another. Most of the cases showed externalizing or both externalizing and internalizing problems; only one showed internalizing problems alone. We concluded from further analysis of the case history profiles that pervasive family relationship problems did not account for the unpredicted finding that a subgroup of securely attached infants developed exceptional numbers of mother-rated behavior problems—the temperament, mother-child interaction, and cognitive development score profiles were generally within the normal range.

Among girls, none of the attachment subgroups showed an impressive ratio of problem cases over nonproblem ones. However, all 3 C girls, from both subgroups, showed problems, and there was a complete absence of problems in the A2 girls. Thus, attachment insecurity in general and its substrates and sequels are evidently not operating to cause behavior problems, as we have measured them, among girls. There is some support for the hypothesized risk status of C girls.

Predictors of Behavior Problems

Having established that attachment has only minimal, and very indirect, implications for psychopathology as we have measured it, we now evaluate a range of other predictor measures.

The following variables were correlated with the CBCL externalizing and internalizing summary scores, with scores from ages 5 and 6 combined, and boys and girls analyzed separately: all of the home observation factor composite scores; the mother perceptions of the child from 6 to 24 months on the ICQ and the MPQ of difficult temperament, unadaptability (fearfulness in new situations), unsociability, and persistence (resistance to control); mother report of behavior problems at 3 years on the Behar PBQ: mother self-reported personality on MMPI scales at 3 years; mother education; family occupation status; and child verbal competence as measured by the Peabody Picture Vocabulary Test at 2 years.

Because of our exploration goal, we selected predictor variables for multiple regression with the criterion that they have $p < .2$ r's with the relevant criterion variable. (The table of bivariate correlations is available on request.) We recognize that this common procedure has the risk of capitalizing on sample-specific relationships, and thus we present the results as a way of describing the path to behavior problems in our sample, not necessarily as a general path. To the extent that our sample and measures do represent other research, however, the current results may be repeated in other studies. In any given analysis, we used only those subjects with all the data for that analysis.

As a way of reducing the number of predictors, and of reducing multicollinearity as well, we averaged the ICQ and MPQ factors across their manifestations at ages 6 to 24 months. The regressions were done hierarchically, with mother-child interaction variables entered first; mother personality, second; and perceptions of the child, third. In doing this, we account for the direct and indirect (via personality and perceptions) influence of interaction on problem ratings, the direct and indirect (via perceptions) influence of personality on problem ratings, and finally the direct influence of perceptions on problems. Based on previous findings of meaningful distinctions between externalizing and internalizing problems, we treat the two kinds of problem in separate regression analyses. However, we must note that the two criterion scales were rather highly correlated ($r = .76$ for boys and .80 for girls). The results can be seen in Tables 8.4 and 8.5.

Boys' Externalizing Problems. Considering the prediction of boys' externalizing problems, the mothers' ratings were crucial predictors. The overall regression equation did not reach significance until the mother perception variables of 6 to 24 month difficult temperament and hostile behavior at 3 years were added. Difficultness and 3-year externalizing problems had been expected to predict 5 to 6-year externalizing problems. Also significant in the final step was the negative beta for observed mother affection and play at 24 months. There was also a negative beta for the

TABLE 8.4
Multiple Regression Results for Boys

	Betas and Rs at Each Step		
Externalizing	*Step 1*	*Step 2*	*Step 3*
1. *Observed Interaction Variables*	(R=.43)	(R=.46)	(R=.78***)
Mother Affectionate Contact, 6m	.13	.12	−.02
Child Disengaged, 24m	−.20	−.20	−.10
Mother Affection and Play, 24m	−.19	−.14	−.23*
Conflict after Power Assertion, 24m	.11	.13	.05
Mother-Child Independence, 24m (obs. rating)	−.26*	−.24	−.14
2. *Mother Personality*			
Mother Depressed (MMPI)		.16	−.10
3. *Mother Perceptions of Child*			
ICQ Persistent ($\bar{x}$ of 13, 24m)			−.14
MPQ Unsociable ($\bar{x}$ of 13, 24m)			.05
ICQ Difficult ($\bar{x}$ of 6, 13, 24m)			.26*
PBQ Hostile			.45*
PBQ Hyperactive			.09
PBQ Anxious			.17

Internalizing	*Step 1*	*Step 2*	*Step 3*
1. *Observed Interaction Variables*	(R=.53***)	(R=.59**)	(R=.77***)
Mother Teaching, 13m	.32*	.39**	.34**
Child Disengaged, 24m	−.19	−.17	−.14
Mother Verbal Stimulation, 24m	−.37	−.38**	−.30**
Conflict after Power Assertion, 24m	.05	.04	−.05
Conflict after Subtle Trouble, 24m	.06	.07	−.02
Mother Nonrestrictive/Nonpunitive	−.20	−.17	−.14
2. *Mother Personality*			
Mother Depressed (MMPI)		.27*	.18
3. *Mother Perceptions*			
ICQ Unadaptable ($\bar{x}$ of 13, 24m)			.01
ICQ Persistent ($\bar{x}$ of 13, 24m)			−.01
MPQ Unsociable ($\bar{x}$ of 13, 24m)			.09
ICQ Difficult ($\bar{x}$ of 6, 13, 24m)			.06
PBQ Anxious			.41**
PBQ Hostile			.07
PBQ Hyperactive			.03

$N = 46$
*$p < .10$
**$p < .05$
***$p < .01$

TABLE 8.5
Multiple Regression Results for Girls

	Betas and Rs at Each Step		
Externalizing	*Step 1*	*Step 2*	
1. *Observed Interaction Variables*	(R=.68***)	(R=.85***)	
Mother Affectionate Contact, 6m	−.58***	−.40***	
Mother Object Stimulation, 6m	.32**	.24*	
Baby Object Communication, 13m	.34**	.36***	
Baby Socially Demanding, 13m	.22	.00	
Mother Affection and Play, 24m	−.16	−.12	
Mother Nonrestrictive/Nonpunitive	.21	.22*	
2. *Mother Perceptions*			
ICQ Persistent (x̄ of 13, 24m)		.12	
ICQ Difficult (x̄ of 6, 13, 24m)		−.12	
PBQ Anxious (3y)		−.02	
PBQ Hostile (3y)		.48***	
PBQ Hyperative (3y)		.18	
Internalizing	*Step 1*	*Step 2*	*Step 3*
1. *Observed Interaction Variables*	(R=.71***)	(R=.76***)	(R=.89***)
Mother Affectionate Contact, 6m	−.47***	−.49***	−.36***
HOME Responsivity, 6m	−.09	−.08	−.14
Baby Socially Demanding, 13m	.03	−.10	−.30**
Baby Object Communication, 13m	.48***	.52***	.43***
HOME Involvement, 13m	−.15	−.28	−.13
Child Self-help and Mastery Attempts, 24m	−.37***	−.36***	−.25**
Conflict after Prohibit Warn, 24m	.01	−.12	.14
Mother Nonrestrictive/Nonpunitive, 24m	.28*	.23*	.14
2. *Mother Personality*			
Mother Depressed (MMPI)		.32**	.39***
Mother MMPI Scales (3 + 4 + 9)		−.06	−.04
3. *Mother Perceptions*			
ICQ Difficult (x̄ of 6, 13, 24m)			.11
ICQ Unadaptable (x̄ of 13, 24m)			−.05
PBQ Anxious, 3y			.27**
PBQ Hostile, 3y			.33**
PBQ Hyperactive, 3y			.07

N = 40
*p < .10
**p < .05
***p < .01

observer rating of mother-child independence at 24 months, which was significant prior to the entry of mother personality and perception variables, and which suggests that there was a tendency toward a restrictive, mother-dominated, perhaps overinvolved relationship in the boys who later showed externalizing problems. In short, 12 predictor variables accounted for about half the variation in the boys' externalizing problem ratings at 5 to 6 years. The predictors were led by observed lack of maternal affection and play with the child at 24 months and mothers' perceptions of early child difficultness and hostility.

Boys' Internalizing.   Interaction variables alone were able to significantly account for internalizing problems in boys. The leading mother-child interaction predictors also played significant roles even when the other kinds of predictors were included in the equation. The interaction variables that best predicted internalizing problems were high levels of cognitive/verbal stimulation at 13 months (Mother Teach), but low levels of a corresponding factor, Mother Verbal Stimulation, at 24 months. On the basis of findings that verbal development is slower in children with internalizing problems at age 3 years (Bates et al., 1985), we might have predicted the 24-month variable's negative correlation with internalizing problems at 5 to 6 years, but would not have predicted the 13-month variable's positive correlation, because both 13 and 24-month variables have been found associated with advanced verbal development (Olson, et al., 1984). However, we offer a post hoc interpretation of the pattern of findings: It is possible that mothers of boys with high internalizing scores were inappropriately high on cognitive/verbal stimulation at 13 months, perhaps because of misexpectations about the boys' developmental level. It is unlikely that the boys themselves were generally eliciting the mothers' behaviors in an obvious, direct way, because the reciprocal child behavior factor (Object Communication) did not correlate with the outcome criterion. Assuming that the mothers' high levels of teaching at 13 months reflected erroneous expectations, it is possible that by 24 months the mothers had overreacted to their ineffectual stimulation at 13 months by avoiding such stimulation at 24 months. An empirical support for this speculative interpretation is that mother depression was part of the predictor equation, and neurotically depressed people are often oversensitive to failure experiences. The role of the child in the process is not obvious because the reciprocal child verbal characteristics did not predict internalizing problems. However, there may have been subtle effects due to the child's anxiety tendencies or subtle speech deficits. For example, the 13-month-old destined to develop internalizing problems, already at an age-related high level of stranger anxiety, might show extra sensitivity to the presence of the observer by maintaining close proximity to the mother, giving her extra occasions to teach the child at this age, even if the child were not playing his or her part in the teaching interactions. However, by 24 months, the child would not be so reactive to the presence of the observer, even if still predisposed to anxiety problems in other situations, and thus, the mother's more natural tendency not to verbally stimulate, or the child's lack of receptivity to verbal stimulation would operate to keep the level of such mother behavior low.

The best mother perception predictor of boys' internalizing problems was the 3-year perception of anxious problems. This is quite understandable, given the conceptual similarity between the predictor and outcome variables, and given that the 3-year variable would be expected to more closely correlate with the outcome variable than the 6 to 24-month analogs of anxiety. The earlier indicators would be dropped from the equation due to their redundancy with the 3-year variable.

In summary, about half the variance in boys' internalizing problems at age 5 to 6 was accounted for by 14 predictor variables, with the leading predictors being, first, conceptually analogous behavior perceived in the first 3 years and, second, a pattern of high verbal stimulation by the mother at 13 months, but low verbal stimulation at 24 months—a pattern perhaps related to inappropriate expectations and then withdrawal of efforts to stimulate verbal development.

Girls' Externalizing.   As can be seen in Table 8.5, mother-child interaction variables predicted girls' externalizing problems even when they were considered in conjunction with the mother-perceived child characteristics. Girls who developed externalizing problems had unaffectionate interactions with their mothers at 6 months of age, but they did receive relatively high levels of stimulation via objects at that age. They also were active in such things as bringing and showing objects to their mothers at 13 months. The active involvement with objects, and the relative lack of affectional involvement would appear consistent with the development of behavior problems, in that behavior problems usually reflect a deficit in social relationship development, and it is possible that a child who learns to communicate mainly via objects would not have the kind of deep affective bond with the mother that would allow the control necessary to prevent externalizing behavior problems. Contrary to what we would have expected, there was no evidence of greater trouble and reactive control in the families where later externalizing problems were seen—in fact, if anything, the mothers in such families impressed the observers as being somewhat less likely to use restrictive, punitive means. Perhaps this correlation reflects a lack of maternal interest in establishing controls on the girls' behavior, but again, we note that the girls' levels of trouble behavior were not associated with the outcome.

Because there were no mother personality predictors here, mother perceptions were entered second. The mother perception variable that best predicted the girls' externalizing scores was the corresponding variable, hostile problems at 3 years. Of course, the earlier analogs of this predictor, difficultness and resistance to control, would have been eliminated by the regression procedure due to their overlap with the predictor more proximal in time.

In summary, more than 70% of the variance in the girls' externalizing outcome scores at age 5 to 6 was accounted for by 10 predictor variables, led by the age 3-year analog of perceived externalizing problems and by observed interactions, which were low in affection but emphasized use of objects at 6 and 13 months, and were low in punishment at 24 months.

Girls' Internalizing. The mother-child interaction predictors of girls' internalizing problems were similar to those for girls' externalizing problems, with low affectionate contact at 6 months, yet high infant object communication at 13 months, and also a relative absence of hard punishment at 24 months. (In the present instance, this last predictor was significant only before the perceived child characteristics were added to the equation.) There is one notable difference between the externalizing and internalizing equations in mother-child interaction predictors, despite the high overlap between the two criterion variables: Internalizing problems were predicted by low levels of self-help and mastery attempts at 24 months, whereas externalizing problems were not. Girls' anxiety-type problems had mother-child interaction origins similar to those for acting-out problems, except that they were also predicted by an indicator of passive, nonindependence. This is consistent with the difference between externalizing and internalizing problems. There is also a significant beta for infant social demandingness at 13 months; however, we chose not to interpret this as meaningful because the beta weight is of opposite sign from the bivariate correlation, suggesting that this beta is an artifact due to correlations among the predictor variables.

Mother depression was a significant predictor of the internalizing outcome for girls. This could be interpreted as an internalizing disorder in the mother being genetically transmitted to the daughter or transmitted via their interactions. It could also be seen as an indicator of the dysphoric mother being biased toward perceiving negative characteristics in her daughter; however, it is interesting to note that if this is so, there is a differentiated bias, in that mother depression does not correlate at all with girls' externalizing problems, and although it does have a nonsignificant correlation with boys' externalizing problems, it is a smaller correlation than it has with boys' internalizing problems.

Both kinds of age 3-year behavior problems, anxious and hostile, made significant contributions to the prediction of girls' internalizing problems. This contrasts with the other 3 prediction equations, where only the conceptually appropriate prior problem score made a significant contribution. From the regression analyses and the more qualitative analyses we did, we are coming to the conclusion that purely internalizing or purely externalizing behavior problem syndromes are rare in our sample, especially when one considers patterns across ages 3 to 6, even though we can draw distinctions between the two dimensions. Perhaps internalizing disorders in girls are more mixed in their antecedents than the other problem dimensions. This might be a good example of Chess' observation (Thomas, Chess, & Birch, 1968) that child anxiety is more a consequence of unresolved management issues than the cause of them, as had been traditionally assumed.

In summary, 15 predictor variables accounted for about 80% of the variance in girls' internalizing problem outcomes at 5 to 6 years. The leading predictors were internalizing and externalizing symptoms at 3 years, mother depression, and mother-child interactions characterized by a lack of affection at 6 months, high levels of infant object communication at 13 months, and a lack of child self-help and mastery attempts at 24 months.

Considering all four regression equations, the analyses indicate that there are conceptually understandable antecedents of later behavior problems—it is clear that the problems seen by the mothers at 5 to 6 years have not appeared from nothing. Perceived temperament/personality in the first 2 years, especially difficultness, negative adaptation, and resistance to control, predicted problems. There were also some advance indicators in observed mother-child interaction within the first 2 years, even if we might not have been able to anticipate the pattern. Mother depression at 3 years was a fairly consistent predictor, which converges with the literature on mother personality concurrent with clinical behavior problems. The early indicators of behavior problems, the 3-year PBQ scores, were also correlated with the outcomes in generally predictable ways. However, we must view the results with caution, too. The pattern of correlations was not entirely clear, even in post hoc interpretation; the individual variables' correlations with the criterion indexes were generally quite small, even when significant, and the numbers of subjects were small relative to the number of predictor variables. Ultimately, the question of how meaningful are the current results will be answered by comparison with other studies.

Clearly, the most consistent predictors were mother perceptions of the child from 6 to 36 months. It might be suggested that this merely reflects continuity in biased perception by the mother. However, because of the clear tendency toward consistent, meaningful differentiation of mother ratings into several dimensions, and because we have previously found that the objectivity of the mother's perception of the child is not overshadowed by subjective biases (Bates & Bayles, 1984; Pettit & Bates, 1984), we are not inclined to reduce this continuity in mother descriptions of the child to mere method variance. Even if the mother's early perceptions play a role in the creation of the child's characteristics, it is still important that the mother is able to see very early characteristics that are conceptually and empirically related to what she sees as much as 5 years later.

DISCUSSION

There are two central questions for organizing the discussion of the results just presented:

1. Did attachment security at 13 months predict mother reports of behavior problems in their 5 and 6-year-olds? Basically, no. The predictions we derived from a straightforward model of continuity in the developmental effects of attachment security were not confirmed. This is essentially the same conclusion we drew in our age 3 follow-up of attachment (Bates et al., 1985). How should this basic finding be reconciled with the prior studies and theory? We have not attempted to decide which of the studies is right. Each of the relevant studies, including our own, gives a picture of development with distortions and limitations, along with its current and future-useful information. In our study, anxious attachment did not, overall, predict mother Achenbach scores. Other researchers have found attachment to predict behavior problems, although not in the same way in any two different studies (even when the studies were based on overlapping samples).

We suggest two reasons why attachment security was not predictive in the present study. First, its effects may depend on correlated, third variables. The variables may have operated in the previous studies but not in the present. For example, general family stress and coping levels were probably better in the present sample than in the Minneapolis study, and this could have played a direct role in the production of behavior problems versus adjustment. We maintain the hypothesis that areas of positive family functioning mitigate the effects of insecure attachment. (Despite the possible role of third variables, however, we still assume that particular qualities of the attachment relationship played roles in the Sroufe/Egeland (Erickson et al., 1985; Sroufe, 1983) study. The fact that specific types of anxious attachment predicted appropriately specific patterns of behavior problems, e.g., the resistant children appeared more disorganized and the avoidant ones more devious [Sroufe, 1983], suggests that anxious attachment classification was not merely an index of a generally poor relationship, but rather of distinctive problems in the relationship.)

What might be the third-variable difference between the present sample and that of Lewis et al. (1984) is harder to guess. One could inferr from Lewis et al.'s description of their sample that ours would be less exclusively middle-class and interested in research than theirs. The effect of this difference might be that our sample had less continuity in the social conditions that attachment security reflects. Perhaps we had more families than Lewis et al. who functioned well in infancy but not in the preschool era, or vice versa. Differential continuity may have also been part of the discrepancy between the present study's results and those of Sroufe (1983) and Erickson et al. (1985), especially considering the Minneapolis study's tendency to select high-continuity subjects for follow-up.

However, besides sample life adjustment and continuity differences, a second reason for the discrepancies might be in the definition and measurement of behavior problem outcomes. Sroufe et al. measured these variables via preschool classroom observation and teachers' reports. We have learned from other parts of our own study that different kinds of measurement can produce different results. We have preliminary findings that suggest our sample's securely attached children were notably less impulsive than anxiously-attached children in several standard laboratory tests at age 6 years (Olson, Bayles, & Bates, in preparation). Impulsiveness could be a building block in the later development of behavior problems.

The mothers' reports at age 6 years might not yet be sufficiently well-tuned to the difficulties of an impulsive child in school, but will perhaps later be more attuned. Mothers appear to base their reports of behavioral adjustment on different aspects of the child than do the teachers. This is shown by the finding of low correlation between mother and teacher Achenbach scores (also see Bates et al., 1985). We also have support for the Sroufe finding of classroom behavior effects of attachment, in the finding of teacher report correlations with attachment. The Olson et al. (in preparation) data suggest that the teachers' ratings of behavioral adjustment were predicted by attachment security.

We are allowed by the foregoing considerations to maintain the possibility that attachment security may yet have some role in the development of behavioral adjustment, even in our own sample. Furthermore, the fact that we did find some variation in mother-report behavior problem scores according to attachment subgroup, e.g., the excess of problems in the A1 boys, also makes us maintain the basic hypothesis that attachment security is somehow related to development. However, from the pattern of current results and from the discrepancies in the prior literature on which gender and which insecure group showed which kinds of behavior problems, we also reserve the possibility that attachment security does not play a direct role. Further research should take pains to consider relevant third variables, such as general coping style, specific parent-child interactions relevant to a given developmental phase, and differential continuity in family stress and coping and attendant socialization processes. Future research should also attempt to compare different kinds of outcome assessments systematically, too. The present study makes a contribution toward this goal. Following, we consider the systematic, replicated meanings in our own study's outcome assessments.

2. The second question for discussion, then, is that origins do the current study's measures of behavior problems have? Mother perceptions of both acting out and anxiety-type problems are predicted best by early mother ratings of difficult temperament. So far, we have learned that difficult temperament marks a tendency to frequently express negative emotion, and that it is often attributed by mothers to infants' need for attention and inability to entertain themselves. We have not settled on a single scenario for how difficult temperament might lead to behavior problems. There could be different reasons for externalizing and internalizing problems, with tendencies to coercively demand stimulation/attention central in externalizing problems and general tendencies toward dysphoria central in internalizing problems. Mother perceptions of acting out behaviors are predicted also by early temperament ratings of fearful/negative reactions to novelty, but externalizing problems were not as well predicted by this early analog to anxiety. On the other hand, externalizing problems were predicted better by early ratings of resistance to maternal attempts to manage the child's activity than by early unadaptability. This pattern of continuity has held for both the 5 to 6-year and the 3-year assessments, even though the internalizing and externalizing dimensions were not independent.

In addition, there were a few links between behavior problem scores and early mother-child interactions, with the relative absence of affectively positive, educative interactions predicting both kinds of problems better than the hypothetically direct analogues of behavior problems, such as rates of child trouble and mother restrictive control.

Just as the antecedents of mother ratings of behavior problems at 6 years were similar to those at 3 years, the antecedents of teacher ratings at 6 years were similar to the antecedents of secondary caregiver (preschool, daycare teacher, regular babysitter, etc.) ratings at 3 years. As the preliminary data of Olson et al. (in preparation) show, the teacher ratings of social and academic competence and nonaggressiveness were predicted best by the child's early rates of verbal development and the verbal, educationally stimulating kinds of mother-child interaction that forecast that cognitive development (as described in Olson et al., 1984). This was also the interpretation at 3 years (Bates et al., 1985), except that lower social class, associated with lower verbal development, also predicted behavior problems, both acting-out and anxious ones.

In summary, the current longitudinal study of a sample of normal families does not find support for the hypothesis that attachment security at 13 months predicts mothers' ratings of behavior problems at ages 5 and 6 years. Early child characteristics as perceived by the mother did predict problems or their absence, however, in a conceptually appropriate way, and so did maternal warmth and stimulation, at a more modest level.

CONCLUSION

The central question of the present volume, and of the study group that launched it, is what are the clinical implications of attachment? We can address this question in two parts, one pertaining to clinical science and the other to practice. On the scientific side, we conclude that the concept of attachment security is a valuable one, despite our own negative findings. From the theoretical considerations, prior empirical work, and our own positive findings, we tend to believe that attachment security is somewhere close to the center of the social developmental process, at least closer than any other operational construct in the field. However, we can also see, via the same sources, that attachment security does not relate so consistently and strongly to other markers of social development that we should regard it as the "mother lode" of the social development research enterprise. We are open to the possibility of a direct role for attachment in the development of behavior problems, e.g., perhaps via the core attitudes the child develops about people. However, we also recommend increased effort to measure ways in which the attachment variable's predictions are modified by other variables. Much of value remains to be learned about the meaning of the secure attachment variable in the development of behavioral adjustment.

On the clinical practice side, we find it useful to consider that some behavior problems could be related to insecure attachment, even if it is clear that not all are. In several instances in our clinical work with 2 to 6-year-olds, we have seen problems partly fueled by attachment insecurity. In these cases, without using attachment terms directly with the family, we promoted changes to increase the child's sense that the parents would be supportive in times of stress. We also tried to reduce the parents' natural tendency to react negatively to child avoidant and resistant behavior in separation and reunion-type situations. In other cases, where we were helping a family through a stressful period, we have found it useful to give special emphasis to the child's attachment needs.

However, our current conclusion from the evidence is that there is not sufficient justification for regarding attachment insecurity as a clinical problem in itself. Nor is there justification for using it, except on an experimental basis, as a screening index for preventive intervention. There is too small a rate of correct predictions. In some cases insecure attachment may indeed represent a developmental process gone seriously wrong, but in others, the insecure attachment does not seem to have such important implications. Eventually, perhaps, we will know more about how to distinguish the two kinds of situation, and thus will know how to target early interventions.

ACKNOWLEDGMENTS

This research was supported in part by NIMH grant MH28018. The authors thank the families who participated and others whose help was essential: D. Pfenninger, T. Rowlison, B. Ridge, T. Triplett, J. Harness, B. Hohman, and J. Alberts.

REFERENCES

Achenbach, T. M. (1979). The child behavior profile: An empirically based system for assessing children's behavior problems and competencies. *International Journal of Mental Health, 7*, 24–42.

Ainsworth, M. D. S., Blehar, M. C., Waters, E., & Wall, S. (1978). *Patterns of attachment: A psychological study of the strange situation.* Hillsdale, NJ: Lawrence Erlbaum Associates.

Arend, R., Gove, F. L., & Sroufe, L. A. (1979). Continuity of individual adaptation from infancy to kindergarten: A predictive study of ego-resiliency and curiosity in preschoolers. *Child Development, 50*, 950–959.

Bates, J. E. (in press). Temperament in infancy. In J. D. Osofsky (Ed.), *Handbook of infant development* (2nd ed.). New York: Wiley.

Bates, J. E., & Bayles, K. (1984). Objective and subjective components in mothers' perceptions of their children from age 6 months to 3 years. *Merrill-Palmer Quarterly, 30*, 111–130.

Bates, J. E., Freeland, C. A. B., & Lounsbury, M. L. (1979). Measurement of infant temperament. *Child Development, 50*, 794–803.

Bates, J. E., Maslin, C. A., & Frankel, K. A. (1985). Attachment security, mother-child interaction, and temperament as predictors of behavior problem ratings at age three years. In I. Bretherton & E. Waters (Ed.,) *Growing points of attachment theory and research. Monographs of the Society for Research in Child Development, 50* (1-2, Serial No. 209).

Bates, J. E., Miller E. M., & Bayles, K. (1984, April). *Understanding the link between difficult temperament and behavior problems: Toward identifying subtypes of difficultness.* In I. St. James-Roberts & D. Wolke (organizers). Difficult temperament: Toward an integration of parental, clinical and research perspectives. Symposium at International Conference on Infant Studies, New York.

Bates, J. E., Olson, S. L., Pettit, G. S., & Bayles, K. (1982). Dimensions of individuality in the mother-infant relationship at six months of age. *Child Development, 53,* 446–461.

Behar, L. B. (1977). The preschool behavior questionnaire. *Journal of Abnormal Child Psychology, 5,* 265–275.

Bell, R. Q. (1979). Parent, child, and reciprocal influences. *American Psychologist, 34* 821–826.

Bowlby, J. (1969). *Attachment and loss:* Vol. 1: *Attachment.* New York: Basic Books.

Bradley, R. H., Caldwell, B. M., & Elardo, R. (1979). Home environment and cognitive development in the first two years: a cross-lagged panel analysis. *Developmental Psychology, 15,* 246–250.

Bretherton, I. (1985). Attachment theory: Retrospect and prospect. In I. Bretherton & E. Waters (Eds.) *Growing points of attachment theory and research. Monographs of the Society for Research in Child Development, 50* (1-2, Serial No. 209).

Erickson, M. F., Sroufe, L. A., & Egeland, B. (1985). The relationship between quality of attachment and behavior problems in preschool in a high-risk sample. In I. Bretherton & E. Waters (Eds.) *Growing points of attachment theory and research. Monographs of the Society for Research in Child Development, 50* (1-2, Serial No. 209).

Feiring, C., (1983). Behavioral styles in infancy and adulthood: The work of Karen Horney and attachment theorists collaterally considered. *Journal of the American Academy of Child Psychiatry, 22,* 1–7.

Frankel, K. A., & Bates, J. E. (1984). *Mother-toddler interactions while solving problems: Correlations with attachment security, and interaction at home.* Unpublished manuscript, Indiana University, Department of Psychology.

Goldsmith, H. H., Bradshaw, D. L., & Rieser-Danner, L. (1986). Temperament as a potential developmental influence on attachment. In J. V. Lerner & R. J. Lerner (Eds.), "Temperament and social interaction in infancy and childhood". *New directions for child development,* no. 31 (March). San Francisco: Jossey-Bass. pp. 5–34.

Goldsmith, H. H., & Campos, J. J. (1982). Toward a theory of infant temperament. In R. Emde & R. Harmon (Eds.), *The development of attachment and affiliative systems* (pp. 161–193). New York: Plenum.

Hinde, R. A. (1982). Attachment: Some conceptual and biological issues. In C. Parkes & J. Stevenson-Hinde (Eds.), *The place of attachment in human behavior* (pp. 60–76). New York: Basic.

Horney, K. (1945). *Our inner conflicts.* New York: Norton.

Kagan, J. (1982). *Psychological research on the human infant: An evaluative summary.* New York: W.T. Grant Foundation.

Kagan, J., Kearsley, R., & Zelazo, P. (1978). *Infancy: Its place in human development.* Cambridge, MA: Harvard University Press.

Kelley, H. H., & Stahelski, A. J. (1970). Social interaction basis of cooperators' and competitors' beliefs about others. *Journal of Personality and Social Psychology, 16*, 66–91.

Kiser, L. J., Bates, J. E., Maslin, C. A., & Bayles, K. (1986). Mother-infant play at six months as a predictor of attachment security at thirteen months. *Journal of the American Academy of Child Psychiatry, 25*, 68–75.

Kohlberg, L., Ricks, D., & Snarey, J. (1984). Childhood development as a predictor of adaptation in adulthood. *Genetic Psychology Monographs, 110*, 91–172.

Lamb, M. E., Thompson, R. A., Gardner, W., & Charnov, E. L. (1985). *Infant-mother attachment.* Hillsdale, NJ: Lawrence Erlbaum Associates.

Lee, C. L., & Bates, J. E. (1985). Mother-child interaction at age two years and perceived difficult temperament. *Child Development, 56*, 1314–1325.

Lerner, J. V., & Lerner, R. M. (1983). Temperament and adaptation across life: Theoretical and empirical issues. In P. B. Baltes & O. G. Brim (Eds.), *Life-span development and behavior* (Vol. 5, pp. 198–231). New York: Academic Press.

Lewis, M., Feiring, C., McGuffog, C., & Jaskir, J. (1984). Predicting psychopathology in six-year-olds from early social relations. *Child Development, 55*, 123–136.

Main, M., & Weston, D. R. (1982). Avoidance of the attachment figure in infancy: Descriptions & interpretations. In C. M. Parkes & J. Stevenson-Hinde (Eds.), *The place of attachment in human behavior.* New York: Basic.

Maslin, C. A. (1983). *Anxious and secure attachments: Antecedents and consequences within the mother-infant system.* Unpublished doctoral dissertation, Indiana University.

Matas, L., Arend, R. A., & Sroufe, L. A. (1978). Continuity of adaptation in the second year: The relationship between attachment and later competence. *Child Development, 49*, 547–556.

Olson, S. L., Bates, J. E., & Bayles, K. (1982). Maternal perceptions of infant and toddler behavior: A longitudinal construct validation study. *Infant Behavior and Development*, 5, 397–410.

Olson, S. L., Bates, J. E., & Bayles, K. (1984). Mother-infant interaction and the development of individual differences in children's cognitive competence. *Developmental Psychology*, 20, 166–179.

Olson, S. L., Bayles, K., & Bates, J. E. (in preparation). *Measurement of self-control in early childhood*. Unpublished Manuscript, Department of Psychology, University of Maine.

Patterson, G. (1982). *Coercive family process*. Eugene, OR: Castilia.

Pettit, G. S., & Bates, J. E. (1984). Continuity of individual differences in the mother-infant relationship from six to thirteen months. *Child Development*, 55, 729–739.

Rutter, M. (1981). *Maternal deprivation reassessed* (2nd ed.). Middlesex, England: Penguin Books.

Sameroff, A. J., & Chandler, M. J. (1975). Reproduction risk and the continuum of caretaking casualty. In F. D. Horowitz (Ed.), *Review of child development research* (Vol. 4). Chicago: University of Chicago Press.

Schnieder-Rosen, K., Braunwald, K. G., Carlson, V., & Cicchetti, D. (1985). Current perspectives in attachment theory: Illustration from the study of maltreated infants. In I. Bretherton & E. Waters (Eds.) *Growing points of attachment theory and research. Monographs of the Society for Research in Child Development*, 50, (1-2, Serial No. 209).

Spanier, G. B. (1976). Measuring dyadic adjustment: New scales for assessing the quality of marriage and similar dyads. *Journal of Marriage and the Family*, 38, 15–28.

Sroufe, L. A. (1979). The coherence of individual development: Early care, attachment, and subsequent developmental issues. *American Psychologist*, 34, 834–841.

Sroufe, L. A. (1983). Individual patterns of adaptation from infancy to preschool. In M. Perlmutter (Ed.), *Minnesota Symposia on Child Psychology* (Vol. 16). Hillsdale, NJ: Lawrence Erlbaum Associates.

Sroufe, L. A. (1985). Attachment classification from the perspective of infant-caregiver relationships and infant temperament. *Child Development*, 56, 1–14.

Stevenson-Hinde, J., & Simpson, A. E. (1985, April). *Attachment and temperament*. Paper presented at the Society for Research in Child Development, Toronto.

Thomas, A., Chess, S., Birch, H. G. (1968). *Temperament and behavior disorders in children*. New York: New York University Press.

Tyler, L. (1978). *Individuality: Human possibilities and choice in the psychological development of men and women*. San Francisco: Jossey-Bass.

Waters, E., Wippman, J., & Sroufe, L. A. (1979). Attachment, positive

affect, and competence in the peer group: Two studies in construct validation. *Child Development, 50,* 821–829.

Werner, E. E., & Smith, R. S. (1982). *Vulnerable but invincible.* New
York: McGraw-Hill.

Wolkind, S. N., & Desalis, W. (1982). Infant temperament, maternal
mental state and child behavioural problems. In R. Porter & G. Collins
(Eds.), *Temperamental differences in infants and young children, Ciba
Foundation symposium 89,* London: Pitman.

Young, R. D. (1975). The abused child and his parents. *Iustitia, 3,* 59–87.

9

Avoidance and its Relation to Other Defensive Processes

Jude Cassidy
University of Illinois

R. Rogers Kobak
University of Denver

An infant's avoidance of the parent during reunion in Ainsworth's Strange Situation procedure is a striking phenomenon. Whereas the majority of infants seek proximity or at least interaction with the parent following a brief laboratory separation, a substantial minority of infants actively avoid the parent. Avoidant infants ignore the parent's bid for approach or interaction, become preoccupied with a toy, actively turn or move away from the parent, or, if picked up, stiffly hold their bodies away from the parent (Ainsworth, Blehar, Waters, & Wall, 1978). In a situation in which high activation of the attachment system is normally expected, avoidant infants show a marked absence of distressed affect and attachment behavior; such infants can be viewed as cutting off affective responses. The presence of the avoidant pattern of attachment in approximately 25% of both middle-class and high-risk samples is a well-replicated finding (Ainsworth et al., 1978; Main & Weston, 1981; Waters, 1978), as is the stability of avoidance during infancy (Connell, 1976; Main & Weston, 1981; Owen, Easterbrooks, Chase-Lansdale, & Goldberg, 1984; Waters, 1978).

Avoidance has been viewed as a behavioral manifestation of an underlying attachment-related pattern of organization, and, in particular, as a defensive strategy in response to parental rejection (Ainsworth, 1984; Bowlby, 1973, 1980; Main, 1981). If there is a defensive component in the organization of the attachment system of the avoidant infant (with a behavioral manifestation of avoidance in the strange situation), it is possible that such a defensive component remains, albeit in a modified form, in the personality organization of some children and adults. The question arises: How is this defensive component manifested in the organization of

300

older individuals? Evidence for the persistence of avoidance during early childhood, and for the stability of avoidance from infancy to early childhood, has emerged from observations of child-parent reunions when children are 6 years of age (Cassidy & Main, 1984; Main & Cassidy, 1986; Main, Kaplan, & Cassidy, 1985). In Main's longitudinal Berkeley Social Development Project, 6 of 8 (75%) of the children classified as avoidant of mother in infancy were also avoidant of her at age 6 (Cassidy & Main, 1984; Main & Cassidy, 1986). This high degree of stability of avoidance has recently been replicated with a southern German sample, in which 6 of 6 (100%) of the children classified as avoidant of the mother in infancy were again avoidant at age 6 (Wartner, 1986). Although the specific behavioral manifestations of avoidance at age 6 differ from those in infancy, the underlying patterns of organization are quite similar. At age 6, the avoidant organization is identified by behaviors that function to maintain or increase physical or affective-emotional distance between child and parent. These behaviors include shifting attention away from the parent and attending to other activities, conversations, or objects. The child is polite but cool, and treats the parent as he might treat a next-door neighbor or teacher with whom he is willing to share social amenities. The child speaks when spoken to, but true interest is missing from the interaction. The tone of avoidance is neutral. Both affection and anger are hidden.

With the extension of attachment research to early childhood and adulthood, there as been an increasing use of methods relying on self-report and representational processes. This new focus raises a second question: How is the defensive component manifested in the organization of older individuals, *at the level of representation*? There are presently only a few studies examining attachment organization at the representational level rather than at the behavioral level. Because of the limited number of such studies, findings must be interpreted with caution. However, when the findings from these studies are examined as a group, a pattern suggestive of associations among various manifestations of avoidance and defensiveness emerges. Findings suggestive of these connections emerge from studies from several laboratories that examine individuals of different ages, use different measures, and explore different content areas. It may be useful for researchers to consider the possibility that these connections exist, particularly given the likelihood that the existence of such connections might have pervasive implications for future empirical work in terms of measurement construction, research design, and interpretation of findings.

The goal of this chapter is to explore the connection between behavioral avoidance as a defensive process and other forms of defensive processes. We begin by describing the experiential precursors of avoidant organization and the development of what Bowlby calls "working models." In particular, we describe the ways in which avoidance can be viewed as a strategy adaptive within a relationship with a particular parent. Next, avoidant organization at the behavioral level is interpreted as involving early defensive repression (or falsification) of affective responses. Then, in reviewing research on avoidant attachment during early childhood, adolescence, and adulthood, we describe two defensive strategies at the representational level—one of deactivation of the attachment system and one of idealization—that parallel behavioral avoidance in infancy. Finally, we discuss methodological and clinical implications that follow from our consideration of defensive processes associated with avoidance.

EXPERIENCES WITHIN THE PARENT-CHILD RELATIONSHIP AND WORKING MODELS OF ATTACHMENT

Bowlby's observations of children's lack of response to their mothers following long separations led him to consider the defensive nature of this behavior. Bowlby viewed this behavior, which he called "detachment," as a protective defensive mechanism by children whose attachment needs had been so long unmet (Bowlby, 1960, 1980; Robertson & Bowlby, 1952). Ainsworth, in the early 1960s, studying a small subsample of 1-year-olds, observed avoidance that looked similar to detachment on reunion following a brief laboratory separation. Such avoidance was found to relate to maternal rejection, lack of maternal emotional expression, unpleasant experiences related to close bodily contact, and rigidity in the home environment over the first year of life (Ainsworth et al., 1978; Main, 1977). Fraiberg (1982) reported total or near total avoidance of the mother in the home in a sample of infants who had been neglected or abused. According to Bowlby, the activation of attachment behavior that is not met with comfort or support arouses anger and/or anxiety. However, this arousal can be prevented if input that would normally activate attachment behavior is defensively excluded from conscious processing. Bowlby (1980) and Ainsworth (1984) have theorized that avoidance serves the function of preventing processing of information that would trigger attachment behavior.

Main (1981) has elaborated on the function of avoidance, suggesting that avoidant behavior may serve to maintain the attachment relationship. In the context of a history of rejection, attachment behavior may have dangerous consequences for the child. If he/she overtly expresses the anger associated with rejected attachment behaviors, he/she might risk alienating the attachment figure. If he/she makes further demands and becomes more clingy, he/she might risk being rebuffed further. Avoidance reduces the infant's arousal level and thereby prevents the direct, and possibly dangerous, expression of anger to the attachment figure. Avoidance simultaneously protects the infant from the rebuff that often results from attempts to seek contact as well as from the painful fear of alienating the attachment figure upon whom she/he depends for survival. Cognitive disconnection of input that might activate behavior potentially displeasing to the attachment figure serves to maintain organization during times of stress, and serves to maintain proximity to the attachment figure.

The child's use of avoidance as a strategy is based upon her/his expectations about a particular parent's response to attachment behaviors. Bowlby (1969, 1980) has suggested that these expectations, or "working models," are based on the child's daily experiences. These models provide the child with a guide for the workings, properties, and characteristics of the attachment figure, the self, and the relationship, and can serve a useful purpose for the child when he/she faces new situations. Although Bowlby views working models as remaining open to new input and to change, he believes that because they tend to operate outside the realm of consciousness, they become increasingly resistant to change (Bowlby, 1980; see also Bretherton, 1985; Main et al., 1985). Bowlby proposed that the foundations of working models are laid during the infant's first year, and there is substantial support for the notion that the working models are reflected in infant-parent reunion behavior with the Strange Situation. Ainsworth (Ainsworth et al., 1978) has suggested that infants who avoid the attachment figure on reunion are expecting rebuff or rejection, and that those who seek contact in a nonambivalent way are expecting comfort and reassurance. That the infant's expectations accurately reflect his/her experiences with a particular parent has been supported by observations in several studies of parent-infant interactions in the home during the year preceding the Strange Situation assessment (Ainsworth et al., 1978; Belsky, Rovine, & Taylor, 1984; Grossmann, Grossmann, Spangler, Suess, & Unzer, 1985; Maslin & Bates, 1983).

AVOIDANCE, DEFENSIVENESS, AND INAPPROPRIATE AFFECT DISPLAYS

Infant avoidance in the Strange Situation can be viewed as a form of masking of negative affect. We propose that just as the infant uses avoidance in the Strange Situation as a defensive strategy designed to reduce anticipated conflict, he/she may use a masking of negative affect as a defensive strategy in order to reduce conflict in other situations as well. Just as the infant's avoidance in the Strange Situation serves to maintain the relationship (Main, 1981), masking of negative affect may also serve to maintain the relationship in other settings. Such masking can be viewed as a distortion of normally expected affect display, and may be inappropriate for the situation. Fraiberg (1982) noted a similar phenomenon in infants, which she interpreted as a masking of anxiety by "giddy, theatrical laughing." She referred to such behavior as a "transformation of affect." The processes through which a strategy of masking negative affect may evolve, the nature of a relationship in which it may be adaptive, and implications for the organization and regulation of affective experience are discussed briefly in the following paragraphs. (See Kobak, 1987a, 1987b, for a more extensive discussion of these issues.)

The quality of affective communication in the parent-child relationship and the corresponding working model of the relationship can be viewed as providing the context in which the child comes to understand and organize his/her affective experience. For the child who interacts with a parent sensitive to his/her signals, affects will be experienced as useful in alerting the parent during times of distress. Sensitive parental response will in turn enhance the child's sense of efficacy in modulating his/her feeling states (Bell & Ainsworth, 1972). In this type of dyad, the child's experience of negative affects such as fear and anger comes to be associated with expectations of ameliorative parental response. As a result, the experience of negative affect may be less threatening to the child. The experience of security is not based on the denial of negative affect, but on the ability to temporarily tolerate negative affects in order to achieve mastery over threatening or frustrating situations (Kobak, 1985).

In contrast, the child who experiences a relationship in which there is a high level of parental insensitivity to affective signals experiences a unique dilemma. The expression of anxiety and anger, which optimally function to elicit caregiving from the parent, may become dysfunctional and may threaten the relationship. In order to reduce anticipated conflict with the parent, the child may learn to cut-off, repress, or falsify the expression of negative affect. Rather than communicate distress, the child attempts to control her/his affective state, and uses an avoidant strategy.

A process through which avoidant infants may learn to mask negative affect has been identified through observations of maternal and infant behavior. Escher-Graub and Grossmann (1983), using a mother-infant free-play situation, found that mothers of avoidant infants joined in play when the infant was content, but withdrew when the infant expressed negative affect. The pattern was reversed among mothers of securely attached infants, who were more likely to join the play (in a facilitative way) when the infant expressed negative affect. In addition, a study that examined infants' behavior in the Strange Situation suggested the avoidant infants behaved as if guided by a model stating that negative affects must be masked in order to preserve the relationship (Grossmann, Grossmann, & Schwan, in press). Observations of the communication patterns of mother-infant dyads revealed that avoidant infants communicated directly with their mothers only when they (the infants) were feeling well. When distressed, these infants tended not to directly signal the mother, and they did not seek bodily contact.

Although the avoidant strategy of affect regulation (i.e., masking of negative affect) may be adaptive in the context of the attachment relationship, it may be maladaptive in other contexts. In particular, an avoidant individual's display of affect in social and problem-solving contexts may appear inappropriate and maladaptive. The two studies described below provide examples of the use of restricted affect by avoidant individuals; this restriction can be viewed as a defensive communication that these individuals are unaffected by others. In an experimental study, Lutkenhaus (Lutkenhaus, Grossmann, & Grossmann, 1985) analyzed the affect and behavior of 3-year-olds who had been assessed in the Strange Situation with mother at 12 months. An unfamiliar adult visitor engaged the children in a competitive tower-building game. The children's affective reactions to winning and losing were analyzed. The avoidant children manifested sadness about losing while they were still engaged in the game. This affective display ceased when the game was over and the experimenter was available for social communication. In fact, during the social communicative exchange, there was a tendency for the avoidant children to replace sadness with smiling. In contrast, securely attached children showed their sadness after the game when the adult was more available. It is not the case that avoidant children simply did not feel (or display) sadness, because sad expressions were evident before the game was finished when there was no child-adult eye contact. Lutkenhaus interpreted his findings as suggesting a greater hesitancy on the part of avoidant children to display their sad feelings in social situations. It is striking that this masking of true feelings of sadness is evident as early as 3 years of age. It is also striking that this pattern of masking emotions is used so readily with a new social partner, with someone with whom the child has no history of social interaction.

Defensive restriction in affective expression among avoidant children is also evident in the drawings of these children. Children participating in the Berkeley Social Development Project were asked to "draw a picture of your family" as part of the 6-year follow-up (Kaplan & Main, 1985). Children who had been classified as insecurely attached/avoidant to mother in infancy tended to draw figures that were carbon copies of each other with little or no individuality. The bodies were tense and rigid. Family members often had no arms: individuals were independent, and were literally unable to reach out to each other. This signaling of "emotional unavailability" (Emde, 1980) is congruent with a style of affective communication organized around the attempt to withhold affect. Another characteristic of this group of drawings was that facial expressions often involved stereotyped, overemphasized smiles. This exaggeration of positive affect in the drawings, with the accompanying masking of negative affect, parallels the behavior of the avoidance children in the Lutkenhaus study described earlier.

AVOIDANCE AND DEACTIVATION OF ATTACHMENT

For Bowlby (1980), the infant's avoidance in a stressful situation represents a defensive effort on the part of the child to "deactivate" the attachment system. With increasing control over the environment, the child and adult can defensively deactivate the attachment system not only at the behavioral level, but also in more complex and elaborated ways involving representational processes. In particular, deactivation of attachment may become anticipatory in two ways. First, the individual may selectively exclude from processing information leading to feelings of anxiety or distress that generally elicit attachment behavior. Second, the individual may develop views of relationships that minimize or dismiss the importance of attachment processes such as giving and receiving care. In effect, these individuals develop information processing biases that serve the function of denying or controlling affective distress (Bowlby, 1980). In older children and adults these processes may combine to form behavior and attitudes that Bowlby has termed "compulsive self-reliance" (Bowlby, 1973).

The existence of both kinds of processes has been suggested by findings from recent studies. Cassidy (in press) explored the connection between child-mother attachment and the child's working models of the self in a sample of 52 white middle-class 6-year-olds. Quality of attachment was assessed on the basis of the child's reunion behavior with the mother following a 1-hour separation, using Main and Cassidy's 6-year reunion procedure (Cassidy & Main, 1984; Main & Cassidy, 1986; Main et al., 1985). The child's working model of the self within the relationship with the mother was assessed by doll play procedures in which the child was asked to complete six stories. Two stories dealt with emotionally-charged and relationship-focused interactions between the child and mother. Two additional stories (taken from Walsh, 1956), dealt with conflict within the family, principally with the mother, and two stores dealt with conflict or a threat from outside the family. Each story was accompanied by a series of probes. Stores were rated on 5-point scales, and each was placed into one of three classificatory groups: secure/confident, avoidant, or hostile/negative. Stories were classified secure/confident when the doll protagonist was described as someone valuable and worthy, and the relationship with the mother was important, special, and warm. In stressful situations related to mother, there was open negotiation and a sense of fair play; in stressful situations related to an external source there was the ability to turn to the mother for safety and protection and a positive outcome. These stories were most characteristic of children judged secure in the reunion episode. Stories were classified avoidant in which the doll protagonist was isolated and/or rejected and the importance of relationships was denied. In stressful situations stemming from both inside and outside the family, the existence of conflict was denied, as was the need for help; when there was a successful resolution, it was brought about entirely by the child without assistance from the mother. These stories were most characteristic of children judged avoidant in the reunion episode. Thus, the stories of the avoidant children showed a tendency to minimize the experience of distressing affect on the part of the child and a tendency to dismiss the importance of the relationship with parents as a source of comfort or support.

Findings from the Berkeley Social Development Project provide partial support for processes associated with the deactivation of attachment in avoidant children (Kaplan, 1984; Kaplan & Main, 1985; Main et al., 1985). Children who had been classified in the Strange Situation at 12 months with mother and at 18 mothers with father returned to the laboratory with their parents at 6 years for a follow-up assessment. One way in which the child's working models of attachment were examined was with the Klagsbrun and Bowlby adaptation of the Hansburg Separation Anxiety Test (Klagsbrun & Bowlby, 1976). Children were shown a series of six photographs of young children in situations related to separation; the least stressful showed a child and parents at bedtime, and the most stressful showed a child whose parents were leaving for a 2-week trip. Responses were scored on scales devised by Kaplan (1984). Scores at the high end of the scale were given to children who expressed a balance between feelings of vulnerability, sadness, or anger related to separation, and feelings of a constructive ability to cope with these feelings. Scores at the low end were given to children who responded in passive, depressed, or disorganized ways—who were unable to offer spontaneous feelings or possible responses. Responses were analyzed in relation to the child's 12-month Strange Situation classification with mother. The pattern most characteristic of avoidant children was for the child to acknowledge feelings of vulnerability and/or sadness, but to be unable to suggest possible adaptive coping strategies. Thus, although these 6-year-olds were able to acknowledge distress in their stories, they were unable to suggest related attachment behavior or the use of others as sources of comfort and support. It is conceivable that these problem-solving deficits resulted from their not processing all relevant information, and particularly from the exclusion of information that would activate attachment needs.

Behavioral avoidance of the parent is associated with an attitude dismissing of attachment not only by the child, but by the parent as well. Main and Goldwyn (1984) used the Adult Attachment Interview (George, Kaplan, & Main, 1984) to explore the connection between infant attachment and parents' abilities to recall and reflect upon their own childhood attachment experiences. The 1-hour semi-structured interview was administered to parents in the Berkeley Social Development Project during the 6-year follow-up assessment. Interview topics included attachment experiences during childhood such as memories of being upset or ill, memories of separations and losses, and early feelings of rejection. Subjects were asked to provide general descriptions of their relationships with parents and to integrate specific memories with these more general descriptions. The interview provides a method for studying how working models of the attachment relationships may control the ability to represent and integrate thoughts and feelings associated with the attachment system. Three patterns of organization were identified: secure/autonomous, preoccupied, and dismissing.

The majority of interviews of parents whose children had been classified as avoidant in the Strange Situation 5 years earlier fell into the dismissing group. These individuals tried to limit or completely dismiss the influence of attachment relationships and experiences from thoughts, feelings, and daily functioning by viewing attachment relationships as unimportant and inconsequential. When negative experiences were described, there was often an accompanying denial of the effects upon the self. Or, when the effects were acknowledged, understanding remained on a cognitive level; pain and sadness were missing. This inability to relate attachment experiences to the self, i.e., the disconnection of cognitive representation of an event from the normally accompanying affect, is similar to what Anna Freud (1966) called "isolation of affect." Another characteristic of individuals placed in the dismissing group was an inability to remember specific events related to attachment during childhood, an inability similar to what Anna Freud called "repression."

The finding that avoidant infants tend to have mothers placed in the dismissing category also emerged from Eichberg's (1987) study in which the Strange Situation and the Adult Attachment Interview were completed during the same month. Thus, interview findings from two studies provide support for the notion that parents of insecurely attached/avoidant infants tend to "deactivate" thoughts and feelings relevant to their own attachment experiences. Whereas those who cannot remember attachment events in childhood show evidence of a bias toward excluding attachment-relevant memories, those who cognitively represent attachment experience isolate the feeling normally expected to accompany such memories. Analysis of interview transcripts revealed that individuals in this group have often experienced considerable rejection or lack of love in their relationships with their own parents. Thus, by excluding information relevant to attachment, these individuals may be using a defensive strategy to control and minimize negative affects associated with working models of their parents.

Use of the Adult Attachment Interview has also revealed a connection between avoidance and deactivation of attachment in a sample of adolescents (Kobak & Sceery, in press), Kobak interviewed 53 first-year college students in the fall, collected self-report measures of perceptions of self and others over the course of the first year, and obtained peer ratings of adjustment in the spring. On the basis of the interview, students were classified into the three groups identified by Main and Goldwyn (1984). Peer ratings of the avoidant individuals (i.e., those in the dismissing group) indicated that they were viewed by their peers as less ego-resilient, more anxious, and more hostile than were secure individuals. However, on self-report measures, the avoidant individuals reported no more self-related distress than did secure individuals. This finding was interpreted as representing a cognitive bias among avoidant individuals toward minimizing the acknowledgment of distress or difficulty in adjustment. Avoidant individuals also reported receiving much less social support from their families than did secure individuals. Together, the biases toward minimizing problems in adjustment and toward minimizing perceptions of support from family were viewed as contributing to maintenance of an image of compulsive self-reliance based on deactivation of attachment thoughts and feelings.

MULTIPLE MODELS AND IDEALIZATION OF PARENTS AND SELF

A second defensive process involving representation is idealization of parents and self. It is assumed that the subject's refusal to perceive and/or report normal human and expectable limitations prevents the processing of information that would distress him/her. Idealization is, in a sense, the individual's avoidance of flexible, realistic, investigation and perception of self or other. To maintain idealization, information must be selectively ignored—in particular, information about negative components of self or other. Because both self and other are viewed as free of problems or distress, the attachment system is not activated; activation of the attachment system is, in fact, considered not relevant.

Bowlby's notion of "multiple models" is useful for understanding the origins of idealization. In families characterized by parent-child difficulties, parents may systematically omit, suppress, or falsify aspects of the parent-child relationship in discussions with their children. By misrepresenting themselves, such parents foster the development of multiple models that the child may hold of the parent (Bowlby, 1973). At the level of verbal reflection and discussion, the parent may be represented in the child's mind as a good parent, despite actions that are experienced quite negatively by the child. The creation of a "good" parent at the level of representation may be perpetuated by the child as a mean of reducing negative affects that would be associated with reflection about the true nature of the relationship. Idealization may also serve to reduce the child's sense of alienation from the parent in a manner similar to what Anna Freud (1966) termed "identification with the aggressor."

In the design of the Adult Attachment Interview (George et al., 1984), idealization was operationalized by examining the extent to which positive characterizations of parents at a general level of description were or were not supported by the recall of specific experiences. Subjects with high idealization claimed, at a global level, an idyllic past with nearly perfect parents. However, careful reading of the interview revealed either a lack of specific examples to substantiate these generalizations or actual contradictory indications of lack of support or rejection of the child by the parent. In two studies, a high rating on the idealization scale was found to be particularly characteristic of individuals with dismissing attitudes toward attachment (Kobak & Sceery, in press; Main et al., 1985). The defensive nature of this idealization has been underscored by the finding of a strong correlation between the subject's idealization of the parent and rejection by that parent in childhood (Main & Goldwyn, 1984). The finding that emerged from Main and Goldwyn's study that mothers of insecure-avoidant infants were more likely than other mothers to idealize their parents and childhood also emerged from a similar study by Eichberg (1987).

Further support for the relation between idealization of parents and avoidance is reported in a study by Ricks (1985). Using a sample of 44 mother-infant dyads from intact middle-class families, Ricks found that mothers of children who had been insecurely attached at 12 months (principally avoidant infants) were more likely to idealize their own mothers on Epstein's (1983) mother-father-peer scale during an assessment when the children were 5 years old. Items tapping idealization included phrases such as, "My mother was close to a perfect parent." In addition, maternal defensiveness on the O'Brien-Epstein Self-Report Inventory (O'Brien, 1981) was found to be more common among mothers of insecurely attached children. These differences had not been found in an earlier study with a smaller sample in which all assessments were made at 12 months (Ricks & Noyes, 1984).

A third study, by Lyons-Ruth and her associates (Lyons-Ruth, Connell, Grunebaum, Botein, & Zoll, 1984), also reported a connection between avoidance and maternal claims of a relatively "better" childhood. Forty-six mothers completed a maternal family history interview, consisting of questions in eight areas: (a) childhood economic status; (b) major psychopathology of adults in the family; (c) parental warmth; (d) peer friendships; (e) conflict and violence; (f) structure and supervision; (g) family health problems; and (h) liking and attendance at school. The authors note that this interview reflected the mother's perception of her history rather than her actual history. Mothers of infants classified at 12 months as insecurely attached/avoidant reported significantly *less* conflict and *more* liking of school than did other mothers. In fact, the group means for these mothers in all areas tapped by the family history interview were in the more adaptive direction. The authors hypothesized that mothers of avoidant infants are more likely than other mothers to deny negative feelings. They also suggested that the behavior of these mothers may actually consist of an "avoidance of overt conflict." It is equally possible, however, that these mothers merely perceive or admit less conflict; that is, the report of less conflict reflects the mother's working model, but does not reflect her (or her family's) actual behavior. Indeed, there is a good deal of evidence to suggest that individuals with avoidant organizations are, in fact, observed to be *more* hostile and aggressive than are others (Kobak & Sceery, in press; Main, 1973; Pastor, 1981).

Bowlby has proposed that working models of attachment figures are associated with complementary working models of the self (Bowlby, 1973; Sroufe, in press; Sroufe & Fleeson, 1986). This raises the question of whether defensively idealized models of the parent may be related to defensively idealized representations of the self in children with avoidant patterns of attachment. Support for a connection between idealization of the self and avoidance emerged in Cassidy's (in press) investigation of the connection between attachment to mother and the child's working model of self in 6-year-olds. One component of the study involved an interview with a large hand puppet (a frog named Bix) for whom the child spoke. The interview questions were about the child. Sample questions included: (1) Bix, do you like (child's name)?; (3) Do you like (child) the way he/she is, or do you want to make him/her better? How?; (9) Tell me Bix, do you want (child) to be your friend?; (16) Do you think (child) is important or not important?; and (17) Do you care what happens to (child)?

Interviews were scored on a 5-point rating scale and were placed into one of three classificatory groups: (a) perfect—the child insisted, even when repeatedly pressed, that he was perfect in every way; (b) negative—

the child made global negative comments about the self; and (c) open/ flexible—the child revealed an overall positive acceptance of the self, but when pressed, realistically admitted minor flaws. The interviews of children classified as secure in their reunions with mothers were split between the open/flexible and perfect categories. The interviews of children classified avoidant were likely to be placed in the perfect category. Although the perfect responses were more characteristic of the avoidant children than of the securely attached children, there were a substantial number of the latter whose responses were in the perfect category. Like many self-report measures, this measure has difficulty distinguishing defensive from nondefensive reports of optimal functioning. In a replication with a smaller German sample (Wartner, 1986), a priori contrasts revealed securely attached children to have significantly higher scale scores than avoidant children (with high scores given for open/flexible responses and low scores given for either perfect or negative responses). Pattern of response, however, did not significantly distinguish groups, although there was a tendency for more securely attached than avoidant children to fall into the open category.

Additional areas open to defensive idealization include quality of life circumstances, level of stress, and level of social support. These areas are extremely complex, and the existing literature presents no clear picture of their connections with attachment (Crockenberg, 1981; Durrett, Otaki, & Richards, 1984; Egeland & Farber, 1984; Goldberg & Easterbrooks, 1984; Kobak & Sceery, in press). However, it is possible that mothers of avoidant infants defensively idealize these aspects of their lives. For example, with a sample of 60 high-risk mothers and infants, Spieker and Booth (this volume) found that mothers whose infants avoided them in the Strange Situation reported more social support and less depression during pregnancy than other mothers. The authors hypothesized that these mothers used denial as a coping strategy in dealing with the same stresses and difficulties experienced by others in this high-risk sample. Certainly, there is variation in the extent to which people within the same sample are exposed to stressful events, and in the extent to which this exposure is perceived as stress. Nonetheless, examination of the case histories of the mothers of avoidant infants revealed that "they coped by being tough, distant, and unemotional, and by not acknowledging the extent to which their life situations were chronically difficult." This connection, however, did not hold over time: at 6 weeks postpartum, the mothers of infants who were to become insecurely attached/avoidant reported the greatest dissatisfaction with their lives; at 3 months postpartum there were no significant differences among groups of mothers. In a study in which amount of stress specifically related to parenting was explored (Green, 1980), it was again the mothers of avoidant infants who reported experiencing the least stress.

METHODOLOGICAL IMPLICATIONS

The majority of attachment-related research has centered on the infancy period. As a result, behavioral observation of infants and their parents has served as the principal means of assessment. Recently, attachment researchers have extended research to include the study of attachment organization during the childhood, adolescent, and adult periods of development. These shifts have led to the use of methods other than observations of behavior, including interview and self-report methods, and new methodological considerations have become necessary. Measurement construction, research design, and interpretation of results should be conducted with consideration of the possibility that the avoidant attachment pattern may be associated with defensiveness in a variety of forms.

Measurement construction can be carried out in a way that facilitates assessment of defensiveness. The attention to *organization* of behaviors and the *context* in which these behaviors occur (rather than frequency counts of behavior) that has characterized attachment research with infants (Sroufe & Waters, 1977) remains critical to the sensitive use of observational methods with older individuals. For instance, in discussing his study of affective communication, Lutkenhaus (Lutkenhaus et al., 1985) emphasized that attachment groups did not differ with respect to frequency of affective display, but differed strikingly in the *context* within which the display occurred; it was only the attention to context that suggested the defensive nature of the affective display of avoidant children. Measures tapping organization at the level of representation can also focus not only on factual events or outcomes, but on organization, process, and relationships, as well. For instance, with the Adult Attachment Interview (George et al., 1984), although the actual experiences in the subject's childhood were somewhat important, the quality of organization and integration of experience were more important. Similarly, when scoring the child's completions of Cassidy's (in press) incomplete doll stories, the outcome of the story and the competence of the doll protagonist's behavior were not as important as the means by which the outcome was achieved, or as important as the relationship context in which activities took place.

The tendency of avoidant individuals to cut-off negative affect suggests that measures should not be designed in which there is a simple linear relation between number of positive statements and optimal functioning. Standard defensiveness items tapping idealization and perfection can also be included in questionnaires. In addition, specific items that probe for normal human limitations and complexities of the self, other, and relationships can be included. Responses can be monitored for selective exclusion of particular components of relevant information; all components of relationships should be processed—not only positive ones, but ambivalent and negative ones, as well. Carefully worded self-report items, designed with an awareness of the tendency of avoidant individuals to dismiss attachment, can also help provide information related to defensiveness. For instance, in a study in which college students provided self-classifications for avoidant, secure, and ambivalent types, Hazan and Shaver (in press) reported that avoidant students did not receive higher loneliness scores than their secure counterparts. However, when items from the loneliness scale were divided into those that explicitly mentioned loneliness and those that simply mentioned "distance" from others, an important pattern became clear: Although the items that referred to distance from others were endorsed more often by the avoidant individuals than by secure individuals, the items that explicitly mentioned loneliness did not differentiate groups. In this instance, avoidant individuals admitted to an objective state (tapped by "distance from others"), but denied that such a state activated attachment needs or had emotional meaning for them (tapped by "I'm lonely").

Research design is another methodological component critical to assessing defensiveness. For instance, the discrepancies revealed in multimethod studies, with information from multiple perspectives, can be informative. In Kobak's study (Kobak & Sceery, in press) conclusions based on either the self-report or the peer-report measures *alone* would not have provided the information provided by the juxtaposition of the two; for those in the dismissing group only, there was a discrepancy between self and other-report. Dismissing individuals viewed themselves in a more positive light than others viewed them. Similar information useful in identifying defensiveness may be provided by comparing the child's self-report with sociometric data, teachers' reports, or naturalistic observations. Incoherency within and across self-reports can also be assessed. For example, the juxtaposition of claims that one's parent is perfect with simultaneous evidence of rejection by that same parent suggests a defensive idealization (Main & Goldwyn, 1984).

Third, consideration of the connection between avoidance and defensiveness is important in the interpretation of findings. Because the influence of experimental observation on the subject's behavior may vary according to attachment organization, such a framework may be useful when considering findings using observational methods. For instance, this framework may be relevant when considering findings that mothers of avoidant infants interact with their infants (Belsky et al., 1984; Smith & Pederson, 1983) and choose kissing as the means of displaying affection to their infants (Tracy & Ainsworth, 1981) *more* often than other mothers; mothers with a defensive need to be viewed as "perfect mothers" may alter their behavior under observation in order to portray such a picture (J.

Belsky, personal communication, June 12, 1986). Such a framework may also be useful when considering findings using self-report methods. It may explain seemingly anomalous findings—e.g., a lack of difference in social adjustment between avoidant and secure individuals (e.g., see earlier description of Kobak & Sceery, in press). The defensiveness of those in the avoidant group may also explain a lack of convergence between measures. For instance, this may explain the apparent discrepancy between the finding that those in the avoidant group report less conflict (Lyons-Ruth et al., 1984; Main & Goldwyn, 1984), yet are observed by others as having greater hostility (Kobak & Sceery, in press), aggression (Main, 1973; Main & Weston, 1981; Pastor, 1981), and negative affective expression (LaFreniere & Sroufe, 1985).

CLINICAL IMPLICATIONS

Present research provides a limited understanding about the relation between attachment organization and later behavioral difficulties. From a theoretical perspective, attachment organization is likely to include self-fulfilling expectations about self and others (Bowlby, 1973). However, this organization itself may be subject to change when the quality of the attachment relationship is altered. The conditions that foster naturally occurring changes in relationships are of considerable interest to clinicians who try to create therapeutic change. Research in early childhood suggests that improvements in family life conditions may mitigate the influence of early attachment organization on later behavioral difficulties. For instance, in Sroufe's Minnesota sample, not all children who had been insecurely attached to their mothers in infancy developed behavioral problems in preschool. The mothers of insecure infants who *did not* develop behavioral problems reported more social support than did the mothers of insecure infants who *did* develop problems. In addition, mother-child interaction at age 4 was associated with the presence or absence of behavioral problems. In particular, children who did not develop behavioral problems demonstrated more positive behavior with their mothers during a problem-solving situation than did other insecure children (Erikson, Sroufe, & Egeland, 1985). It might be inferred that these insecure children had undergone a positive alteration in their attachment relationships as a result of improved family circumstances. Unfortunately, methods for assessing attachment organization at age 4 were not available to determine whether attachment organization had also changed among these formerly insecure children. As new methods for assessing attachment in early childhood develop (e.g., Cassiday & Marvin, 1987; Main & Cassidy, 1986), longitudinal studies can examine the extent to which reorganization of attachment occurs, and what factors contribute to such reorganization.

Even when avoidant organization remains stable over time, difficulties associated with this pattern of attachment may be manifested only in limited circumstances. For instance, individuals may derive a sense of continuity and satisfaction from intimate relationships in which there is relatively little affective exchange. In addition, an avoidant pattern of attachment may have little influence on productive functioning outside the sphere of intimate relationships. In view of the many variables impinging upon human development, we cannot predict with certainty the ultimate outcome of avoidant behavioral patterns. However, despite these qualifications, research on the social correlates of avoidant attachment during infancy and early childhood suggests that this pattern of insecurity may leave individuals vulnerable to behavioral difficulties. Especially during times of stress or transition, the avoidant individual's inability to gain comfort from others or to use emotion to share and reflect upon experience may result in symptomatic behavior. There is some evidence that avoidant children tend to behave in a hostile and antisocial manner and tend to show impairments in empathy (Erikson et al., 1985; Main & Weston, 1981; Sroufe, 1983). These impairments may be early precursors of affectionless character and antisocial personality (Bowlby, 1944). Difficulties in emotional communication and impairments in the establishment and maintenance of age-appropriate peer contacts are also experienced by some avoidant children and may contribute to antisocial difficulties (Pastor, 1981; Sroufe, Schork, Motti, Lawroski, & LaFreniere, 1984).

For the clinician working with individuals or families, several clinical indicators of problems associated with avoidant attachment are likely to be evident. In particular, feelings of distress or vulnerability, even in conjunction with presenting problems, are likely to be minimized. This may limit an individual's or family's abilities to trust and rely on the clinician for support. In addition, both avoidant individuals and their families may evidence considerable displaced hostility. Although this anger may not be manifest in overt conflict, it is likely to be manifest in passive–aggressive or antisocial behavior on the part of the child. Such behavior serves, in turn, as a source of irritation to the parents, and may justify parental anger and rejection of the child. This pattern may, in turn, foster a family myth in which the parent is viewed as good and the child is viewed as bad. Whereas family therapy allows the clinician to directly observe such family interactions, individual therapy can also provide a context within which problems of trust and displaced anger can be assessed. In both types of clinical setting, the clinician should pay attention to the nonverbal dimensions of interaction, particularly to the expression of support and affection, to the level of overt and covert anger, and to the parents' reactions to signs of distress in the child.

The attachment perspective also provides a framework within which the therapeutic goals for working with avoidant individuals and their families can be derived. Because avoidant defenses involve the cut-off of negative affect, a primary therapeutic goal is to increase the individual's ability to acknowledge and communicate emotions. In individual work, the therapist can demonstrate special sensitivity and responsiveness to hidden or unacknowledged aspects of an individual's affective experience. In the family therapy setting, the clinician's sensitivity can provide a model to other family members of the constructive potential inherent in genuine emotional exchange. It is important for clinicians to respect the adaptive function of avoidant defenses and to recognize that such defenses often evolve in order to maintain relationships threatened with dissolution. As a result, an important therapeutic goal is to reduce the sense of threat that avoidant individuals and their families associate with emotional expression. This can be accomplished by establishing a "safe" therapeutic environment in which the acknowledgment and expression of negative emotion does not lead to the anticipated consequences of unresolved conflict and rejection (Kobak & Waters, 1984). The establishment of safety in therapy is likely to be evident when the individual or family experiences a sense of trust and security with the clinician. From this therapeutic "secure base" (Bowlby, 1979), the individual or family can explore the origins of "dangerous" emotions and can work toward viable alternatives to dissatisfying interactions.

SUMMARY

With the extension of attachment research into periods beyond infancy, new questions about the nature of attachment organization have been raised. This chapter has attempted to integrate what is known about attachment organization in infancy and early childhood with more recent research on later periods of development. In particular, we tried to identify processes that characterize avoidant organization at both the behavioral and the representational levels. At the behavioral level, avoidant organization has been discussed in terms of infant behavior within the Strange Situation, and in terms of affective repression and falsification. At the representational level, research has been reviewed that points to the existence of information processing biases that serve to deactivate the attachment system and to create idealized images of self and attachment figure. Research relying on self-report and representational processes is in an early phase of development. Nonetheless, our literature review presents a pattern of findings that suggests that researchers should proceed with increased awareness of the possible role of defensive processes. It is particularly important to consider whether individuals with an avoidant organization have tendencies to dismiss attachment, to idealize self and other, or to mask negative emotions. These tendencies, which may operate selectively with regard to attachment organization, can conceivably influence the measurement of constructs related to attachment. The connection between attachment organization and defensive processes can have important implications not only for methodology, but for theory and clinical practice as well. The study of this connection opens up new research opportunities for collaboration between developmentalists and clinicians.

ACKNOWLEDGMENTS

The authors are grateful to Mary D. Ainsworth, Jay Belsky, Elsie R. Broussard, and Ilo Milton, who provided helpful comments on an earlier draft of this chapter. Preparation of this chapter was supported by the NIMH Postdoctoral Training Grant to the Consortium on Family Process and Psychopathology.

REFERENCES

Ainsworth, M. D. (1984). Attachment. In N. S. Endler & J. McV. Hunt (Eds.), *Personality and the behavior disorders* (Vol. 1, 2nd ed., pp. 559-602). New York: Wiley.

Ainsworth, M., Blehar, M., Waters, E., & Wall, S. (1978). *Patterns of attachment*. Hillsdale, NJ: Lawrence Erlbaum Associates.

Bell, S., & Ainsworth, M. D. (1972). Infant crying and maternal responsiveness. *Child Development, 43,* 1171-1190.

Belsky, J., Rovine, M., & Taylor, D. (1984). The origins of individual differences in infant-mother attachment: maternal and infant contributions. *Child Development, 55,* 718-728.

Bowlby, J. (1944). Forty-four juvenile thieves: Their characters and homelife. *International Journal of Psychoanalysis, 25,* 19-52, 107-127.

Bowlby, J. (1960). *Grief and mourning in infancy and early childhood. The psychoanalytic study of the child. Vol. XV.* New York: International Universities Press.

Bowlby, J. (1969). *Attachment and loss.* Vol. 1: *Attachment.* New York: Basic Books.

Bowlby, J. (1973). *Attachment and loss.* Vol. 2: *Separation.* New York: Basic Books.

Bowlby, J. (1979). *The making and breaking of affectional bonds.* London: Tavistock Press.

Bowlby, J. (1980). *Attachment and loss. Vol. 3: Loss, sadness, and depression.* New York: Basic Books.

Bretherton, I. (1985). Attachment theory: Retrospect and prospect. In I. Bretherton & E. Waters (Eds.), *Growing points in attachment theory and research, Monographs of the Society for Research in Child Development, 50,* 3–38.

Cassidy, J. (in press). Child-mother attachment and the self in six-year-olds. *Child Development.*

Cassidy, J., & Main, M. (1984, April). *Quality of attachment from infancy to early childhood: Security is stable but behavior changes.* Paper presented at the International Conference on Infant Studies, New York.

Cassidy, J., & Marvin, R. S. (1987). *Attachment organizations at three-years of age: A classification system.* Unpublished manuscript.

Connell, D. (1976). *Individual differences in attachment behavior.* Unpublished doctoral dissertation, Syracuse University.

Crockenberg, S. (1981). Infant irritability, mother responsiveness, and social support influences on the security of infant-mother attachment. *Child Development, 52,* 857–865.

Durrett, M., Otaki, M., & Richards, P. (1984). Attachment and the mother's perception of support from the father. *International Journal of Behavioral Development, 7,* 167–176.

Egeland, B., & Farber, E. (1984). Infant-mother attachment: Factors related to its development and changes over time. *Child Development, 55,* 753–771.

Eichberg, C. (1987). *Security of attachment in infancy: Contributions of mother's representation of her own experience and child-care attitudes.* Unpublished doctoral dissertation, University of Virginia, Charlottesville.

Emde, R. (1980). Emotional availability: A reciprocal award system for infants and parents with implications for prevention of psychosocial disorders. In P. Taylor (Ed.), *Parent-infant relationships* (pp. 87-116). New York: Grune & Stratton.

Epstein, S. (1983). *The mother–father–peer scale.* Unpublished manuscript, University of Massachusetts, Amherst.

Erickson, M., Sroufe, L. A., & Egeland, B. (1985). The relationship between quality of attachment and behavior problems in preschool in a high-risk sample. In I. Bretherton & E. Waters (Eds.), *Growing points in attachment theory and research, Monographs of the Society for Research in Child Development, 50,* 147–167.

Escher-Graub, C., & Grossmann, K. E. (1983). *Bindungssicherheit im zweiten Lebensjahr-die Regensburger Querschnittuntersuchung*

[Attachment security in the second year of life: The Regensburg cross-sectional study]. Research report, University of Regensburg, West Germany.

Fraiberg, S. (1982). Pathological defenses in infancy. *Psychoanalytic Quarterly, 51,* 612–635.

Freud, A. (1966). *The ego and the mechanisms of defense.* New York: International Universities Press.

George, C., Kaplan, N., & Main, M. (1984). *Attachment interview for adults.* Unpublished manuscript, University of California, Berkeley.

Goldberg, W., & Easterbrooks, M. A. (1984). The role of marital quality in toddler development. *Developmental Psychology, 20,* 504–514.

Green, J. (1980). *Stress and infant-mother attachment.* Unpublished doctoral dissertation, University of Virginia, Charlottesville.

Grossmann, K. E., Grossmann, K., & Schwan, A. (in press). Capturing the wider view of attachment: A reanalysis of Ainsworth's Strange Situation. In C. Izard & P. Read (Eds.), *Measuring emotions in infants and children* (Vol. 2). New York: Cambridge University Press.

Grossmann, K. E., Grossmann, K., Spangler, G., Suess, G., & Unzer, L. (1985). Maternal sensitivity in Northern Germany. In I. Bretherton & E. Waters (Eds.), *Growing Points in Attachment, Monographs of the Society of Research in Child Development.*

Hazan, C., & Shaver, P. (in press). Romantic love conceptualized as an attachment process. *Journal of Personality and Social Psychology.*

Kaplan, N. (1984). *Internal representations of separation experiences in six-year-olds: Related to actual experiences of separation.* Unpublished master's thesis, University of California, Berkeley.

Kaplan, N., & Main, M. (1985, April). *Internal representations of attachment at six years as indicated by family drawings and verbal responses to imagined separations.* In Main, M. "Attachment: A Move to the Level of Representation," Symposium presented at the meeting of the Society for Research in Child Development, Toronto, Canada.

Klagsbrun, M., & Bowlby, J. (1976). Responses to separation from parents: A clinical test for young children. *British Journal of Projective Psychology, 21,* 7–21.

Kobak, R. (1985). *Attitudes towards attachment relations and social competence among first year college students.* Unpublished doctoral dissertation, University of Virginia, Charlottesville.

Kobak, R. (1987a). *Attachment as a theory of affect regulation.* Unpublished manuscript.

Kobak, R. (1987b, April). Attachment, affect regulation, and defense. In J. Cassidy, *Attachment and defensive processes,* Symposium presented at the meeting of the Society for Research in Child Development, Baltimore.

Kobak, R., & Sceery, A. (in press). Attachment in late adolescence: Working models, affect regulation, and perceptions of self and others. *Child Development*.

Kobak, R., & Waters, D. (1984). Family therapy as a rite of passage: The play's the thing. *Family Process, 23*, 89–100.

LaFreniere, P., & Sroufe, L. A. (1985). Profiles of peer competence in the preschool: Interrelations between measures, influence of social ecology, and relation to attachment history. *Developmental Psychology, 21*, 56–68.

Lutkenhaus, P., Grossmann, K. E., & Grossmann, K. (1985). Infant-mother attachment at 12 months and style of interaction with a stranger at the age of three years. *Child Development, 56*, 1538–1572.

Lyons-Ruth, K., Connell, D., Grunebaum, H., Botein, M., & Zoll, D. (1984). Maternal family history, maternal caretaking, and infant attachment in multiproblem families. *Journal of Preventive Psychiatry, 2*, 403–425.

Main, M. (1973). *Play, exploration, and competence as related to child-adult attachment*. Unpublished doctoral dissertation, Johns Hopkins University, MD.

Main, M. (1977). Analysis of a peculiar form of reunion behavior seen in some day-care children. In R. Webb (Ed.), *Social development in childhood* (pp. 651-693). Baltimore, MD: Johns Hopkins University.

Main, M. (1981). Avoidance in the service of attachment: A working paper. In K. Immelman, G. Barlow, M. Main, & L. Petrinovitch (Eds.), *Behavioral development: The Bielefeld interdisciplinary project* (pp.651–693). New York: Cambridge University Press.

Main, M., & Cassidy, J. (1986). *Categories of response to reunion with the parent at age six: Predictable from infant attachment classification and stable over a one-month period*. Manuscript submitted for publication.

Main, M., & Goldwyn, R. (1984). Predicting rejection of her infant from mother's representation of her own experiences: A preliminary report. *International Journal of Child Abuse and Neglect, 8*, 203–217.

Main, M., Kaplan, N., & Cassidy, J. (1985). Security in infancy, childhood, and adulthood: A move to the level of representation. In I. Bretherton & E. Waters (Eds.), *Growing points in attachment theory and research, Monographs of the Society for Research in Child Development, 50*, 66–106.

Main, M., & Weston, D. (1981). The quality of the toddler's relationship to mother and to father: Related to conflict behavior and the readiness to establish new relationships. *Child Development, 52*, 932–940.

Maslin, C., & Bates, J. E. (1983, April). *Precursors of anxious and secure attachments: A multivariate model at age six months*. Paper presented at the biennial meeting of the Society for Research in Child Development, Detroit.

O'Brien, E. (1981). *The self-report inventory: Construction and validation of a multidimensional measure of the self-concept and sources of self-esteem.* Unpublished doctoral dissertation, University of Massachusetts, Amherst.

Owen, M., Easterbrooks, M. A., Chase-Lansdale, L., & Goldberg, W. (1984). The relation between maternal employment status and the stability of attachments to mother and father. *Child Development, 55,* 1894–1901.

Pastor, D. (1981). The quality of mother-infant attachment and its relationship to toddler's initial sociability with peers. *Developmental Psychology, 17,* 326–335.

Ricks, M. (1985). The social transmission of parental behavior: Attachment across generations. In I. Bretherton & E. Waters (Eds.), *Growing points in attachment theory and research, Monographs of the Society for Research in Child Development, 50,* 211–230.

Ricks, M., & Noyes, D. (1984). *Secure babies have secure mothers.* Unpublished manuscript, University of Massachusetts, Amherst.

Robertson, J., & Bowlby, J. (1952). Responses of young children to separation from their mothers. *Courrier du Centre Internationale de l'Enfance, 2,* 131–142.

Smith, P., & Pederson, D. (1983, April). *Maternal sensitivity and patterns of attachment.* Paper presented at the meetings of the Society for Research in Child Development, Detroit.

Sroufe, L. A. (1983). Infant-caregiver attachment and patterns of adaptation in preschool: The roots of maladaptation and competence. In M. Perlmutter (Ed.)., *Minnesota symposium on child psychology* (Vol. 16, pp. 41–85). Hillsdale, NJ: Lawrence Erlbaum Associates.

Sroufe, L. A. (in press). An organizational perspective on the self. In D. Cicchetti & M. Beeghly (Eds.), *Transitions from infancy to childhood: The self.* Chicago: University of Chicago Press.

Sroufe, L. A., & Fleeson, J. (1986). Attachment and the construction of relationships. In W. Hartup & Z. Rubin (Eds.), *Relationships and development* (pp. 51-71). Hillsdale, NJ: Lawrence Erlbaum Associates.

Sroufe, L. A., Schork, E., Motti, E., Lawrosky, N., & LaFreniere, P. (1984). The role of affect in emerging social competence. In C. Izard, J. Kagan, & R. Zajonc (Eds.), *Emotion, cognition, and behavior* (pp. 155–192). New York: Cambridge University Press.

Sroufe, L. A., & Waters, E. (1977). Attachment as an organizational construct. *Child Development, 48,* 1184–1199.

Tracy, R., & Ainsworth, M. (1981). Maternal affectionate behavior and infant-mother attachment patterns. *Child Development, 52,* 1341–1343.

Wartner, U. (1986). *Attachment in infancy and at age six, and children's self-concept: A follow-up of a German longitudinal sample.* Unpublished doctoral dissertation, University of Virginia, Charlottesville.

Walsh, A. M. (1956). *Self-concepts of bright boys with learning difficulties.* New York: Teachers College, Columbia University.

Waters, E. (1978). The reliability and stability of individual differences in infant-mother attachment. *Child Development, 49,* 483–494.

IV
CLINICAL APPLICATIONS

10

Clinical Applications of Attachment Theory

Alicia F. Lieberman
Jeree H. Pawl
Infant–Parent Program
University of California San Francisco

The field of infant mental health includes a broad spectrum of disciplines and approaches to promoting the well-being and development of infants. Activities within the field range from clinical interventions of various kinds of research efforts intended to explore the different parameters of development and their possible vicissitudes. Researchers and clinicians alike share an interest in elucidating how maturation and development unfold in the context of diverse sociocultural conditions, varying human relationships, genetic and temperamental differences, and the mutual influences among these factors. Another common interest is the effort to understand how early development influences later development. There is a broad professional consensus that early functioning and experience affect later functioning, although there may be disagreement about the potency of these influences and about the nature of the causal mechanisms underlying this effect.

Among infant mental health clinicians, an additional endeavor is to promote societal concern for the developing infant and to educate and intervene in instances where the infant's well-being is at risk. Even within the clinical realm, however, there is a wide spectrum of approaches to intervention. A major difference among programs is the extent to which the parent–child relationship is the primary focus of the intervention. In many infant programs, focus is either on the parent or the infant as individual recipients of treatment. Some programs emphasize direct work with the infants, as in settings where an "infant curriculum" is used to encourage attainment of developmental milestones. Other programs seek to alleviate the parent's personal difficulties as a means of reducing stress and improving the environmental conditions for the infant. Methods of intervention may involve concrete assistance (i.e., help in securing food stamps, emergency assistance, or adequate housing), emotional support, and/or individual psychotherapy or family therapy (see Nezworski et al., this volume).

In programs where the parent–child relationship becomes a major focus of the intervention, treatment approaches are equally varied. The clinician may rely on didactic methods such as modeling or the structured provision of developmental and child-rearing information. Parent support groups may also be used to decrease parental isolation and promote discussion about problems of child-rearing. These approaches are based on the premise that lack of information and support constitute a major reason for difficulties in parenting. Whereas this may well be the case in some instances, in many other situations the sources of the problem are such that information and support alone would prove ineffective.

The goal of the present chapter is to describe a conceptual approach to infant mental health that involves a synthesis of attachment theory, object relations and psychoanalysis. In this approach, the concept of disorders of attachment is used as a pivotal organizing construct to understand problems in the parent–infant relationship that may have a negative effect on the infant's socioemotional development and hence on his/her mental health. We discuss the usefulness of this concept as a guide to intervention, and describe its clinical applications at the Infant-Parent Program, the infant mental health program of the University of California, San Francisco. In this context, clinical vignettes are used to illustrate the assessment and treatment of infants at risk for disorders of attachment and their families.

THE CONCEPT OF DISORDERS OF ATTACHMENT

As Bowlby (1969) and Ainsworth (1969, 1972; Ainsworth, Blehar, Waters, & Wall, 1978) describe it, a secure attachment is an emotional relationship with a specific figure that is characterized by feeling safe and protected in the presence of that person and by feelings of longing and the desire to restore proximity and contact when that person is absent. Although attachment relationships include other dimensions as well (such as playfulness and socialization), what makes them attachments instead of friendships or social acquaintances is the emotional core of felt security and perceived protection from danger in the presence of the attachment figure (Bretherton, 1985). In this sense, disorders of attachment in infancy may be defined as distortions in the parent–child relationship that result in the baby's inability to experience the parent as emotionally available and as a reliable protector from external danger or internal distress.

It is not possible to talk about disorders of attachment without at least commenting on the issue of the age by which one might properly speak of attachment as having occurred. Bowlby (1969) described three phases of attachment, and notes that by Phase 3 (6 to 7 months), attachment should have occurred under most circumstances. He emphasized that this conclusion is arbitrary and entirely dependent upon how attachment is defined. Bowlby chose Phase 3 behavior as clearly indicating that an attachment has been formed because at this time the systems mediating a child's behavior to the mother become organized on a goal-corrected basis, "and then his attachment to his mother-figure is evident for all to see" (p. 267). Both Bowlby's awareness of the arbitrariness in the criteria for attachment, and his statement that Phase 3 is the time when attachment becomes obvious, underline the dynamic process involved in the formation of an attachment. Unfortunately, the concept of attachment is often used in ways that violate this notion, as if the child's experience does not matter in any significant way until the magical 6 or 7 months of age have been achieved, and not before. Examples to the contrary abound. In a study of 3-month-old babies in face-to-face interaction, Blehar, Lieberman, and Ainsworth (1977) found that babies whose mothers encouraged interaction and were contingently responsive to their cues showed more delight in their response to the mother than to the observer. Infants whose mothers were impassive or abrupt did not show this early differential response. Moreover, these early individual differences were related to later differences in quality of attachment as assessed in the strange situation at 12 months. Infants later classified as securely attached were more positively responsive to the mother than to the observer in early face-to-face episodes, whereas anxiously attached infants were not. A study by Yarrow and Goodwin (1973) of babies who were transferred to adoptive homes at different ages highlights how even very young infants respond negatively to a change in mother figures. A full 40% of infants between 3 and 4 months of age showed moderate to severe reactions to separation. By 4 months, 72% of the infants did so. By 6 months, 91% of the infants showed disturbance, and by 9 months all the infants in the sample were showing marked negative reactions. These findings are consistent with the observations of Sander, Stechler, Burns, and Julia (1970) on the remarkable adaptations to caregiving conditions made by newborns, and the pronounced shifts in regulation of biological rhythms that they may experience when transferred from one caregiving condition to a different one.

The recurrent message of these findings is that the potential to form an attachment is present from birth, and is exercised and developed continuously at a pace that is influenced by the unique characteristics of the infant, the parent, and the quality of their interaction. It is a disservice both to the theory and to individual babies to view attachment as an attribute of a relationship that exists only at a point in time when it becomes "obvious," rather than as a complex process that begins at the beginning and is immediately subjected to multiple vicissitudes. Yet this latter approach has become all too common in actual practice, to the detriment of preventive and therapeutic endeavors in addressing the earliest symptoms of deviations in the parent–infant relationship and the infant's socioaffective development.

If forming an attachment begins at birth, so does the process by which deviations in attachment may emerge. This clinical tendency to view disorders of attachment as a condition that may be observed even before 6 or 8 months of age is apparent in the work of Fraiberg (1977, 1980) and Greenspan (1979, 1981; Greenspan & Lieberman, 1980; this volume), both of whom have written extensively about the early manifestations of affective disturbances in infants. This theoretical position finds clinical application in the field of infant mental health. Fraiberg and her colleagues pioneered a demonstration research project (e.g., Fraiberg, Adelson, & Shapiro, 1975; Fraiberg, 1980; Fraiberg, Lieberman, Pekarsky, & Pawl, 1981) and subsequently established an infant mental health program (e.g., Lieberman & Pawl, 1984; Lieberman, 1985) where infants could be treated from birth for disorders of attachment. Greenspan and his colleagues (Greenspan, 1981; Greenspan & Lieberman, 1980; Greenspan, Wieder, Lieberman, Nover, Lourie, & Robinson, in press) set up a research program of preventive clinical intervention with multipara pregnant mothers whose unborn babies were deemed to be at risk for a variety of socio-affective deviations that included disorders of attachment.

Disorders of attachment may be classified under three major categories: (a) nonattachment; (b) anxious attachment; and (c) disrupted attachments. These conditions have been extensively studied and discussed in theoretical and research contributions (e.g., Ainsworth, 1973; Ainsworth eta l., 1978; Bowlby, 1969, 1973, 1980, 1982; Main, 1982; Main, Kaplan, & Cassidy, 1985; Sroufe, 1979, 1983, 1985); a review of this vast literature is beyond the scope of this chapter. Our purpose instead is to clarify the clinical manifestations of disorders of attachment in the context of the assessment and treatment of infants and their parents in an infant mental health program, and to highlight the contributions of attachment theory to our work. It should be emphasized that although the classifications describe the quality of the infants' attachment, the contributions to this quality reside in characteristics of both the infant and the parent and may express chronic situational stresses as well (see Belsky & Isabella, this volume).

Disorders of Nonattachment

This term is used to describe the condition of infants reared with no opportunity for forming emotional connections with other human beings. Development shows impairment in three major areas: interpersonal relationships, cognitive functioning, and impulse control and the regulation of aggression (Fraiberg, 1977). These children are considered to suffer from a structural ego deficiency that seriously handicaps their long-term capacity to establish emotionally meaningful human relationships. Their connections to people are based on need and satisfaction of need, regardless of the specific personal qualities of the partner. There is no apparent emotional claim for one partner over another, and no signs of longing or distress when one caregiver leaves and another arrives. Thus, one person can easily replace another provided the child finds her/his needs and wishes satisfied. Cognitively, nonattached children tend to show impairments of intellectual functioning, particularly of language. Finally, there is a marked deficiency in the child's ability to regulate aggressive impulses and to modulate responses to frustration and displeasure.

The specific etiology of each of these areas of dysfunction has been the subject of lively debate regarding the role of maternal deprivation per se as a pathogenic factor (Rutter, 1972). In our view, maternal deprivation often involves a paucity not only of physical care and emotional sustenance, but of cognitive stimulation as well, because in the first years of life the mother figure is the primary mediator between the child and the environment. Thus, "maternal deprivation" has become a shorthand descriptive term for deprivation of many types of care and stimulation. Theoretically, such different forms of stimulations may stem from a variety of sources, but in real life and ordinary circumstances a substantial portion of this environmental input is provided by a "good enough mother" (Winnicott, 1941/1975) in the course of her daily ministrations.

The classical studies of children showing disorders of nonattachment are those of infants in institutions (e.g., Provence & Lipton, 1962; Spitz, 1945), and the powerful descriptions of their behavior still stand as models of careful clinical observation. Whether infants reared in severely neglecting home environments may fail to become attached and whether they may suffer from disorders of nonattachment is debatable. On one hand, it is possible that the developing impetus to form an attachment is so strong that infants may select even a minimally responsive but contingently available caregiver as an attachment figure. On the other hand, it is at least theoretically plausible that infants reared by caregivers who are extremely emotionally unavailable (due, for example, to mental illness or substance addiction) may be deprived of the minimal human responsiveness necessary to help them establish a reciprocal relationship with a discriminated and preferred partner. It is quite likely that even when a depriving home experience results in a form of nonattachment, the specific affective manifestation of the condition will be different from the type of nonattachment shown by children subjected to many anonymous, serial caregivers. In other words, whereas a child raised in an institution and one raised in a severely neglecting home may both be considered nonattached, the long-term consequences for the formation of the self may be different in each of these two types of situations.

Anxious or Ambivalent Attachment

This category describes the condition of infants who have been able to form a focused relationships with a discriminated and preferred partner, but whose attachments show an unusual amount of conflict regarding the perceived physical and emotional availability of the attachment figure. Ainsworth and her colleagues have provided detailed descriptions of the behavioral patterns and developmental correlates of anxious attachment among one year-olds in a nonclinical population (e.g., Ainsworth et al., 1978). Also using a nonclinical sample, Sroufe and his colleagues have provided long-term follow-up of children identified at one year of age as anxiously attached, and have shown that these children differ from securely attached children in their negotiations of age-appropriate developmental tasks (e.g., Matas, Arend, & Sroufe, 1978; Sroufe, 1979, 1983; Waters & Sroufe, 1983).

Working with a clinical population, Lieberman and Pawl (in press) used Ainsworth's concept of "secure base" as a basis for explaining some maladaptive behavioral patterns repeatedly observed among severely disturbed infants and their mothers. They suggested that deviations from the contextually determined, dynamic balance between attachment and exploratory behaviors represent distortions in the individual organization of secure base behavior. These distortions may be viewed as defensive adaptations, which protect the child against anxiety about the mother's unavailability as a secure base from which to explore.

Lieberman and Pawl (in press) have described three major patterns of distortion in secure base behavior. These patterns have been observed vis-á-vis the mother, and so we use this term instead of the more anonymous and less affectively compelling label of *caregiver.*

Recklessness and Accident Proneness.   A major manifestation of this pattern is the child's tendency to leave the mother's side and wander away for prolonged periods without either checking back with her or returning to her for reassurance. For example, the toddler may open the front door of the home and walk down the street; or she/he may take off alone in unfamiliar places, such as stores. Customarily, the child shows no distress and makes no effort to restore proximity or contact with the mother. It is usually the mother who, in a panic, finds that her child is gone and starts a search in an effort to restore proximity.

A second manifestation of recklessness is the child's tendency to get repeatedly hurt in the course of exploration: the child may cut himself/ herself in the course of playing with a sharp object, or fall down while climbing on furniture, or bang against furniture or walls in the course of running.

Recklessness and accident-proneness can be interpreted as the predominance of exploration at the expense of attachment behavior. The child's safety is endangered because exploratory behavior is not balanced by the protection usually provided by the complementary pull of attachment behaviors. Children showing this pattern may be developing counterphobic defenses against anxiety in the sense that they attempt to manage their uncertainty over the mother's availability as a protector by taking off on their own and courting danger, rather than seeking protection from a source they perceive as unreliable.

There is evidence that a similar but less extreme pattern of deviations in patterns of exploration is present in a nonclinical population. Cassidy (in press) described what she termed "negotiation of the environment" in 18-month toddlers observed in the Strange Situation. She reported that toddlers classified as anxiously attached, ambivalent (C babies) have more difficulty in negotiating the environment than either securely attached (B) or anxiously attached, avoidant (A) infants. Cassidy defines "negotiation of the environment" as the "ability to move safely through space, to be relatively comfortable in the understanding of the physical properties and boundaries of objects, to be aware of weight and balance, to be careful when testing the limits of one's physical skills, and to begin to foresee the consequences of one's physical actions". This definition is thoroughly congruent with our own conceptualization of a child's ability to protect himself/herself in the course of exploration.

Inhibition of Exploration.   This pattern is characterized by the exaggerated suppression of exploration, accompanied by deviations in the incidence and quality of attachment behaviors. Children showing this pattern are hesitant to approach, touch, and manipulate objects, and withdraw from social interaction with unfamiliar persons. They are often immobile in unfamiliar situations even in the presence of the mother and show a marked restriction of the affective range. This affective constriction is diagnostically important because it distinguishes inhibited children from those who may be temperamentally "slow to warm-up" or otherwise reserved in their approach to a new situation. Some inhibited children may cling to the mother and refuse to separate from her even after becoming familiar with a setting; others tend to avoid proximity to the mother as well as exploration. The choice of pattern is likely to reflect the child's working model of the attachment relationship. Our clinical observations have shown that inhibition of exploration is found in two major groups of children. One group has mothers who are gratified by their child's dependence and who discourage their unfolding autonomy through exploration by either withdrawing emotionally or becoming punitive. These children are likely to equate exploration and physical distance from the mother with maternal emotional unavailability and lack of protection. The second group comprises children living in chaotic situations where they are repeatedly and unpredictably punished for actions that displease the mother. These children may perceive the mother herself as a source of danger, and keep their distance both from the physical environment and from the mother in an effort to avoid the danger from either source.

Precocious Competence in Self-Protection. This pattern is characterized by an apparent reversal of roles between mother and child, so that the child engages in protective behaviors normatively performed by the mother and is unusually aware of the mother's wishes and needs. This pattern has long been recognized as an indication of developmental disturbance by psychoanalytically oriented clinicians (Settlage, personal communication, January 22, 1986) and some aspects of it are receiving increasing attention from attachment theory researchers (e.g., the "compulsive caregiving" pattern described by Crittenden, this volume). These children seem to internalize sooner than developmentally expected the protective role of the mother. This pattern does not involve a marked alteration of the contextually determined balance between attachment and exploration, but it can nevertheless be considered as a distortion of secure base behavior because the child does not rely on the mother as the primary protector but incorporates in his/her own behavior substantial portions of the mother's role.

The conceptualization described previously illustrates the potential clinical applications of attachment theory for understanding affective disturbances in infancy. In our work with disturbed infants and their parents, it has often been useful to understand symptoms in the child as deviations in the ability to internalize the role of the parent as a reliable protector. The distortions in secure-base behavior in toddlerhood described previously are one manifestation of this process. The emerging self must then resort to costly adaptive mechanisms to cope with the experience of insecurity and anxiety. The growing knowledge about these very early defenses is particularly important because it shows that, according to Fraiberg

(1982), at much younger ages than was previously imagined, "pain can be transformed into pleasure or obliterated from consciousness while a symptom stands in place of the original conflict" (p. 612). This new awareness, which carries such important theoretical and therapeutic implications for our understanding of the subjective experience of infants, has been made possible in large part by the cross-pollination between psychoanalysis, object relations, and attachment theory.

Disrupted Attachment: Separation and Loss

Separation is defined in this context as the premature and prolonged removal of a child from his/her attachment figure. Loss is a permanent separation. Both terms, used in this way, represent extremes in a continuum of experience. In ordinary circumstances, the child encounters many gradations of separation experiences, ranging from the mother leaving the room for a few minutes to her going away for a period of days, weeks, or even months. This variety of separation experiences illustrates two different but related uses of the term "separation": as a normal developmental process of gradual psychological differentiation from the mother, and as an event resulting in the mother's physical unavailability to the child (Allen, 1955).

As events, separations vary greatly in their psychological impact on the child (Provence, in press). Depending on the specific factors involved, a separation from the mother may encourage psychological growth or, alternatively, it may trigger such intense anxiety that the child's coping mechanisms are overpowered and the event may have long-term negative consequences for personality development and the capacity to form enduring and basically trusting human relationships. In this latter situation, a separation becomes a pathogenic experience.

The contributions of attachment theory have been crucial in focusing attention on the extreme manifestations of separation experiences, and in heightening understanding about the anxiety-producing potential of even minor separations (e.g., Ainsworth et al., 1978; Bowlby, 1973). Attachment theory has also generated valuable information and lively controversy about the psychological consequences and long-term repercussions of loss in infancy (Bowlby, 1980). In particular, there was been intense debate about the infant's ability to experience grief, mourning, and depression in response to the loss of the attachment figure, and about the similarities and differences between the subjective experience of loss in infancy, childhood, and the adult years. (e.g., Bowlby, 1960, 1961, 1980; A. Freud, 1960; Spitz, 1960). Regardless of the theoretical stance one chooses to espouse, the work of Bowlby, Ainsworth, and their colleagues make it quite clear that we can no longer disparage the meaning of the intense distress that may be experienced by even young infants upon separation from or loss of the attachment figure. We have also become much more knowledgeable about the factors that may heighten or serve as palliatives to the negative psychological repercussions of these events (e.g., Ainsworth, 1962; Provence, in press; Robertson & Robertson, 1971). It behooves the agencies and professionals charged with promoting the welfare of infants to encourage the application of this knowledge to social policy and clinical situations where the long-term placement of infants is at stake.

THE TREATMENT OF DISORDERS OF ATTACHMENT AT THE INFANT–PARENT PROGRAM

The Infant–Parent Program is located at the San Francisco General Hospital, a teaching county hospital in the University of California, San Francisco system. Every year, the program serves approximately 200 families who are referred when there is concern about infant abuse, neglect, and disorders of attachment. The infants range in age from prebirth to 3 years old. The main referral sources are local hospitals and the San Francisco Department of Social Services, but families are also referred by a large number of legal, social, and community agencies, including the court system. The families tend to be of low socioeconomic status, and 70% of them receive some form of social assistance. There is a high incidence of socioeconomic stress such as poverty, unemployment, and cultural uprooting through immigration, and a high incidence of psychological problems such as mental illness and substance abuse.

Conceptual Background

In the current program (Lieberman, 1985; Lieberman & Pawl, 1984), as well as in the original research demonstration project from which this program grew (Fraiberg, 1980; Fraiberg et al., 1981), the notion of disorders of attachment has played a pivotal conceptual role in developing methods for the assessment and treatment of infants and families at risk. These clinical methods represent a coalescence of the respective contributions of object relations, psychoanalytic theory, and attachment theory. Psychoanalytic theory provides a framework for understanding the psychodynamics of the parents and the genetic history of the parental experience of the baby and attitudes toward caregiving. In addition, it illuminates the vicissitudes of the parents' real and transferential relationship with the therapist, which is essential to the establishment of a working alliance, and hence to the success of treatment. Attachment theory, as a theory of dyadic relationships, provides a framework for understanding the affective meaning of the infant's behavior as a measure of the quality of the relationship with each parent. The concept of "disorders of attachment" has allowed us to examine the contributions that the parent and the infant make to problems in their relationship. On this basis, we have developed treatment methods geared to ameliorating disorders of attachment by focusing on their roots in the parent–child interaction and in the infant's caregiving experience.

Observations of the infant show that she/he is often a powerful contributor to the problems in the interaction with the parent. This may be due either to constitutional characteristics such as unusually low sensory threshholds, irritability, and excessively high arousability (Brazelton, 1973; Clemente, Purpura, & Mayer, 1972; Escalona, 1968; Korner, 1974; Thomas, Chess, Birch, & Hertzig, 1963), which may make it unusually difficult for the parent–infant dyad to help the infant achieve a smooth regulation of neurophysiological processes (Emde, Gaensbauer, & Harmon, 1976; Greenspan, 1981; Sander, 1962, 1975). The infant may also put stress on the relationship through behaviors that may themselves be the result of early interactional difficulties with the parent, but now also contribute to them, such as food refusal, night waking, frequent and protracted temper tantrums, and persistent negativism. It is in understanding these maladaptive patterns that attachment theory makes a powerful contribution to our approach. Concepts such as "differential response to the attachment figure," "secure base behavior," "avoidance," "resistance," and "secure and anxious attachment" (Ainsworth, 1969, 1972; Ainsworth et al., 1978; Bowlby, 1969, 1973, 1980) have been invaluable in complementing the working vocabularies of psychoanalysis and object-relations theory because such concepts provide a unique framework for observing infant behavior and for understanding both the normative and defensive qualities of that behavior (Lieberman & Pawl, in press).

In the parental experience, the baby often emerges as a powerful negative transference object. This means that important aspects of the parents' relationship with the infant may be understood as reenactments of their childhood experiences. The baby may be unconsciously perceived as a representative of key childhood figures or of repudiated aspects of the self, and these distorted perceptions mar the parents' empathetic response to the baby and the quality of their caregiving (Fraiberg, 1980). The distorted parental perceptions and caregiving behaviors may reflect the influence of socioemotional stresses such as poverty, family instability, and cultural uprooting. Caregiving difficulties may also stem from psychological conditions in the parent, ranging from neurotic conflicts to character disorders and psychotic processes. The prognosis for alleviating distortions in the parental perception of the baby and improving the quality of

caregiving is strongly influenced by the overall level of parental functioning and his/her emotional investment in treatment as a means of
improving the relationship with the baby and facilitating the baby's
development.

Services Provided

The conceptual background outlined previously provides the basics for
our clinical treatment methods (Fraiberg, 1980; Fraiberg et al., 1981;
Lieberman, 1985; Lieberman & Pawl, 1984). The underlying assumption
is that, on an individual basis, the mental health of the infant can best be
served by promoting the positive emotional investment of the parents and
by facilitating parental understanding of an appropriate responsiveness to
the infant's idiosyncracies. This involves exploring with the parents the
obstacles they face in responding to the baby's needs, in developing a satisfying and growth-promoting relationship with the baby, and in expressing
their emotional commitment to the baby in a relatively unconflicted manner. It also means that the therapist makes an ongoing effort to understand
and translate the baby's affective experience in terms that can be of use to
the parents. Particularly with toddlers and preschoolers who have some
use of language, we may also speak directly to the child, explaining our perception of the family situation and of the child's experience in terms that
she/he can understand—either verbally or through play.

All interventions begin with an assessment that takes place primarily in
the home and involves between five and seven weekly visits. An office visit
is also scheduled routinely to conduct a videotaped developmental assessment of the child (using either the Bayley Scales of Infant Development or
the Stanford-Binet Intelligence Test, depending on the child's age) and an
unstructured play session between the infant and the parents.

The assessment period has two primary goals. One goal is to provide an
evaluation of the infant's affective, social, and cognitive functioning. The
presence or absence of age-appropriate responses in each of these areas is
carefully assessed, with emphasis on the quality of attachment behaviors,
social responsiveness, the range and modulation of affect, and the adaptive coping mechanisms used by the baby. The second goal involves
appraising the parents' caregiving skills, their emotional investment in the
baby, the areas of conflict in social and intrapsychic functioning, and the
implications of these factors for the infant's development. The parents'
willingness and ability to make use of clinical services are also evaluated in
the course of the assessment through the use of preliminary interventions
and trial interpretations.

At the end of the assessment period, the parents are appraised of our
findings and invited to enter treatment if this is considered the appropri-

ate course of action. The treatment modalities involve nondidactic developmental guidance, emotional support, and infant–parent psychotherapy. These methods evolved as part of an effort to develop a psychoanalytic understanding of the plight of infants at risk for abuse, neglect, disorders of attachment, and deviations of affective development. The methods involve an interweaving of psychoanalytic principles with the traditional social work techniques of emotional and concrete support and educational intervention (Fraiberg, 1980).

In the course of developmental guidance, information about the needs of infants is provided in the context of the parents' spontaneous questions and of the specific difficulties they experience in raising their child. Joint observation of the baby by the parents and the therapist is a focal point of the sessions, with comments about the baby's behavior and the parents' experience of it flowing naturally from the observations. There is no developmental curriculum for the parents to learn, and there is no overt modeling by the clinician of appropriate modes of interaction with the baby. There is, however, a deliberate emphasis on expanding the parents' understanding of the process of forming attachments in infancy, the psychological meaning of separation protest and wariness of strangers, and the centrality of the relationship to the parents in shaping the interpersonal and affective world of the child. Suggestions about childrearing are geared to the parents' individual needs as they perceive them; these are tailored to what the parents consider a comfortable, ego-syntonic way of interacting with the child. In this sense, the developmental guidance follows the clinical tradition of respecting "the patient's definition of the problem," keeping in mind that here the patient is not only the parent but also the infant, who may be defining the problem in ways that need to be translated by the clinician into a language that the parent can understand. In this process, the clinician provides emotional support and expresses empathy for the family's plight.

When developmental guidance in the context of emotional support proves insufficient to bring about improvement in the infant–parent relationship and in the infant's development, we expand our treatment methods to incorporate infant–parent psychotherapy. This modality is offered when the conflicts between parent and infant are deeply rooted in the parent's past and can only be addressed through an exploration of the parents' intrapsychic difficulties. This approach differs from individual psychotherapy in its explicit focus on the baby and on the family conflicts involving the baby. Parents are encouraged to recollect their own childhood, and as these memories emerge the therapist looks for and addresses the links between the parents' past experiences and their current feelings and behaviors towards the baby. This technique helps to generate parental insight into the sources of their current difficulties in caregiving, and this insight in turn permits the parents to stop reenacting with their baby the conflicts of their own past.

In the treatment of a particular infant and family, one or another of the clinical modalities described previously may predominate, but in many situations developmental guidance, emotional support, and infant–parent psychotherapy blend and coalesce with each other in the course of treatment. Regardless of the specific modalities used, the format of the treatment has two main components: the sessions ordinarily take place in the home, and the baby is regularly present during the visits. The conjunction of the baby's presence and the home setting enables the clinician to assess and treat the baby and family in the environment where most of their interactions occur, where they are likely to feel least self-conscious, and where an understanding of the family's everyday circumstances and hence of the baby's experience can be most expeditiously achieved through direct observation.

Two clinical cases are used to illustrate how attachment theory is used in understanding the infant's experience and to provide brief illustrations of our assessment and treatment methods.

Clinical Illustration.   This case is a typical example of a failure in the mother's contribution to the early dyadic exchanges with the baby that, in the normative course of development, contribute to the formation of a secure attachment. Although the baby's contribution to the developing relationship can never be overlooked, in this case the mother's muted affect and mechanical handling of the baby were found to be the major contributors to the interactional difficulties, and for the sake of clarity this is the focus of the description that follows.

Andy was referred to the program for nonorganic failure to thrive when he was 6 weeks old. He had had a normal birth and an uneventful postnatal course. However, he had failed to gain weight from the third week of life and was hospitalized at 5 weeks for extensive medical testing. He was discharged 1 week later after gaining weight rapidly while in the hospital. This medical course ruled out an organic etiology for the child's condition and led the pediatrician to recommend treatment in our program.

Andy's mother, Mrs. Bradley, was an intelligent and resourceful woman who seemed paradoxically at a loss when she needed to think about formulas and feeding schedules, as if the complexity of the topic were beyond her ability to understand. Initial efforts to provide developmental guidance were met with an apparent willingness to learn that belied a profound resistance; Mrs. Bradley found herself unable to put into practice even the simplest suggestions about how to perceive her baby's states of hunger and satiation. This inability to respond appropriately to the baby was by no means confined to feeding. Mrs. Bradley was stiff and mechanical in her physical handling and tended to be efficient but matter-of-fact in her physical care of the baby. There was little face-to-face interaction and very little pleasure in social exchanges with the baby. From these observations, the therapist inferred that there were intrapsychic impediments to Mrs. Bradley's ability to form a relationship with her child, and that the quality of the unfolding attachment was endangered. This prognosis received support when ongoing observations of the infant made clear that at 3 months he tended to avoid his mother's gaze, had a bland facial expression, and was delayed in the onset of the social smile. Andy could respond to the social overture of the therapist after an initial period of vacant staring. These observations suggested that, although healthy, Andy was an undemanding, relatively passive baby who would make no strong claims for attention or for need satisfaction. These characteristics made is easy for Mrs. Bradley to overlook the infant's very subtle signals, including those that indicated hunger or other forms of discomfort.

Because Mrs. Bradley did not seem to profit from developmental guidance, the therapist inferred that her difficulties in caregiving originated in psychological conflicts over mothering. Acting on this assumption, the therapist began to address Mrs. Bradley's feelings about the baby, and to search for the sources of her ambivalence and her muted emotional investment as a mother. This in turn led to Mrs. Bradley's recollections of her own childhood, which helped to illuminate the origin of her current difficulties.

Mrs. Bradley had been abandoned by her biological mother and had always felt misunderstood and rejected by her adoptive mother. Although she had been adopted a 4 weeks of age, Mrs. Bradley described herself as "motherless" and spoke repeatedly of having never had a mother. She perceived her adoptive mother as a barely adequate substitute. Mrs. Bradley recalled having been hungry for the first 2 years of her life due to a minor malformation in the oral cavity that was not corrected as early as medically indicated. The physical hunger she vividly recalled had an emotional counterpoint in a feeling of emptiness that constantly haunted her; Mrs. Bradley felt that her needs and her feelings were of no importance to anyone, and therefore should be of no importance to herself.

The theme of hunger and its many layers of psychological meaning, both in the present and in the past, were a focal point of the therapy; Mrs. Bradley spoke with much sadness of her lack of pleasure and fulfillment in many areas of her life, including a striking absence of interest in food and a long-standing inability to prepare meals for her husband and herself.

The intervention consisted of helping the mother recognize and explore the links between her long-buried feelings of being empty, worthless, and unwanted and her present difficulties in feeding her infant, giving the proper importance to his signals, and taking pleasure in interacting with him. This approach to treatment helped to free the mother's ability to become more aware of her own needs, and more attuned and responsive to her infant's needs. The baby's weight stabilized and striking improvements were observed in the mother–child interaction as a result of this intervention. When the baby was 12 months old, he displayed all the major criteria for judging that he had a secure relationship with his mother, including unambivalent approach and contact in situations of stress and the appropriate use of the mother as a secure base from which to explore. Mrs. Bradley in turn took much pleasure in her child and was appropriately responsive to his signals.

This case illustrates the kind of treatment outcome that may be achieved when therapeutic exploration of psychological conflicts can take place in a relatively stable family constellation with little socioeconomic upheaval. However, many of our cases must be treated in the context of great social and psychological instability. In a large proportion of our client population, the parents are not only poor but also unskilled, untrusting and isolated. Many of them are so unable to provide adequate care that their children have been removed and placed in temporary or permanent foster homes. Such placement may occur at our instigation when the therapeutic efforts to help the parents become more adequate caregivers have failed (e.g., Lieberman & Pawl, 1984). In other situations, we may not be initially involved in the case, but are called in by the legal system after a child has been removed from the home as an emergency measure. In these situations, we may be asked to assess the quality of the relationship between the baby and the foster parents, and to compare it to the baby's relationship with the biological parents in order to make long-term placement decisions. We may also be asked to assess and make recommendations in cases where a baby with a very difficult history is failing to develop adequately in a foster or adoptive home. In all such circumstances, it is necessary to try to understand, from the baby's history and past and present behavior, what the vicissitudes of his/her attachment relationships have been, how they are affecting current functioning, and what caregiving arrangements present the best hope for adequate development.

The following clinical vignette illustrates the use of attachment theory in our clinical understanding of these difficult and chaotic cases. This case highlights the degree to which the infant's behavior may contribute to problems in the relationship with sensitive and emotionally invested parental figures. The case also illustrates how the three conceptual categories of disorders of attachment—nonattachment, anxious or ambivalent attachment, and broken attachment—must be considered in their reciprocal relationships when they are applied to real life situations. The categories of attachment disorder often merge with each other when the actual experiences of a child are being considered.

Clinical Illustration. Sarah was referred to our program by the Department of Social Services with a request for an evaluation of her behavior and for our recommendations regarding the long-term placement of the child. The concerns prompting the referral involved the child's indiscriminate friendliness and her lack of a differential response to her primary caregivers. Sarah was 21 months old at the time of referral. She was living with foster parents who were willing to adopt her should this become legally feasible.

The child's history from birth to the time of referral comprised a series of broken human relationships. Sarah had been conceived in a mental hospital, where both her parents had been committed with a diagnosis of paranoid schizophrenia. After their release from the hospital, the parents had hitchhiked across the country and appeared in a emergency room when the mother was in labor. There had been no prenatal care. Although there was professional concern about the home care this child would receive, the parents could not be persuaded to accept services of any kind. In spite of this Sarah was discharged to them. At one month, she was hospitalized for a week with a serious respiratory ailment. Again, there were professional concerns about the quality of the care she was receiving, but again the parents did not want any help. By the time Sarah was 2 months old, her mother had abandoned the home. Soon after this, Sarah's father left the child in the care of a very casual acquaintance and failed to pick her up. The Department of Social Services was called in and the father was contacted by them. The father explained that he was having great difficulty caring for Sarah since his wife had left. Sarah was 3 months old.

With the father's agreement, Sarah was placed in shelter care for 2 weeks. She was then transferred to a foster home, where she remained for 3 weeks until the foster family left town for a vacation and could not take the child with them. She was then placed in a second foster home, where she stayed from 4½ months to 10 months of age. At that time the social worker discovered that the care in this foster home was, in her words, "minimal," and placed Sarah in a potentially adoptive home under the appropriate assumption that the child was likely to be freed for adoption. Sarah remained with this family for 2 months, until she was 12 months old. The care was excellent, but the placement was disrupted because of unforeseeable practical circumstances, and Sarah was moved yet again, this time again to a potentially adoptive foster home. Sarah had been at this home for 9 months at the time of referral to our program. In the opinion of the social worker, these foster parents were excellent and should become Sarah's permanent parents if the child were freed for adoption.

By 12 months, then, Sarah had been cared for by her parents, hospital staff, casual acquaintances of her parents, a shelter care family, two foster care families, and two potentially adoptive families. There had been at least 7 different major shifts in caregiving for the first 12 months of her life. In addition, the quality of care had varied greatly. The Infant–Parent Program agreed to do an assessment of Sarah's functioning, to make recommendations, and to work with the foster family if necessary.

The observations from the home visits were striking. Sarah was described by her current foster parents as having entered their home at 12 months "as if she owned it." She was friendly, comfortable, took to them easily, and showed no hesitation in interacting with them. When we questioned the foster parents they did reveal that Sarah had had some initial problems in eating, that sleep patterns were initially irregular, and that sleep was still easily disrupted. The foster parents explained that initially they had been pleased with Sarah's friendliness to everyone and with her lack of anxiety about new people with whom she came in contact. Later, however, they felt less pleased with this behavior because it seemed to them that Sarah should be friendlier with them than with strangers. In her first visit, the Infant–Parent Program therapist noted no anxiety or hesitation on Sarah's part in interacting with her and noted also that twice Sarah approached her rather than her foster parents when she was crying. In addition, at the end of this visit, Sarah made active efforts to leave with the therapist.

On the second home visit, Sarah continued to be overly friendly to the therapist, showed no preference for her foster parents, and this time actually cried when the worker left. During this visit the foster father arrived unexpectedly and in response Sarah became markedly disorganized. She seemed not to know where to go, turned in circles, cried desperately, and finally sought a corner of the room in which to comfort herself. She persistently rebuffed the foster parents' efforts to console her.

On the third home visit, Sarah still showed no preference for her foster parents, and remained friendly with the therapist but did not attempt to leave with her or cry. Held by her foster mother, she waved "good-bye" pleasantly and seemed uninterested in the separation.

The fourth encounter with Sarah took place in the playroom at the Infant–Parent Program when she was being formally evaluated using the Bayley Scales of Infant Development. Present in the room were Sarah; the foster mother; the examiner, with whom the infant was already familiar; and the videotape cameraperson. Throughout the testing, Sarah's attention was continuously centered on the cameraperson. Although the examiner could engage her to some extent in the testing materials, the child's primary focus was on the only stranger in the room. She approached him indirectly and somewhat shyly, occasionally flirtatiously, but with clear anxiety. He was minimally responsive and relatively unengageable, yet he was clearly, in Sarah's view, the most compelling figure in the room; she had eyes only for him and paid progressively less attention to the test. We interpreted this to mean that the child was responding to the twin stresses of the unfamiliar setting and the unresponsive stranger by becoming more and more anxious and simultaneously more invested in interacting with him. Once, as Sarah stood next to the cameraperson naming a picture on the wall and looking hesitantly toward him, he softly repeated the word she spoke. In response, Sarah pointed out to her foster mother, said "mama," and quickly ran toward her, stopping short of reaching her, however. She then began turning in circles, unable to find a solution to her dilemma: Who should she go to? Sarah's anxious expression clearly conveyed the quandary she found herself in.

As we survey Sarah's history and current behavior, it is worthwhile to note how complex a task it is to categorize this child's experiences. Are we dealing with a problem of nonattachment? Could she not approach the foster mother because she was unable to form an attachment to her? If not now, would this have been the major category applicable to her when Sarah was 4 months? At that time Sarah had been cared for in succession by her parents, strangers, hospital personnel, a shelter care mother, and a foster care family. The question arises as to whether or not the child had subjectively experienced those separations and losses as stressful and what effect they had had. Was the biological mother's departure when Sarah was 2 months experienced as a loss? We might well agree that until 4 months Sarah had little opportunity to do anything other than to begin establishing the initial dialogue of a reciprocal relationship, only to have it disrupted again and again. She might have had opportunities to build certain expectancies around some familiar modes of handling, a voice, a smell, a face, or a way of making eye contact. She might have registered shifts and changes with some distress, upset, and a sense of violation of expectations, but given the frequent changes in caregivers, the opportunity to form a coherent pattern of expectation centered around one or two familiar persons cannot have been there. This may be one of the circumstances that creates the quality of nonattachment. What these circumstances contribute as an anlage for later opportunities for attachment remains a question. The possibilities range from a vulnerability regarding later attachments to a sustained rupture of the possibility for focused, discriminated relationships. Certainly, some vulnerability would be expected in the area that Erikson termed "basic trust" and psychoanalysts have referred to as "libidinal object constancy." It is likely, then, that at 4 months Sarah was affectively disorganized, somewhat unresponsive and withdrawn, but not depressed as a result of the loss of a central, discriminated figure. Nonattachment is likely to have been the most accurate descriptive category for her at that time.

From 4 months of 10½ months, Sarah's care was inadequate but consistent. She had a caregiver around with whom she could organize herself affectively and with whom an attachment could be formed. However, this caregiver was neither contingently responsive, nor sensitive, nor greatly emotionally invested in Sarah. This is the likeliest construction that we can place on the worker's description of the care Sarah received as "minimal." Under these circumstances, the quality of the attachment that Sarah might have been able to create was probably anxious at best. At 10½ months, then, Sarah experienced her first loss of an attachment figure, though an inadequate one. This attachment figure was replaced by a contingently responsive and deeply invested caregiver who offered Sarah a new kind of commitment. This new situation probably ameliorated some of the immediate acute effects of the previous loss. Given her early experiences, however, it seems likely that Sarah's anxiety around attachment would persist despite the actual quality of the new parental behavior. In any case, when this barely formed new accommodation was again disrupted, there was yet another assault on Sarah's capacity for a secure attachment. It is 9 months after this final disruption that we have our first opportunity to observe Sarah.

During the course of our assessment we changed our initial view of Sarah as nonattached to her current foster parents to seeing her as "counterphobic" and anxiously attached. We believe that over the 9 months previous to our first meetings, Sarah's feelings of closeness to her current foster parents and possibility of attachment to them had grown. As this process unfolded, the child's early experiences began to interfere seriously with her developmental impetus toward attachment. The disruption of her incipient relationships of varying qualities had resulted in a expectation of and a basic adaptation to shifts, changes, separations, and loss. Thus, as the potential attachment to her new foster parents was activated, and as their responsiveness and sensitivity matched her still available natural tendencies to form an attachment, Sarah's anxiety over loss increased and her defenses became mobilized. She began to seek out the experience of separation and loss that she expected and to which she had learned to adapt, but which she also feared. After 9 months in this excellent home she started showing increasingly marked behavioral interest in and preference for strangers—any stranger. This was a new level of creative adaptation, but a costly and disturbing one that neither mastered the anxiety nor really solved the conflict. Sarah was no longer neutral in her approaches. Instead, she sought out strangers and only when they became familiar did they lose their compulsive attractiveness to her. We believe that it was not her intent to persuade the stranger to let her stay where she was. Instead, she was attempting to master the newly felt anxiety and pain about her expectations of loss by taking control of the situation. Each time she encountered a stranger she readied herself for a new separation and loss. Sarah now had something meaningful to lose, and there was no doubt in her mind that she would lose it. In this scenario, Sarah attempted to experience a sense of effectiveness rather than helplessness by actively seeking the contact with the stranger and offering herself rather than being passively taken away. This pattern was apparent both in her behavior towards the therapist in the first three assessment visits and in her behavior towards the cameraperson during the testing session. There seemed little question that this behavior was a direct result of Sarah's growing natural preference for an attachment to her foster family, her expectation of loss, and her defense against the pain and anxiety created by that expectation. Offering herself to strangers was Sarah's way of mastering her history.

It was of vital important in our treatment that we recognize the defensive aspect of Sarah's behavior and not accept it as a straightforward expression of a presumed lack of attachment to her foster parents. The foster parents needed to understand this as well, and they also needed help in dealing with the situation in order to remain emotionally available and not to feel unloved and betrayed by Sarah's behavior.

By 30 months Sarah's relatability toward her foster parents was much more positive and age-appropriate, though sequelae of her earlier experience were still very evident. She still sought out strangers, but with a brave swagger. It was as if she felt that she would confront a stranger and hope against hope that the worst would not happen. This was the new message in this behavior. Still vulnerable, still anxious, but now with some hope. This behavior persisted despite the fact that she had been in a excellent, stable situation for 19 months—three fifths of her life.

It remains impossible to know to what degree and in what ways the experiences of her first year of life will manifest themselves when Sarah begins to form new relationships later in life. The intent of this description, however, is less to predict than to illustrate the usefulness of attachment concepts in a clinical setting. It was by focusing on the behavior of the child in the context of attachment and understanding her experience in terms of the development of attachment that we were able to make some sense of her current dilemma and that of her foster parents.

CONCLUSION

We have outlined some contributions of attachment theory to the treatment of disorders of attachment in an infant mental health program. We find that the application of concepts from attachment theory to a clinical setting is of great value in understanding the behavior of infants who are at risk for or already experiencing disorders of attachment. Although psychoanalytic and object relations theories provide accounts of the development of the self and of the processes of internalization and defense formation in the context of human relationships, attachment theory contributes a useful framework for understanding infant behavior as a manifestation of these affective processes and as a response to caregiving experiences. A clinical synthesis of these theoretical approaches has been of great value in our work for understanding the subjective experience of infants in situations of emotional stress.

REFERENCES

Ainsworth, M. D. (1962). The effects of maternal deprivation: A review of findings and controversy in the context of research strategy. In *Deprivation of maternal care: A reassessment of its effects*. Public Health papers, 14. Geneva: World Health Organization.
Ainsworth, M. D. (1969). Object relations, dependency and attachment: A theoretical review of the infant-mother relationship. *Child Development, 40*, 969–1025.
Ainsworth, M. D. (1972). Attachment and dependency: A comparison, In J. L. Gerwitz (Ed.), *Attachment and dependency*. Washington, DC: V. H. Winston.
Ainsworth, M. D. (1973). The development of infant-mother attachment. In B. M. Caldwell & H. N. Ricciuti (Eds.), *Review of child development research* (Vol. 3). Chicago: University of Chicago Press.
Ainsworth, M. D., Blehar, M. C., Water, E., & Wall, S. (1973). *The strange situation: Observing patterns of attachment*. Hillsdale, NJ: Lawrence Erlbaum Associates.
Allen, F. H. (1955). Mother-child separation—process or event. In G. Caplan (Ed.), *Emotional problems of early childhood* (pp. 325–331). New York: Basic Books.
Blehar, M. B., Lieberman, A. F., & Ainsworth, M. D. (1977). Early face-to-face interaction and its relation to later infant-mother attachment. *Child Development, 48*, 182–194.
Bowlby, J. (1960). Grief and mourning in infancy and early childhood. *The Psychoanalytic Study of the Child, 15*, 9–52.
Bowlby, J. (1961). Processes of mourning. *International Journal of Psycho-Analysis, 42*, 317–40.
Bowlby, J. (1969). *Attachment and loss,* Vol. 1: *Attachment*. New York: Basic Books.
Bowlby, J. (1973). *Attachment and loss,* Vol. 2: *Separation*. New York: Basic Books.
Bowlby, J. (1980). *Attachment and loss,* Vol. 3: *Loss, sadness and depression*. New York: Basic Books.

Bowlby, J. (1982). Attachment and loss: Retrospect and prospect. *American Journal of Orthopsychiatry, 52.* 664–678.

Brazelton, T. (1973). Neonatal Behavioral Assessment. *National Spastic Society Monographs, Clinics in Developmental Medicine, 50.* London: W. Heinemann & Sons.

Bretherton, I. (1985). Attachment theory: Retrospect and prospect. In I. Bretherton, & E. Waters (Eds.), *Growing points of attachment theory and research. Monographs of the Society for Research in Child Development, 50* (1 & 2), pp. 3–38.

Cassidy, J. (in press). The ability to negotiate the environment: An aspect of infant competence as related to quality of attachment. *Child Development.*

Clemente, C. D., Purpura, D. P., & Bayer, F. E. (Eds.). (1972). *Sleep and the maturing nervous system.* New York: Academic Press.

Emde, R. N., Gaensbauer, T., & Harmon, R. J. (1976). Emotional expression in infancy: A biobehavioral study. *Psychological Issues, Monograph 10.* New York: International University Press.

Escalona, S. K. (1968). *Roots of individuality.* Chicago: Aldine.

Fraiberg, S. (1977). *Notes on infant and preschool programs in Jerusalem.* Unpublished manuscript.

Fraiberg, S. (Ed.). (1980). *Clinical studies in infant mental health: The first year of life.* New York: Basic Books.

Fraiberg, S. (1982). Pathological defenses in infancy. *Psychoanalytic Quarterly, 51,* 612–634.

Fraiberg, S., Adelson, E., & Shapiro, V. (1975). Ghosts in the nursery: A psychoanalytical approach to the problems of impaired infant-mother relationships. *Journal of the American Academy of Child Psychiatry, 14,* 387–422.

Freud, A. (1960). Discussion of Dr. John Bowlby's paper. *The Psychoanalytic Study of the Child, 15,* 50–52.

Goldstein, J., Freud, A., & Solnit, A. J. (1973). *Beyond the best interests of the child.* New York: Free Press.

Goldstein, J., Freud, A., & Solnit, A. J. (1979). *Before the best interests of the child..* New York: Free Press.

Greenspan, S. I. (1979). *Intelligence and adaptation: An integration of psychoanalytic and Piagetian developmental psychology.* New York: International Universities Press.

Greenspan, S. I. (1981). Psychopathology and adaptation: Principles of clinical diagnosis and preventive intervention. *Clinical Infant Reports, #1 National Center for Clinical Infant Programs.* New York: International Universities Press.

Greenspan, S. I., & Lieberman, A. F. (1980). Infants, mothers and their interaction: A quantitative approach to developmental assessment. In

S. Greenspan & G. Pollock (Eds.), *The course of life, Vol. I: Infancy and early childhood* (pp 271-312). U.S. Department of Human Services.

Greenspan, S. I., Wieder, S., Lieberman, A. F., Nover, R., Lourie, R., & Robinson, M. (in press). *Multiproblem families.* New York: International Universities Press.

Korner, A. (1974). The effect of the infant's state, level of arousal, sex and ontogenetic stage on the caregiver. In M. Lewis & L. Rosenblum (Ed.), *The effect of the infant on its caregiver* (pp. 105-121). New York: Wiley.

Lieberman, A. F. (1985). Infant mental health: A model for service delivery. *Journal of Clinical Child Psychology, 14*(3), 196-201.

Lieberman, A. F., & Pawl, J. H. (1984). Searching for the best interests of the child: Intervention with an abusive mother and her toddler. *The Psychoanalytic Study of the Child, 39,* 527-548.

Lieberman, A. F., & Pawl, J. H. (in press). Disorders of attachment in the second year: A Clinical developmental perspective. In M. Greenberg, D. Cicchetti, & M. Cummings (Eds.), *Attachment beyond infancy.* Chicago: University of Chicago Press.

Main, M. (1982). Avoidance in the service of attachment: A working paper. In K. Immelman, G. W. Bariow, I. Petrinovich, & M. Main (Eds.), *Behavioral development: The Bielfield interdisciplinary project.* Cambridge: University Press.

Main, M., Kaplan, N., & Cassidy, J. (1985). Security in infancy, childhood, and adulthood: A move to the level of representation. In I. Bretherton & E. Waters (Eds.), *Growing points in attachment. Monographs of the Society for Research in Child Development, 50* (1 & 2), 66-106.

Matas, L., Arend, R., & Sroufe, A. L. (1978). Continuity of adaptation in the second year: The relationship between quality of attachment and later competence. *Child Development, 49,* 547-556.

Provence, S. (in press). Psychoanalytic perspectives on separation. In J. & S. Bloom-Feshbach (Eds.), *The psychology of separation through the life span.* San Francisco: Josey-Bass.

Provence, S., & Lipton, F. (1962). *Infants in institutions.* New York: International Universities Press.

Robertson, J., & Robertson, J. (1971). Young children in brief separations: A fresh look. *The Psychoanalytic Study of the Child, 26,* 264-315.

Rutter, M. (1972). *Maternal deprivation reassessed.* London: Penguin Books.

Sander, L. (1962). Issues in early mother-child interaction. *Journal of the American Academy of Child Psychiatry, 1,* 141-166.

Sander, L. (1975). Infant and caretaking environment: Investigation and conceptualization of adaptive behavior in a system of increasing complexity. In E. J. Anthony (Ed.), *Explorations in child psychiatry* (pp. 129–166). New York: Plenum Press.

Sander, L. W., Stechler, G., Burns, P., & Julia, H. (1970). Early other-infant interaction and 24-hour patterns of activity and sleep. *Journal of the American Academy of Child Psychiatry, 9,* 104–123.

Spitz, R. A. (1945). Hospitalism: An inquiry into the genesis of psychiatric conditions in early childhood. *The Psychoanalytic Study of the Child, 1,* 53–74.

Spitz, R. A. (1960). Discussion of Dr. Bowlby's paper. *The Psychoanalytic Study of the Child, 15,* 86–94.

Sroufe, A. L. (1979). The coherence of individual development: Early care, attachment, and subsequent developmental issues. *American Psychologist, 34,* 834–841.

Sroufe, A. L. (1983). Infant-caregiver attachment patterns of adaption in preschool: The roots of maladaption and competence. In M. Perlmutter (Ed.), *Minnesota Symposium in Child Psychology* (Vol. 16, pp. 41–83). Hillsdale, NJ: Lawrence Erlbaum Associates.

Sroufe, A. L. (1985). Attachment classification from the perspectives of infant-caregiver relationship and infant temperament. *Child Development, 56,* 1–14.

Thomas, A., Chess, S., Birch, H., & Hertzig, M. (1963). *Behavioral individuality in early childhood.* New York: New York University Press.

Waters, A., & Sroufe, A. L. (1983). Social competence as a developmental construct. *Developmental Review, 3,* 79–97.

Winnicott, D. W. (1975). The observation of infants in a set situation. In D. W. Winnicott (Ed.), *Through Paediatrics to Psychoanalysis.* New York: Basic Books. (Reprinted from International Journal of Psychoanalysis, Vol. 22)

Yarrow, L. J., & Goodwin, M. S. (1973). The immediate impact of separation: reactions of infants to a change in mother figures. In L. J. Stone, H. T. Smith, & L. B. Murphy (Eds.), *The competent infant.* New York: Basic Books.

11

Intervention in Insecure Infant Attachment

Teresa Nezworski
University of California, Santa Barbara

William J. Tolan
The Meadows Psychiatric Center
Centre Hall, Pennsylvania

Jay Belsky
The Pennsylvania State University

Accumulating research over the last decade has demonstrated that insecurely attached infants function less well that their securely attached peers on a variety of tasks during their toddler and preschool years (Main, 1973; Pastor, 1981; Sroufe, 1979, 1983). The youngsters studied appeared less effective in interpersonal relations and less successful in their efforts to master challenging tasks (Arend, Gove, & Sroufe, 1979; George & Main, 1979; La Freniere & Sroufe, 1985; Londerville & Main, 1981; Main & Weston, 1981; Matas, Arend, & Sroufe, 1978; Nezworski, 1983; Sroufe, Schork, Motti, Lawroski, & La Freniere, 1984; Waters, Wippman, & Sroufe, 1979). These findings have provided important empirical support for the theoretical propositions that link the quality of infant-parent attachment to child personality development and subsequent adjustment.

INSECURE ATTACHMENT AS AN INDEX OF
RISK STATUS

Recent publications from two independent longitudinal investigations have underscored the importance of these earlier studies by further documenting a significant relationship between the quality of infant-parent attachment and the incidence of child behavioral problems in the beginning school years (Erickson, Sroufe, & Egeland, 1985; Lewis, Feiring, McGuffog, & Jaskir, 1984. For details see Belsky & Nezworski,

352

this volume). This work is particularly important in that it lays the foundation for a more extensive bridge from attachment status in infancy to the development of psychopathology. Bowlby (1973, 1977, 1982, 1985) clearly predicted that such disturbances of the attachment relationship would cause psychopathology by engendering pervasive anxiety and distrust in the child. Up until this point, however, support for this connection has been based primarily on clinical case studies (Bowlby, 1977, 1980; Guidano & Liotti, 1983; Liotti, 1984). Due to their retrospective and nonexperimental nature, these case studies have inherent methodological problems that limit their warrant for causal inferences.

On the basis of the Lewis et al. (1984) and Erickson et al. (1985) data, there would seem to be some grounds for expecting that attachment classification may prove of special diagnostic value in the area of early developmental intervention. Early intervention in the developmental years has been identified as the strategy of choice for reducing the overall incidence of adult psychopathology and the comparatively higher costs for treatment at later life stages. What is especially attractive about using attachment data for clinical purposes is the relative paucity of indicators (except in the most extreme circumstances such as autism and apart from those assessing biological or socioeconomic risk) that can serve as powerful diagnostic indices of psychological vulnerability so early in life.

The developmental period of infancy appears to provide a unique intervention opportunity in that the family system is at this time inherently open as it struggles to adapt itself to the presence of the new member. The spontaneous family reorganization that occurs with its requisite change in membership roles and responsibilities allows for greater flexibility than at many other life stages. At few other times are parents so motivated to consciously examine their own behavior and feeling patterns as when they are caring for a baby who depends on them for physical survival.

Parents of infants voraciously seek out child care information from books, magazine, friends, neighbors, pediatricians, and almost anyone who seems to have experience or expert knowledge (Clarke-Stewart, 1978). They want to know which parenting techniques offer their child greatest happiness and health and they crave information that will help them evaluate their child's status and their own parenting success. This general eagerness to take responsibility for their child's development reflects a unique period in both infant and parental development. The new parents' active search for information and input on their nascent privilege and responsibility represents a natural context in which to offer intervention services, especially for children at risk.

THE IMPETUS TO INTERVENE

With the dissemination of the Lewis et al. (1984) and the Erickson et al. (1985) preprints in 1983, the authors of this chapter met to consider the utility and feasibility of offering some type of intervention program to participants in the longitudinal Infant and Family Project at Penn State (see Belsky & Isabella, this volume). The design of this ongoing project called for attachment status to be routinely assessed using the Ainsworth Strange Situation. As an incentive for participation, families in the study had been promised information about the practical implications of their child's performance on the various experimental measures. Most important from the standpoint of the intervention we eventually came to offer (and describe later in this chapter) was our promise to families when we enrolled them in the project that if we developed any cause for concern about the child's development over the course of our data collection that we would share it with them.

With the appearance in the peer-reviewed research literature of two reports linking insecure attachment and subsequent behavioral problems, we were forced to consider our professional and ethical responsibility to include some information about the possible risk of insecure attachment in the descriptive feedback routinely provided to all parents. We anticipated, however, that telling parents that their child might be at risk could have an unintended negative impact if this information were not supplemented with an offer of optional professional assistance aimed at reducing the likelihood of the risk. Located in a small university town surrounded by rural communities, low cost mental health services were minimal and designed primarily for maintenance of the chronically ill. There were, in fact, no infant-parent intervention programs of any type. We were faced, therefore, with the ethical dilemma of choosing between violating our agreement to fully disclose information to our subjects about their child's functioning or sharing this emotionally charged information within a virtual vacuum of clinical referral sources. After serious deliberation with colleagues and university ethics committees, we decided that we were obligated to provide the parents with information about the risks associated with insecure attachment. We could not do so in good conscience, though, without offering at least a minimal service to help parents understand the personal implications of such information for the individual families.

It should be noted that we seriously considered not sharing the information on the potential risk of insecurity at all, given its probabilistic nature. After much soul searching, however, we realized that we could not do this. To our way of thinking, this was the parents' information to have, not simply ours which we could decide to keep from them. How could we face ourselves, or the families we were studying, if it turned out at follow-up that those children thought to be at risk did indeed turn out to be developing patterns of behavior that are clearly troublesome—to children, parents, and research scientists? Wouldn't families wonder why we had not shared with them what we were concerned about years earlier? How would the explanation that "we could not be certain" sound at that time? Ultimately, what led us to talk with parents about insecurity (but never in those terms) and to offer an intervention program was the obligation we felt to uphold the initial promise we had made to share concerns with them, were they to develop in the course of studying their child.

In the remaining portion of this chapter we describe our attempts to resolve these ethical issues through the initiation of a parent program designed to reduce both the overall risks associated with infant insecurity and the potential problems that could result from labeling a child as a problem so early in life. We outline the theoretical issues that served as a rationale for our decisions to focus primarily on the mother as the target for intervention and to offer psychotherapy as the medium by which to promote change in attachment organization. Our efforts in implementing the Penn State Family Intervention Program including our experiences in informing parents about risks associated with insecurity and enlisting their participation in this pilot intervention program are reported. Clinical impressions regarding parenting style, marital problems, and maternal personality factors related to insecure attachment and subsequent developmental risk are also discussed and illustrated with case examples. The chapter concludes with evaluative comments concerning the program's original goals.

CONCEPTUAL ISSUES IN ATTACHMENT INTERVENTION

Targeting the Mother

Ainsworth and colleagues' (Ainsworth, Bell, & Stayton, 1971; Ainsworth, Blehar, Waters, & Wall, 1978) early work was based on extensive observations of mothers and infants in the home and provides clues to the behavioral markers preceding anxious attachment in infancy. Maternal sensitivity and responsiveness to an infant's signals during feeding, play, and distress during the course of the first 3 months were found to be predictive of the quality of attachment at the end of the child's first year of life. Mothers who had shown insensitivity to their babys' signals in a variety of caretaking and play situations were more likely to have children who were later characterized by the anxious-avoidant (A) pattern of attachment. It was noted also that these mothers verbalized dislike for close physical contact with their infants and were observed to have been generally low in emotional expressiveness. Although mothers of infants later classified as anxious-resistant (C) had also been rated as insensitive during the early months, their patterns of insensitivity were less consistent over time and these mothers did not report an aversion to physical contact with their babies. These findings on maternal antecedents of attachment status have received support in other longitudinal studies and are consistent with Bowlby's (1982) assertions concerning the mother's disproportionately powerful influence on the development of the mother-child relationship (Belsky, Rovine, & Taylor, 1984; Egeland & Farber, 1984; Egeland & Sroufe, 1981; Grossmann, Grossmann, Spangler, Suess, & Unzer, 1985; Main & Stadtman, 1981; Main, Tomasini, & Tolan, 1979; Maslin, 1983; see also Lamb, Thompson, Gardner, Charnov, & Estes, 1985 for a different reading of the relevant literature).

The Pathogenic Mechanism

The process by which very early maternal insensitivity is transformed into an insecure mother-infant relationship (with its associated developmental risks) is of particular relevance when contemplating how to intervene. Bowlby (1980) conjectures that the evolutionary function of infant attachment lies in its securing protection from physical and psychological danger. This interpretation suggests that early parental insensitivity may be particularly pathogenic because it encourages the child to construct his/her first model of the social environment as essentially hostile or unresponsive and that of the self as inadequate or unworthy of help and comfort. These preconscious models of self and world necessarily engender chronic anxiety as they are used to anticipate, order, and assimilate future experience, especially in instances of ambiguity, novelty, and crisis. Thus, future experience, especially in times of stress, is construed from this negative viewpoint.

As long as the social environment remains truly unsafe, this internal model may prove adaptive in facilitating the avoidance of danger. The problem arises when the capabilities and needs of the child change as development proceeds, or when the sensitivity, availability, or responsiveness of caretakers improves. The parent may now be better able to appropriately nurture and respond to the child's current set of needs. The previously neglected or rejected child, however, may still be experiencing from the context of her original negative model. Such a child will not be likely to anticipate, recognize, or assimilate such a change in support and nurturance from parents or other caregivers. So, for example, the babies who consistently experience mothers as unresponsive to signals of distress may in later childhood frequently refrain from communicating their psychological needs to others because they now expect significant others (e.g., parents, teachers, friends, etc.) to fail them. This negative model of self and world becomes in some sense self-perpetuating. These children will, therefore, become avoidant of closeness to ward off the anxiety generated in social interaction and, thus, develop inadequate social skills. It is through this interpretive process, then, that the cognitive affective models initially constructed during infancy may play a powerful role in the organization and development of personality as well as psychopathology.

Conditions Supporting Change in Attachment Organization

Although these internal models are hypothesized to operate at a level outside of conscious awareness, their operation may be observed in an individual's consistent pattern of response to stress such as that observed in infants in the Strange Situation. Researchers have verified that there is stability within individuals in their attachment behavior throughout infancy (Connell, 1976; Main & Weston, 1981; Waters, 1978) as well as the preschool period (Main, Kaplan, & Cassidy, 1985). Accumulating evidence indicates, however, that changes can occur in attachment organization and, presumably, in the corresponding models of self, world, and future developmental trajectory.

Life stress was identified by several early researchers as a key factor that was predictably associated with changes in attachment classification and other measures of personality development (Thompson, Lamb, & Estes, 1982; Vaughn, Egeland, Sroufe, & Waters, 1979). It seems likely that life stress appears so influential only because it varies predictably—and possibly causally—with availability and nurturance.

The primacy of parenting factors in producing change in attachment status as well as future personality development is suggested by the longitudinal studies directed by Sroufe (Erickson et al., 1985) and Lewis et al. (1984). Although these investigators found similarly significant relations between insecurity during infancy and the later incidence of behavioral problems, exceptions were also discovered. When Erickson et al. looked for ways to explain deviations from the predicted relationship, some of the most powerful variables identified were those reflecting parental effectiveness in facilitating the child's negotiation of subsequent developmental tasks (involvement in the home, provision of age-appropriate play materials, support and encouragement, respect for child autonomy, clarity of instructions, consistency in limit setting, low hostility, etc.). In their sample, the few children with insecure attachment relationships who failed to develop behavioral problems were those who appeared to have received good quality parenting during the preschool years. Although Lewis and his colleagues did not have observational data on parenting quality for a comparative analysis, their questionnaire data suggested that a child's status as a "planned birth" and family stress were associated with level of risk. These data also provide support for the notion that improvements in the quality of parenting may be crucial for altering the developmental trajectory of the insecurely attached infant. To the extent, then, that developmental processes work as suggested, it becomes important to better understand—and affect—those personal and contextual factors that shape parenting.

Determinants of Parent Effectiveness

The influential role of the parent in the development of infant security and later personality adjustment has received considerable theoretical attention and empirical focus. The parental factor most frequently discussed— maternal insensitivity—has been shown to precede and hypothetically cause insecure attachments (Ainsworth et al., 1978; Belsky et al., 1984; Egeland & Farber, 1984; Egeland & Sroufe, 1981; Grossmann et al., 1985; Main & Stadtman, 1981; Main et al., 1979; Maslin, 1983). The determinants of maternal insensitivity as well as other parent effectiveness variables, however, have been relatively ignored. Isabella and Belsky's (this volume) longitudinal investigation represents one notable exception to this trend.

Belsky (1984) outlined a process model of the determinants of parenting that posits that the quality of the parent-child relationship is a direct result of the interrelationships among three behavioral subsystems: (a) that of the individual parent (resulting from child-rearing history and personality; (b) the individual child; and (c) the broader social context (parents' marital adjustment, social support networks, occupational experiences, etc.). Using this model of the determinants of parenting, these investigators provided evidence that parent characteristics (maternal interpersonal affection, ego strength, nurturance, self-esteem), child characteristics (parent perception of infant adaptability), and the social context (marital adjustment, neighborhood supportiveness) are all influential in the development of attachment security. A path analysis provided support for Isabella and Belsky's predictions regarding the particularly important role played by maternal personality in directly and indirectly influencing infant attachment organization through changes in marital adjustment. Although parental marital adjustment appears to be a significant contributor to infant security, a portion of its influence appears to be determined by maternal personality. These authors also note that their child characteristic (infant adaptability) and social context variables (neighborhood supportiveness) all derive from parent questionnaire data. They, therefore, represent parent perceptions that are likely to also have been shaped by the parent's personality organization.

If parental personality does indeed serve such a pivotal function in the development of security, then the origins of this structure in the parent's own early child-rearing experience deserves serious consideration. Several theoreticians, including Bowlby (1969), hypothesize that there is intergenerational continuity in the quality of parenting and that the factors originally responsible for producing insecurity in infancy (deficits in parental sensitivity and supportiveness) are also responsible, in part, for the subsequent maladaptive personality organizations and resultant parenting styles.

Retrospective investigations of intergenerational continuity of insecurity by Ricks (1985) and Main and Goldwyn (in press) found support for Bowlby's thesis. Mothers' recollections of their own acceptance and rejection by their parents reliably distinguished their own children's attachment classifications. In both studies, a few parents with clear histories of rejection were found, contrary to prediction, to have children who were securely attached. Surprisingly, they also reported having satisfying, stable marriages and strong social support systems. These mothers were notably able to recognize the deprivations they had experienced as children and appeared able to express righteous anger regarding their treatment. Ricks suggested that taking an autonomous stance toward the parent in consciously working through the past experience may be one means of exiting the pathogenic cycle.

A Model For Intervention

Bowlby's theory (1973), Ainsworth et al.'s (1978) work on the antecedents of security, and the empirical investigations of the correlates of sensitive and effective caretaking uniformly point to the parents as the logical locus for intervention efforts. Perhaps because of their culturally determined role as primary caregivers, mothers appear to be key figures in the attachment process and are therefore likely to be crucial in any intervention project aimed at promoting child security or its subsequent developmental impact.

In light of the provocative findings of Erickson et al. (1985) regarding the apparent effect of good quality parenting in ameliorating the impact of early insecurity, we sought to design an intervention program that would facilitate effective parenting. Our review of the relevant theory and research suggested that mothers of insecurely attached children were facing many obstacles, the foremost of which was a personal history of loss through early emotional rejection and/or separation. The scars of their childhood difficulties, manifest in negative models of self and the world, were probably interfering with not only their relationships with their children, but with many other significant social relationships, as well, most notably with their marriages. Because it seemed that the parenting deficits that originally resulted in the insecure mother-child attachment were influenced strongly by the mother's personality organization, we believed that a didactic approach to parent training would not be optimally effective by itself. Instead, we hypothesized that a strategy primarily aimed at dealing with the presumed problem source—the mother's negative representations of self and world—would have a greater chance for success, in part, by indirectly facilitating improvements in her ongoing relationships (i.e., marriage, family of origin, friendships, etc.). Transactions within these relationships could then be expected to better meet the mother's needs for emotional support and practical assistance with the everyday challenges of parenting.

We agree with Bowlby (1980), Mahoney (in press) and other cognitive therapists that the deep structural change we were targeting is most likely to occur within the context of an emotionally significant relationship that challenges and disconfirms early unconscious assumptions (e.g., "I am unworthy of nurturance, the world is dangerous" or their coping derivatives (e.g., "Don't trust anyone, I don't need help"). In this view, a significant ingredient for change involves the nurturing actions of the therapist. The therapist strives to establish a secure, safe, and caring relationship. Within this interpersonal setting, the therapist helps create a context from which the client can explore past and emerging representations of self and world. This therapeutic stance derives its power from its implicit contradiction of the client's negative core beliefs and its explicit but gentle challenge regarding the current reality base of those initial self/world assumptions.

Fraiberg's (1980) therapeutic work with disturbed mothers and their infants also persuaded us that infant participation in the therapy itself could be a valuable asset. In her experience, the presence of the infant allowed the therapist to observe quickly the current workings of the mother's negative models as they were played out in her ongoing caretaking during the therapy session. We were particularly attracted to this therapeutic modality because of the ease with which such developmentally rich content could be accessed and used to work through both the mother's earliest psychological insults and her current parenting problems.

We wanted to include the infant in our therapy sessions for the aforementioned reasons. However, we also wanted to retain the flexibility necessary for allowing the mother to discuss personally intimate issues that did not require and sometimes could not benefit from the baby's presence. We were ultimately seeking a therapeutic structure that would facilitate sensitive responses to the mother's needs at any given point in therapy. We, therefore, wanted to encourage mothers to bring their babies to the therapy hour while at the same time conveying to them that there might be times when they would find coming alone to the therapy session more meaningful. This flexible position corresponded, in general, with our assumption that in order for psychotherapy to be effective in building self-esteem and improving marital harmony and effective parenting, it had to be progressively tailored to the continually changing needs of each individual mother.

Consistent with this assumption, we anticipated that these mothers would also have variable needs regarding many other issues, including the amount of therapeutic contact desired. In order to be sensitive to the mother's need for more or less contact, and afford them a sense of control over their progress in the intervention program, we built three choice points into the therapeutic regimen. At each of these choice points mothers were encouraged to consider the value of continuing therapeutic contact (within an overall time limitation of 12, one-hour, weekly sessions). Studies of psychotherapy effectiveness have repeatedly noted that encouraging the client's awareness of therapeutic time limits with formal contracting can be a powerful technique in facilitating personal change within relatively brief periods of time (cf. Frank, 1974; Johnson & Gelso, 1980; Mann, 1973).

Our therapy model represented an initial attempt to provide mothers of insecurely attached infants with "corrective emotional experiences" (Alexander & French, 1946) that could facilitate change in self-esteem, relationship functioning, and parenting effectiveness. These are lofty goals for any intervention program. Because of our extensive and longitudinal involvement with these families, however, we felt free to entertain such therapeutic goals. As ongoing witnesses to these parents' joys and tribulations in child-rearing, we were convinced that each one was already "reaching for the stars" in trying to do the best for their child and that with some help at this crucial period, the developmental consequences could be significant.

Our principal goal was thus to provide immediate help for these particular families. Data collection on the intervention process was carried out for exploratory purposes and as the preliminary stage to the implementation of more formal attempts at attachment intervention. In this pilot program, we did not attempt to follow state of the art psychotherapy research guidelines in rigorously equating treatment groups or treatment delivery. Conclusions about the program's effectiveness and active ingredients must therefore be drawn cautiously and with these constraints in mind.

As developmental researchers, we secondarily viewed the intervention program as a promising opportunity for learning more about the family dynamics operating in the cross-generational transmission of insecurity. We hoped that analysis of the content revealed in the psychotherapy sessions might provide information, usually difficult to obtain, about the emotionally sensitive issues connected with personal and marital distress and its impact on parental functioning. Although this type of data collection was only a subsidiary goal, we anticipated that it might well prove invaluable in terms of advancing our understanding of both individual personality and family development.

THE PENN STATE FAMILY INTERVENTION PILOT PROJECT

Sample Characteristics

The Penn State Family Intervention Study began in late spring of 1984 as an off-shoot of Belsky's longitudinal Infant and Family Development Project. All participating parents were working or middle-class, and in intact marriages. That they were highly committed to their children is reflected in their voluntary participation in the longitudinal study for the reported purpose of gaining information about their child's developmental progress. (See Isabella & Belsky, this volume, for further elaboration of the characteristics of the entire sample.)

Pilot Program Design

Infants in this project were regularly assessed at 12 months of age using the standard Ainsworth Strange Situation procedure. When infants in the third cohort of the longitudinal study were classified as insecurely attached (major classification A or C) by two independent raters, the questionnaire, intervention, and observational data gathered on the family from the last trimester of pregnancy through the infant's ninth month were scrutinized. Our policy was to assign each insecurely attached infant's mother to an experimental or no-treatment control group if additional evidence of stress, other than attachment classification, could be found in the data gathered prior to the Strange Situation assessment. In each and every case, corroborative evidence of difficulty in the personality or family system of the mother was in evidence. For instance, in one case, the questionnaire data on child-rearing history revealed that the mother perceived her parents love for her to be totally conditional, based primarily on her achievements in school and other specified areas. In another identified case, a review of responses to questions concerning social support showed that the mother felt isolated except for her neighboring mother-in-law, who she experienced as critical and rejecting. In a third case, marital adjustment questionnaire responses indicated a pattern of increasing conflict and hostility.

A total of 31 infants were classified as insecure (16 A's, 15 C's). Four families moved out of the area shortly after the assessment at 1 year and became unavailable for further study (1 A, 3 C's). Of the remaining insecure sample, 14 were invited to participate in the clinical treatment phase (8 A's, 6 C's).

Each family in the experimental group was invited to enroll in the clinical phase after they were given feedback by the principal investigator, Jay Belsky, about their child's performance during the 12-month assessment. In the feedback, the parents were told that their child had shown a pattern of behavior in the laboratory situation that some researchers indicated was, to a degree, predictive of patterns of child behavior in later years that parents often found difficult. It should be noted that in a concerted effort not to alarm parents, the terms *insecure* (in all of its varieties) and *behavioral problems* were never employed. Further, it was repeatedly pointed out to parents: (a) that we were by no means certain that their child would develop these difficulties; (b) that the research evidence was not absolutely conclusive; (c) that change was possible; and (d) that we shared this information with parents because we had promised to at initial program enrollment and felt it was theirs to have, not ours to keep. In describing the service we would be offering, we further noted that we could not be certain of its effectiveness and that parents should feel totally free to decline participation at the outset or terminate it at any point they desired. The intervention program itself was described as an opportunity to talk with someone about day to day experiences and events involving their infant or possibly affecting him/her. Because of fiscal constraints and experiential limits of personnel, we made it clear that the service would be short-term and could not involve the entire family.

During the feedback/enrollment session, two thirds of the couples contacted spontaneously reported that they indeed experienced significant personal stress. Typically, mothers were more open initially about difficulties than were fathers. In two cases, mothers clearly acknowledged problems and seemingly welcomed the opportunity to discuss them, but the fathers' conflicting perspectives apparently led them to decline participation. A total of four families refused the initial invitation (1 A's, 3 C's) whereas another three (3 A's) accepted but then declined after only one or two meetings. The remaining seven subjects (4 A's, 3 C's) participated in 8 to 12 therapy sessions.

One of the mothers who participated for only two sessions declined to participate further because she believed that only marital therapy would be effective in alleviating the significant distress in her family. Disputes between parents about their perceptions of child/family problems or the potential helpfulness of the project may have also played a role in other refusals to pursue our intervention. Several mothers appeared eager to participate upon first contact and only later declined after they had discussed the matter with their husbands. Nevertheless, our refusal rate was slightly higher than the 37% to 45% rate typically found in other psychotherapy process studies involving clients who have themselves initiated professional contact (Fiester & Rudestam, 1975).

Although the invitation to participate in the clinical treatment phase was presented to both parents, the program was specifically designed only for mother and mother-infant participation. Fathers were excluded primarily due to the limited pool of therapists and our belief that dealing with couples together required more expertise than our therapists possessed. Mothers were offered a series of up to 12 individual counseling sessions that were divided into three contracts of four sessions per contract period. The sessions followed a standard model of brief psychotherapy (Koss, Butcher, & Strupp, 1986; Strupp & Bender, 1984). Weekly meetings lasting 60 to 90 minutes took place in a treatment room near the laboratories with which the mothers were familiar from their participation in the earlier phases of the longitudinal study.

Three graduate students with clinical training (2 females, 1 male) served as therapists. The students audiotaped each therapy session and kept detailed therapy process notes. Intensive supervision, amounting to a minimum of ½ hour for every 1 hour of client contact, was provided to the students on a weekly basis by two of the authors (T.N., W.J.T.) who are trained clinical psychologists.

The Minnesota Multiphasic Personality Inventory (MMPI) was initially administered to all mothers who enrolled in the intervention program in order to screen for the presence of severe psychopathology. At the conclusion of each four-session contract period, mothers were also asked to complete an open-ended questionnaire on changes they were currently experiencing in their relationships with their infant, husband, family of origin, friends, etc. Measures of personality, marital function, child-rearing history, parenting style, etc. were also available from the files of the original longitudinal study.

In addition to the audiotapes and therapy process notes, therapists were required to maintain problem lists for each mother. Using their case notes and tapes, therapists documented the occurrence of problems that either the therapist or mother judged to be significantly influencing their parenting effectiveness.

The Treatment Program

The first therapy sessions contained some awkwardness on both the parts of the mothers and the student therapists. This may have been due to the mothers' initial conceptualizations of treatment as primarily didactic in nature. During this phase, the mothers viewed the therapists as authorities with expert knowledge on all of the problems in child-rearing. As such, they came to the therapy sessions with pragmatic questions about parenting, e.g., "How do I entertain my child at this age?," "Why is my baby so clingy?," "What does it mean when he screams?," "What is the best way to handle temper outbursts?," etc. The therapists did not provide any immediate answers but instead attempted to explore with the mother the antecedent conditions, consequences, and potential problem solutions while empathizing with the difficulties they presented. In this manner, the therapeutic focus was shifted away from the sharing of expert knowledge and enlarged to include cooperative exploring of the mother's experiences of stress and support as it affected her parenting behavior.

Providing Emotional Support. The role of the therapist in these early sessions was to engage the mothers in an emotionally supportive, nonjudgmental relationship. In the beginning, this most often took place in the context of gathering information about the mother's current concerns. Although there was no formal plan regarding the content or sequence of topics to be covered, the same general issues were addressed by all of the therapy subjects. These content areas derived from their common roles as mothers, wives, offspring, workers, and friends.

As the therapeutic relationship became more firmly established, the therapist was more direct in eliciting and probing for the feelings associated with the mother's concerns. Revelation of such feeling states was seen as crucial for elucidating the core assumptions associated with the mother's poor self-esteem and insensitive caretaking. In the case of one mother who originally brought up her child's clinginess as a parenting problem, for example, sensitive probing revealed that this situation often inspired rather intense anger. In her perception, the child's continual desire to cling represented an "unfair" attempt to restrict the mother's movement, especially her leave-taking. This mother recalled that she habitually responded to the clinging by moving more quickly to put the baby down saying, "After all, I can't let him control me!" The influence of the emotive dimension was suggested by the fact that this revealing material had been inaccessible in the first session when clinginess was first discussed as a parenting difficulty. Although the antecedents and consequences of the baby's clinging were explored in some detail, the mother's perceptions of the baby's behavior as unfairly controlling were outlined only after she had been helped in exploring her emotional reaction to the clinginess.

As the therapeutic focus turned more frequently toward eliciting the mothers' emotional reactions, the relationship between the therapist and client appeared to grow in trust and intimacy. This development was typically marked first by a new level of comfort in the helping relationship and was often reflected in the synchrony of conversational style and (later) by mothers initiating discussion of stressful events in their past and present.

Countertransference Problems. When they began to more fully understand the extent of the mothers' past pains and the intensity of their day to day struggles, the therapists reported that at times they were feeling inadequate in the therapeutic role. Difficulties in managing client dependency or countertransference issues were not uncommon. In their subsequent interactions with the mothers, their problems in dealing with their countertransference were also manifest in their subtle avoidance of emotionally provocative material and with attempts to take care of or undo the associated negative feeling state. At this point in the therapeutic course, they often requested more frequent and lengthy supervisory guidance to deal with their fears of failing to meet their clients' needs and expectations.

Perhaps due to the therapists' relative inexperience, difficulties with the countertransference occurred frequently throughout the latter sessions despite the additional supervisory attention. No therapist ever overtly refused to discuss any issue with their client. Rather, they sometimes simply failed to directly acknowledge or emphasize the emotionally intense aspects of the event. For example, when one mother appeared to come close to tears as she shared her deep disappointment that her son did not seem to enjoy being held or cuddled, her therapist uncomfortably responded by asking the mother to describe in detail her typical manner of holding the baby. Through her questions, the therapist led the mother to consider that perhaps her perception of the baby's lack of cuddliness was actually incorrect. She intended with this inquiry to encourage the mother to try other styles of expressing her physical affection. The mother, however, was so discouraged that she resisted all of these suggestions.

When the therapist presented the incident in supervision, she wanted help in understanding why the mother had shown little interest in trying the suggested alternatives. In her eagerness to reduce the mother's distress as well as her own, the student had not only ignored the tears but had also failed to explore with the mother the significance she felt in the baby's lack of cuddliness. This kind of insensitivity could obviously be expected to undermine the positive impact of the treatment, but we were impressed with the resolution each mother showed in repeatedly attempting to share the heartfelt story of her life.

Termination. Clients were formally encouraged to consider terminating their participation in the treatment program after the fourth and eighth sessions. As a prelude to this discussion, each mother completed a lengthy questionnaire on her experience in therapy and changes that were occurring in her feelings, attitudes, and relationship experiences. The therapists assumed a neutral attitude while facilitating their clients' explorations regarding the helpfulness of the program and the advisability of continuation. Guidance in dealing with the positive and negative feelings associated with leaving the intervention program was provided when termination was chosen. As part of the termination process, the therapists also emphasized the positive attributes and strengths they had observed in the course of their work with the mother and expressed appreciation for the valuable contribution each had made toward the research project.

CLINICAL PATTERNS

We reviewed the therapy case notes and tapes in hopes that the mothers' revelations during therapy would provide new information about the intrapersonal and interpersonal dynamics involved in the development of insecurity during infancy and early childhood. With this goal in mind, we initially searched the records for content directly related to parenting style and childcare.

Childcare Issues

Disparity Between Parents in Household and Childcare Responsibilities. We were particularly interested in the mothers' comments during therapy about their parenting experiences. Surveys of the content of the initial therapy sessions indicated that all of these mothers had significant resentment toward their partners over their perception of disparity in the division of childcare and related household responsibilities. Every mother interviewed described herself as the primary caregiver and indicated that she had taken on this responsibility in addition to her other duties as primary homemaker. The majority of these women were also either working outside the home or planning to go back to work in the near future. They uniformly described their partners as making little effort to help with the additional work created by the birth of their child.

Although the intensity of the resentment appeared to be significant, all but one of the mothers refused to target the issue of cooperation in childcare as one that they wished to work on during therapy. In response to this suggestion, a few mothers disowned their feelings by saying it really wasn't that big of a problem. Others clearly stated that they felt certain that their husbands would never be more helpful, and so preferred not to "waste time" discussing it. Despite both types of disclaimers, the importance of this issue was underlined by the mothers continuing to comment throughout the course of therapy on their husbands lack of helpfulness or, more frequently, sharing feelings of being overwhelmed with the household and childcare work.

In these latter cases, the feelings of being overwhelmed seemed to rise not only from the quantity of work but also from the disorganization of it all. These mothers appeared to cope with their resentment toward their husbands' uninvolvement by refusing to accomplish any task in a predictable manner or at an anticipated time. They seemed to live in perpetual anticipation that their husbands might take more responsibility if they made the household needs painfully obvious. For these families, laundry piled up until there were no more clothes in the closets, grocery shopping occurred when the cupboard was bare, and meals were prepared when someone was well beyond hungry. These mothers did indeed appear to be living on the edge of chaos, constant prey for the most immediate need and most intense call.

This style of household (dis)organization exacted its toll not only in breeding tension and frustration within the parents, but also in its sapping their nurturing energy. The child was responded to only when its cries were intense and salient in relation to the other pressing needs. These parents could not characteristically enjoy playing with their child; they were too busy coping with the latest crisis.

In the one case in which the mother openly acknowledged problems with her husband over childcare responsibilities, the intensity of this conflict appeared so strong that the needs of the child were often sacrificed. This mother described a morning routine that involved both parents heatedly arguing over whose turn it was to get up with the baby and change its diaper. The argument typically lasted from 15 to 30 minutes with the baby's cries in the background. It was very important to this mother that she not appear to give in, so she made a point of not picking up the baby— despite its cries—until the argument was concluded by her husband getting out of bed and stomping off to the bathroom. On the occasions when this mother felt she had won the argument, the verbal exchange was the same but the mother got to the bathroom first, leaving the husband to cope with the crying baby. In this marriage in which the baby appeared to frequently play the role of "hot potato," the child's signals were not simply ignored but the stimulus for active avoidance and emotional conflict. Clearly, these dynamics could create a negative understanding of self, others, and world. And, in particular, they might well teach a child to restrain or hide any overt signs of her/his needs or feelings in order to prevent parental fighting and unavailability.

Disagreements Over Parenting Style: Responsiveness and Protection. In addition to the simple disparity in sharing the childcare work, several mothers reported frequent disagreements with their partners over parenting style. Three couples had major disagreements over the appropriate response to their child's cries. One mother reported that her husband believed that their baby's cries were signs of misbehavior. This father instructed the mother to respond by moving the baby to a far away room with the door closed in order to teach the baby not to cry. Although the mother often responded in this manner when the father was nearby, she admitted that she preferred to "see if I can fix what's troubling him" whenever she was alone with the baby. In further discussion, this mother described an episode when she had tried to attend to the baby's cries in opposition to her husband's wishes. The mother thought that her caretaking had fueled the father's brewing anger over another incident and resulted in his hitting her, smashing furniture, and threatening to do more harm. Although this mother believed her style of responding to the baby's cries was better than that of her husband, she was clearly afraid of asserting herself because of the hostility and violence that could result.

Other mothers reported conflicts with their husbands over how to organize play activities in order to insure safety. These disagreements were never identified by the responsive mothers as concerns in and of themselves, but rather were shared as background information in the telling of other stories. In describing her feelings of emptiness and helplessness, one mother mentioned in an off-hand manner that she couldn't even spend time alone with her husband because he didn't like to leave the baby playing without supervision. On questioning, this mother explained that after dinner she preferred to leave the baby playing on the kitchen floor while she and her husband watched television a few rooms away. The therapist gently queried about the issue of safety because, in a previous therapy session, the mother had shared that the baby was becoming very clever at removing the protective caps from the electric sockets, climbing the baby gate, opening the refrigerator, etc. She told her therapist that she was sure the child was "safe enough" because she could tell by his sounds when he was getting into anything dangerous. The conflict between the parents arose because the father felt uncomfortable with the arrangement and regularly moved the baby to the TV room despite the mother's protests. Although the mother's lack of appropriate protectiveness for the child's physical well-being was significant in itself, the fact that the parental conflict was reenacted almost nightly may have represented an even more serious risk factor for the child's emotional health.

Insensitivity to the Child's Expanding Cognitive Organization. As babies enter their second year of life, their growing mobility and dexterity allow their curiosity about the world to take more sophisticated forms. For some mothers in our project, these new exploratory efforts were seen as problematic and often identified as an issue they desired help with in therapy. Their anxiety about these behaviors often resulted in premature and unsuccessful efforts to train the "proper" behavior with verbal instructions, modeling, and also with punishment, i.e., sometimes they spanked, but often they simply told the child, "Bad!"

These mothers typically asked their therapist to teach them how to control their baby so that they could eliminate these "messy" tendencies. The exploration of food during meal time was an area that was particularly troublesome to many. One mother complained that she was so embarrassed by her child's table manners that she refused to feed him when anyone else was present. She described her then 14-month old son as seeming to take delight in removing new foods from his mouth and smearing them all over his high chair tray. When the therapist attempted to reframe the child's behavior as an exploratory exercise to discover the respective food's taste, texture, color, etc., the mother rigidly replied that she wanted her baby to explore with its toys, not with food.

The creation of messes with food, cupboard contents, clothes, and sometimes even with toys, seemed unacceptable to some mothers under any label. These women were clearly not intending to stifle their child's cognitive growth, but it appeared that they simply could not believe that this kind of exploration might be developmentally appropriate and even beneficial. For them, their child's messes seemed to signify an additional and unnecessary burden of cleaning and, perhaps, more importantly, cause for public embarrassment. One mother commented, "I know if anyone sees him doing that, they will think I am a bad mother." The powerful influence of this fear of social criticism suggests that at least in this case, insensitivity to the child's exploratory needs can be understood in terms of the mother's own needs to protect her ego.

Maternal insensitivity to the child's cognitive level of development was also manifest in a disregard for the child's expanding memory and understanding of time and sequences. Three mothers reported frustration with their children over the clinginess they had begun to demonstrate. In two of these cases, the mothers had adopted a strategy of trying to leave without being noticed. One mother described a daily scene where she brought her daughter into the babysitter's house, gave her some toys with which to play, and then walked out while the girl wasn't looking. These women thought that their children would cry less if they did not draw their attention to the approaching separation. They failed to realize that the children could remember the order of events and anticipate very well the final act—Mom leaving them.

Several mothers also showed insensitivity through their general lack of support for their child's new attempts to discover order and predictability, especially in regard to caretaking routines. Not only were the household activities disorganized in these families, but the children also did not have

established meal times or sleeping schedules, and each child also had multiple babysitters. Childcare arrangements were often made on the spur of
the moment and were never the same week to week. One mother utilized
an average of three different caregivers each day. This mother had no
explanation for this arrangement; it just never occurred to her to plan
otherwise.

*Poor Support for the Child's Emotional Differentiation and Budding
Autonomy.*   Many mothers in the project appeared to find their child's
expanding experience of emotion, including desire, frustration, and anger,
very threatening. This was most often described by the therapists as "difficulty handling temper tantrums." Although almost no parent finds
handling tantrums a pleasant experience, this group of mothers seemed to
find them more troubling. Four mothers asked specifically for advice on
how to prevent the occurrence of *any* angry outburst. The majority of this
group reported becoming angry themselves in response to their child's acting out and resorting to a variety of techniques to end the outburst
including screaming, spanking, isolation, and giving in to the child's
desire. All of the mothers reported that they had great difficulty in handling the tantrums in a consistent manner despite efforts to do so.

In discussions with their therapists, most of these mothers indicated
that they believed all angry feelings were unnecessary and in some sense
bad. They viewed their child's angry acting out as an intentional act meant
to manipulate, embarrass, and anger them. Caught in this perspective,
these women could not affirm their children's emotional experience or
help them find comfortable ways to express these feelings.

Although these mothers may have been threatened by their children's
displays of emotional intensity, some of the mothers found mild expressions of negativity difficult to cope with, as well. One mother reported that
she was troubled by her son's inattentiveness during reading time. Every
night before bedtime she tried to hold the boy in her lap and show him a
story book. Although the boy didn't cry, he often squirmed to get down or
tried to grab a toy. He rarely looked at the book or got involved with the
reading. The mother tearfully described him as "always interested in
someone, something else." As the therapist attempted to clarify the woman's feelings about the incident, it because obvious that she had
interpreted the baby's rejection of the reading activity as a rejection of her.
When the mother was asked about how she handled these feelings, her
mood seemed to brighten and she replied, "It's okay, I get back at him later.
I wait until he's asleep in his crib, then I pick him up and have him all to
myself." For this woman, the child's negativity represented his
individuation from her, and this was intolerable. The mother's outright
rejection of the child's budding autonomy can be seen both in her

preference for his unconscious state and in her need to retaliate for the hurt he had caused her.

Four other mothers showed similar difficulties in supporting their children's moves toward separation and individuation. As a group, however, these women were not as overtly concerned with tantrums or negativity, but instead seemed preoccupied with the affection their children showed to other caregivers. They spoke jealously of how their children enjoyed their babysitters. Several mothers described feelings of disappointment and even sadness when they discovered their baby happy and content in the arms of another woman. It seemed almost as if the child's ability to relate and gain comfort from another led them to doubt the significance of their own relationship. Two mothers recalled that they decided to quit their jobs specifically because they could not tolerate their baby becoming attached to the babysitter. One mother was especially jealous of the relationship developing between her husband and her daughter. This woman stated that she felt "left out" because she was not the "chosen comforter." She was not at all pleased with her baby's growing attachment to his father despite her earlier statements about wanting her husband to be more involved in childcare. Each of these mothers seemed to equate the expansion of their child's social network as a personal rejection instead of the developmental advance it represented.

Marital Issues

Poor Communication and Sharing.   All of the parenting problems described previously, including parental conflicts over style of child-rearing, appeared to arise in a larger context of marital difficulty. In these families the potential for conflict appeared to be ever ready—almost waiting—for content to give it form. The propensity for misunderstandings and disagreements seemed highly related to the amount of time couples spent in common activity or in direct communication. Most mothers had complaints in both of these areas but they were very hesitant to admit them to themselves or share them with their husbands. They talked of being lonely and wishing they could spend more time with their husbands but were quick to make excuses for their husbands' unavailability. One woman complained that her husband spent much more time in front of the television than with her but then rationalized that he needed that kind of mindless activity in order to relax after work.

Several mothers excused their husbands' lack of involvement as the result of work commitments. One described her husband as working long and hard hours but "enjoying every minute of it" and then added the following postscript: "It's just too bad he couldn't be there when (the baby) was born." Through careful questioning the therapist discovered that the father had not been present at the birth and had not visited his wife or baby until 24 hours later, even though he could have gotten off work. The wife attempted to project her disappointment and anger over the event on to her husband's employer but she also wondered aloud if she was "less important" to her husband than his work. She admitted that she had never openly shared her disappointment about his uninvolvement in the birth to anyone. The same woman also commented that she had been quite surprised by the "blues" that had plagued her for weeks following the birth of her daughter.

Over half of the mothers participating in our clinical project had similar problems with failing to share significant concerns with their partners. They found it most difficult to share emotional needs and ask for support. One woman came into a therapy session asking for help in understanding a recurring nightmare. She reported that she had been troubled by the dream almost every night for at least a year. The dream involved bitterly fighting with her own mother and was so stressful that she always awoke in tears and was "down about it for hours every morning." When the therapist asked how her husband responded to her nightmare and tears, the woman quietly replied, "He's never noticed. I don't think he knows about it." This woman was troubled not only by the disturbing dream but also by her inability to share it with her partner. She kept waiting and hoping that he would ask about her tears but he never did. At that point, she could only imagine that he didn't ask because he didn't want to know. She felt painfully rejected by him despite the fact that she had never directly tried to talk to him about the dream or her feelings.

Sexual Difficulties.   The most common problem mentioned in this area concerned infrequency of sexual intimacy. Four women said that they wished their husbands would initiate sex more often. Initially, they explained their husbands' infrequency in making sexual overtures as due to not having enough time or energy. When one therapist encouraged her client to invite her husband to set aside a specific time for a sexual encounter with her, the woman resisted saying, "But then I won't know if he really wanted to or if he was just giving in to me." This woman could only believe her husband was honestly wanting her if he initiated without provocation. On questioning, the therapist discovered that on another level this woman feared that her husband's lack of amorous behavior was due to her own unattractiveness. She both blamed herself for failing to work harder at getting her figure back in shape and felt resentful at the conditional nature of her husband's affection. Two other women eventually shared their secret fears about their husbands' apparent losses of sexual interest. They believed for various reasons that their husbands were sexually involved with other women. None of these mothers were willing to talk with their husbands about their inferences and, thus, their fears took on a life of their own as if they were established truth.

Despite all of these mothers' statements about wanting more sex, their resistance to making attempts to verify their inferences or solve these sexual problems suggested that most were intensely ambivalent about their desires to have sexual contact with their partners. On one hand, they seemed to think that if their husbands' initiated sex, it might feel reassuring and indicate that the marriage commitment was still intact, but on the other hand, they appeared afraid of sharing that very vulnerable part of themselves in such a context of distrust.

Problems in Conflict Resolution.   Most of the couples who had difficulty in resolving sexual problems also had trouble in working through the misunderstandings and conflicts inevitable in any marriage. Not one of the mothers believed her marital conflicts could be satisfactorily resolved through discussion. They expected that their husbands would basically ignore them, ridicule them for their feelings, reject, and/or leave them if they were open about their anger, or become physically abusive if they did not "give in." They preferred to minimize disagreements and let them be solved "by time." This strategy was exemplified in how several mothers handled the disagreements over whether they should participate in our therapy project. When the father stated that he preferred that his partner decline participation, as happened in at least three cases of those who participated in all 12 intervention sessions in addition to the early terminators and refusals, the mother typically said she would like to go in once just to see what it was like. Then she set up future appointments while her husband was at work and refrained from mentioning the project or her therapy sessions unless the husband asked about it directly. These women did not see their behavior as dishonest but rather as self-protective. Nevertheless, their inability to relate the significance of the experience to their husbands must have contributed to their sense of isolation and emotional distance.

At this point in their lives these women seemed to view their marriages as good enough, even if not blissful, and thus preferred not to take risks by instead adopting a passive stance. They worked hard at convincing themselves that "things are really not that bad" and became confused about their feelings. This was particularly true of the one mother who reported that her husband was chronically unemployed, a cocaine addict, and physically abusive to her (but not to the child). Even with these circumstances, the woman rationalized staying in the relationship by saying, "At least my son will have a father."

This woman was one of four mothers who admitted that they had fantasized from time to time about leaving their husbands or seeking a divorce.

Several were puzzled about why they should have such daydreams. These women were also the most resistant to making efforts to change the dynamics in their marital relationship. They appeared stuck in a web of fear and unhappiness with little hope for anything better. Perhaps they unconsciously hoped that a second child would help strengthen their marital relationship or at least alleviate their loneliness because half of this group were among those who became "unexpectedly" pregnant again before their first baby was 18 months old.

Three of the four who had divorce fantasies did believe that marriage counseling could be helpful, but they all doubted that their husbands would be willing to talk openly to a therapist. Two of the women had been troubled enough that they had asked their husbands to go with them to marriage counseling prior to the beginning of our program. In both cases, the husband immediately rejected the idea and the wives had pursued the issue no further.

Extended Family Problems

Stressful Childhood History. Due to the time-limited nature of the therapy program, therapists did not directly initiate discussions concerning the mothers' childhood histories. Nevertheless, almost all of the mothers talked some about their early experiences in their family of origin, often in the context of drawing a contrast to their husband's childhood background. Only one mother gave the impression of having a happy childhood, and in this case the woman gave so vague an account, similar to Main and Goldwyn's (in press) description of idealizing mothers, that it was impossible to evaluate.

The majority of women recalled specific events from childhood that suggested that their early years were troubled, painful times. This finding corroborates the findings of Morris (1980) and Ricks (1982, 1983) on the intergenerational transmission of attachment patterns. Three mothers described their own parents as extremely critical and rejecting .They remembered feeling "no good," "always wrong," and "unloved." Another told of spending a great deal of time alone and lonely, saying of her parents, "It seemed like they were never there." Two mothers had been physically abused throughout their childhoods; one by her mother and one by her father. When they talked of those experiences, it almost sounded as if it had happened to someone else. The therapists were impressed, however, with the fact that not one of these mothers displayed any negative affect while sharing these memories. Even though they recalled experiences such as "mostly being afraid" and "wishing I just could be good enough," their faces showed no sign of hurt, sadness, or anger. They seemed to have coped with the pain by distancing themselves and acting tough with comments such as, "It never really hurt; I knew how to take a good beating."

Failure to Currently Provide Emotional and Instrumental Support. Although the accuracy of this information about the mothers' childhood histories is questionable due to its retrospective nature, at the least, it seems clear that most of the mothers did not *feel* appropriately nurtured as children. This failure to feel accepted and supported was also a common theme when mothers discussed their current interactions with their parents and mother and father-in-laws. Some mothers spoke of feeling continually criticized about their household organization and parenting style. Others were frustrated by parents' offers of instrumental support, especially child care, which never materialized. Two appeared to be jealous of the attention their parents directed toward their child, saying, "They give her way too much—I never got anything like that. She's going to be spoiled for sure."

In contrast to their nearly flat affect when talking of their childhoods or current interactions with their own parents, these mothers were often quite animated when sharing their frustration, anger, and resentment toward their husbands' parents. Mothers-in-law, in particular, were common targets of anger, often for some perceived failure to provide instrumental assistance with housework, childcare, or in times of special need, e.g., family illness, moving, going back to work, etc. Intense feelings of rejection were also engendered on occasions when the mother-in-law failed, for instance, to buy the mother a birthday gift, introduce the mother at a party, or remember the mother's dress size. In most cases, the mothers' expectations regarding their relationships with their mothers-in-law seemed excessive when compared with the expectations they had for their own mothers, but this may have been due to some unconscious hopes that this second mother would make up for the nurturing they had never received from their own parent.

Maternal Personality Functioning

Common Characteristics. The mothers who participated in this intervention project were commonly troubled by worries and guilt that they could not control their feelings, especially in regard to anger and sadness. Seven mothers reported that they had very bad tempers that frequently got them into trouble. Two were especially concerned that they might lose control and hurt their children. Four women also expressed embarrassment that at times they could not control their tears. The entire group of mothers appeared to work very hard to keep their feelings in balance, though all too often their efforts were in vain. In fact, they perceived themselves to be ineffective in most other domains as well, and this contributed, no doubt, to their predominantly low self-esteem. Finally, these mothers appeared to have very little psychological insight into themselves, their motivations, problems, or stumbling blocks.

Working Models. Not only did these women generally view themselves in negative terms, but they also showed some similarities in what they specifically did not know about themselves or their world. These areas of "unknowing" or ambiguity generally conformed to the four core themes of power, value, identity, and reality identified by Mahoney (in press) in his theory of identity construction and were the areas in which the mothers' perceptions were most distorted.

The mothers with problems around the issue of power typically misperceived what events could be controlled, how to exert control over them, or how to know when others were trying to affect control. These ever-present ambiguities concerning themselves and their world contributed to their difficulties in assuming an appropriate amount of responsibility—they sometimes assumed too much, as with the mothers who wanted to prevent their children or themselves from ever being angry, and sometimes too little, as with the mothers who failed to organize their households or attempt to make changes in areas where they were dissatisfied. Those with open questions about how to recognize who was in control often made errors by incorrectly attributing intentionality and power to others, as when the mother interpreted her mother-in-law's forgetfulness about her birthday as "she meant to hurt me" or perceived her crying baby as "trying to control me."

When the mother's working model showed core deficits around the these of value, she had difficulty in accurately perceiving the goodness or badness of a situation. This confusion typically was the source of her characteristically poor judgement and decision making. Problems with this issue were best exemplified by the mother who justified staying with her abusive husband by saying, "At least my son will have a father," despite the personal pain this caused her and the obviously negative environment it created for her child.

Identity issues were expressed in mothers' doubtfulness about their basic nature or personality. With this type of core organization, the mother's lack of self-knowledge was balanced by overemphasizing the opinions of others and being very sensitive to social norms. In these cases, the mothers' seemed inordinately concerned with their appearances (rather than their internal state) while characteristically misperceiving social cues. Thus, they were preoccupied with avoiding social criticism, because for them, it was equivalent to self-hate. Identity was clearly at stake for the mother who needed to prevent her child's messiness because, "I know if anyone sees him doing that, they will think I am a bad mother." Given her working model with its vacuous self-structure, if *anyone* thought she was *anything*, she was predisposed to believe them.

When mothers had concerns around the core theme of reality, they showed gaps in their ability to perceive themselves and the world as orderly and consistent. Instead they felt threatened by chaos. These women typically coped through a general avoidance of intimacy because of their distorted view of others as undependable or untrustworthy. This basic issue seemed most responsible for the mothers' unwillingness to communicate their needs and feelings with their husbands and inability to tolerate their children's affection for others.

In summary, all of the mothers who participated in our clinical treatment program appeared to have substantial personality problems of longstanding duration. Their consistent patterns of "unknowing" suggested that their working models had reached representational homeostasis (Bowlby, 1980), probably as the result of defensive exclusion of early painful experiences. This interpretation was supported by the mothers' pervasively inappropriate affect during the recall of their troubled childhoods.

These women viewed themselves and the world in not only negative terms, but also with consistent perceptual distortions, indicating repeatedly the inadequacies of their model of reality. Each mother's individual pattern of distortion seemed to contribute in predictable ways to her problems with her own parents, her husband, and now also with her child. In approximately half of the cases, the problems were so severe that the mothers additionally showed signs of clinical pathology through their depression, anxiety, alcohol and other substance abuse, and psychosomatic disorders, i.e., migraine headaches, gastric ulcers, and colitis, etc., as evidenced both in their MMPI responses and spontaneous self descriptions during therapy.

INTERVENTION PROGRAM EVALUATION

Maternal Change

When the idea of providing clinical intervention for families of insecure children was first introduced, many researchers, including ourselves, were doubtful about the real need for such services. Although attachment theory has suggested from its beginning that parental personality problems play a large role in the transmission of insecurity, there was very little documentation aside from Bowlby's original case studies (1973, 1977, 1982) on the parents' personal levels of distress during their children's formative years. The clinical case studies presented here show clearly that these mothers of insecurely attached children were themselves chronically stressed, but fearful of reaching out for help.

Almost every mother was initially skeptical of the value of our treatment program; they had doubts concerning its helpfulness for their child and for themselves. Many commented during their initial sessions on how they could not see how talking about their family situation could change anything. The majority of mothers felt differently about "the talking cure" by the conclusion of their last session.

From the immediate perspective of the therapists, their clients had only begun to become attached and to form a working alliance with them by the time termination was near. Because little attention was directed toward the basic maladaptive parenting style or stressed marital relationship, which together continued to place the child at risk for the problems associated with infant insecurity, the intervention program appeared ineffective.

Most mothers, however, showed a gradual change toward their therapists and the therapy process itself. Several of the women were not ready to terminate and asked for referrals to other treatment programs. Other spoke of how they would miss having the special time when they *knew* that they could always find someone interested in listening to them. A few mothers indicated that they would readily consider going to a therapist again, especially for help in going through hard times. All of these developments suggested that indirectly, there had been significant progress concerning the basic issue of trust. Indeed, given the participants' apparent increases in openness toward getting help, the therapy appeared to have successfully provided a short, but significant, "corrective emotional experience" and showed promise for producing more changes in core personality functioning and current relationship problems if it made it possible for mothers to later seek more intensive therapy.

Impact on the Child

Despite the promising suggestions of intervention effectiveness observed with the mothers, the success of any such program can ultimately be evaluated only in terms of its beneficial impact on the child. Post-treatment changes in child functioning, however, could not be assessed due to our limited resources. The original longitudinal study of family adjustment and child competence continues though, and it is possible that we may be able to observe some treatment effect in future observations. Unfortunately, the intervention program design and our small sample sizes together necessarily restrict any future conclusions concerning the effectiveness of our intervention program in reducing the risks of infant insecurity.

Active Ingredients Promoting Change

The most powerful elements in our intervention program were undoubtedly our student therapists. Although their relative inexperience was sometimes a disadvantage, as in dealing with intense affect and countertransference issues, they were deeply committed to understanding these mothers as individuals. The sincerity of their interest and care were probably responsible, in large part, for the mothers' general changes in attitudes toward therapy.

The use of unit contracting appeared useful in facilitating the efficient use of therapeutic time, but the overall limitation to a total of 12 sessions proved unreasonable given the extensiveness of the problems presented by the mothers. Documentation of further case work in attachment intervention could prove valuable in estimating more accurately the optimal therapeutic contract period; the appropriate range seems more likely to span months rather than weeks.

The ability of the therapeutic encounter to produce personality reorganization and changes in current relationships could probably be strengthened through the adoption of the developmental process emphases of the constructivist cognitive therapies (Guidano & Liotti, 1983; Mahoney, in press; Mahoney & Nezworski, 1985). This would involve specific exploration of current difficulties in intimate relationships as well as early memories of attachment relationships in an attempt to explicitly identify core patterns of misperception and distortion within the context of an emotionally supportive relationship.

Clinical Discoveries

In addition to providing therapeutic service, we noted earlier our hope that the clinical format of our program would provide us with a unique opportunity to observe the intimate family processes involved in the transmission of insecurity. The clinical case records showed incontestably, to us at least, that these mothers of insecurely attached babies were indeed encountering many of the stresses and strains that have been presumed to underly insensitive caretaking and that have been empirically linked to the development of an insecure attachment relationship. The case studies additionally elucidated specific parenting patterns (disparity between parents in child care responsibilities, disagreements over responsiveness and protection, insensitivity to the child's expanding cognitive organization, and poor support for the child's emotional differentiation and budding autonomy), common marital problems (poor communication and resolution), extended family difficulties (stressful childhood experiences), and maternal personality issues that appeared to contribute to the babies' insecurity. Perhaps one of the most important discoveries in this area concerned the fact that every mother of an insecure child showed vulnerability or difficulty in many areas. This observation suggested to us that child insecurity does not result from small, isolated deficits in parenting but may be determined by a pervasive pattern of insensitivity and family difficulty.

CONCLUSION

What remains unclear, given the fact that no treatment was made available to mothers of securely attached babies was whether they would report comparable stresses and strains as those women who did share their lives with our student therapists. In many respects, the complaints and difficulties that the clients of this pilot program expressed were normative with regard to what is routinely encountered during the transition to parenthood. What we suspect is different in the case of women whose children establish insecure attachments, however, is the degree of stress encountered and the lack of support experienced. This formulation is clearly supported in the companion chapter from our project (included in this volume) that empirically documents consistent differences between families in which infants develop secure and insecure relationships with their mothers (Belsky & Isabella, this volume).

The fact that the insecure attachment classifications used in the original identification of this sample seemed to index women and families under stress, and that most of these stressed mothers appeared to gain some benefit from the intervention program, raises some very important issues. Most significant in this regard is whether the Strange Situation classifications are useful for identifying families in need of this kind of psychological support. Like Greenspan and Lieberman (this volume), it is our opinion that the Strange Situation is by no means sufficient in and of itself for identifying families in need of help. Our experience here has suggested, though, that information on the security of the mother-child relationship could be very valuable to the clinician if the results were used cautiously in concert with other critical information on family history, parental stress, and support systems. At this point, a great deal of empirical work concerning the relative utility of attachment classification in diagnosis and treatment planning needs to be done before Strange Situation classifications could be considered relevant in routine clinical assessment of children and their families.

In this regard, it must be recalled that our own motivation for inviting families to participate in our intervention program was as much dictated by ethical considerations as it was by scientific theoretical ones. In view of the fact that we had promised families that we would share any concerns with them and, in the face of emerging data linking insecurity with subsequent developmental difficulties, we felt obliged to raise the prospect of subsequent risk, and we really had little choice but to offer some service that we believed might reduce this risk. Even though we were unsure of the severity of the risk involved, we can conclude that there was sufficient pain and suffering in the participating families to indicate that our offer of help was not misguided. To the extent that we offered even some temporary relief, we feel confident that we did the right thing. Only more extensive and careful future research will determine, however, whether this approach to service delivery can be of long-term assistance to families rearing young children.

REFERENCES

Ainsworth, M. D. S., Bell, S. M., & Stayton, D. J. (1971). Individual differences in strange situation behavior of one-year-olds. In H. R. Schaffer (Ed.), *The origins of human social relations* (pp. 17–57). London: Academic Press.

Ainsworth, M. D. S., Blehar, M. C., Waters, E., & Wall, S. (1978). *Patterns of attachment: A psychological study of the Strange Situation.* Hillsdale, NJ: Lawrence Erlbaum Associates.

Alexander, F., & French, T. M. (1946). *Psychoanalytic therapy.* New York: Basic.

Arend, R., Gove, F., & Sroufe, L. A. (1979). Continuity of individual adaptation from infancy to kindergarten: A predictive study of ego-resiliency and curiosity in preschoolers. *Child Development, 50,* 950–959.

Belsky, J. (1984). The determinants of parenting: A process model. *Child Development, 55,* 718–728.

Belsky, J., Rovine, M., & Taylor, D. G. (1984). The Pennsylvania Infant and Family Development Project, 3: The origins of individual differences in infant-mother attachment: Maternal and infant contributions. *Child Development, 55,* 718–728.

Bowlby, J. (1969). *Attachment and loss:* Vol. 1: *Attachment.* New York: Basic.

Bowlby, J. (1973). *Attachment and loss:* Vol. 2: *Separation.* New York: Basic.

Bowlby, J. (1977). The making and breaking of affectional bonds. *British Journal of Psychiatry, 130,* 201–210, 421–430.

Bowlby, J.   (1980). *Attachment and loss:* Vol. 3: *Loss, sadness and depression.* New York: Basic.

Bowlby, J.   (1982). Attachment and loss: Retrospect and prospect. *American Journal of Orthopsychiatry, 52,* 664–678.

Bowlby, J.   (1985). The role of childhood experience in cognitive disturbance. In M. J. Mahoney & A. Freeman (Eds.), *Cognition and psychotherapy* (pp. 181–200). New York: Plenum.

Clarke-Stewart, K. A.   (1978). Popular primers for parents. *American Psychologist, 33cf5. 359–369.*

Connell, D. B.   (1976). *Individual differences in attachment: An investigation into stability, implication and relationships to structure of early language development.* Unpublished doctoral dissertation, University of Syracuse.

Egeland, B., & Farber, E. A.   (1984). Infant-mother attachment: Factors related to its development and changes over time. *Child Development, 55,* 753–771.

Egeland, G., & Sroufe, L. A.   (1981). Developmental sequelae of maltreatment in infancy. In R. Rizley & D. Cicchetti (Eds.), *Developmental perspectives in child maltreatment* (pp. 77–92). San Francisco: Jossey-Bass.

Erickson, M. F., Sroufe, L. A., & Egeland, B.   (1985). The relationship between quality of attachment and behavior problems in preschool in a high-risk sample. In I. Bretherton & E. Waters (Eds.), *Growing points of attachment theory and research. Monographs of the Society for Research in Child Development, 50,* (1-2, Serial No. 209).

Fiester, A. R., & Rudestam, K. E. A.   (1975). A multivariate analysis of the early dropout process. *Journal of Consulting and Clinical Psychology, 43,* 528–535.

Fraiberg, S.   (1980). *Clinical studies in infant mental health.* New York: Basic.

Frank, J. D.   (1974). Therapeutic components of psychotherapy: A 25-year progress report on research. *Journal of Nervous and Mental Disease, 159,* 325–342.

George, C., & Main, M.   (1979). Social interactions of young abused children: Approach, avoidance, and aggression. *Child Development, 50,* 306–318.

Grossmann, K., Grossmann, K. E., Spangler, G., Suess, G., & Unzer, L.   (1985). In I. Bretherton & E. Waters (Eds.), *Growing points in attachment theory and research. Monographs of the Society for Research in Child Development, 50,* (1-2, Serial No. 209).

Guidano, V. F., & Liotti, G.   (1983). *Cognitive processes and emotional disorders.* New York: Guilford.

Johnson, D. H., & Gelso, C. J.   (1980). The effectiveness of time limits in counseling and psychotherapy: A critical review. *The Counseling Psychologist, 9*(1), 70–83.

Koss, M., Butcher, J., & Strupp, H. H.   (1986). Brief psychotherapy methods in clinical research. *Journal of Clinical and Consulting Psychology, 54,* 60–67.

LaFreniere, P., & Sroufe, L. A.   (198). Profiles of peer competence in the preschool: Interrelations between measures, influence of social ecology, and relation to attachment history. *Developmental Psychology, 21,* 56–68.

Lamb, M. E., Thompson, R. A., Gardner, W. P., Charnov, E. L., & Estes, D.   (1984). Security of infantile attachment as assessed in the "strange situation": Its study and biological interpretation. *The Behavioral and Brain Sciences, 7,* 127–147.

Lewis, M., Feiring, C., McGuffog, C., & Jaskir, J.   (1984). Predicting psychopathology in six-year-olds from early social relations. *Child Development, 55,* 123–136.

Liotti, G.   (1984). Cognitive therapy, attachment theory, and psychiatric nosology: A clinical and theoretical inquiry into interdependence. In M. A. Reda & M. J. Mahoney (Eds.), *Cognitive psychotherapies: Recent developments in theory, research and practice* (pp. 211–232). Cambridge, MA: Ballinger.

Londerville, S., & Main, M.   (1981). Security of attachment, compliance, and maternal training methods in the second year of life. *Developmental Psychology, 17,* 289–299.

Mahoney, M. J., & Nezworski, M. T.   (1985). Cognitive-behavioral approaches to the treatment of children's problems. *Journal of Abnormal Child Psychology, 13,* 467–476.

Mahoney, M. J.   (in press). *Human change processes: Notes on the facilitation of personal development.* New York: Basic.

Main, M.   (1973). *Play, exploration and competence as related to child-adult attachment.* Unpublished doctoral dissertation, Johns Hopkins University, MD.

Main, M., & Goldwyn, R.   (in press). Predicting rejection of her infant from mother's representation of her own experiences: A preliminary report. *International Journal of Child Abuse and Neglect.*

Main, M., Kaplan, N., & Cassidy, J.   (1985). Security in infancy, childhood, and adulthood: A move to the level of representation. In I. Bretherton & E. Waters (Eds.), *Growing points of attachment theory and research. Monographs of the Society for Research in Child Development, 50,* (1-2, Serial No. 209).

Main, M., & Stadtman, J.   (1981). Infant response to rejection of physical contact by the mother: Aggression avoidance and conflict. *Journal of the American Academy of Child Psychiatry, 20,* 292–307.

Main, M., Tomasini, L., & Tolan, W.   (1979). Differences among mothers of infants judged to differ in security. *Developmental Psychology, 15*, 472–473.

Main, M., & Weston, D. R.   (1981). The quality of the toddler's relationship to mother and to father: Related to conflict behavior and the readiness to establish new relationships. *Child Development, 52*, 932–940.

Mann, J.   (1973). *Time-limited psychotherapy.* Cambridge: Harvard University Press.

Maslin, C. A.   (1983). *Anxious and secure attachments: Antecedents and consequences in the mother-infant system.* Unpublished doctoral dissertation, Indiana University.

Matas, L., Arend, R. A., & Sroufe, L. A.   (1978). Continuity of adaptation in the second year: The relationship between quality of attachment and later competence. *Child Development, 49*, 547–556.

Morris, D.   (1980). *Infant attachment and problem solving in the toddler: Relations to family history.* Unpublished doctoral dissertation, University of Minnesota.

Nezworski, M. T.   (1983). *Continuity in adaptation into the fourth year: Individual differences in curiosity and exploratory behavior of preschool children.* Unpublished doctoral dissertation, University of Minnesota.

Pastor, D. L.   (1981). The quality of mother-infant attachment and its relationship to toddler's initial sociability with peers. *Developmental Psychology, 17*, 323–335.

Ricks, M. H.   (1982, April). *Origins of individual differences in attachment: Maternal, familial and infant variables.* Paper presented at the International Conference on Infant Studies, Austin, TX.

Ricks, M. H.   (1983). *Individual differences in the preschoolers' competence: Contributions of attachment history and concurrent environmental support.* Unpublished doctoral dissertation, University of Massachusetts, Amherst.

Ricks, M. H.   (1985). The social transmission of parent behavior: Attachment across generations. In I. Bretherton & E. Waters (Eds.), *Growing points in attachment theory and research. Monographs of the Society for Research in Child Development, 50*, (1-2, Serial No. 209).

Sroufe, L. A.   (1979). The coherence of individual development. *American Psychologist, 34*, 834–841.

Sroufe, L. A.   (1983). Infant-caregiver attachment patterns of adaptation in preschool: The roots of maladaptation and competence. In M. Perlmutter (Ed.), *Minnesota symposium in child psychology* (Vol. 16, pp. 41–81). Hillsdale, NJ: Lawrence Erlbaum Associates.

Sroufe, L. A., Schork, E., Motti, E., Lawroski, N., & LaFreniere, P.   (1984). The role of affect in emerging social competence. In C.

Izard, J. Kagan, & R. Zajonc (Eds.), *Emotion, cognition and behavior* (pp. 289–319). New York: Cambridge University Press.

Strupp, H. H., & Bender, J. L. (1984). *Psychotherapy in a new key: A guide to time-limited dynamic psychotherapy.* New York: Basic.

Thompson, R. A., Lamb, M. E., & Estes, D. (1983). Stability of infant-mother attachment and its relationship to changing life circumstances in an unselected middle class sample. *Child Development, 53,* 144–148.

Vaughn, B., Egeland, B., Sroufe, L. A. & Waters, E. (1979). Individual differences in infant-mother attachment at twelve and eighteen months: Stability and change in families under stress. *Child Development, 50,* 971–975.

Waters, E. (1978). The reliability and stability of individual differences in infant-mother attachment. *Child Development, 49,* 483–494.

Waters, E., Wippman, J., & Sroufe, L. A. (1979). Attachment, positive affect, and competence in the peer group: Two studies in construct validation. *Child Development, 50,* 821–829.

12

A Clinical Approach
to Attachment

Stanley I. Greenspan, M.D.
Dept. of Health & Human Services

Alicia F. Lieberman, Ph.D.
University of California, San Francisco

Attachment patterns in infants have been of enormous interest to clinical and research psychologists because of the patterns' importance in understanding human survival, coping strategies, and psychological health and illness. How infants learn to relate to others and organize emotional experiences of these relationships may be viewed from a number of different perspectives. These perspectives include the way in which the infant and caregiver initiate their relationship in terms of individual differences in sensory, motor, cognitive, and affective patterns; the manner in which the relationship is sustained and recovered from disruptive stresses (e.g., separations, illness, etc.); the range of affects incorporated into the relationship pattern (e.g., the degree and balance of pleasure, assertiveness, anger, sadness, etc.); and the emerging unique character or identity of the relationship pattern (e.g., preferred affects and themes). Various clinical and research approaches derived from differing theoretical assumptions have focused on one or another of these perspectives, sometimes with the assumption that one perspective is a window on others. This chapter discusses these various approaches to attachment patterns in the context of: its broader clinical roots (in the context of infant psychopathology), current definition of attachment, and the current empirical literature on one well-studied type of attachment pattern. It also presents an integrated developmental model that can incorporate both clinical and research perspectives. In this model, attachment is viewed as an ongoing process that has specific attributes related to the challenges of each developmental phase in the first 4 years of life.

CLINICAL ROOTS AND CURRENT CLINICAL
PERSPECTIVES ON ATTACHMENT

The study of psychopathology in infancy is a new area, even though the historical foundation for describing early relationship patterns and identifying disturbances in the early years of life is very impressive. Clinical reports, naturalistic observations, empirical studies, and animal experiments in which conditions can be altered, converge on the central role of early experiences and the importance of constitutional and environmental factors that influence these early experiences. Constitutional and maturational factors that influenced the formation of early relationship patterns were already noted in the early 1900's, and included descriptions of "babies of nervous inheritance" who exhaust their mothers (Cameron, 1919) and infants with "excessive nerve activity and functionally immature" nervous systems (Rachford, 1905). Winnicott (1931), who, as a pediatrician in the 1930's, began describing the environment's role in early relationship problems, was followed in the 1940's by the well-known studies describing the severe developmental disturbances of infants brought up in institutions or in other situations of emotional deprivation (Bakwin, 1942; Bowlby, 1951; Hunt, 1941; Lowrey, 1940; Spitz, 1946). Spitz's films resulted in laws in the United States prohibiting care of infants in institutions.

The role of individual differences in the infant based on constitutional, maturational, and early interactional patterns, i.e., "nervous" infants described by Cameron (1919) and Rachford (1905) in the early 1900s, became a focus of inquiry again during the 1940s and 1950s. Clinical observations of affective reactions to stress were made by Burlingham and Freud 1942), who observed and worked with children separated from their parents. Bergman and Escalona's (1949) descriptions of infants with "unusual sensitivities" and work by Escalona and Heider (1959) highlighted constitutional differences. Escalona's clinical reports of infants with severe sensory hypersensitivities indicated that they were at risk for severe psychopathology. Murphy and Moriarty's overview (1976) presenting Murphy's vulnerability index, created a broader framework for considering an infant's coping capacity. Thomas, Chess, and Birch's temperament studies (1968) focused on the joint role of perceived temperament and environment in influencing development. Cravioto and DeLicardie's (1973) descriptions of the role of infant individual differences in malnutrition highlighted most convincingly the infant's contribution to the infant-caregiver interaction. They focused on the impact of infant patterns on parental perceptions and in turn, on such basic adaptive functions such as gaining weight.

An extensive current literature on the emotional development of presumed normal infants builds on this impressive foundation and sets the stage for a developmental approach to the concept of attachment in both its normative and disordered patterns. It is now well documented that the infant is capable, even at birth and/or shortly thereafter, of organizing experience in an adaptive fashion. He/she can: respond to pleasure and displeasure (Lipsitt, 1966); change behavior as a function of its consequences (Gewirtz, 1965, 1969); form intimate bonds and make visual discriminations (Klaus & Kennell, 1976; Meltzoff & Moore, 1977); organize cycles and rhythms, e.g., sleep–awake, alertness states (Sander, 1962); evidence a variety of affects or affect proclivities (Ekman, 1972; Izard, 1978; Tomkins, 1963); demonstrate organized social responses in conjunction with increasing neurophysiologic organization (Emde, Gaensbauer, & Harmon, 1976); and, from the early months, can demonstrate a unique capacity to enter into complex social and affective interactions (Stern, 1974a, 1974b, 1977; Brazelton, 1974). It is interesting to note that this empirically documented view of the infant is, in a general sense, consistent with Freud's early hypothesis (1911/1958) and Hartmann's postulation (1939/1958) of an early undifferentiated organizational matrix. That the organization of experience broadens during the early months of life to reflect increases in the capacity to experience and tolerate a range of stimuli, which includes responding in social interaction in stable and personal configurations, is also consistent with recent empirical data (Brazelton, Koslowski, & Main, 1974; Emde et al., 1976; Escalona, 1968; Murphy & Moriarty, 1976; Sander, 1962; Sroufe, Waters, & Matas, 1974; Stern, 1974a, 1974b). That increasingly complex patterns continue to emerge as the infant further develops is indicated by complex emotional responses such as surprise (Charlesworth, 1969) and affiliation, wariness and fear (Ainsworth, Bell, & Stayton, 1974; Bowlby, 1969; Sroufe & Waters, 1977), observed between 7 and 12 months; exploration and "refueling" patterns (Mahler, Pine, & Bergman, 1975); behavior suggesting functional understanding of objects (Werner & Kaplan, 1963), observed in the middle to latter part of the second year of life; and the eventual emergence of symbolic capacities (Bell, 1970; Gouin-Decarie, 1965; Piaget, 1962).

In these studies, there is a consensus on a central point (and there are no dissenting studies): By 3 or 4 months of age at the latest, healthy babies are capable of a complex relationship characterized by pleasure and joy, and illustrated by responding to their caregivers' faces, smiles, and voices with brightening or alert faces and, often, with a pleasurable smile and reciprocal vocalizations (suggesting positive affect), as well as other reciprocal responses. Furthermore, the infant-caregiver interaction patterns become progressively characterized by more complex social interaction (e.g., see Charlesworth, 1969; Sroufe, 1979; and review article by Hesse &

Cicchetti, 1982). These studies of presumed normal infants, therefore, create an impressive set of behavioral parameters for expectable infant-caregiver patterns at different ages, and suggest guidelines for determining when behavior is outside the range of these expected patterns. How to define disordered attachment patterns from a developmental understanding of presumed normal patterns is discussed later.

In addition to studies of presumed normal infants, animal studies, where conditions can be experimentally altered, also provide valuable insights into both normal and disordered early attachment patterns. Recent primate studies add further information to the behavioral and biological features of attachment patterns. As Reite and Short (1980) pointed out, the affective reactions of nonhuman primates to the disruption of an affective relationship to their caregivers or peers is well documented and includes in the most extreme instances death (Goodall 1971a, 1971b, 1979), agitation and despair, inhibition of growth, and a variety of related behavioral manifestations (Harlow & Soumi, 1974; Hinde, Leighton-Shapiro, & McGinnis, 1978; Hinde & Spencer-Booth, 1970; Kaufman & Rosenblum, 1967a, 1967b; Mineka & Soumi, 1978; Seay, Hansen, & Harlow, 1962).

Recent studies of physiological and neurochemical reactions to disturbances in attachment are especially interesting and reveal the interactive nature of biological and behavioral systems. Three-month-old primates separated from their mothers for 10 days show profound changes in heart rate (e.g., bradycardia and arrythmias), EEG patterns, sleep patterns, sarcadian rhythms, and cellular immune responses (e.g., decreased lymphocyte response on challenge), and approximately 10% of monkeys do not return to baseline functioning after their mother is returned (Reite, 1981). Norepinephrene metabolism, including response to administration of imiprimine, appears to be associated with differential responses to peer separation in infant nonhuman primates (McKinny, 1977).

There is a large literature relating separation experiences in infant nonhuman primates with cortisol secretion (see Coe & Levine, 1981). Of special interest is the relationship between lack of handling, states of hyperarousal, and increased cortisol secretion in rodents (Weinberg, Smother, & Levine, 1979). In dogs reared in isolation, behavior similar to extreme masochistic behavior in humans was noted, including repeatedly returning to a lighted match and becoming burned and returning to a needle to be stuck (Melzack & Scott, 1957).

The highly specific effect of early physical contact, including forms of tactile stimulation, is highlighted in an intriguing finding that, in rat pups, tactile stimulation influences polyamine biosynthesis and the production of and tissue response to growth hormones (Butler, Suskind, & Schanberg, 1978). Also interesting in animal studies is the finding that

N-acetylneuraminic acid, in brain tissue (a compound found in many receptor sites), is sensitive to both poor nutrition and lack of human stimulation (Morgan, Boris, & Winick, 1982; Morgan & Naismith, 1982, Morgan & Winick, 1980). Because this compound has not been measured in humans and its measurement is a relatively simple procedure, it presents a promising area for further inquiry. Understanding the challenging relationship between biology and behavior obviously requires further study. Early in life when attachment patterns are being established, there are suggestions that a foundation of related biological and behavioral-psychological structures are being created.

Whereas the animal studies cited above are based on environmentally induced deprivation, there is evidence that individual differences in human infants may lead to different patterns of early human contact. For example, as indicated earlier, in studies performed in Mexican villages with mothers breastfeeding twins, Cravioto found that one baby would develop protein deficiency and the other would not. This difference was often related to infant characteristics, which influenced affective interaction (Cravioto & DeLicardie, 1973).

There are a few studies that do look at the clinically relevant situation of overstimulation or inappropriate stimulation that results in an overloading or overwhelming of the immature nervous system. For example, in rats, inconsistent mothering (induced by shocks to the maternal rat), as well as interchanging mothers repeatedly, resulted in decreased motor activity and increased defecation in the infant rats (Ottinger, Denenberg, & Stephens, 1963). In another series of experiments that contain implications for our understanding of the environmental role in ameliorating or intensifying unique constitutional patterns, it was observed that strains of very reactive, aggressive mice retained this behavior when reared with their own mothers (who are behaviorally known to be low on comforting in terms of physical contact). However, they grew up with good regulation of their aggressive behavior when reared either by a rat mother, or with a virgin "aunt" rat in the cage in addition to their own mother to offer extra comforting (rats are apparently more comforting in terms of physical contact; Denenberg, 1982).

Animal studies, where experiences can be experimentally manipulated, support the observations that either deprivation or overstimulation can lead to disordered functioning and that "special" environments may be able to compensate for certain maturational tendencies. The ability of the environment to alter early constitutional patterns in a favorable manner is also suggested by observations made in clinical settings. In our work with multirisk families (Greenspan et al., 1987), as indicated earlier, we were impressed with the infant's contribution to attachment problems, and the caregiver's ability to "woo" even an easily overstimulated infant. For example, if the infant with tactile and auditory hypersensitivities could experience a modulated, firm, tactile presence and gentle, low vocalizations, he could learn to find the human world pleasurable rather than aversive. In this context, Evelyn Toman reported (personal communication, December, 1984) an interesting case of an infant she observed daily since birth as part of a systematic study of infants, and documented an aversion to any kind of physical handling (as evidenced by back arching, gaze aversion, and other types of pulling away behavior). She suggested to the cooperative and enlightened parents that they permit physical distance, but use lots of visual and eventually verbal and auditory contact. Apparently, at approximately the age of 1½, the infant did well using what we have termed as distal communication modes (Greenspan, 1981), rather than the proximal modes. Work in progress by Soumi (personal communication, February, 1986) on nonhuman primates relates directly to the issue of individual differences in response tendency. Under nonchallenge situations, his animals look similar behaviorally and endocrinologically. With challenges such as separation experiences, novel settings, or new peer animals, some groups of monkeys evidence behavioral differences and increased cortisol secretion, whereas others seem to handle the stress quite well with little or no behavioral or endocrinologic changes. The "reactors" seem to remain "reactors" over a period of years. It also appears that certain mothers tend to produce the reactors and other mothers produce the nonreactors. This latter hypothesis is currently being explored systematically (Soumi, personal communication, February, 1986).

Considering human infants, one clinically observes that some infants seem especially vulnerable to patterns in the caregiver milieu. However, if the environment is highly stressful, it may result in disordered functioning even in very competent infants. Therefore, an important goal of future research is to identify both the specific infant and the environmental characteristics that contribute to an attachment disorder. Although additional research will facilitate clarification of infant, caregiver, and interactional characteristics of both normal and disordered attachments at each stage of development, it is important to focus on how to best classify attachment disorders based on the current "state-of-the-art."

THE DEFINITION AND CLASSIFICATION OF ATTACHMENT DISORDERS

The current state-of-the-art of psychopathology in infancy has been limited to descriptions of selected disorders and very insightful clinical case studies (e.g., Fraiberg, 1979; Greenspan et al., 1987; Provence, 1979, 1983). Recently there have been attempts at comprehensive diagnostic schemes (Greenspan, 1981, 1986; Greenspan & Lourie, 1981; Greenspan, Lourie, & Nover, 1979).

In comparison to adult disorders, research on psychopathology in infants is, ironically, both in a very early state of development and comparatively well advanced. It is early, in the sense that, as described earlier, classifications of major syndromes such as attachment disorders are only beginning to find their way into the psychiatric nomenclature (e.g., DSM III/Diagnostic & Statistical Manual of Mental Disorders, III). It is relatively advanced in the sense that in the last 14 years there has been an enormous amount of research documenting presumed normal infant emotional patterns (more than on any other period in the life cycle, including adulthood). There are new techniques to reliably assess infant behavior and physiological response patterns, which can be used to understand important features of maladaptive infant behavioral patterns. Furthermore, new developments in the basic sciences provide potential assays that may prove useful in the search for biological correlates of infant disturbances. The study of infant psychopathology, while at an early stage in the descriptive sense, can make use of technologies that were not available in the early studies of adult psychopathology.

In contemplating new directions, however, we have to consider two important issues: the degree to which we can reliably operationalize our criteria for identifying disorders in infancy, and the validity of these disorders. Here, too, the comparison with adult disorders is informative. On the positive side, it is possible to develop criteria for identifying certain disturbances in infancy. Clinicians can make reliable judgments and thereby partition presumed maladaptive groups of babies from adaptive groups (the criteria for a specific disorder—that of attachment—is discussed later). Although this may seem like a small positive factor, it is an essential beginning and only recently has been achieved for many of the adult disorders. The DSM-III and evolving DSM III-R are considered major advances, because they allow for reliable judgments about whether individuals do or do not evidence a disorder and which disorder, among the many potential disorders, is in evidence.

For many disorders in adults, children, and infants, however, there is not yet sufficient information on the natural history of the disorder or about the behavioral, physiological, and biochemical correlates of the disorder. Many of the disorders exist on theoretical groups or on general clinical grounds (that is, if the functioning of the individual is sufficiently different than that which is presumed normal and/or from other disorders), such as when a person is sufficiently depressed so that he is not able to sleep, eat, work, or engage in the expected range of human interactions.

Disorders in infancy exist at a similar state-of-the-art. There are, at present, not a sufficiently large enough group of studies documenting the natural history of these disorders or their biochemical and physiological correlates to provide for a sense of clinical confidence regarding their natural history. Yet, there is growing interest in attachment problems in infancy. These problems have received attention in the context of normal infant behavior (e.g., Ainsworth et al., 1974; Brazelton, Koslowski, & Main, 1974; Emde et al., 1976; Sroufe, 1979; Stern, 1974a) and of psychopathology, (e.g., Bowlby, 1969; Fraiberg, 1980; Provence, 1979, 1983; Rheingold, 1961; Spitz & Cobliner, 1965). Additional interesting, but less well-known, trends are also being reported informally. For instance, a recent survey at Boston Children's Hospital listed physical symptoms with no identified organic cause as the tenth leading reason for admissions (personal communication with Child Development Unit, May, 1985). The impression of the Child Development Unit staff, as has been the general clinical view of such cases, was that most of these cases involved attachment problems.

It is possible to identify these disorders reliably and make a strong case that the functioning of babies who have these presumed disorders is sufficiently different than the well-documented normative milestones of babies. More work needs to be done on differentiating infant disorders; as a general criterion of "disturbance," we have found the following principle clinically useful:

> An infant is experiencing a disorder when his behavior at a given developmental phase is sufficiently different from the norm and interferes with the accomplishments of the tasks of that phase, and the opportunity to pursue the challenges of the next phase. For example, a baby who is totally disinterested and unresponsive to the human world at 4 months is unlikely to master the task of developing a joyful intimate attachment (the phase-specific expectation), and subsequently, by 7 or 8 months, is unlikely to enter into the expected pattern of the phase concerned with purposeful, cause-and-effect-type, affective interactions.

On the basis of this principle, a number of disorders of infancy *can be delineated* and will be described later (Greenspan, 1981; Greenspan & Lourie, 1981; Greenspan, Lourie, & Nover, 1979; Greenspan et al., 1987).

Unfortunately, as indicated earlier, little is known about the incidence, prevalence, and natural history of this disturbance. Clinical case histories of autistic children often reveal that, as babies, these children were less socially responsive than other children in the same family or than expected normative patterns. But retrospective case studies, although informative, also have obvious limitations. One attempt, using family films of autistic children, to systematically rate infant behavior and compare the findings with normal controls, supports the notion that early social responsiveness is disturbed in these children (Massie, 1978a, 1978b). However, the limited number of subjects and the methodological problems experienced, also limit the value of this study.

In the context of the historical review, overview of relevant human and animal research, and definitional issues, and prior to exploring the laboratory assessment of attachment and discussing an integrated developmental perspective, it proves useful to note and briefly discuss the current clinical criteria in the formal psychiatric nomenclature. The current formal clinical criteria are an outgrowth of both the historical human and animal studies, and focus on the most extreme types of disordered attachment—the withdrawn infant.

CURRENT CLINICAL CRITERIA FOR DIAGNOSING ATTACHMENT DISORDER

In this section is is evident that the DSM-III represents a phenomenological approach that suggests concrete operational criteria, but ignores the most recent developmental findings. The laboratory approach (the Strange Situation) is discussed in a subsequent section and it is seen that, although this approach creates a valuable research paradigm for attachment, it also is limited from a clinical developmental perspective. An integrated developmental approach follows which attempts to combine the assets of these approaches.

Two sets of criteria are already established: (I) DSM III, attachment disorders; and (II) DSM III, autism (i.e., the items relevant to infants less than 1 year of age).

I. Reactive Attachment Disorder (DSM III)
   A. Onset before 8 months.
   B. Lack of signs of social responsiveness as indicated by several of the following:
      1. visual tracking of eyes and faces;
      2. smiling in response to faces;
      3. visual reciprocity;
      4. vocal reciprocity (infant of more than 5 months of age);
      5. alerting and turning toward caregiver's voice by infant of more than 4 months;
      6. spontaneous reaching for the mother by an infant of more than 4 months;
      7. anticipating reaching when approached to be picked up by an infant of more than 5 months;
      8. participation in playful games with caregiver by an infant of more than 5 months.

C. Evidence of three or more of the following:
   1. weak cry;
   2. excessive sleep;
   3. lack of interest in the environment;
   4. hypomobility;
   5. poor muscle tone;
   6. weak rooting and grasping in response to feeding attempts.
D. Weight loss or failure to gain weight, unexplained by a physical disorder.

II. Autism (DSM III)—Items relevant to infants under 12 months of age.
   A. Pervasive lack of responsiveness to other people.
   B. Gross deficits in language development (preverbal vocalizations normally expected in last half of the first year).
   C. Bizarre responses.

As can be seen, both categories in DSM-III focus on striking clinical features of a lack of attachment, manifested by a lack of expected social and emotional behaviors ordinarily seen in relationship to the development of human relationships.

Although limited, from a developmental point of view, the clinical approach to attachment was derived from attempts to categorize clinical phenomena. Another approach to attachment has been the laboratory study of aspects of attachment, illustrated for the most part by the Strange Situation paradigm. Although limited to a certain age range (12 months old) and to certain infant and parent behavior, this procedure has facilitated a detailed focus on aspects of the attachment process and contributes a valuable research paradigm, creating a part of the necessary empirical foundation for a truly clinical-developmental approach to attachment that is considered in the final section.

LABORATORY ASSESSMENT OF ATTACHMENT: THE STRANGE SITUATION

In the context of the foregoing discussion of clinical approaches to the assessment of attachment disorders, it is pertinent to focus also on the Strange Situation (Ainsworth, Blehar, Waters, & Wall, 1978; Ainsworth & Wittig, 1969), currently the most widely utilized research method for evaluating the quality of the infant's attachment to the caregiver. This section offers a brief review of the conceptual underpinnings of the Strange Situation and of the research findings it has generated. We then discuss the issues raised by the possible application of the Strange Situation to clinical settings as an extension of its current use as a research instrument.

The Strange Situation was originally designed by Ainsworth and her colleagues as a standardized procedure to investigate the normative patterns in mother–infant interaction. The early findings made clear that the instrument was also useful in the investigation of the individual differences among mother–infant dyads that had been detected in the course of extensive home observations during the first year of life (Ainsworth, Bell & Stayton, 1971; Ainsworth, Bleher, Waters, & Wall, 1978; Ainsworth & Wittig, 1969). The design of the Strange Situation is based on the conceptualization of attachment as a behavioral control system, with the set goal of gaining or maintaining proximity to the attachment figure (Bowlby, 1969). Ainsworth (1973) elaborated on this view by highlighting the secure base phenomenon, whereby the infant uses the attachment figure as an anchor for exploration and as a haven to which she/he returns for comfort and for security when frightened or distressed. This balance between exploration and attachment is influenced by contextual and psychological factors. Children tend to explore when they feel secure and perceive the surroundings as safe; conversely, they tend to seek proximity to the mother when they feel a need for protection and reassurance. Ainsworth (1973; Ainsworth et al., 1971) has suggested that secure base behavior in a variety of settings and across time is the most reliable indicator of attachment in infancy. She also believes that securely and anxiously attached infants differ in their ability to use the mother as a secure base from which to explore.

As a laboratory procedure, the Strange Situation incorporates these premises, because it is designed to first encourage exploration and to later elicit attachment behaviors by introducing cumulative sources of stress. These sources of stress are: first, the unfamiliarity of the laboratory playroom, followed by the entrance of an unfamiliar female (the stranger) and then by two 3-minute separations from the mother, each followed by a reunion with her. Infants' responses to the reunion with the mother following these increasingly stressful events tend to reflect individual differences in the organization of the attachment system. Briefly, infants considered to be securely attached tend to greet the mother upon reunion and to seek proximity and contact with her (Group B). Infants deemed anxiously attached show two main patterns of reunion behavior. One group of infants tends to avoid proximity, contact, and distal interaction with the mother upon reunion (Group A, anxiously attached, avoidant). The second group tends to show a mixture of reunion behaviors: they may seek proximity and/or contact, only to resist it when actually achieved, showing a mixture of anger and difficulty in being comforted (Group C, anxiously attached, resistant). Each of these three groups (A, B, C) comprises smaller but conceptually intriguing subgroups characterized by specific particularities within the broader similarities in their behavior. More recently, Main and Solomon (1987) have described a newly identified group of anxiously attached infants characterized by disorganized behavior and odd mannerisms upon reunion (Group D— disorganized).

The taxonomic classification of infants into major groups on the basis of Strange Situation reunion behavior has given major impetus to research on individual differences in quality of attachment. The usefulness of the Strange Situation as a research instrument is supported by findings in four major areas: the correspondence between Strange Situation and antecedent home behavior, the temporal stability of classification and the conceptual intelligibility of departures from such stability, the correspondences between Strange Situation classifications and infant behavior in concurrent areas of functioning, and the correspondence between Strange Situation classification and later competence in a variety of measures of adaptation in toddlers and in early childhood.

Infant behavior in the Strange Situation shows conceptually coherent links with mother–infant interaction and with infant behavior as observed in frequent home visits during the first year both in a Baltimore, Maryland, and in a Bielefeld, North Germany, sample (Ainsworth, Bell, & Stayton, 1971; Ainsworth et al., 1978; Grossmann, Grossmann, Spangler, Suess, & Unzner, 1985). Further evidence of the validity of the Strange Situation procedure is the temporal stability of the classifications (Waters, 1979), coupled with findings that infant classification does change when family circumstances improve or deteriorate in ways that tend to affect the quality of the attachment (Thompson, Lamb, & Estes, 1982; Vaughn, Egeland, Sroufe, & Waters, 1979). These data suggest that infant behavior in the Strange Situation tends to reflect the dynamic quality of the mother–infant interaction.

Quality of attachment as assessed by the Strange Situation is also associated with competence in concurrent areas of infant functioning. Securely attached infants tend to be more competent in play than anxiously attached infants (Belsky, Gardugue, & Hrncir, 1982). Quality of attachment is also related to peer competence both among infants and among representation of the self in relation to attachment. They found that securely attached infants showed greater security of attachment at 6 years of age, regardless of the modality in which this security was expressed.

The preceding findings, which were derived from stable, middle-class samples unless otherwise specified, are consonant with findings from a high-risk sample of 267 infants and their mothers, the Minnesota Mother–Child Interaction Project. In this sample, secure attachment in infancy was found to predict later competent functioning. Securely attached infants were, as toddlers, more sociable with their peers (Pastor, 1981) and more compliant with their mothers (Erickson & Crichton, 1981) than anxiously attached infants. As preschoolers, they were more compliant with their nursery teacher (Erickson, Farber, & Egeland, 1982), were less dependent on her (Sroufe, Fox, & Pancake, 1983), and showed fewer behavioral problems in preschool (Erickson, Sroufe, & Egeland, 1985). Using a selected subsample of 40 children, Sroufe (1983) reported that preschoolers who had been classified as securely attached during infancy score higher than anxiously attached peers in a variety of mental health and socio-affective measures, including self-esteem, expression of affect, and impulses, social competence, classroom deportment, and empathy.

The value of the Strange Situation in documenting the continuity of patterns of adaptation and maladaptation in nonclinical samples has led to its application to the study of special groups of infants as well. Some of these studies have used modified versions of the Strange Situation. The overwhelming direction of the evidence is that groups of infants in at-risk categories for mother–child interaction tend to show higher proportions of preschoolers (Easterbrooks & Lamb, 1979; Lieberman, 1977). In addition, securely attached infants tend to be more compliant (Stayton, Hogan, & Ainsworth, 1971) and to have more internalized controls than insecurely attached infants (Londerville & Main, 1981).

Finally, the Strange Situation classification has been useful in predicting later infant competence in a series of studies linking the quality of the infant attachment at 12 months and social and emotional functioning as a toddler and in the preschool years. Matas, Arend, and Sroufe (1978) showed that securely attached 12-month-olds became toddlers who, at 24 months, were less easily frustrated, more persistent, more cooperative, and more enthusiastic in efforts to master a task than toddlers who had been anxiously attached. These findings were replicated with a poverty sample (Sroufe, 1979). Waters et al. (1979) found that securely attached infants became highly competent preschoolers, both with peers and in exploration of their surroundings. Arend, Grove, and Sroufe (1979) found that securely attached children had more ego resilience at 54 to 70 months than anxiously attached children when assessed by their nursery school or kindergarten teacher as well as in a laboratory situation. In a study focusing on the links between early quality of attachment and psychopathology at 6 years of age, Lewis, Feiring, McGaffog, and Jaskir (1984) found that anxious attachment at 12 months was significantly related to later psychopathology (as defined by behavioral problems) for males, although no such relationship was observed for females. Main, Kaplan, and Cassidy (1985) have provided striking evidence of the continuity of anxious attachment (using control groups). This is the case for failure-to-thrive infants (Gordon & Jameson, 1979), infants of mentally ill mothers (Gaensbauer, Harmon, Cytryn, & McKnew, 1984; Naslund, Persson-Blennow, McNeil, Kaiij, & Malmquist-Larsson, 1984; Radke-Yarrow,

Cummings, Kuczyniski, & Chapman, 1985; Sameroff, Seifer, & Zax, 1982; Zahn-Waxler, Chapman, & Cummings, 1984), and maltreated, abused, and neglected infants (e.g., Crittendon, 1981, 1985a, 1985b; Egeland & Sroufe, 1984a, 1981b; Gaensbauer & Harmon, 1982).

Although it may be possible to find fault with one or another methodological shortcomings of individual studies (e.g., Lamb, Thompson, Gardner, Charnov, & Estes, 1984), the general picture of adaptation and maladaptation in infancy and early childhood acquired through the research use of the Strange Situation is impressively consistent. It is also consonant with clinical studies of disturbed infant–mother dyads (Fraiberg, Adelson, & Shapiro, 1975; Greenspan, 1981; Greenspan & Lieberman, 1980; Lieberman, 1985; Lieberman & Pawl, in press).

This superb performance as a research instrument has raised the possibility of extending the application of the Strange Situation or modified versions of it to the clinical assessment of individual infants and toddlers (e.g., Gaensbauer & Harmon, 1981). This raises a variety of issues regarding the clinical use, with individual children, of a research instrument designed for group assessments. The attractiveness of the Strange Situation as an assessment instrument is certainly compelling. It presents the infant and mother, in the course of approximately 20 minutes, with a cross-section of the stressful situations and stresses that they may encounter in an ordinary week. In addition, the scoring system is based on actual observation, a clear advantage for assessment instruments in infancy (Gaensbauer & Harmon, 1981). In addition, the usefulness of the instrument is supported by a massive body of research findings, as described earlier.

Are these virtues sufficient to warrant the use of the Strange Situation as a clinical assessment instrument for individual children? If it were to be used as a single instrument, our answer is a definite "no". The reasons are outlined below.

1. The Strange Situation shows clear differences in quality of attachment between groups of children considered to be at risk on the basis of external criteria (e.g., failure to thrive; maltreatment, abuse, and/or neglect; maternal mental illness) and control groups. Such a finding does not imply reliable differences at the individual level. Although the risk groups tend to have higher proportions of anxiously attached infants than the control groups, there is a wide array of individual differences within each group. In other words, a substantial number of children in the risk groups are classified as securely attached, and, conversely, a substantial number of children in the control groups are classified as anxiously attached. There may be a variety of reasons for this: (a) errors in classification; (b) undetected situational factors, such as child illness, which temporarily affects the child's behavior; or (c) the fact that different chil-

dren manifest malfunction in different forms and under different conditions, and many children may not display their anxiety (or their felt security) in the patterns already recognized in the Strange Situation classification. Clearly, the research use of the Strange Situation is not seriously hampered by the different sources of error, since the group findings tend to be statistically significant and reliable. However, such errors, at the level of individual assessments, may well make the difference between recognizing or not recognizing the gravity of a child's situation, and offering or not offering needed intervention. Alternatively, such errors may lead to the false categorization of a securely attached infant as anxious, with the attendant risks of mistakenly labeling the child and unnecessarily alarming the parents about their child's mental health status and about their own child-rearing practices and functioning as parents. Such possibilities are clearly delineated by Gaensbauer and Harmon (1982), who have presented highly informative description of infants whose behavior in a modified version of the Strange Situation was inconsistent with other clinical information and would have led to mistaken conclusions had it been used as the sole intention for evaluation.

2. The Strange Situation was originally designed for use with a middle-class, non-clinical population. Accordingly, the patterns of attachment behavior derived from this sample may not encompass the full variety of attachment patterns that may be found in other populations that may differ in socioeconomic status, child-rearing mores and values, mental health status of the parents, risk factors in the child, and a myriad of other variables. The questions of national, cultural, and/or ethnic differences is a specific aspect of this larger question, and one that is beyond the scope of this paper. We will only point out that, although it is true that the A, B, and C classifications have been found to be applicable in other countries, it is also true that different national samples yield a different incidence of such groupings, a finding that needs further research for a fuller understanding of its significance. It is likely that the greater the departure of the sample under study from the US white middle-class norm, the more difficult the interpretation of the classification findings will be, and the greater the likelihood of the existence of hitherto unrecognized alternative patterns of attachment behavior. The recent identification by Main and Solomon (1987) of a new anxiously attached group (Group D, disorganized) supports the view that alternative manifestations of anxious and secure attachment are likely to exist.

3. Quality of attachment is not isomorphic with socioemotional functioning. These areas do overlap, and the mother–child relationship plays a crucial role in shaping the infant's affectivity. However, attachment is one component of the child's overall functioning, and the part should not be mistaken for the whole in assessing an individual infant. The Strange

Situation is designed to evaluate the child's quality of attachment in terms of the use of the mother as a secure base. It does not incorporate systematic appraisals of other equally important aspects of the child's functioning, such as constitutional make-up, range of affect, predominant affective tone, adaptive modes, tolerance of frustration and anxiety, resistance under stress, "goodness of fit" between infant and mother regarding basic patterns such as activity/passivity or introversion/extroversion, and infant developmental history. These and other factors are important components of the psychiatric evaluation of infants, and need to be incorporated into a comprehensive assessment (Cytryn, 1968; Greenspan, 1981; Greenspan et al., 1987). In this sense, it is extremely unlikely that any one instrument can perform all these functions. Different instruments are needed to succeed at systematizing the thorough clinical and developmental observation that is the basic ingredient of a good infant assessment.

4. The Strange Situation classification system calls for extensive experience assessing infants displaying a wide range of individual differences. Children with the same attachment classification may be very different from each other in sociability, activity level, predominant mood, favored modes of play, and other characteristics that may mislead an inexperienced rater. Consequently, raters need to be rigorously trained to classify infants correctly (Mary Ainsworth, personal communication, December, 1985). It is inaccurate to think of the Strange Situation as an easy "shortcut" that circumvents the need for skilled and well-trained assessors. The procedure is quick and relatively easy to administer, but ascertaining the meaning of the data it yields is a demanding and time-consuming process (Ainsworth, 1980).

5. The Strange Situation classification is relevant for the assessment of quality of attachment in a narrow age range–perhaps as narrow as from 10 to 18 months (Ainsworth, 1980). Hence, the procedure may not be used without further research on the needed modifications for the assessment of attachment throughout the period conventionally considered as infancy—the first 3 years of life.

6. The Strange Situation does not readily lend itself as a clinical instrument because it precludes the dialogue with the parents that is essential in obtaining an accurate picture of the baby's functioning. This dialogue, which Fraiberg (1980) called "the invitation to the parents" hinges on the parents' sense of permission from the children to talk candidly about their perceptions of their infant and about their own positive and negative experience as parents. Since the treatment of infants necessitates parental cooperation, this dialogue is important because it encourages the parents' emotional investment in the therapeutic process and the formation of a working alliance on behalf of the infant. In our experience, this working

alliance with the parents is an integral part of the assessment, and needs to be carefully nurtured by the clinician through an explicit statement of interest in the parents' affective experience with regard to their child. In a procedure such as the Strange Situation, the parents' own perceptions and emotions are not elicited and the parents' behavior is carefully dictated by the needs for standardization. Hence, its use should be considered only after the working alliance with the parents has been well established.

In summary, the Strange Situation has proved to be a very useful instrument for the assessment of the quality of attachment in the context of developmental research. Its application as a clinical instrument cannot, however, be advocated without strong caveats. In Ainsworth's (1980) own words "perhaps its more appropriate use would be as a 'marker' instrument" (p. 45). Such a use would involve using the behaviors identified in the Strange Situation to guide observations of infant behavior and mother–infant interaction in a variety of settings. This information would then be integrated with other knowledge about the infant and his/her socio-affective milieu in order to arrive at a comprehensive clinical account of the infant's functioning that may then guide the planning of treatment.

TOWARD A DEVELOPMENTAL APPROACH TO CONCEPTUALIZING ATTACHMENT PATTERNS

Where does this leave us? Experimental approaches illustrated by the Strange Situation suggest that focusing on aspects of the attachment process at a certain age yields important information that has both predictive and clinical significance, but not a level of specificity necessary for clinical diagnosis. In contrast, DSM-III type criteria derived from clinical work, although useful, is overly general, ignores important features of the infants' constitutional maturational contributions, the caregiver and family interaction patterns, and, most importantly, the changing forms of attachments as a child proceeds up the developmental ladder.

The goal of the following section is to discuss a model within which attachment can be viewed as beginning early in life and undergoing its own progression and differentiation as development proceeds (in comparison to defining attachment only in relationship to stranger anxiety or separation protest). This developmental view has strong empirical support, as described earlier.

This approach to classification is based on the developmental structuralist approach to infant emotional development (Greenspan, 1981). A brief description of the developmental structuralist approach is followed by operational criteria for classifying patterns of attachment at each level of development. This discussion deliberately focuses on the infant side of the infant-caregiver-family equation (see Greenspan, 1981, for a discussion of the stage–specific caregiver patterns and infant caregiver interaction).

Attachment is seen to be a changing process reflective of adaptive or maladaptive trends at each developmental phase in the context of phase-expected tasks and challenges. For example, during the early months of life, the main infant–caregiver task is to form a pleasurable, interesting, comforting relationship. Here, apathy would obviously be a worrisome sign. By 9 to 18 months, the infant learns to interact intentionally with his/ her "loved one" and now organizes more complex behavioral and emotional patterns, including learning to integrate exploration and emotional closeness dependence (e.g., the separation paradigm). At this time, pseudo-independence, anger, avoidance, or clinging dependency may constitute worrisome signs.

By 24 to 36 months, the child already creates internal imagery, reflecting a symbolic concept of a human attachment relationship. The dolls hug, fight, make up, leave each other, return, and so forth. Now, an affective attachment is elevated to the world of internal affects and "ideas." Here, the child who remains concrete, unable to use imagery to "think about" or communicate affects around attachment, may be worrisome (e.g., the 36-month-old who is not able to say "don't go" or play out separation scenes or anger with his/her dolls or toy soldiers, but instead becomes impulsive or despondent).

Although this framework relates to overall adaptation, it is our view that the vicissitudes of attachment are inseparable from overall adaptation in infancy and is best studied as part of the overall progression of the capacity to form, differentiate, abstract and symbolize affective human relationships, (see Greenspan, 1979, 1981; Greenspan et al., 1987, for detailed discussions of theory and clinical cases).

The Clinical-Developmental Classification

Our approach to classification involves elucidating organizational levels and organizational defects. A defect occurs when an age-expected developmental level is not attained, such as when an infant does not enter into reciprocal interaction patterns by 6 to 8 months. It also involves determining optimal experiential ranges and constrictions for each organizational level. A constriction occurs when the full range of age-expected affective-thematic inclinations are not present, even though an expected state has been reached. The type of affective-thematic inclinations one would look for were chosen on the basis of the age-expected "emotional dramas" one would expect to be present at each age and the absence of which would have clinical significance. There was an attempt to avoid double referencing (e.g., assertiveness and tendency toward avoidance). Either assertiveness was present or absent, and, if absent, one would assume that something else such as avoidance or withdrawal was substituted. Similarly, certain affects related to specific phases (e.g., wariness or stranger anxiety) were not included because we found clinically that infants who did not progress to this level of differentiation reflected their limitations in other, more generally observable ways (e.g., a general lack of pleasure or comfort with dependency).

The general descriptive categories of affective-thematic inclinations we found clinically useful include: (a) interest and attentiveness; (b) relaxation and/or calmness; (c) dependency (including holding or comforting-type behaviors, etc.); (d) pleasure or joy (including enthusiasm); (e) assertiveness (explorativeness and curiosity; (f) protest or other distinct forms of unpleasure, including anger; (g) negativism or stubbornness; (h) self-limit setting (often not seen until children are in the middle of the second year of life); and (i) after the age of three, empathy and more stable feelings of love.

It is interesting to note that, although in the first month or two it is difficult to observe all of these affective-thematic areas, by 4 months of age it is possible to clinically observe each of these affective-thematic areas in a series of free exchanges between mother and baby. A healthy 4-month-old, for example, often has no difficulty showing focused attentiveness (particularly to mother's face and voice); using this focused attentiveness to be relaxed or calm; contributing to dependency by holding and finding comfortable positions (the infant holds mother's neck and even begins directing her toward the type of rhythmic movements or sensory experiences that are most comforting); evidencing pleasure and joy (by smiling in synchrony with mother's smile or vocalizations); showing assertiveness and curiosity by somewhat chaotically, but purposely, moving arms to grasp an object; evidencing anger, frustration, or protest with a distinct cry, angry look, and a flailing of arms and legs when a desired object is taken away; and evidencing negativism and even belligerency by refusing to open mouth or by spitting up what the infant does not like. These affective-thematic dimensions, which are differentiated during the first and second year, have been partitioned by investigators into subcategories and subtle gradations (e.g., Ainsworth et al., 1974; Charlesworth, 1969; Sroufe, 1979). Interestingly, adaptive toddlers appear to have all the "moves"; that is, they have the subtle affective expressions, including bewilderment, surprise, anticipation, and even a little smirk as they deliberately behave provocatively or negatively. The disturbed toddler's emotions, in comparison, are somewhat global and dampened.

Each affective-thematic area may have many distinct contents. For example, one 2½-year-old will evidence assertiveness or anger by shooting guns, another by "beating up" his father, and another by winning a car race. Similarly, pleasure may be reflected in the excitement of feeding and undressing the dolls or in the joy of building a huge tower. The contributions of psychoanalytic observers and psychosexual theory toward understanding the phase-specific organizing fantasies or "dramas" are of inestimable importance in the study of what contributes to distinctly human experience.

Stages of Development

In the developmental structuralist classification, the first stage is the *achievement of homeostasis,* i.e., self-regulation and emerging interest through the senses in the world: sights, sounds, smells, touch, etc. Once the infant has achieved some capacity for regulation in the context of engaging the world and as central nervous system (CNS) maturation increases between 2 and 4 months of age, the infant becomes more attuned to social and interpersonal interaction. She/he is more able to respond to the external environment and to form a special relationship with significant primary caregivers.

Thus, a second, closely related stage is that of *forming a human attachment.* If an affective and relatively pleasurable attachment (an investment in the human, animate world) is formed, then, with growing maturational abilities, the infant develops complex patterns of communication in the context of this primary human relationship. Parallel with development of the infant's relationship to the inanimate world where basic schemes of causality (means/ends relationships; Piaget, 1972) are being developed, the infant becomes capable of complicated human communications (Brazelton et al., 1974; Charlesworth, 1969; Stern, 1974a).

When there have been distortions in the attachment process (e.g., if a mother responds in a mechanical, remote manner, and/or projects some of her own dependent feelings onto her infant), the infant may not learn to appreciate causal relationships between people at the level of compassionate and intimate feelings. This can occur even though causality seems to be developing in terms of the inanimate world and the impersonal human world. We have observed infants who are differentiated in the assertive impersonal domain of human relationships, but who are relatively undifferentiated in the intimate, pleasurable domain.

Causal relationships are established between the infant and the primary caregiver, as evidence in the infant's growing ability to discriminate significant primary caregivers from others. She/he also becomes able to differentiate her/his own actions from their consequences affectively, somatically, behaviorally, and interpersonally. Usually by 8 months of age or earlier, the process of differentiation begins along a number of developmental lines: sensorimotor integration, affects, relationships. A third stage, therefore, may be formally termed *somatopsychologic differentiation,* to indicate processes occurring at the somatic (e.g., sensorimotor) and emerging psychological levels. In this context, psychologic refers to higher level mental processes characterized by the capacity to form internal representations or symbols as a way to organize experience. Although schemes of causality are being established in the infant's relationship to the interpersonal world, it is not at all clear whether these schemes exist at an organized representational or symbolic level. Rather, they appear to exist mainly at a somatic level (Greenspan, 1979), even though we do observe the precursors of representational capacities. Some are perhaps even prenatally determined (Lourie, 1971).

With appropriate reading of cues and systematic differential responses, the infant's or toddler's behavioral repertoire becomes complicated and communications take on more organized, meaningful configurations. By 12 months of age, the infant is connecting behavioral units into larger organizations as he/she exhibits complex emotional responses such as affiliation, wariness, and fear (Ainsworth, Bell, & Stayton, 1974; Bowlby, 1969; Sroufe & Waters, 1977). As the toddler moves further into the second year of life, in the context of the practicing subphase of the development of individuation (Mahler et al., 1975), there is an increased capacity for forming original behavioral schemes (Piaget, 1972) and for imitative activity and intentionality.

A type of learning through imitation evidenced in earlier development now seems to assume a more dominant role. As imitations take on a more integrated personal form, it appears that the toddler is adopting or internalizing attributes of his caregivers. To describe these new capacities, it is useful to consider a fourth stage, that of *behavioral organization, initiative, and internalization.*

As the toddler moves into the end of the second year, with further CNS maturation, we notice an increased capacity to form and organize mental representations. Internal sensations and unstable images become organized in a mental representational form, which can be evoked and is somewhat stable (Bell, 1970; Gouin-Decarie, 1965; Piaget, 1972). Although this capacity is initially fragile, between 16 and 24 months it soon appears to become a dominant mode in organizing the child's behavior, and a fifth stage can be documented, that of *forming mental representations or ideas,* such as object permanence.

The capacity for object permanence is relative and goes through a series of stages (Gouin-Decarie, 1965). It refers to the toddler's ability to search for hidden inanimate objects. Representational capacity refers to the ability to organize and evoke internal organized multisensory experiences of the animate object. The capacities to represent animate and inanimate experiences are related and depend both on CNS myelination and appropriate experiences. The process of "internalization" may be thought of as an intermediary process. Internalized experiences eventually become sufficiently organized to be considered representations.

At a representational level, the child again develops her/his capacities for elaboration, integration, and differentiation. Just as causal schemes previously were developed at a somatic and behavioral level, now they are developed at a representational level. The child begins to elaborate and eventually differentiate those feelings, thoughts, and events that emanate from herself/himself and those that emanate from other. She/he begins to differentiate what she/he experiences and does, from the impact of her/his actions on the world. This gradually forms the basis for the differentiation of "self" representations from those that embody the external world, animate and inanimate, and also provides the basis for such crucial personality functions as knowing what is real from unreal, impulse and mood regulation, and the capacity to focus attention and concentrate in order to learn and interact.

The capacity for differentiating internal representations becomes consolidated as object constancy (Mahler et al., 1975). In middle childhood, representational capacity becomes reinforced, with the child's ability to develop derivative representational systems tied to the original representation and to transform them in accord with adaptive and defensive goals. This permits greater flexibility in dealing with perceptions, feelings, thoughts, and emerging ideals. Substages for these capacities include representational differentiation, the consolidation of representational capacity, and the capacity for structural learning—the formation of omitted derivative and multiple derivative representational systems (Greenspan, 1979).

At each of these stages, in varying degrees, pathologic as well as adaptive formations are possible. These may be considered as relative compromises in the range, depth, stability, and/or personal uniqueness of the experiential organization consolidated at each stage. The infant can form adaptive patterns of regulation in the earliest stages of development. His/her internal states are harmoniously regulated and he/she is free to invest himself/herself in the inanimate world, thereby setting the basis for rich emotional attachments to primary caregivers. On the other hand, if his/her regulatory processes are not functioning properly and he/she cannot maintain internal harmony in the context of being available to the world, the infant may withdraw. From relatively minor compromises such as a tendency to withdraw and/or be hyperexcitable under stress, to a major deviation such as an overwhelming avoidance of the animate world, we can observe the degrees to which the infant, even in the first months of life, achieves a less-than-optimal adaptive structural organization.

Thus, the early attachments can be warm and engaging, or shallow, insecure, and limited in their affective tone. In the early reciprocal relationships, we can observe differences between an infant who reads the signals of the caregivers and responds in a rich, meaningful way with multiple affects and behavioral communications to multiple aspects of the communications, and one who can respond only within a narrow range of affect (e.g., protest) or who cannot respond at all in a contingent or reciprocal manner (e.g., the seemingly apathetic, withdrawn, and depressed child who responds only to his/her internal cues). As the toddler, optimally, becomes behaviorally more organized and complex and patterns appear that reflect originality and initiative in the context of the separation and individuation subphase of development, we can observe those toddlers who manifest this full adaptive capacity. They may be compared with others who are stereotyped in their behavioral patterns (reflect no originality or intentionality), who remain fragmented (never connect pieces of behavior into more complicated patterns), or who evidence polarities of affect, showing no capacity to integrate emotions, as when the chronic negativistic aggressive toddler cannot show interest, curiosity, or love.

As a capacity for representational organization is reached, we can distinguish the child who can organize, integrate, and differentiate a rich range of affective and ideational life from one who remains either without representational capacity or undifferentiated. Such a child may have deficits with reality testing, impulse control, and focused concentration. That child may form and differentiate self and object representations only at the expense of extreme compromises in the range of tolerated experience, as when a schizoid child withdraws from relationships. Similar adaptive or maladaptive structural organizations can be observed in later childhood (the triangular phase), latency, and adolescence.

Through videotaped analyses of infant–caregiver interactions (Greenspan & Lieberman, 1980; Hofheimer, Poisson, Strauss, Eyler, & Greenspan, 1983), these patterns can be reliably rated and new raters trained and kept at high levels of reliability. These patterns also evidence short-term temporal stability (Hofheimer, Greenspan, Lieberman, & Poisson, in preparation).

This brief discussion provides the necessary overview of a classification system for disturbances in infancy and early childhood leading to the operational definitions that follow. In this system, attachment problems can occur as part of each organizational level, in the context of either a defect in the achievement of the organizational level or a constriction in the affective-thematic range at that level. As with all systems of classification, this approach should be viewed as a set of hypotheses derived from clinical observations and abstractions of what appear to be relevant clinical patterns. These descriptions are open to further revisions and need to be applied in larger population studies.

OPERATIONAL CRITERIA

I. Homeostasis (concrete attachments, interest in the world and self-regulation, 0 to 3 months)
   A. *Competent Functioning.* Infant is relaxed and sleeps at regular times; recovers from crying with comforting; is able to be very alert; looks at one when talked to; brightens up progressively more when provided with appropriate visual, auditory, and/or tactile stimulation as he/she goes from 0 to 3 months.
   B. *Disordered Functioning.*
      1. Severe:
         a. *Type A*—Disinterested in attachments; sleeps almost all the time; shows no interest in anyone; does not respond to interesting stimuli (e.g., lights, colors, sounds, touch, or movements).
         b. *Type B*—Overly exited and unfocused on attachments; always upset or crying; stiff and rigid; becomes completely distracted by any sights, noises, touch, movement; gets too excited and cries.
         c. *Type C*—Shows a mixture of Type A and Type B.
      2. Moderate:
         a. *Type A*—Seems apathetic and disinterested in everything; responds a little to touch or movement, but not very interested in seeing or hearing objects nearby.
         b. *Type B*—Upset and crying most of the time; is too alert; looks at too many things; gets somewhat distracted by things she/he can see, hear, or feel.
         c. *Type C*—Shows a mixture of Type A and Type B.
      3. Mild: Functioning between competent and moderate range.
II. Attachment (personal [emotional, joyful, syncronous] attachment, 0 to 7 months)
   A. *Competent Functioning.* Infant is very interested in people, especially mother or father, and other caregivers; responds to their glances, smiles, voices, and touches with signs of pleasure and interest such as smiling, relaxing, or cooing; also seems to respond with deep feelings and with multiple sensory modalities (e.g., with vision, hearing, tactile senses, movement, olfactory senses, and so on).
   B. *Disordered Functioning.*

1. Severe:
    a. *Type A*—Disinterested in people, especially mother, father, and/or other primary caregivers (e.g., always looks away rather than at people); looks withdrawn (as though eyes are turned inward); and becomes rigid and more withdrawn with physical contact (i.e., holding).
    b. *Type B*—Insists on being held all the time; will not sleep without being held.
    c. *Type C*—Shows a mixture of Type A and Type B.
2. Moderate:
    a. *Type A*—Only occasionally looks at people, or fleetingly responds to their voices with interest (e.g., a smile, an extended hand, or kicking).
    b. *Type B*—Seems almost too interested in people; clings to mother, father, or other primary caregiver; cries easily if not held; goes to strangers and holds on as if they were parents; not very interested in playing alone (e.g., exploring new toy).
    c. *Type C*—Shows a mixture of Type A and Type B.
3. Mild: Functioning between competent and moderate range.

III. Somatopsychological Differentiation (intentional attachments; purposeful communication, 3 to 10 Months)
   A. *Competent Functioning.* Infant is able to interact in a purposeful (i.e., intentional, reciprocal, cause-and-effect-type) manner, such as smiling in response to a voice; initiates signals and responds purposefully using multiple sensory modalities, the motor system, and a range of emotions (e.g., pleasure, protest, assertion, and so on), while at the same time gets involved with toys and other inanimate objects.
   B. *Disordered Functioning.*
      1. Severe:
          a. *Type A*—May interact, but not purposefully; seems oblivious to caregivers' signals; does not respond to their smiles, voices, reaching out; "marches to the beat of a different drummer."
          b. *Type B*—Demands constant interaction, cannot tolerate being alone at all; has temper tantrums or withdraws if caregiver does not respond to her/his signals or initiate interactive signals all the time.
          c. *Type C*—Shows a mixture of Type A and Type B.
      2. Moderate:
          a. *Type A*—Responds intermittently and unpredictably to caregiver signals, such as smile or sounds; purposeful social

responses limited only to one type of signal, such as caregiver voice, but not smile.

b. *Type B*—Able to interact, but seems overly sensitive to any emotional communication of caregiver; looks sad and forlorn at slightest sign that caregiver is preoccupied; gets very easily frustrated if signal (e.g., smile and hand reaching out) is not responded to; disorganized.

c. *Type C*—Shows a mixture of Type A and Type B.

3. Mild: Functioning between the competent and moderate range.

IV. Behavioral Organization, initiative and internalization (conceptual, integrated attachments, 9 to 18 Months)

A. *Competent Functioning.* Infant manifests a wide range of socially meaningful behaviors and feelings including warmth, pleasure, assertion, exploration, protest, anger, etc., in an organized manner. Is able to go from interacting to separation and reunion with organized affects including pleasure, apprehension, and protest. Initiates complex, organized, emotionally and socially relevant interactions, yet also accepts limits. Continually surprising parents in a "delightful way" with new behaviors, capacities, social skills, complex emotions. Can explore new objects, and after a "warm-up," new people, especially when parents are available.

B. *Disordered Functioning.*

1. Severe:

a. *Type A*—Passive attachments; rarely initiates behaviors and/or emotions; mostly passive and withdrawn, or seemingly uninvolved or excessively negativistic.

b. *Type B*—Chaotic attachment; behavior and affect completely random, chaotic; almost always appears "out of control" with aggressive affects predominating; highly disorganized behaviors.

c. *Type C*—Shows a mixture of Type A and Type B.

2. Moderate:

a. *Type A*—Can manifest a few socially meaningful behaviors in narrow range (e.g., can only protest, or only compliantly "go along"); involved only with social interaction around inanimate world (explores new objects); no capacity for integrating pleasure, warmth, assertiveness and anger in social context; occasionally takes initiative, but usually only responds to others' initiative and may also be negativistic; little or no originality (i.e., no surprises or new emotions or behaviors) and, instead, tends to be repetitive.

b. *Type B*—Lots of behaviors and feelings manifested, but in poorly organized, unmodulated manner; shifts behaviors and moods rapidly; only occasionally involved in socially meaningful interactions; takes initiative, but is demanding and stubborn; tends to repeat rather than develop new behaviors or interactions.

c. *Type C*—Shows a mixture of Type A and Type B.

3. Mild: Functioning between competent and moderate range.

V. Representational Capacity (internalized, ideational [symbolic] attachments, 18 to 36 Months)

A. *Competent Functioning.* Representational elaboration of attachments and relationships. For example, either uses words or word-like sounds to indicate wishes and intentions toward key others; can use dolls or other objects to play out drama (e.g., separation scene, hugging scene, feeding scene, or shooting scene, etc.). Symbolic elaboration appears to cover a range of emotions that characterize human attachments and relationships, including love, closeness, dependency, assertion, curiosity, anger, and protest.

B. *Disordered Functioning.*

1. Severe:

a. *Type A*—No symbolic behavior such as words or symbolic play applied to human attachments and relationships (e.g., no dolls hugging or separating, etc.); no complex actions that imply planning and anticipation, and so on; behavior fragmented or stereotyped.

b. *Type B*—Symbolic activity, but totally disorganized, fragmented, and used in the service of discharge-type hyperactivity; words or play activities never develop into an organized drama.

c. *Type C*—Shows a mixture of Type A and Type B.

2. Moderate:

a. *Type A*—Some symbolic behavior such as words or doll play, limited to descriptive use of symbolic mode (e.g., naming objects or pictures); little or no capacity for socioemotional interactive use of thoughts and ideas (e.g., no "I like you" or "Don't go," etc.).

b. *Type B*—Symbols used (e.g., words or play), but often in chaotic, disorganized fashion; dramas have only fragments of discernible meaning.

c. *Type C*—Shows a mixture of Type A and Type B.

3. Mild: Functioning between competent and moderate range.
VI. Representational Differentiation (internalized [symbolic] differentiated attachments [i.e., self-other differentiation], 30 to 48 Months)
    A. *Competent Functioning.* Uses the representational mode to separate self from nonself and relate to people and things across a range of emotions in a balanced manner (e.g., warmth, assertiveness); is able to be purposeful; knows what is real from unreal; accepts limits; is self-limiting and also feels good about self; switches from fantasy to reality with little difficult.
    B. *Disordered Functioning.*
       1. Severe:
          a. *Type A*—Withdrawn; unrelated to people; uses words or symbolic play only with things; if words or symbolic play with people are used, differentiation of real from unreal is unclear; no sense of purpose or intention in social use of symbolic mode.
          b. *Type B*—Symbolically relates to people and things in a totally chaotic, unrealistic manner; no reality testing or impulse control; self-esteem and mood are labile.
          c. *Type C*—Shows a mixture of Type A and Type B.
       2. Moderate:
          a. *Type A*—Relates slightly to people with words, play or other symbols, but in narrow range of emotions; some purposefulness and reality orientation is present, but are sensitive to the slightest stress.
          b. *Type B*—Relates to people and things using words or play across a range of emotions and themes, but in a chaotic, unreality-oriented manner; can only relate to reality orientation with structure (e.g., needs lots of limits and repeated help with what is pretend and what is real).
          c. *Type C*—Shows a mixture of Type A and Type B.
       3. Mild: Functioning between competent and moderate range.

DISCUSSION/CONCLUSION

The foregoing discussion has reviewed the clinical, human, and animal, research and laboratory approaches to attachment, and highlighted the relative contributions of each. Existing clinical criteria are not sufficiently related to the stages of human development. The laboratory-based approach (Strange Situation), although impressive as a research tool, lacks the specificity of clinical context to be useful as a clinical instrument. Clinical approaches need to be: (a) attentive to the numerous types of data available (from parents' history, feelings, and perceptions; ongoing infant caregiver and family observations; etc.); (b) sensitive to the formation of a therapeutic relationship; and (c) both broad enough to conceptualize the overall adaptive process, and specific enough to pinpoint defects or constrictions in adaptive developmental pathways. A framework based on a developmental structuralist model (Greenspan, 1981) for operationalizing the developmental process was suggested. This framework provides a way of conceptualizing attachment as an ongoing process that becomes organized and reorganized at each stage of development in keeping with new maturational and experiential opportunities.

Concrete attachments, where interest in the world and regulation are key, characterize the first stage of attachments. Personal, joyful, synchronous attachments characterize the second. Purposeful, interactive attachment patterns with a broadening range of affect signify the third stage. The ability to integrate and conceptualize, at the behavioral level, different interpersonal thematic-affective domains (including dependence and independence, passivity, and activity, etc.), characterizes the fourth stage, conceptual integrated attachments. The ability to elevate behaviors and affect to a higher plane (i.e., to create internal emotional imagery) and, therefore, represent attachments and relationships, indicates the emerging of the fifth stage. The ability to differentiate one's internal world of imagery into clear organization of self and nonself, along affective and temperal and spacial dimensions, characterizes the sixth stage.

By viewing attachment as a developmental process at the core of the formation of intrapsychic structure and personality, we avoid unproductive theoretical polarities (e.g., attachment doesn't start until we see separation or stranger anxiety, etc.) and provide a clinical framework that is sensitive to the importance of the human relationship in the formation of psychological structure and function.

REFERENCES

Ainsworth, M. D. S. (1973). The development of infant–mother attachment. In B. M. Caldwell & H. N. Riociuti (Eds.), *Review of child development research* (pp. 1–194). Chicago: University of Chicago Press.

Ainsworth, M. D. S. (1980). Attachment and child abuse. In G. Gerbner, C. Ross, & E. Zigler (Eds.), *Child abuse: An agenda for action* (pp. 35–47). New York: Oxford University Press.

Ainsworth, M. D. S., Bell, S. M., & Stayton, D. (1971). Individual differences in strange situation behavior of one-year-olds. In H. R. Schaffer

(Ed.), *The origins of human social relations* (pp. 17–57). London: Academic Press.

Ainsworth, M. D. S., Bell, S. M., & Stayton, D. (1974). Infant–mother attachment and social development: Socialization as a product of reciprocal responsiveness to signals. In M. Richard (Ed.), *The integration of the child into a social world* (pp. 99–135). Cambridge, England: Cambridge University Press.

Ainsworth, M. D. S., Blehar, M. C., Waters, W., & Wall, S. (1978). *Patterns of attachment.* Hillsdale, NJ: Lawrence Erlbaum Associates.

Ainsworth, M. D. S., & Wittig, B. (1969). Attachment and exploratory behavior of one-year-olds in a strange situation. In B. Foss (Ed.), *Determinants of infant behavior* (Vol. IV, pp. 113–136). London: Methuen.

American Psychiatric Association. (1980). *Diagnostic and Statistical Manual of Mental Disorders* (3rd ed.). Washington, DC: author.

Arend, R., Gove, F. L., & Sroufe, L. A. (1979). Continuity of individual adaptation from infancy to kindergarten: A predictive study of ego-resiliency and curiosity in preschoolers. *Child Development, 50,* 950–959.

Bakwin, H. (1942). Loneliness in infants. *American Journal of Diseases of Children, 63,* 30.

Bell, S. (1970). The development of the concept of object as related to infant–mother attachment. *Child Development, 41,* 219–311.

Belsky, J., Gardugue, L., & Hrncir, E. (1983). Assessing performance, competence, and executive capacity in infant play: Relations to home environment and security of attachment. *Developmental Psychology, 20,* 406–417.

Bergman, P., & Escalona, S. (1949). Unusual sensitivities in very young children. *Psychoanalytic Study of the Child, 3–4,* 333.

Bowlby, J. (1951). Maternal care and mental health *WHO Monograph Series,* No. 2. Geneva: World Health Organization.

Bowlby, J. (1969). *Attachment and loss,* Vol. I: *Attachment.* New York: Basic.

Brazelton, T. B., Koslowski, B., & Main, M. (1974). The origins of reciprocity: The early mother–infant interaction. In M. Lewis & L. Rosenblum (Eds.), *The effect of the infant on its caregiver* (pp. 49–76). New York: Wiley.

Burlingham, D., & Freud, A. (1942). *Young children in wartime.* London: Allen & Unwin.

Butler, S. R., Suskind, M. R., & Schanberg, S. M. (1978). Maternal behavior as a regulator of polyamine biosynthesis in brain and heart of the developing rat pup. *Science, 199,* 445–447.

Cameron, H. C. (1919). *The nervous child.* London: Oxford Medical Publications.

Charlesworth, W. R. (1969). The role of surprise in cognitive development. In E. Elkind & J. H. Flavell (Eds.), *Studies in cognitive development: Essays in honor of Jean Piaget* (pp. 257–314). London: Oxford University Press.

Coe, C. L., & Levine, S. (1981). Normal responses to mother–infant separation in nonhuman primates. In D. F. Klein & J. G. Rabkin (Eds.), *Anxiety: New research and changing concepts* (pp. 155–177). New York: Raven Press.

Cravioto, J., & DeLicardie, E. (1973). Environmental correlates of severe clinical malnutrition and language development in survivors from kwashiorkor or marasmus. In PAHO Scientific Publication No. 251, *Nutrition, the nervous system and behavior,* Washington, DC.

Crittenden, P. M. (1981). Abusing, neglecting, problematic, and adequate dyads: Differentiating by patterns of interaction. *Merrill–Palmer Quarterly, 27,* 201–108.

Crittenden, P. M. (1985a). Maltreated infants: Vulnerability and resilience. *Journal of Child Psychology and Psychiatry, 26*(1), 85–96.

Crittenden, P. M. (1985b). Social networks, quality of child rearing, and child development. *Child Development, 56,* 1299–1313.

Cytryn, L. (1968). Methodological issues in psychiatric evaluation of infants. *Journal of the American Academy of Child Psychiatry, 7,* 510–521.

Denenberg, V. H. (1982). Postnatal stimulation, brain lateralization, and emotional reactivity. In R. J. Mathew (Ed.), *The biology of anxiety* (pp. 87–103). New York: Brunner/Mazel.

Easterbrooks, M. A., & Lamb, M. E. (1979). The relationship between quality of infant–mother attachment and infant competence in initial encounters with peers. *Child Development, 50,* 380–387.

Egeland, B., & Sroufe, L. A. (1981a). Attachment and early maltreatment. *Child Development, 52,* 44–52.

Egeland, B., & Sroufe, L. A. (1981b). Developmental sequelae of maltreatment in infancy. In R. Rizley & D. Cicchetti (Eds.), *Developmental perspectives on child maltreatment* (pp. 77–92). San Francisco: Jossey–Bass.

Ekman, P. (1972). Universals and cultural differences in facial expressions of emotion. *Nebraska Symposium on Motivation.* Lincoln: University of Nebraska Press.

Emde, R. N., Gaensbauer, T. J., & Harmon, R. J. (1976). Emotional expression in infancy: A biobehavioral study. *Psychological Issues,* Monograph No. 37. New York: International Universities Press.

Erickson, M. F., & Crichton, L. (1981, April). *Antecedents of compliance in two-year-olds from a high-risk sample.* Paper presented at the biennial meeting of The Society of Research in Child Development, Boston, MA.

Erickson, M. F., Farber, E. A., & Egeland, B. (1982, August). *Antecedents and concomitants of compliance in high-risk preschool children.* Paper presented at the annual meeting of The American Psychological Association, Washington, DC.

Erickson, M. F., Sroufe, L. A., & Egeland, B. (1985). The relationship between quality of attachment and behavior problems in preschool in the high-risk sample. In I. Bretherton & E. Waters (Eds.), *Growing points of attachment theory and research, Monographs of The Society for Research in Child Development, 50*(1–2), 147–166.

Escalona, S. K. (1968). *The roots of individuality.* Chicago: Aldine.

Escalona, S. K., & Heider, G. (1959). *Prediction and outcome: A study in child development.* New York: Basic Books.

Fraiberg, S. (1980). *Clinical studies in infant mental health: The first year of life.* New York: Basic Books.

Fraiberg, S., Adelson, E., & Shapiro, V. (1975). Ghosts in the nursery: A psychoanalytic approach to the problems of impaired infant–mother relationships. *Journal of The American Academy of Child Psychiatry, 14,* 387–422.

Freud, S. (1958). Formulations on the two principles of mental functioning. *Standard Edition, 12,* 218–226. London: Hogarth Press. (Originally published, 1911)

Gaensbauer, T. J., & Harmon, R. J. (1981). Clinical assessment in infancy utilizing structured playroom situation. *Journal of The American Academy of Child Psychiatry, 20,* 264–280.

Gaensbauer, T. J., & Harmon, R. J. (1982). Attachment behavior in abused/neglected, and premature infants: Implications for the concept of attachment. In R. N. Emde & R. J. Harmon (Eds.), *Attachment and affiliative systems* (pp. 245–279). New York: Plenum.

Gaensbauer, T. J., Harmon, R. J., Cytryn, L., & McKnew, D. H. (1984). Social and affective development in infants with a manic-depressive parent. *American Journal of Child Psychiatry, 141*(2), 223–229.

Gewirtz, J. L. (1965). The course of infant smiling in four child-rearing environments in Israel. In B. M. Foss (Ed.), *Determinants of infant behavior* (Vol. 3, pp. 205–260). London: Methuen.

Gewirtz, J. L. (1969). Levels of conceptual analysis in environment: Infant interaction research. *Merrill-Palmer Quarterly, 15,* 9–47.

Goodall, J. (1971a). *In the shadow of man.* Boston: Houghton Mifflin.

Goodall, J. (1971b). Some aspects of mother–infant relationships in a group of wild chimpanzees. In H. R. Schaffer (Ed.), *The origins of human social relations.* New York: Academic Press.

Goodall, J. (1979). Life and death at Gombe. *National Geographic, 155,* 592–621.

Gordon, A., & Jameson, J. (1979). Infant–mother attachment in patients with nonorganic failure to thrive. *American Academy of Child Psychiatry, 18,* 251–259.

Gouin-Decarie, T. (1965). *Intelligence and affectivity in early childhood: An experimental study of Jean Piaget's object concept and object relations.* New York: International Universities Press.

Greenspan, S. I. (1979). Intelligence and adaptation: An integration of psychoanalytic and Piagetian developmental psychology. *Psychological Issues,* Monograph, 47–48. New York: International Universities Press.

Greenspan, S. I. (1981). Psychopathology and adaptation in infancy and early childhood: Principles of clinical diagnosis and preventive intervention. *Clinical Infant Reports, 1.* New York: International Universities Press.

Greenspan, S. I., & Lieberman, A. F. (1980). Infants, mothers and their interactions: A quantitative clinical approach to developmental assessment. In S. I. Greenspan & G. H. Pollock (Eds.), *The course of life: Psychoanalytic contributions toward understanding personality development, Vol. I – Infancy and early childhood* (DHHS Publication No. ADM 80–786). Washington, DC: U.S. Government Printing Office.

Greenspan, S. I., & Lourie, R. S. (1981, June). Developmental structuralist approach to the classification of adaptive and pathologic personality organization: Application to infancy and early childhood. *American Journal of Psychiatry, 138*(6), 725–735.

Greenspan, S. I., Lourie, R. S., & Nover, R. A. (1979). A developmental approach to the classification of psychopathology in infancy and early childhood. In J. Noshpitz (Ed.), *The basic handbook of child psychiatry* (Vol. 2, pp. 157–164). New York: Basic.

Greenspan, S. I., Wieder, S., Lieberman, A. F., Nover, R. A., Lourie, R. S., & Robinson, M. E. (Eds.). (1987). Infants in multirisk families: Case studies in preventive intervention. *Clinical Infant Reports, 3.* New York: International Universities Press.

Greenspan, S. I., Wieder, S., & Nover, R. (1986). Diagnosis and preventive intervention of developmental and emotional disorders in infancy and early childhood: New perspectives. In M. Green (Ed.), *The psychosocial aspects of the family: the new pediatrics* (pp. 13–52). Lexington, Maine/Toronto: D.C. Heath.

Grossman, K., Grossman, K., Spangler, G., Suess, G., & Unzer, L. (1985) Maternal sensitivity and newborns' orientation responses as related to quality of attachment in northern Germany. In I. Bretherton & E. Waters (Eds.), *Growing points of attachment theory and research, Monographs of The Society for Research in Child Development, 50*(1–2), 233–256.

Harlow, H. H., & Soumi, S. J. (1974). Induced depression in monkeys. *Behavioral Biology, 12,* 273–296.

Hartmann, H. (1958). *Ego psychology and the problem of adaptation.* New York: International Universities Press. (Originally published, 1939)

Hesse, P., & Cicchetti, D. (1982). Toward an integrated theory of emotional development. *New Directions for Child Development, 16,* 3–48.

Hinde, R. A., Leighton-Shapiro, M. E., & McGinnis, L. (1978). Effects of various types of separation experience on Rhesus monkeys 5 months later. *Journal of Child Psychology and Psychiatry, 19,* 197–212.

Hinde, R. A., & Spencer-Booth, Y. (1970). Individual differences in the responses of Rhesus monkeys to a period of separation from their mothers. *Journal of Child Psychology and Psychiatry, 11,* 159–176.

Hofheimer, J., Greenspan, S., Lieberman, A., & Poisson, S. (in prep.). *The Greenspan–Lieberman interaction system: Reliability and stability studies.* Unpublished manuscript. Division of Maternal and Child Health, Dept. of Health and Human Services, Washington, DC.

Hofheimer, J., Poisson, S., Strauss, M., Eyler, F., & Greenspan, S. (1983). Perinatal and behavioral characteristics of neonates born to multi-risk families. *Developmental and Behavioral Pediatrics, 4*(3), 163–170.

Hunt, J. M. (1941). Infants in an orphanage. *Journal of Abnormal and Social Psychology, 36,* 338.

Izard, C. (1978). On the ontogenesis of emotions and emotion—cognition relationships in infancy. In M. Lewis & L. Rosenblum (Eds.), *The development of affect* (pp. 389–413). New York: Plenum.

Kaufman, I. C., & Rosenblum, L. A. (1967a). Depression in infant monkeys separated from their mothers. *Science, 155,* 1030–1031.

Kaufman, I. C., & Rosenblum, L. A. (1967b). The reaction to separation in infant monkeys: Anaclitic depression and conservation-withdrawal. *Psychosomatic Medicine, 29,* 649–675.

Klaus, M., & Kennell, J. (1976). *Maternal–infant bonding: The impact of early separation or loss on family development,* St. Louis: Mosby.

Lamb, M. E., Thompson, R. A., Gardner, W., Charnov, E. L., & Estes, C. (1984). Security of attachment as assessed in the strange situation: Its study and biological interpretation. *Behavioral and Brain Sciences, 7,* 127–147.

Lewis, M., Feiring, C., McGaffog, C., & Jaskir, J. (1984). Predicting psychopathology in six-year-olds from early social relations. *Child Development, 55,* 123–136.

Lieberman, A. F. (1977). Preschoolers' competence with a peer: Relations with attachment and peer experience. *Child Development, 48,* 1277–1287.

Lieberman, A. F. (1985). Infant mental health: A model for service delivery. *Journal of Clinical Child Psychology, 14*(3), 196–201.

Lieberman, A. F., & Pawl, J. H. (in press). Disorders of attachment in the second year: A clinical developmental perspective. In M. Greenberg, D.

Cicchetti, & M. Cummings (Eds.), *Attachment beyond infancy.* Chicago: University of Chicago Press.

Lipsitt, L. (1966). Learning processes of newborns. *Merrill-Palmer Quarterly, 12,* 45–71.

Londerville, S., & Main, M. (1981). Security of attachment, compliance, and maternal training methods in the second year of life. *Developmental Psychology, 17,* 289–299.

Lourie, R. (1971). The first three years of life. *American Journal of Psychiatry, 127,* 1457–1463.

Lowrey, L. G. (1940). Personality distortion and early institutional care, *American Journal of Orthopsychiatry, 10,* 546.

Mahler, M. S., Pine, F., & Bergman, A. (1975). *The psychological birth of the human infant.* New York: Basic.

Main, M., Kaplan, N., & Cassidy, J. (1985). Security in infancy, childhood, and adulthood: A move to the level of representation. In I. Bretherton & E. Waters (Eds.), *Growing points in attachment, Monographs of The Society for Research in Child Development, 50* (1–2), 66–106.

Main, M., & Solomon, J. (1987). Discovery of an insecure, disorganized/disoriented attachment pattern: Procedures, findings, and implications for the classification of behavior. In M. Yogman & T. B. Brazelton (Eds.), *Affective development in infancy.* Norwood, NJ: Ablex.

Massie, H. (1978a). Blind ratings of mother–infant interaction in home movies of prepsychotic and normal infants. *Journal of the American Academy of Child Psychiatry, 135*(11), 1371–1374.

Massie, H. (1978b). The early natural history of childhood psychosis: Ten cases studied by analysis of family home movies of the infancies of the children. *Journal of The American Academy of Child Psychiatry, 17,* 29–45.

Matas, L., Arend, R., & Sroufe, L. A. (1978). Continuity of adaptation in the second year: The relationship between quality of attachment and later competence. *Child Development, 49,* 547–556.

McKinney, W. T. (1977). Animal behavioral/biological models relevant to depressive and affective disorders in humans. In J. G. Schulterbrandt & A. Raskin (Eds.), *Depression in childhood: Diagnosis, treatment and conceptual models* (pp. 107–122). New York: Rowen Press.

Meltzoff, A. N., & Moore, K. M. (1977). Imitation of facial and manual gestures by human neonates, *Science, 198*(4312), 75–78.

Melzack, R., & Scott, T. H. (1957). The effects of early experience on the response to pain. *Journal of Comparative and Physiological Psychology, 50,* 155–161.

Mineka, S., & Suomi, S. J. (1978). Social separation in monkeys. *Psychology Bulletin, 85,* 1376–1400.

Morgan, B. L. G., Boris, G., & Winick, M. (1982). A useful correlation between blood and brain N-acetylneuraminic acid contents. *Biological Neonate, 42*, 299–303.

Morgan, B. L. G., & Naismith, D. J. (1982). The effect of early postnatal undernutrition on the growth and development of the rat brain, *British Journal of Nutrition, 48*, 15–23.

Morgan, B. L. G., & Winick, M. (1981). The subcellular localization of administered N-acetylneuraminic acid in the brains of well-fed and protein restricted rates. *British Journal of Nutrition, 46*, 231–238.

Murphy, L. B., & Moriarty, A. E. (1976). *Vulnerability, coping, and growth: From infancy to adolescence.* New Haven, CT: Yale University Press.

Naslund, B., Persson-Blennow, I., McNeil, T., Kaij, L., & Malmquist-Larsson, A. (1984). Offspring of women with nonorganic psychosis: Infant attachment to the mother at one year of age. *Acta Psychiatrica Scandinavia, 69*, 231–241.

Ottinger, D. R., Denenberg, V. H., & Stephens, M. W. (1963). Maternal emotionality, multiple mothering, and emotionality in maturity. *Journal of Comparative and Physiological Psychology, 56*(2), 313–317.

Pastor, D. (1981). The quality of mother–infant attachment and its relationship to toddler's initial sociability with peers. *Developmental Psychology, 17*, 323–335.

Piaget, J. (1972). The stages of the intellectual development of the child. In S. Harrison & J. McDermott (Eds.), *Childhood psychopathology* (pp. 157–166). New York: International Universities Press. (Originally published, 1962)

Provence, S. (1979, December). *A service-centered study: Methods of intervention and outcome.* Paper presented at the training institute on "Clinical Approaches to Infants and Their Families," sponsored by The National Center for Clinical Infant Programs, Washington, DC.

Provence, S. (Ed.), (1983). Infants and parents: Clinical case reports. *Clinical Infant Reports, 2.* New York: International Universities Press.

Rachford, B. K. (1905). *Neurotic disorders of childhood.* New York: E. B. Treat.

Radke-Yarrow, M., Cummings, E. M., Kuczyniski, L., & Chapman, M. (1985). Patterns of attachment in 2- and 3-year-olds in normal families and families with parental depression. *Child Development, 56*, 884–891.

Reite, M., & Short, R. (1980) A biobehavioral developmental profile (BDP) for the pigtailed monkey. *Developmental Psychobiology, 13*, 243–285.

Reite, M., Short, R., Seiler, C., & Pauley, D. J. (1981). Attachment, loss and depression. *Child Psychology and Psychiatry, 22*, 141–169.

Rheingold, H. L. (1961). The effect of environmental stimulation upon social and exploratory behavior in the human infant. In B. M. Foss (Ed.), *Determinants of infant behavior, 3.* New York: Wiley.

Rheingold, H. L. (1966). The development of social behavior in the human infant. *Monographs of The Society for Research in Child Development*, 31(1).

Sameroff, A., Seifer, R., & Zax, M. (1982). Early development of children at risk for emotional disorder. *Monographs of The Society for Research in Child Development*, 47(2).

Sander, L. (1962). Issues in early mother–child interaction. *Journal of The American Academy of Child Psychiatry*, 1, 141–166.

Seay, B., Hansen, E., & Harlow, H. F. (1962). Mother–infant separation in monkeys. *Journal of Child Psychology and Psychiatry*, 3, 123–132.

Spitz, R. A. (1946). Hospitalism: A follow-up report. *The Psychoanalytic Study of the Child*, 2, 113–117.

Spitz, R. A., & Cobliner, W. (1965). *The first year of life*. New York: International Universities Press.

Sroufe, L. A. (1979a). The coherence of individual development: Early care, attachment, and subsequent developmental issues. *American Psychologist*, 34, 834–841.

Sroufe, L. A. (1979b). Socioemotional development. In J. Osofsky (Ed.), *Handbook of infant development* (pp. 462–516). New York: Wiley.

Sroufe, L. A. (1983). Infant–caregiver attachment patterns of adaptation in preschool: The roots of maladaption and competence. In M. Perlmutter (Ed.), *Minnesota symposium in child psychology* (Vol. 16, pp. 41–81).

Sroufe, L. A., Fox, N. E., & Pancake, V. R. (1983). Attachment and dependency in developmental perspective. *Child Development*, 54, 1615–1627.

Sroufe, L. A., & Waters, E. (1977). Heartrate as a convergent measure in clinical and developmental research. *Merrill-Palmer Quarterly*, 23, 3–28.

Sroufe, L. A., Waters, E., & Matas, L. (1974). Contextual determinants of infant affective response. In M. Lewis & L. Rosenblum (Eds.), *The origins of fear*. New York: Wiley.

Stern, D. (1984a). The goal and structure of mother–infant play. *Journal of The American Academy of Child Psychiatry*, 13, 402–421.

Stern, D. (1974b). Mother and infant at play: The dyadic interaction involving facial, vocal and gaze behaviors. In M. Lewis & L. Rosenblum (Eds.), *The effect of the infant on its caregiver* (pp. 187–213). New York: Wiley.

Stern, D. (1977). *The first relationship: Infant and mother*. Cambridge: Harvard University Press.

Thomas, A., Chess, S., & Birch, H. (1968). *Temperament and behavior disorders in children*. New York: International Universities Press.

Thompson, R. A., Lamb, M. E., & Estes, D. (1982). Stability of infant–mother attachment and its relationship to changing life circumstances in an unselected middle class sample. *Child Development*, 53, 144–148.

Tomkins, S. (1963). *Affect, imagery, consciousness* (Vols. 1 & 2). New York: Springer.

Vaughn, B., Egeland, B., Sroufe, L. A., & Waters, E. (1979). Individual differences in infant–mother attachment at 12 and 18 months: Stability and change in families under stress. *Child Development, 50,* 971–975.

Waters, E., Wippman, J., & Sroufe, L. A. (1979). Attachment, positive affect, and competence in peer group: Two studies in construct validation. *Child Development, 50,* 821–829.

Weinberg, J., Smotherman, W. P., & Levine, J. (1979). Early handling effects on neophobia and conditioned taste aversion, *Physiology and Behavior, 20,* 589–596.

Werner, H., & Kaplan, B. (1963). *Symbol formation.* New York: Wiley.

Winnicott, D. W. (1931). *Clinical notes on disorders of childhood.* London, England: Heineman.

Zahn-Waxler, C., Chapman, M., & Cummings, E. M. (1984). Cognitive and social development in infants and toddlers with a bipolar parent. *Child Psychiatry and Human Development, 15*(2), 75–85.

AUTHOR INDEX

H

Hammond, M. A., 114, 117, *132,* 242, *246*
Hanf, C., 183, *213*
Hansen, E., 390, *423*
Harlow, H. H., 245, *252,* 390, *419*
Harmon, R. J., 78, *91,* 103, 104, 109, *133,*
   337, *349,* 389, 394, 399, 400, 401,
   417, 418
Harris, S. L., 187, *213*
Hartmann, H., 389, *420*
Hartup, W. W., 220, 245, *248, 249*
Hawkins, N., 184, *216*
Hazan, C., *320*
Heatherington, E. M., 221, 225, *249*
Heider, G., 388, *418*
Hertzig, M., 337, *351*
Hertzog, C., 46, *89*
Hesse, P., 389, *420*
Hinde, R. A., 254, 256, *297,* 390, *420*
Hoffman, M., 43, *88*
Hofheimer, J., 409, *420*
Hogan, R., 25, *37*
Holmes, D., 54, *91*
Hops, H., 235, *248*
Horney, K., 257, 259, *297*
Hrncir, E., 398, *416*
Humphreys, L., 186, *213*
Hunt, J. M., 388, *420*
Huston, T., 64, 65, *91, 92*
Hymel, S., 234, 236, 240, *246, 249,*
   251

I

Iannotti, R., 220, *249*
Isabella, R. A., 10, *16,* 76, *92*
Izard, C., 389, *420*

J

Jackson, D., 62, *92*
Jacobson, J. L., 244, *249*
Jacobvitz, D., 23, *35*
Jameson, J., 399, *418*
Jaskir, J., 6, *16,* 27, *36,* 79, *92,* 191, 192,
   194, *214,* 232, 233, *249,* 267, 268,
   292, *297,* 352, 353, 354, 357, *384,*
   399, *420*

Johnson, C., 141, *166*
Johnson, D. H., 361, *383*
Johnson, H., 114, 116, *134*
Johnson, S. M., 184, 186, *212, 213*
Julia, H., 329, *351*

K

Kagan, J., 4, *16,* 22, *36,* 52, *92,* 192, *211,*
   226, 227, 229, 230, 231, *248, 249,*
   250, 263, 268, *297*
Kaij, L., 399, *422*
Kaplan, B., 389, *424*
Kaplan, N., 18, *36,* 106, 107, 125, *133,*
   187, 189, 192, 193, 194, *214,* 301,
   305, 306, 307, 308, 310, 313, *320,*
   321, 330, *350,* 357, *384,* 399, *421*
Katan, A., 202, *214*
Kaufman, I. C., 390, *420*
Kaye, K., 63, *92*
Keane, S., 221, *248*
Kearsley, R., 4, *16, 92,* 263, *297*
Keeley, S. M., 184, *212*
Kegan, R., 187, 196, 198, *214*
Kelley, H., 65, *90*
Kelley, H. H., 262, *297*
Kempe, C. H., 137, *166*
Kemper, T., 225, *249*
Kendall, P. C., 205, *214*
Kennell, J., 389, *420*
King, H. E., 184, *212*
Kiser, L., 44, *92,* 265, *297*
Klagsbrun, M., 307, *320*
Klaus, M., 389, *420*
Klinnert, M. D., 185, *211*
Kobak, R., 304, 309, 311, 317, *320, 321*
Kogan, K. L., 183, *218*
Kohlberg, L. 29, *36,* 264, *297*
Korner, A., 337, *350*
Koslowski, B., 389, 394, 406, *416*
Koss, M., 364, *384*
Kovaks, M., 240, *249*
Kovitz, K., 141, *166*
Kowalski, J., 54, *91*
Krafchuk, E. E., 63, *93*
Krasnor, L. R., 233, 237, 238, *251*
Kuchner, J. F. R., 52, *92*
Kuczynski, L., 96, 103, 104, 105, 109,
   113, 123, 128, *134,* 145, *167,* 188,
   216, 400, *422*

McHale, S., 64, *91*
McKinney, W. T., 390, *421*
McKnew, D. H., 103, 104, 109, *133,* 225,
    252, 399, *418*
McMahon, R. J., 178, 181, 182, 183, 185,
    186, 209, *212, 213*
McNeal, S., 184, *216*
McNeil, T., 399, *422*
Meltzoff, A. N., 389, *421*
Melzack, R., 390, *421*
Metcalf, D., 18, *37*
Michael, C. M., 221, *250*
Miller, E. M., 271, *296*
Mineka, S., 390, *421*
Mitchel, S. K., 114, 117, *132,* 242, *246*
Miyake, K., 43, 44, 52, 54, 70, *93*
Moore, K. M., 389, *421*
Moreland, J. R., 184, *215*
Morgan, B. L. G., 391, *421, 422*
Moriarty, A. E., 388, 389, *422*
Morris, C. P., 221, *250*
Morris, D., 19, *36,* 48, 49, *73,* 209, *215, 385*
Morrison, D. C., 184, *218*
Moss, H. A., 226, 230, *249*
Motti, F., 21, *37,* 316, *322,* 352, *385*
Murphy, L. B., 388, 389, *422*

N

Naismith, D. J., 391, *422*
Naslund, B., 399, *422*
Nesselroade, J., 53, *92*
Nezworski, M. T., 352, 380, *384*
Nover, R. A., 391, 392, 393, 394, 402,
    404, *419*
Noyes, D., 311, *322*

O

Obmascher, P., 144, *167*
O'Brien, E., 310, *322*
Oliver, J. M., 114, *133*
Olson, S. L., 263, 265, 267, 276, 277,
    278, 287, 294, *296, 298*
Olweus, D., 177, *215*
Otaki, M., 46, 56, 77, *90,* 312, *319*
Ottinger, D. R., 391, *422*
Overton, W. F., 186, *216*
Owen, M. T., 19, *35,* 189, *215,* 300, *322*

P

Palermo, M., 53, *92*
Pancake, V. R., 20, 21, 33, *37,* 188, 190,
    217, 244, *250,* 399, *423*
Parke, R., 6, *16*
Parrish, J. M., 185, *211*
Parten, M. B., 235, *250*
Pastor, D. L., 244, *250,* 311, 316, *322,*
    352, *385,* 398, *422*
Patterson, G. R., 178, 180, 181, 184, 185,
    204, *215, 216,* 245, *250,* 259, 262, *298*
Pauley, D. J., *422*
Pawl, J., 196, 209, *214,* 330, 336, 338,
    342, *350, 420*
Pederson, D., 314, *322*
Peed, S., 185, *216*
Persson-Blennow, I., 399, *422*
Peterson, R. F., 178, 184, *216, 218*
Pettit, G. S., 263, 265, 276, 278, 291,
    296, 298
Phelps, R., 184, *216*
Piaget, J., 220, 238, *250,* 389, 406, 407, *422*
Pine, F., 187, 193, 197, 198, 202, 204,
    214, 216, 389, 407, 408, *421*
Plomin, R. A., 226, 227, 242, *247, 248, 250*
Poisson, S., 409, *420*
Pressley, M., 64, 65, *93*
Prinz, R. J., 221, *252*
Provence, S., 331, *350,* 392, 394, *422*
Purpura, D. P., 337, *349*

Q

Quay, H. C., 177, *216,* 221, 224, *250*

R

Rachford, B. K., 388, *422*
Radke-Yarrow, M., 8, *17,* 96, 103, 104,
    105, 109, 113, 123, 128, *134,* 145,
    167, 188, *216,* 225, *252,* 399, *422*
Radloff, L. S., 107, *134*
Rahe, D. F., 245, *248*
Rajecki, D. W., 144, *167*
Reese, H. W., 186, *216*
Reichler, M., 225, *249*
Reid, J. B., 180, 185, *216*
Reite, M., 390, *422*

Waters, D., *321*
Waters, E., 13, *17,* 19, 23, 25, 31, 32, *35,*
38, 43, 45, 54, 59, 70, *88, 94,* 95, 97,
98, 110, 126, 131, *132, 134,* 138, 145,
157, 162, *165,* 187, 188, 189, 202,
210, 217, 218, 228, 229, 244, *246,*
252, 255, 257, 258, 259, 260, 265,
266, 277, 282, *295, 298,* 300, 302,
303, 313, 317, *318, 322, 323,* 328,
330, 332, 335, 337, *348, 351,* 352,
355, 357, 358, 359, *382, 386,* 389,
396, 397, 398, 399, 407, *416, 423, 424*
Watson, D., 129, *134*
Weber, R. A., 45, 50, 53, 55, 56, *92, 94*
Webster-Stratton, C., 185, *218*
Weinberg, J., 390, *424*
Weinert, C., 114, 115, *132*
Weingarten, C. G. T., 114, 115, *133*
Weinstein, H., 52, *90*
Weisfeld, G. D., 141, *165*
Weiss, R., *135*
Wells, K., 185, 186, *212, 218*
Wells, R. T., 184, *215*
Werner, E. E., 262, *299*
Werner, H., 389, *424*
Weston, D., 95, 98, 106, *134,* 145, *166,*
188, *215,* 255, *297,* 300, 315, 316,
321, 352, 357, *385*
Wieder, S., 330, *349,* 391, 392, 402, 404, *419*
Wille, D. E., 244, *249*

Willerman, L., 226, *247*
Wiltuner, L., 183, *217*
Wimberger, H. C., 183, *218*
Winick, M., 391, *421, 422*
Winkle, G. H., 184, *218*
Winnicott, D. W., 205, *218,* 331, *351,*
388, *424*
Wippman, J., 266, *298,* 352, *386,* 399,
424
Wittig, B., 59, *88,* 396, 397, *416*
Wolkind, S. N., 270, *299*

Y

Yarrow, L. J., 329, *351*
Yates, A., 137, *167*
Young, R. D., 255, *299*

Z

Zahn-Waxler, C., 198, *211,* 225, *252,* 400,
424
Zax, M., 103, 104, 105, 109, *134,* 400, *423*
Zeilberger, J., 184, *218*
Zelazo, P., 4, *16, 92,* 263, *297*
Zoll, D., 45, 48, 49, *93,* 97, 98, 99, 100,
102, 103, 106, 107, 109, 123, 125,
133, 311, 315, *321*

SUBJECT INDEX

A

Adaptation,
  and developmental change, 147–150,
    163–164
  quality of, 22
Ambiguity,
  and issues with power, 377
Anger,
  adaptive expression, 359
  and attachment, 8, 21, 23, 200, 244–
    245, 255–257, 259, 301
  maternal, 376–377
  toddlers' expression, 199, 204, 371–372
Anxiety, *see* Separation
Assessment,
  of relationships, 137–147
Attachment,
  and IQ, 27
  and language acquisition, 27
  and psychopathology, 28–30, 254–265
    prior empirical data, 265–268
  and self-recognition, 27
  parent-child relationship, 302–303
Attachment antecedents, 9–11, 265; *see*
    also Determinants
  A classification, 125–126
  B classification, 128–129
  C classification, 126–127
  D classification, 127–128
  maternal, 106–110, 140–147, 153–161,
    198–199, 206–208, 355–356, 398
  quality of childrearing, 157–159
Attachment assessment,

power as predictor, 26, 398–400
  use of the Strange-Situation,
    396–403
Attachment classification,
  and maltreatment, 99–103, 137–139,
    140, 144–147
  diagnostic value, 353
  in high risk samples, 97–99
  need for system expansion, 95–103,
    144–147, 159, 162–163, 398
  reliability, 110–113
Attachment consequences, 11–14, 21,
    265–266, 352
  behavior problems, 266–268, 353–355
  developmental models, 192–203
  individual differences in empathy, 25
Attachment determinants, *see* Attachment
    antecedents; Determinants
Attachment disorders,
  age of onset, 330, 395
  anxious attachment
    accident proneness, 332–333
    inhibition of exploration, 333–334
    precocious competence, 334–335
  classification
    clinical criteria, 392–396, 410–414
    use of Strange-Situation, 396–403
  disrupted attachment, 335–336
  distortions in parent-child relationship,
    328–331
  nonattachment, 331–332
Attachment history,
  and type of symptoms, 29
Attachment insecurity,